WOMEN IN LEADERSHIP

A PARADIGM SHIFT

Boaz, Meet Ruth

JOY GRAETZ

WOMEN IN LEADERSHIP: A Paradigm Shift... Boaz, Meet Ruth

ISBN: 0-924748-55-9
UPC: 88571300025-3

Printed in the United States of America
© 2005 by Joy Graetz

Milestones International Publishers
4410 University Dr., Ste. 113
Huntsville, AL 35816
(256) 536-9402, ext. 234; Fax: (256) 536-4530
www.milestonesintl.com

1 2 3 4 5 6 7 8 9 10 11 / 10 09 08 07 06 05

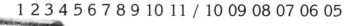

DEDICATION

꧁꧂

To my father, Lloyd Averill, whose reverence of the pulpit and competence in its practice are my internal measures.

CONTENTS

FOREWORD

STOP! You are about to enter a journey of spiritual truths that are revealing, enlightening, profound and impacting. The truths of this book can release many into ministries God has planted in them.

Joy Graetz uniquely develops a theme from the biblical book of Ruth on female leadership—one of the most complex and emotional subjects facing the church today. She takes it away from misinformation, mistranslations and traditions.

She is not sidetracked by specious arguments, diversions of opinion, perplexities, cultural barriers, varying interpretations, convictions or conclusions. Biblical interpretation takes precedence over cultural impact or contemporary doctrines.

There is profound discovery of dormant or neglected principles, suddenly aroused by this fresh insight concerning male-female bias in church leadership.

When neglected truth is rediscovered, it often results in overemphasis, which is as harmful as neglect. However, Joy with her warmth, serving spirit, entertaining style and authoritative pen, takes a very controversial subject to new meaning and significance.

She doesn't allow the Truth to become a caricature, which happens if one feature of a portrait is exaggerated. This is not an exaggerated portrait! It is a subject desperately needing to be addressed and is done so with positive balance, skill and the weight of the Scriptures being its guide.

As a result, I feel many who live with secret condemnation and frustration by being "called" but seemingly without "portfolio," will awaken and own their spiritual mantles.

There is a tremor being felt throughout the body of Christ. It's women with divine ordination being awakened and rising. An anticipation is racing through them because their hope is again ignited that, "Yes, there is a placement for me to serve as my calling designates."

As a woman who has been in full-time ministry for 47 years, I've walked alongside many brothers in ministry. I've seen how ministry of male-female complements and challenges instead of creating chasms through conflict and competition.

My heart's cry is, "Let us not call unfit those whom God has qualified, gifted and placed among us for His honor and glory. Let us realize leadership in church is based on calling and anointing, not gender."

My first introduction to Joy was quite poignant. Her mother, Edith Averill, had been appointed to serve at a conference I was preaching in Brisbane, Queensland. She left such a rich deposit of "fragrance" in me that at the close of the conference I asked if there was a heart concern I could share with her in prayer. She spoke of her daughter, Joy, who was battling the long-term effects of a contracted fever.

Three years later at a Preacher's Intensive I was conducting in Springbrook, Queensland, there was a striking, tall, slender, dark-haired, jubilant face with dancing eyes introducing herself. In polished English but with a definite Australian brogue she said, "Hello, Joy here."

From that moment throughout the week, God continued to speak to me about Joy. I invited her to take a "prophetic walk" with me. As we walked together through the manicured gardens, God spoke of things past, things present and things future, as if we were tripping over treasure. Among "things future" was the releasing of this voice to her nation as well as to other nations.

I've seen Joy own her call, her intellect, her humor, her home, her rich heritage, her inner voice, her strength, her skills, etc. and step onto platforms that God continues to prepare and reserve for her.

So from this delightful and delighted heart, this message comes...

From this heart that treasures Father's voice, this message comes...

From this heart who loves and was raised in the church, this message comes...

From this heart who has no ax to grind, this message comes...

WOMEN IN LEADERSHIP

...to us and the world,

...to awaken ALL of us to our spiritual possibilities.

Lois E. Burkett, D.M., D.D.
New Creation International Church Ministries
Phoenix, Arizona. USA

PREFACE

⊰✿⊱

In 1962, my father was in his sixth year as the pastor of Glad Tidings Tabernacle in downtown Brisbane, Queensland. At the time, it was one of the largest Pentecostal churches in Australia. (This is not mentioned to brag, but to add weight to the story that follows.) I was 11 years of age.

A Canadian ministry family moved to our laid-back city—an evangelist father, a highly intelligent and creative mother and twins my age, Becky and Robbie. This intersection of my parochial life with the lives of people who had lived *overseas* fueled dreams and enriched my journey. Now, nearly 40 years later, I readily remember the sounds, sights and styles of our Canadian friends.

One Sunday morning, those many years ago, my father stood in the pulpit and introduced "Mary Tregenza," the mother, as the morning service preacher. I sat bolt upright in my seat.

I remember feeling a sense of horror, sure that Dad was about to get into awful trouble from... from... from.... Well, surely someone was going to be mightily concerned about flooding the pulpit with a woman! In all my 11 years, such a thing had never happened, and I knew that, of all the things a woman could do in church, preaching wasn't one of them.

As it happened, not only was my father's introduction stately and without apology, but Mrs. Tregenza went on to deliver what I regarded as a perfect message. I was transfixed, perhaps by the warmth of her Canadian accent, but definitely by her content and by the image, now slightly blurred in my mind, of a woman standing behind the pulpit.

The Tregenza family departed Australia in the winter of '62 and life sank back to its comfortable predictability.

But it had happened. In a time and season when women rose to the lofty heights of Sunday school teaching and making fried rice and sweet and sour entrées for the youth banquets, my father had opened a door and let one of them creep out onto the hallowed turf of the platform.

It was to be a few years before Dad repeated this act of bravery. We moved to Christchurch, New Zealand. A womanly duo arrived from a far-flung country. They were devout in behavior and in their clothing.

I can't remember their speaking messages, but I can remember their instrumental messages. One wound up her presentation using a saw and violin bow, while the other played the piano in a triumphant style.

The highlight of their instrumental message was the sinking of the Titanic. I sat dumbfounded and wide-eyed as the ship gurgled its way to the sea bottom, leaving only a frothy rendition of an altar call hymn in its wake.

I recall marveling at three things simultaneously: first, at how embarrassing it all was; second, at how they ended up in our town; and third, at how different they were to Mary Tregenza.

You see, like most ministers' kids who have met with the intelligence of the Holy Spirit, by 15 years of age I had a taste for the real thing—and a comparable distaste for anything else.

My father allowed the real thing—Mary—into the pulpit, and from that Sunday in 1962 until now, I have known two things:

1. A woman can stand as God's oracle, and
2. She can stand alongside men in leadership in the church, with dignity, as a peer.

This book has been written from the perspective—my perspective—of four decades of watching, listening and wondering about the Mary Tregenza-factor in the church. These observations and insights have come through the filter of my personal experiences (specifically acknowledged throughout) but more so through the experiences of others, gleaned over the course of these four decades.

I thank and honor God and men and women in leadership for the diverse opportunities given me to speak, write and lead. As a result, I have been allowed a glimpse into the potential magnificence of the church wonderfully led in the health and wholeness that comes when a Boaz meets a Ruth.

INTRODUCTION

❧

Every Christian is called to the ministry, the priesthood. First Peter 2:9 is an emphatic and vivid description of the task that is given to all believers: *"But you are a chosen people, a royal priesthood, a holy nation, a people belonging to God, that you may declare the praises of him who called you out of darkness into his wonderful light."*

Whether our conversion to Christianity took place a week ago or half a century ago, that descriptor is valid and cannot be diminished by our circumstances.

It is a task that is accompanied neither by a sense of slavery nor by an imposed requirement that speaks of coercion.

It is, rather, our act of joyful obedience from a grateful heart.

The act? *We declare His praises*. We work it out in our daily lives.

For those in the armed services, it is worked out in combat uniform. For the young father and mother, it is worked out through the constancy of parenthood. For the para-plegic, it is worked out of a wheelchair. For the business person, it is worked out in boardrooms and around negotiating tables. For the believer in war-ravaged lands, it is worked out through the daily grind of finding food, staying alive and caring for the oppressed.

We work it out...joyfully...whatever our gender, race, stage of life, level of responsibility and socio-economic status—and our effectiveness in doing so is not diminished or dismissed by any one of those variables. When we awake each day, we receive His fresh mercy and we have an evident task for that day.

There is never nothing to do as a believer.

The work of the believer could be described as sitting on the cube of life like this:

- Side 1—Love God fully.

- Side 2—Love each other enthusiastically.

- Side 3—Walk in the way of the righteous consistently.

- Side 4—Care for the needy selflessly.

- Side 5—Introduce people to Jesus Christ normally.

- Side 6—Grow these people into disciples of Jesus Christ wisely.

The question then is this: Who teaches believers to do all those things?

And the answer is this: To His body, God has given gifts. These gifts are men and women who equip believers so that they can function as His emissaries on earth. These people are, by God-invented labels, pastors, teachers, evangelists, apostles and prophets.

Very few church systems have followed God's labels. In rare instances, they do have "Prophet John" or "Evangelist Sam," but mostly these people are labeled "Reverend" or "Father" or "Pastor."

If only the title "Equipper" looked snappier on a passport. (If only it was a word!) That is, after all, the catchall label: one who equips the believers to do the work of the ministry.

Women in Leadership focuses on the world of those who equip believers.

Before you read any further, however, here are two things you should know.

First, this is not a theological exposé of the issues of women/ascension gifts or women/church government. Many such books speaking for and against the recognition and release of women in the church are available. This book is not intended to join their shelf in the library as an assertive doctrinal commentary.

Second, I have five strong men in my life:

- My father, a veteran minister of the Gospel who will, forever, stand before me as an example of a true shepherd of the sheep.

- My husband, a man of integrity and wisdom whose generosity has freed me to roles of leadership and influence.

- My brother, a statesman in Christian education and in the church who has committed himself to a lifetime of learning.

- My elder son, a creative thinker who loves God deeply.

- My younger son, a gentle and devoted young man who walks before God and man with honesty and loyalty.

Because they are strong, they have flavored my life accordingly.

The biblical book of Ruth provides insights and foresights into the plight of women who are called by God to enable the Christian community to do the work of the ministry.

In writing this book, I have endeavored to give these two sights a voice, and in so doing perhaps I have provided a voice for such women also.

Part One

YOUR PEOPLE WILL BE MY PEOPLE

Ruth 1 (KJV)

Now it came to pass in the days when the judges ruled, that there was a famine in the land. And a certain man of Bethlehemjudah went to sojourn in the country of Moab, he, and his wife, and his two sons. And the name of the man was Elimelech, and the name of his wife Naomi, and the name of his two sons Mahlon and Chilion, Ephrathites of Bethlehemjudah. And they came into the country of Moab, and continued there. And Elimelech Naomi's husband died; and she was left, and her two sons. And they took them wives of the women of Moab; the name of the one was Orpah, and the name of the other Ruth: and they dwelled there about ten years. And Mahlon and

1

Chilion died also both of them; and the woman was left of her two sons and her husband.

Then she arose with her daughters in law, that she might return from the country of Moab: for she had heard in the country of Moab how that the LORD had visited his people in giving them bread. Wherefore she went forth out of the place where she was, and her two daughters in law with her; and they went on the way to return unto the land of Judah. And Naomi said unto her two daughters in law, Go, return each to her mother's house: the LORD deal kindly with you, as ye have dealt with the dead, and with me. The LORD grant you that ye may find rest, each of you in the house of her husband. Then she kissed them; and they lifted up their voice, and wept. And they said unto her, Surely we will return with thee unto thy people. And Naomi said, Turn again, my daughters: why will ye go with me? are there yet any more sons in my womb, that they may be your husbands? Turn again, my daughters, go your way; for I am too old to have an husband. If I should say, I have hope, if I should have an husband also to night, and should also bear sons; would ye tarry for them till they were grown? would ye stay for them from having husbands? nay, my daughters; for it grieveth me much for your sakes that the hand of the LORD is gone out against me. And they lifted up their voice, and wept again: and Orpah kissed her mother in law; but Ruth clave unto her. And she said, Behold, thy sister in law is gone back unto her people, and unto her gods: return thou after thy sister in law. And Ruth said, Entreat me not to leave thee, or to *return from following after thee: for whither thou goest, I will go; and where thou lodgest, I will lodge: thy people shall be my people, and thy God my God: where thou diest, will I die, and there will I be buried: the LORD do so to me, and more also, if ought but death part thee and me. When she saw that she was stedfastly minded to go with her, then she left speaking unto her.*

So they two went until they came to Bethlehem. And it came to pass, when they were come to Bethlehem, that all the city was moved about them, and they said, Is this Naomi? And she said unto them, Call me not Naomi, call me Mara: for the Almighty hath dealt very bitterly with me. I went out full, and the LORD hath brought me home again empty: why then call ye me Naomi, seeing the LORD hath testified against me, and the Almighty hath afflicted me? So Naomi returned, and Ruth the Moabitess, her daughter in law, with her, which returned out of the country of Moab: and they came to Bethlehem in the beginning of barley harvest.

Chapter 1

RESPONDING TO FAMINE

꧁꧂

Elimelech, Naomi and their two sons decide that they don't like their life or their town. Nothing is working. They are in the grip of a famine and they want to get out.

It would seem that most of their neighbors stay and, not surprisingly, at least some of them survive. These are the people who aren't prepared to throw out what they *do* have, to chase after what they *don't* have. Despite the evident example of hope in friends and family for a brighter tomorrow, Elimelech and his family pack up and leave.

KEEPING "MY GOD IS KING" ON THE THRONE

The story of Ruth's epic life takes place in the time of the judges. God's jealousy for His own sovereignty has kept the land under the care and oversight of judges. God will not share His glory with another. He alone is King.

Discontented with living under the gaze of an unseen God, the children of Israel will eventually demand a man-king.[1] Almighty God deals with His people with mystical benevolence, but most of these kings and their queens will live below the waterline of the mystical and many will be malevolent in their treatment of their people. Israel will pay a huge price for setting up earthly kingdoms. Every time they pay lip service to their sovereigns, saying, "Saul is king" or "David is king" or "Solomon is king" and so on, they will be sealing their position as lesser mortals to these sovereigns, thus reducing their personal authority. Sovereignty will only be inherited by those of the earthly bloodlines (exclusivity), and these hand-overs will often be accompanied by distress, betrayal and intrigue.

The bloodline of heaven leans to inclusion, not exclusivity. This truth sandwiches the Bible from God's magnanimous handing of the earth to us in Genesis 1:28, *"God blessed them and said to them, 'Be fruitful and increase in number; fill the earth and subdue it...' "* to His final plea for relationship with us in Revelation 22:17, *"The Spirit and the bride say, 'Come!' And let him who hears say, 'Come!' Whoever is thirsty, let him come; and whoever wishes, let him take the free gift of the water of life."*

Our need for exclusivity, at any level of life and ministry, tarnishes the glow of His glory.

The setting up of leadership and, through leadership, holy-inspired order in the church must never creep into the territory of making man-kings. Because worshipping is as much part of the human psyche as loving or having or achieving or belonging, it is all too easy to place people on the throne that should be reserved for God alone.

From person to person or nation to nation, we are pre-disposed to making objects of worship out of certain entertainers, certain athletes, certain strong personalities, certain ideologists. Because of this predisposition, we need to be wary of feeding it in the church by the creating of labeled hierarchies. However benign we regard the labels we employ to denote authority levels, there will always be a risk that the elevation of an office will be accompanied by the elevation of the human spirit.

Somehow, it seems to be the human pattern to drift away from "my God is King" to anything or anyone we can see and touch becoming king.

The children of Israel did this when they demanded the visible focus of worship in the form of a golden calf.[2] This bovine masterpiece was totally devoid of any ability whatsoever. It couldn't even produce a moo, let alone answer a prayer. In fact, the calf was formed out of jewelry that should have been adorning the people, the dining tables and, eventually, the tabernacle. Talk about a misuse of resources!

After the calf incident, the Israelites go quiet on the subject of needing something visible to worship for a while. They at least pretend to be content to be ruled by judges—God's best option for them—which brings us back to the Elimelechs and the famine.

EXPECTING TO THRIVE IN TIMES OF FAMINE

When church works, it is the most exhilarating, exciting place to be. We arrive with expectation written all over our faces, just from the sheer joy of belonging. The people, the

7

pastor, the program, the praise—we love it all and are fully alive and alert to everything that God is observably doing.

It is the famines in our churches that leave us puzzled. We feel hunger pangs and blame them on the pastor because he can't preach, the youth group because it isn't meeting the needs in our children, the noise of the harps and lyres, and the fact that we are no longer singing Miriam's hymn every second Sunday. We go home each Sunday miserable with the pain in our empty spirits.

What we often fail to realize is that the promises of both fulfillment and nourishment are contained in our name: Christian. We contain Christ—living water, bread of life. For the Elimelechs who are Ephrathites, their name contains "fertility," and they live in Bethlehem, which means "house of bread."[3]

A famine amongst fertile people who live in a breadbasket? It doesn't make sense to be in a famine. It is an alien concept from the hope and promise contained within our churches.

We cast our gaze at our fellow parishioners who don't look fertile and who don't feel fed, wondering if we will ever bear the image of a fertile, life-bearing God.

A fervent preacher once implored his congregation to "be a friend and bring a friend" as his method of plumping out church attendance. A relative was visiting the church with his family for the first time and heard this plea. After the meeting was over, he said, "If you were a really good friend, you'd keep quiet about that place." He was recognizing that this particular church was struggling to exist in a famine.

So what is the answer to *"there was a famine in the land."* Leave? Stay and starve? Everything within us fights the pull to create a Moab situation (forming a liaison with the wrong church or the wrong people out of desperation to produce spiritual seed).[4] But equally intense is the need for our heart hunger to be sated. Leave? Stay and starve? Either way, we have to make a decision.

A church with a moderate congregation had gone through a time of instability. During a fairly short period, it had undergone many changes in its leadership style and structure. Although people had come and gone, a solid core stayed during seasons of rain and seasons of dryness. Then the church came into a time of great famine. Many of the previous stayers became leave-ers. Elimelechs and their families walked out. Some ended up in other fertile breadbaskets. Others didn't do so well. Some simply stayed home. The last I heard about this church, it had leveled out, but was not yet thriving.

There is no easy answer to this dilemma. Stay and die? Leave and hope for the best?

Why not stay and look for the declaration of God's heart for His church?

But the LORD Almighty will be exalted by his justice, and the holy God will show himself holy by his righteousness. Then sheep will graze as in their own pasture; lambs will feed among the ruins of the rich (Isaiah 5:16-17).

MASTERING THE ART OF INTELLIGENT WAITING

There is an art in waiting that takes all the pus and pain out of life. I call it "intelligent waiting." The best understanding of intelligent waiting is found at the end of the famous communion chapter of 1 Corinthians 11. Halfway through that chapter, Paul took his cautionary and disciplinary comments about the immature and self-serving behavior of the congregation to another level. He was rebuking but he softened the rebuke by bringing the involvement of heaven into his reprimand. *"For I received from the Lord what I also passed on to you..."* (verse 23).

Then he wrote the famous scriptures that usually accompany our communion times, finishing with the instruction of 1 Corinthians 11:33-34: *"So then, my brothers, when you come together to eat, wait for each other. If anyone is hungry, he should eat at home, so that when you meet together it may not result in judgment...."*

"Wait," he said. The Greek word that has been translated as "wait" is *ekdechomai.* Other English terms used in the translation of *ekdechomai* are "expect," "look" or "tarry for."[5]

In the context of the last verses in chapter 11, it sounds as though Paul was encouraging the simple courtesies of hanging around for five minutes or so until everyone shows up. However, it is the use of *ekdechomai,* now loaded by its context, that sends the waiting into orbit.

Here are other verses that contain *ekdechomai:*

*"In these lay a great multitude of impotent folk, of blind, halt, withered, **waiting** for the moving of the water"* (John 5:3 KJV). This is waiting in forced inactivity. The immobile people knew that healing would come when the waters moved, but they couldn't do anything to precipitate that moment.

*"While Paul was **waiting** for them in Athens, he was greatly distressed to see that the city was full of idols"* (Acts 17:16). This is waiting for a defined period of time. Paul

knew that the others would eventually arrive in Athens, but for now nothing that he could do would hurry them up.

*"For he was **looking** forward to the city with foundations, whose architect and builder is God"* (Hebrews 11:10). This is waiting or searching or questing. Abraham knew that the city he was waiting for was not going to be found in his tent, so he had to *ekdechomai*...for his whole earthly life.

*"Be patient, then, brothers, until the Lord's coming. See how the farmer **waits** for the land to yield its valuable crop and how patient he is for the autumn and spring rains"* (James 5:7). This is waiting during a natural process of events. The farmer knows that the planted crop will grow but won't appear until a series of unhurried, ordained events transpire.

*"Who disobeyed long ago when God **waited** patiently in the days of Noah while the ark was being built"* (1 Peter 3:20a). This is waiting for others to play their part. God knew that the ark would be built but chose not to move beyond the pace set by Noah.

Forced inactivity; people yet to arrive where you are already; looking for something beyond the familiar; patiently waiting for the unseen to become seen; waiting for someone else to play his part...these oh-too-familiar characteristics of the famine times in the church are softened for us when we remind ourselves that the day will come when the waiting will be over.

So how do we handle a famine? In each of these scriptures, there is a measure of intelligent knowing.

• The immobile people know that healing will come.

• Paul knows that the others will eventually arrive in Athens.

- Abraham knows that the city he is waiting for is not going to be found in his tent.

- The farmer knows that the planted crop will grow.

- God knows that the ark will be built.

If you are a leader, you think and plan. You may have original thought, as opposed to a cut 'n' paste approach to vision getting or sermon getting. You may shrink back from an institutional approach to anything. If most of the men and women in leadership with whom you associate are not where you are, what do you do? The answer is found in mastering the art of intelligent waiting:

- waiting in forced inactivity

- waiting for others to catch up

- waiting...searching...questing

- waiting during a natural process of events

- waiting for others to play their part

Sometimes, despite our awareness that we are *ekde-chomai*-ing, we can be as busy as we have ever been; God can be blessing our output as much as He ever has; there can be evidence of blessing on the things we touch. Yet, we know that we are waiting for something way beyond what we see. We are waiting for a break in the famine.

EATING AT HOME

Where does the intelligent part come into this waiting? Simply, we master the art of eating at home. Paul told the Corinthians that the best way to cope with a famine—or with lack of sufficient food in the church—is to eat at home before they arrive, so that they won't let their starvation create uncouth behavior.

That is how we wait intelligently during the famine times. We draw from the wells of water that have been sunk during our times of weeping. We draw from the provision of food that others have threshed and packaged up for our consumption. Then, when we come together, we aren't as anguished or as "angsty" at leadership who, by the way, are also aware of the famine and are doing everything they know to do to provide for the people in their care.

It is an awesome thing to find a place, person, or association where we can be nourished so that the feast of love, the feast of remembrance, is not reduced to chaos and judgment.

When we hold church leadership as the sole providers of our spiritual food, we do them an injustice, and we keep ourselves at the level of high-chair Christianity.

Here is the extraordinary truth: Elimelech owns land. Elimelech is meant to be a leader in his community. Can I say it again? Elimelech owns land. He is meant to be growing things, tending things and feeding his family with what he grows. Oh, it is dry all right, and every day he walks out of his house knowing the prophecy from the Lord about fertility and bread only to lift his gaze to a sky devoid of rain clouds. But, Elimelech, you own the land. Walk away from it, and you walk away from your inheritance, which still carries the promise of God despite what you see.

Furthermore, Elimelech, every time Naomi or the boys call your name, they are stating the highest truth under which any man or woman, boy or girl, can ever live. They are saying, "my God is King," for this is what your name, *Elimelech*, means.

Do you really want to go to Moab, a land populated out of an incestuous relationship? Do you really want to live in a land that the psalmist described as a washbasin?[6] The fruit in that land has weakness in its makeup.

Don't leave, Elimelech. Find a way to nourish yourself in the famine. There is a worse fate waiting for you if you are unwilling to suffer the pangs of hunger. Those pangs will pass, but death is final. The message of redemption is to come out of your own land...out of Bethlehem, not Moab. By staying, you remain part of the glorious procession of life. Do you really want to turn your back on that? Won't you allow "my God is King" to provide you with a miracle diet? Hasn't He done that before for your ancestors? Don't the words *manna* and *quail* mean anything to you?

Okay, go. But your sons will never make it back to their land of promise...to their portion of their divine inheritance. And forever their names will carry a message that perhaps need not have been (*Mahlon*, "invalid"; *Kilion*, "pining, wasting away").

And in your leaving, Elimelech, you are uprooting one of the most treasured gifts ever given by a relational God to His children: the gift of community. Your sons won't be marrying girls from your Christian community. They'll get married, but those marriages won't produce any offspring, let alone offspring who carry the seed that contains the redemptive message. God, the masterful economist, will position the right woman with the right man to produce generational seed-carrying, but you and your sons are now sidelined.

When churches are in famine, the words of Psalm 11:1-4 must be more our truth than the circumstances around us.

14

In the LORD I take refuge. How then can you say to me: "Flee like a bird to your mountain. For look, the wicked bend their bows; they set their arrows against the strings to shoot from the shadows at the upright in heart. When the foundations are being destroyed, what can the righteous do?" The LORD is in his holy temple; the LORD is on his heavenly throne....

Although it is always good to ask what righteous people can do in the face of destruction, this friend of the psalmist perhaps got it wrong. He saw that foundations were being destroyed and his response was escape. Today, legions of believers are following the same line. They see the foundations of their faith being diluted; they see the foundations of their church system being eroded; they see the foundations of their own church being undermined, and they flee like birds. What if, instead, they stayed and declared the truth emphatically stated by the psalmist...the truth that is far greater than the evidence of destruction, the truth that God is our refuge and we can choose to hide in that refuge, which is His holy throne. That holy throne is our sacred land. It is our possession.

Elimelech has the land, but he flees like a bird. Instead of producing food as his part in generational responsibility and blessing, he walks away just because times get a bit tough. His life is a denial of the statement of the greatest truth that man can ever encounter: the truth that "my God is King."

TURNING GRAIN INTO BREAD— OUR RESPONSIBILITY

We need to pause here and remind ourselves of a crucial piece of information. Even if he had stayed in Bethlehem,

Elimelech would have only grown grain, not bread. He is a landowner in the town and his assignment is to use that land wisely as part of the process of feeding those for whom he is responsible. He is not a landowner for prestige, power or pride, but for provision. He is a landowner because God needs providers. Elimelech has to till, fertilize, plant, tend, harvest, separate, thresh, grind, form and bake before anyone is going to eat bread.

Yet hasn't God prophesied that there will be bread in his house? Yes. But "my God is King" has placed the responsibility for significant parts of that process into Elimelech's hands. God provides the land. God creates the seed. God waters the land. And He entrusts the one in charge with the responsibility to form it into something edible that will feed those in his care.

The partnership between God and man was always going to be risky business on God's part. He has chosen to tie Himself down to our understanding of life. (In a way, He is still waiting while we are building the ark that will save our generation.)

The feeding and tending of sheep is of the highest priority to God. Just hours away from the crucifixion, there is a wrangling session going on between certain disciples about prestige, power and pride. Just who, they argue, is going to sit where in this great new kingdom? The Lord yet again tries to break through carnal thinking and introduce them to their assigned role as providers (or, equippers).

Here is how that moment plays out. As the curtain closes on the writings of John, Christ gives the most impacting plea to those to whom He is entrusting the building of His church: "Follow Me."[7] It is the second last impacting plea in John 21:15-17 that we must equally heed.

When they had finished eating, Jesus said to Simon Peter, "Simon son of John, do you truly love me more than these?" "Yes, Lord," he said, "you know that I love you." Jesus said, "Feed my lambs." Again Jesus said, "Simon son of John, do you truly love me?" He answered, "Yes, Lord, you know that I love you." Jesus said, "Take care of my sheep." The third time he said to him, "Simon son of John, do you love me?" Peter was hurt because Jesus asked him the third time, "Do you love me?" He said, "Lord, you know all things; you know that I love you." Jesus said, "Feed my sheep."

Feed My sheep. Don't get bogged down on issues of position and prestige. Instead, focus on gathering grain and threshing it into edible food. Feed the sheep.

In his days as a young pastor, my father traveled to Britain to seek enrichment in his life and ministry. While there, he met with a titan in faith. Nelson Parr was a small man with a giant ability to feed sheep. My father asked him how he got his weekly sermons for which he was famous. Parr's reply was, "I start reading the Word until something bites me, and then that is what I preach." This is a simple description of the process of taking the Word to which our spirit is quickened, assimilating it into our heart and then forming it into a digestible meal for the sheep.

Dr. Lois Burkett puts it like this: "Receive the Word of revelation from the Lord. Research it thoroughly, and then preach out of the revealed Word, supported by the researched Word."

There is nothing quite as disconcerting as preacher's block. For the man and woman called to equip believers, it is a really bad moment to sit before the Word, armed with pen and paper, and feel an enveloping blankness. Already hopelessly uninspired, a slow walk to the mailbox, followed by the all-important and pressured task of, well, anything, fails to kick start any spiritual substance. Stalling doesn't help. What *must* take place is a deliberate choice to push past the famine, find something to work with, and turn it into food. We *will* find something. Kind David observed, in Psalm 37:25: *"I was young and now I am old, yet I have never seen the righteous forsaken or their children begging bread."*

Back to the Elimelechs. They now walk out of one famine into another. The Bethlehem famine made their stomachs ache from emptiness. The second famine is more harsh than the first. It makes their wombs ache with emptiness. Moreover, the second famine takes place in a land of dubious origins—Moab.

FINDING HOPE IN MOAB

The Moabite ancestry finds its origins in the incestuous relationship between Lot and his daughter. Their liaison wasn't the result of lust but of a desperate attempt to ensure the survival of the family line. Is it this pull of the elemental need for survival that draws Elimelech to this particular faraway place? Of everywhere that he could choose, he chooses a place that exists because a woman opted for a carnal solution to her barrenness.

The inclusion of the Moab details in the story of Ruth has got to be an encouragement to us rather than a slap in the face. We look at our needy circumstances and we cast about for a solution. The more immediate the solution, the better. "There is no man to give me a son, so I will find my

18

own solution." "There is no food in the land, so I will find my own solution." In so doing, we create a Moab out of our own frenetic solution-seeking.

Is it God's highest for us? No.

Can we find redemption in it? Absolutely. (In this narrative, I am using Elimelech's decision-making to address the "do-I-go-or-do-I-stay" dilemma that faces many. For us to see the bright side of Elimelech's migration, we must remind ourselves that it was this very migration that wove a Ruth into the lineage of Christ. Redemption? Absolutely.)

We are God's workmanship. Our confidence must always be in His capacity to re-work the circumstances of our life. There is really only one condition, and that is our yieldedness. A favorite scripture of mine is Jeremiah 31:18: *"I have surely heard Ephraim's moaning: 'You disciplined me like an unruly calf, and I have been disciplined. Restore me, and I will return, because you are the LORD my God.' "*

God's gentle but insistent re-creating abilities can eventually place us back in our Bethlehems.

Here is another reason to find courage in our Moab moments. Moab is contained in a natural fortress. A chasm to the north, perpendicular cliffs to the west and a semicircle of hills to the south and east create a sense of fortification. For its inhabitants, there is a lulling security provided by the created surroundings.[8]

How typical of the goodness of God that, even in times when we have drifted from a higher way, He shelters us.

As a young woman, I found myself, on several occasions, in risky situations. Almost always I got there through miscalculated decision-making. Once, during my student years, I hitchhiked in the late afternoon and into the night from a port in the South Island of New Zealand, down its eastern coastline, toward the city in which I was living. Not the brightest move at all. In hindsight, I think I was surrounded by a "natural fortress" as I hitchhiked.

Thirty years later, our youngest child, as a 16-year-old, was working for his older brother in Thailand. During a morning off, he walked, on his own, into a neighboring town, hired a scooter and, in his own words, "fanged all over Pataya at 80k, Mum!" There was not a lot that I could say. Perhaps he was encased in the same "natural fortress."

Although these two examples speak more of recklessness than desperation or hunger, they illustrate the protective power of God over His people during times of shaky decision-making. Our heavenly Father provides safe places in the middle of our chaos that can be found even when we have drifted away from where we should be because of desperation or soul hunger.

Not only will Moab provide a protected environment for the Elimelech family, it also is going to provide so much more. Out of this rather blighted nation will come a woman whose resolute disposition will guarantee her the most lofty position possible in any household in Bethlehem.

Even if our Moabs have been self-induced, our great confidence is this: We can find God there.

Back to the Elimelechs. For a season in Moab, death will be more real to them than their rightful inheritance of life and living. In the future, life will once again produce life, but that victory is over ten years away.

God, who keeps the promises He makes Himself (one such promise being that He *will* have a people who bear His image), will turn this disaster into delight. He always does. But for now, this little family is in for a miserable time. We, the readers, know that a pearl is hidden in their irritation, but they don't know that, and now they have moved a long way from the place where they are meant to be.

Several years ago, I had been thinking about the constant movement of the body of Christ amongst the churches in our city. In their search for food, so much of the body of Christ gathered itself up like a deck of cards each Sunday and dealt itself out to the various buildings! Fresh pews; same famine. One day the Lord spoke to me and said, "You have been called to a vineyard, not to a man." Although, at that time, we were not considering changing churches, we contentedly stayed put (along with many others, I must say). Time went by, and the famine didn't seem to be lifting. In fact, it began to feel to me like a forced famine brought about through faulty decision-making by a few in leadership, rather than a natural famine brought about because of the seasons and timings of God.

One day, God spoke to my husband saying, "I release you to think about your future." He shared this with me, and our considered response was, "Thank You, Lord, for giving us that freedom, but where would we go?" God may have been testing us, but we don't think so. We think that Father was genuinely giving us the freedom of choice based on our best understanding of our journey. Well, we stayed. God has been, and still is, our refuge. We might get in our car and drive to a particular building on a Sunday, but our whole lives are lived out of the land that we possess—His throne.

If the sound of His voice calls for migration, go. Without that sound, a good idea is to stay put.

REMEMBERING TO LIVE

To get from the famine-riddled Ephrath to Moab, they need to go around or over the Salt Sea. We know this stretch of water as the Dead Sea. Selah.

As residents in Moab, Mr. and Mrs. E. set about creating their new life. They need food, somewhere to live, furnishings and relationships. We can take heart from this phrase used in the telling of their story: They *"lived there"* (Ruth 1:2). We worship a God who doesn't just create an existence for us. He creates life for us. Although they are in the wrong church, in the wrong town, amongst people who carry the stigma of shameful origins, they *live.* Now that's worthy of praise.

However, as is the way of things, amongst life is death. Elimelech passes away, taking with him unfulfilled promises, untilled land, unplanted crops, unharvested fields and misplaced loyalties.

A few generations later, his wife's great-grandson by adoption will write in Psalm 33:18-19, *"But the eyes of the LORD are on those who fear him, on those whose hope is in his unfailing love, to deliver them from death and keep them alive in famine."* In Psalm 37:19, he will write, *"In times of disaster they will not wither; in days of famine they will enjoy plenty."*

Perhaps amongst the stories that comprised the oral history of David's family tree was the hushed and morbid tale of his ancestor-by-marriage who could have proven God in the same way that the rest of the Ephrathites did, but allowed desperation to send him to Moab.

LOOKING FOR LIFE IN BARRENNESS

The boys marry. Mahlon and Kilion need, as we all do, love and relationships. Because this family are foreigners, the usual arrangements for marriage probably haven't been made. The family has no history here. However, God has made provision for these young men in the form of two available maids, Ruth and Orpah.

It says a huge amount about Naomi that she keeps a sweet and winning relationship with her daughters-in-law even though they are married and she is now a widow.

Naomi means "pleasant."[9] Well done, Naomi. You have resisted the temptation to become numb to engaging in life, even in the face of the death of your husband and dislocation from your inheritance. As a result, you are sowing something wonderful into your near future. (Her bitterness isn't apparent until the end of her arduous journey home.)

Single men and women create a better world of connections for themselves when they learn to enjoy the marriages and families of those around them. Although they live in their own homes on their own, they choose, by their pleasant disposition and active participation in life, to stay sweet. In so doing, they give others the freedom to also enjoy life.

Mary Slessor, a 20th-century missionary to Calabar, is quoted as saying, "We lose nothing of ourselves when we rejoice in the achievements of another."[10]

We have a valued friend who has never married. She attends many of our children's special events. In fact, our children, now adults, feel quite robbed of something special if she is not part of our family Christmases. Her unfailing pleasure in the achievements of our family members has made her a welcome and happy part of our family circle, and the family circles of everyone in her world. How wise of her to choose to keep doors of connection open with her many married friends because of this outlook on life.

The passing of time reveals that Mahlon and Kilion are not going to experience the joy of fatherhood. For ten long years, Ruth and Orpah watch month by month for the promise of children. In a culture where women need children for their own security, these girls are facing a grim future. There are few agonies like the fruitlessness of the womb. At least for those ten years, they have someone to hug!

In the same way that Ruth has the marriage experience without fertility, so we can have a church experience or a small group experience without any sense of fertility—without any sense that something is growing inside us that speaks of reproductive life. We long to live in a place named "fertility" or "house of bread" but, instead, we are left wondering why the growth we crave never seems to come. Like Ruth, the marriage is giving us relationship; it is satisfying our God-placed needs for love and affection; we belong somewhere; we can get a hug; but there is a possibility that the union, for whatever reason, will never produce a child.

Stay, Ruth. Without even knowing that you are doing so, stay put. God is at work and is preparing the "house of bread" for you. It is there that your real future lies. You see, Ruth, some relationships must die before we gain access to strong and seed-yielding relationships.

Which is exactly what happens. Mahlon and Kilion die, having never fully lived.

DISCOVERING A NEW FACET OF GOD'S CHARACTER

Word now comes across the hills and across the Salt Sea that God has again visited His people in Bethlehem with the miracle of provision. Faithful God always comes to the aid of His people. Bread, part of the DNA of Naomi's homeland, is being found again. Although Elimelech, "my God is King," has passed away, the Lord plans to show Himself to Naomi in the same way He declared Himself to Abraham on Mount Moriah: as Jehovah-Jireh, my God is Provider.[11] In other words, she is being asked to allow God to reveal Himself to her in a new way.

In our spiritual youthfulness, we require God to reveal Himself in the same way week after week and year after year. The security of the known is desired more than the headiness of the unknown. Luke 5:37-39 says, *"And no one pours new wine into old wineskins. If he does, the new wine will burst the skins, the wine will run out and the wineskins will be ruined. No, new wine must be poured into new wineskins. And no one after drinking old wine wants the new, for he says, 'The old is better.' "*

It is possible to build the ethos of local churches or even church systems on *"the old is better"*—on a couple of man-ifestations of God's presence that have to take place every meeting, or else, in the vernacular, "God hasn't shown up."

In recent years, God has visited the western church as the joy-filler, as the restorer of lost dreams and, in the world of women, as the Father of princesses. There is no question, no doubt at all about the timeliness of these visitations. However, if that is where we stay, we remain giggling, goo-ey, starry-eyed portraits who end up where all portraits end up—over the fireplace, occasionally toasted!

God is ever wanting to test our readiness for adventure. He wants us to reflect His multifaceted character rather than be a two-dimensional portrait. He wants us to be transportable with His message, not forever frozen onto just one canvas.

To Naomi, "my God is King" is now revealing Himself as "my God is Provider." There are so many facets of God's character that it is in our best interests for us to be willing to meet Him outside of the familiar rut of past blessings. A sense of adventure makes the Christian life worth living.

It is a providential God, the Dispenser of prevenient grace, who ensures that the message comes over the mountains and the seas to those who will heed it. "How beautiful on the mountains are the feet of the one who brings news that God is greater than a famine!" (Isaiah 52:7, more or less!)

Naomi hears this wonderful news and prepares to change the course of her life. She packs up to return home. Praise God that she hasn't forgotten where home is.

There have been occasions when I have met with people who have left the church that our family calls home, but have now returned. A not uncommon reflection from them is, "We're back home. We should never have left." It seems that something inside of us is never fully at rest until the little homing device of the Spirit ceases beeping because our return brings our nomadic days to a close.

GOING FORWARD BY GOING BACK

The Scriptures so cutely say that Naomi returned home *"from there"* (Ruth 1:6). Carrying the hurt of displacement through the famine in Ephrath and with the etched lines of grief through the loss of husband and sons on her face, Naomi sets forth. She is armed with resolution and with two relationships that are, as far as we can tell, her only legacy of her Moabite years. I wonder if she also has a sense of déja vu, that familiar thought: "Here I go again, seeking bread."

In the stretch of ministry life, we rarely pick things up from where we left off. Process; process; process. When we are away from our place of God's appointment, we can't expect to wake up one morning and find ourselves fully returned. It may take some packing up, some good-bye hugs and some trekking to get "from there" back to our intended "here." Although it is not always possible, pausing to tie up loose ends can free up the future from unnecessary entanglement.

WHERE THINGS ARE RIGHT NOW

For now, all that matters to us in our passion to stand in the place of our appointment is the truth that the famine is over. In Bethlehem, crops have been sown; they have grown; and the harvest is soon to begin. Elimelech is dead. Mahlon and Kilion are dead. Naomi, on the other hand, is very alive and has yet to play a vital role in this narrative.

❧

RESPONSES TO FAMINE

- Keep "my God is King" on the throne.
- Expect to thrive.
- Master the art of intelligent waiting.
- Eat at home.
- Turn grain into bread.
- Find hope in Moab.
- Remember to live.
- Look for life in barrenness.
- Discover a new facet of God's character.
- If necessary, go forward by going back.

ENDNOTES

1. *They said to him, "You are old, and your sons do not walk in your ways; now appoint a king to lead us, such as all the other nations have"* (1 Samuel 8:5).

2. *Then the LORD said to Moses, "Go down, because your people, whom you brought up out of Egypt, have become corrupt. They have been quick to turn away from what I commanded them and have made themselves an idol cast in the shape of a calf. They have bowed down to it and sacrificed to it..."* (Exodus 32:7-8).

3. *Fausset's Bible Dictionary*, electronic database (copyright © 1998 by Biblesoft).

4. *Lot and his two daughters left Zoar and settled in the mountains, for he was afraid to stay in Zoar. He and his two daughters lived in a cave. One day the older daughter said to the younger, "Our father is old, and there is no man around here to lie with us, as is the custom all over the earth. Let's get our father to drink wine and then lie with him and preserve our family line through our father." That night they got their father to drink wine, and the older daughter went in and lay with him. He was not aware of it when she lay down or when she got up. ... The older daughter had a son, and she named him Moab; he is the father of the Moabites of today* (Genesis 19:30-33, 37).

5. *Biblesoft's New Exhaustive Strong's Numbers and Concordance with Expanded Greek-Hebrew Dictionary* (copyright © 1994 by Biblesoft and International Bible Translators, Inc.).

6. *Moab is my washbasin, upon Edom I toss my sandal; over Philistia I shout in triumph* (Psalm 60:8; also Psalm 108:9).

7. *Jesus said this to indicate the kind of death by which Peter would glorify God. Then he said to him, "Follow me!"* (John 21:19)

8. *Fausset's Bible Dictionary*, electronic database (copyright © 1998 by Biblesoft).

9. *Biblesoft's New Exhaustive Strong's Numbers and Concordance with Expanded Greek-Hebrew Dictionary* (copyright © 1994 by Biblesoft and International Bible Translators, Inc.).

10. W.P. Livingstone, *Mary Slessor of Calabar: Pioneer Missionary* (New York: George H. Doran, Co.)

11. *So Abraham called that place The LORD Will Provide. And to this day it is said, "On the mountain of the LORD it will be provided"* (Genesis 22:14).

Chapter 2

RESPONDING TO OPPORTUNITY

⁂

These three women now provide us with a picture of life for both believers and those who equip believers.

We have the older woman who is called by God to be a landowner. Naomi, miles from the land she should be working, is now returning home with the dream of her own ministry now dead. There is nothing to show for the promise that was contained in her loins. No sons. No hope of ever having her own grandchildren. No husband who can provide doors of opportunity for other forms of ministry. Nothing. At least she has known the feeling of birthing something in God, even though what was birthed is now dead.

We also have two younger women who are joining the older woman because of loyalty, because of relationship and because of an attraction to her encouraging, pleasant disposition. They have never known the birthing of anything, let alone the joy of seeing it live or the horror of seeing it die. And now they choose to join the older woman who *has* known these things—the birth, life and death of a dream— and who has managed to keep an air of sweetness about her life regardless. They are not joining her because of a promise of an easy or secure future.

We need to know three things in this situation.

First, it is only Naomi who knows where to go and how to get there. She sets out on the right road—the road that will take them home—and takes the younger women with her.

Second, Ruth and Orpah follow willingly. They haven't been coerced. They just want to be with the one who knows more about life than they do.

Third, there is no mention made of servants. Technically, there may have been. However, we are talking about three widows here—and one of them has lived in a famine in her recent past. Naomi, Ruth and Orpah almost surely have to personally manage everything that they will need for this journey. It is this third point that is mirrored by a current reality in many parts of the church.

MANAGING YOUR OWN LOAD

So many mature-aged women who equip believers to do the work of the ministry are managing the load of all that is required of them, unaided. Whether they stand with their husbands in ministry or function in ministry or leadership roles on their own, they often manage the load of maintaining their homes, caring for dependents, endeavoring to develop their own ministry call and so on.

30

I was asked to speak to a group of pastors about the value of identifying and releasing their wives to rise in the call and anointing that God had placed upon them. I suggested that some of them could even consider paying people to do the housework in order to provide space for developments in their wives' ministries. As my eyes ran quickly across this room of men, I noticed quite a few heads nodding in agreement, but then the leader in the front seat dictated the expected response from the room by a loud and derisive snort. Perhaps he had a lot to give up in order to make way for the development of his wife's call to equip and lead the church. (Perhaps he just had a sinus problem.)

It is my observation that men seem to more commonly have the kind of assistance that frees them to focus on their call. Also, often these men are enabled by wives who are taking care of matters that have been deemed women's work such as children, friendships, upkeep of the home and managing of the family finances (things that also have eternal value and that most wives undertake willingly, happily and competently).

Up until now, in the church, this has been an easy or uneasy status quo, depending on the motivational gifting of the various players. However, a new breed of woman, working at a new kind of marriage, is emerging. The biblical marriage components of honor, submission and love set in a home where order, not chaos, reigns are still sought and highly valued. But the traditional roles, which are more cultural than biblical, are under review. Twenty-first century first world economies are demanding a double income in the average home. Many young women are putting themselves through the rigorous discipline of college study because of a strong sense of vocation and are capably supplying one of those incomes. Consequently, Christian marriages are helped along by load-carrying assistance such as paid housework, ironing, eating out and so on. Young men and women are working together to make their marriages and families the homes of honor that bring glory to God.

In other words, it is no longer the post-war culture of one income with defined boundaries of what is woman's work and what is man's work.

We need to make way for this paradigm within the dynamics of Christian leadership. Today, and in line with the unfolding sharing of ministry platforms, both men and women must serve at times, and both men and women must sit at times— in both the home and the church. It's okay.

I was sitting beside a pastor's wife who manages the private world of her family capably. Her husband was preaching a good message. He was certainly being faithful to the Word, and God sees to it that such energy never returns to heaven void. As he produced the bread for the sheep to enjoy that Sunday, his wife leaned over to me and said, without rancor, "That is all he does." In their home, she told me, her business was to manage everything that the family needed for living— food, clothing, discipline and comfort of children, counsel and comfort of husband and even the garden upkeep. His business was to get the Sunday message and deliver it as well as he could. Perhaps those dynamics worked for that couple, but I was interested and saddened to note that in that particular church, there was no systematic ministry to women and no vision for releasing them to levels of leadership.

Perhaps one of the reasons we have seen so much of this solo load-managing by women within the church is that managing heavy loads is something women do well—and mostly without complaint (as do many men, but we are focusing on two women at this point in the narrative).

So, back to our story. In a few months' time, Ruth is going to have a heavier-than-normal load placed upon her by her soon-to-be lover, but it will only rest upon her head for a short while because God never intended either men or women to manage the load of ministry upon their heads alone. After all, while we are balancing those loads, our hands are tied up from reaching out to others who need our touch of life's experience.

In today's church, like Naomi, Ruth and Orpah, if need be, women called to equip believers continue to willingly manage the load in order to get to where they have to go.

RESISTING SECOND BEST

After some time, Naomi tells the young women to return to the safety of their mothers' homes and find rest through marriages to other men. "Girls," she says, "what you need to do is...."

Naomi, you are wasting your time. It's not going to happen. Ruth and Orpah will never find marital and relational rest outside of God's sovereign plans. They have already each lived in an infertile marriage. Don't push them into another. Stop clutching at a fix-and-dismiss style of leadership. Perhaps there is a higher plan that will require your long-term involvement in their lives.

Many women, for centuries, have heard the voice of God calling them to become one who equips believers and have set about to respond obediently to that voice.

They have shared their story with, say, their youth group leaders, their small group leaders, their husbands or even their senior pastors. Of course, there have been instances where this has resulted in the recognition and fulfillment of their divine destiny.

However, so often, tragically, they have been told to go home and try to find rest in another "marriage"/another passion. Well-intentioned alternatives are encouraged, such as: "What you need to do is work in the nursery." "What you need to do is prove yourself by cleaning the church." "What you need to do is stop going after the wrong thing." "Women can't do what you are wanting to do, so what you need to do is this other thing."

And so these women have returned to the "house"/place of containment that they should by now have left, to wait for someone to notice them—a second "husband"—who will offer them a second-best life.

Oh, the men in charge usually mean it in a kindly way, and it is intended for the well-being of these called, gifted and anointed women. It is just that they are being sent to the wrong home to await the wrong outcome that will produce second-rate fruitfulness.

Sometimes, there also has been an accompanying stigma created by private conversations between men in leadership about the woman's pushiness, or lack of order, or wrong theology.

The Naomis and the Ruths of our church systems have often been an awkward feature and it has been the church's loss that their lives have not been as fulfilled as God intended.

Often, they have refused to return meekly to the second-rate option. And a cycle of frustration and misunderstanding has set in.

Many times, if they have taken up the second-best option under the mistaken belief that they are correctly submitting to those in authority, they have failed to find rest. And it is this very restlessness that has added fuel to the stigma of their lives.

The Naomis and the Ruths of our church systems have often been an awkward feature and it has been the church's loss that their lives have not been as fulfilled as God intended.

Before moving on, I want to enlarge on the earlier phrase of "a fix-and-dismiss style of leadership." Having worked in churches all my adult life, I have observed many ill-conceived solutions or evaluations being handed down. Quite often this is the result of busy-ness...of too much needing to be done in too little time. Desperation, rather than anything dark, has produced the "what you have got to do is..." response.

However, there have been times when the fix-and-dismiss style of leadership has been the product of something other than a hectic schedule. It has been the product of intimidation, ignorance or insecurity on the part of the existing leadership. As leaders, there are times when we need to pause long enough to examine our motive for the fix-and-dismiss approach.

35

Getting back to our story, what we do know is that God has a plan for Naomi and Ruth that they won't stumble upon without a long, arduous, hot, painful journey on their own, burdened by their own load in life.

OWNING PAIN WITHOUT BITTERNESS

Naomi now makes a wrong call about her circumstances. She colors the character of God in black by making Him responsible for her dilemma. She tells Ruth and Orpah that everything that has happened is because God is against her.

No, He's not, Naomi! Elimelech's decision-making—and your willingness to go along with it—has put you in this dilemma.

You are speaking out of hurt and gut-wrenching disappointment to lay blame at the Father's door for something that was the mistake of the human element.

And Naomi, your former pleasantness is now masked by another smell. It is the acrid smell of bitterness. Stop blaming God.

One of the marks of adulthood is taking responsibility for those things for which we must take responsibility, and shedding responsibility for those things that are someone else's responsibility.

It is not uncommon for women who are chronologically mature to be spiritually and emotionally stunted because of a "girly" culture in the church, or because of an inability of those around them to deal effectively with this weakness.

This produces the spoilt, temper tantrum that blames some-one else for things not going the way they want.

(After a lifetime in pastorates, my mother has observed to me that many of the women who created the most diffi-culties in church life were spoilt as little girls.)

It is healthy for women to revel in a girlish Daddy-God relationship with Father at an appropriate point in their pil-grimage—but only for a while. Father wants to commune with us as grown-ups and, if we are serious about the call on our lives, in the church or in the community, we need to move past the princess stage into a queenliness under God, for it is kings and queens who rule and reign.

THINKING ABOUT LIVING, NOT DYING

As the girls process Naomi's instructions, it becomes apparent that Orpah's hunger for a new life is not strong enough, nor is her vision clear enough, for her to face the hard times ahead.

She is not to be criticized unduly. Naomi isn't exactly painting a rosy picture of the church, of her Maker or of the life to come. Because of this, someone on his or her way toward salvation most probably never makes it.

Senior women with the call of God on their lives, partic-ularly those who have been dealt with in a disappointing way, need to be so careful about how they behave, espe-cially around emerging leaders.

I refer again to my own mother. In her early 80's, God spoke to her during her morning walk, "Think living, not dying." When she told me about His message to her, I was inspired to write the following. Naomi, this is for you.

"THINK LIVING, NOT DYING"

My mother was born in 1922. Recently, during her daily morning walk, the Holy Spirit spoke clearly to her saying, "Think living, not dying." Most of her days have two basic occupations: caring for my elderly father and being the receptionist in our family business. She does both enthusiastically and capably, her latest achievements being mastering emailing and whizzing around the suburbs in her natty new car.

What she values:

- *wearing classy jewelry*

- *matching her nail polish with her lipstick*

- *matching snappy trousers with sharp tops*

- *giggling like a teenager when her adult grandson calls her a foxy chick*

- *attending anything that the younger women of our fellowship convene (At her age, everyone else is younger. By "younger," in this context, I mean anyone under 55 years.)*

- *being enthusiastic about life*

- *keeping a sweet spirit*

- *singing all the latest songs*

- *living in, and breathing, the Word of God*

- *the house of God*

- *relationships with friends old and new*

- *giving time to younger women who want to talk with her*

- *listening to preaching that contains revelation*

What she doesn't value:

- *attending seniors events ("They are just for old people.")*
- *cardigans*
- *brooches*
- *dishonesty*
- *ungodliness*
- *politics in church life*
- *pretense*
- *listening to preaching that has no revelation*

Her generation, and the generation that followed, fought and won some amazing battles.

The battle of "the adornment of a godly woman":

- *They buried the brown-wrinkled-potato fashion statement.*
- *They were the first generation to color their hair. (The previous generation had, interestingly, found scriptural license to have tight little curly perms—they just had to be gray tight little curly perms.)*
- *They began to wear makeup.*
- *They began to wear trousers.*
- *They began to wear tasteful jewelry.*

- *They stopped wearing hats as a sign of submission and godliness. (In the death throes of that battle, not even the most legalistic preacher was trying to find scriptural support for millinery.)*

- *They were the generation that saw the fading out of the matching shoes and handbag, the matching hat and gloves and the "ensemble" as crucial Sunday morning regalia.*

The battle of "the little ladies' meeting":

- *They faced the need for women to be well founded in the Word of God, starting weekly Bible studies for the women of their churches.*

- *They began to face the need for women to meet in a context that fed the soul as well as the spirit, so they began dinners, dessert and coffee nights and special guest nights.*

- *They recognized the need to resource small groups or individuals with Bible studies, so they wrote and published them for our churches.*

- *They took the "little ladies' meeting" out of the church basement—figuratively or literally—giving it a greater air of dignity and stature.*

The battle of status:

- *They began to see that God's call and anointing are without gender bias, and so sought to fulfill the destiny that was on their lives.*

- *For some, this led to credentialing for ministry.*

- *For some, this led to the pulpit.*

- *For some, this led to the marketplace, where our top-class women of God became significant players in business and service industries in particular.*

- *They became valued members of church leadership teams.*

- *They came head-to-head with the real issue of keeping home and family while walking in integrity to the call of God on their lives.*

Answers were few and hard to find, but they began the journey for the next two generations that are currently functioning in leadership in our churches.

Perhaps the saddest observations of those women—chiefly pastors' wives—who are now in their late 50's and older are these:

- *Many of them were brilliant cooks, cleaners, home-makers, husband supporters, child rearers. This was what they did and this is all they wanted to do.*

- *Many of them were, **in addition**, able to play the piano, lead the choir, teach Sunday school, visit the sick and hostess the continual stream of guest speakers and missionaries who came through the town. (Commercial accommodation was never used.)*

My mother was one such woman.

BUT

- *Some pastors' wives and key women in the local churches had another call burning in their hearts.*

41

- *They were called to preach and to lead; they were called to run businesses, to nurse, to teach, to be in government.*

- *They received nil or minimal recognition or understanding for this longing and, if they dared to voice it, were quickly labeled as being a "strong" woman, or a "difficult" woman, or "a handful."*

IN FACT

- *Pulpit preachers often fired shots at women who failed to walk "in submission."*

- *Ignorance of God's viewpoint of equality and strident interpretations of Paul's call to submission and right order in the godly home led to great pain and grief for these women.*

- *It is these very women who now have to stand on the sidelines and watch the two current generations of female leaders in our churches receive opportunity, recognition and reward for doing the kinds of things that they longed to do.*

- *The temptation is there for sorrow to turn to bitterness and meanness of heart.*

These older generations also had some battles that were not fought and won. These are the battles that they bequeath to those of us in significant leadership in our churches today.

The battle of balancing home and family with the call of God:

- *There are still leadership homes where all the energy goes toward getting the man of God into the pulpit with a clean shirt every Sunday.*

- *There are still leadership homes where domestic duties are mostly or completely fulfilled by the wife and mother, thus enabling the husband and father to score his goals, with resulting frustration if the woman's call is otherwise.*

- *There are still ministerial homes where the wife's highest call is to enable her husband to be the pastor. (However, this narrow-minded restriction on ministers' wives is a stronghold that is weakening.)*

- *There are still ministerial homes that have not yet hit the glorious air-current of synergistic leadership of the home.*

The battle of equality in churches:

- *A great and current danger is the advocating of the perfect model as being the husband and wife in strategic leadership of the local church. Although this is wonderful when both have the mantle/anointing for leadership of their church, to regard this as a perfect model, or as an assumption, may place women (perhaps even men) outside of their anointing.*

- *Great stand-alone women are still an awkward feature of many local churches. Yet, Paul said that it was better not to marry because then the devotion of the single person to the ministry could be unimpeded. When and why did we start overlooking such scriptures?*

- *While a staggering percentage of our churches can only afford to pay a senior pastor and, possibly, some administrative assistance, we do have churches who have paid staff as their leadership teams. It is a tragic fact that a youth leader and a creative ministries leader will often be paid before a women's leader will be paid. This demonstration of the low value of women is still in the thinking of some of our younger pastors, not just a few older pastors.*

Values that keep older women qualified for active service:

- *current hairstyle*

- *appropriate hair coloring*

- *appropriate makeup*

- *money (Many of our fabulous older women are on hopeless pensions and can't afford gas or transport, tickets to events, decent shoes, dental work, and so on. If I was a widow on a pension, the lack of these things would cause me distress, and the widow in her distress is to be looked after by the New Testament church.)*

- *appropriate clothing (often all they can afford are shapeless polyester numbers from a budget store)*

- *enthusiasm*

- *a sweet spirit*

- *freshness in the Word*

- *sending little notes or cards congratulating current leadership on victories won*

- *keeping socially attractive (appropriate levels of couth)*

- *smiling at younger women and, wherever a younger person will let them (this is such a two-way street), stopping for a brief chat before and after the meetings to take an interest in the life of that younger woman*

Behavior that may disqualify an older woman from active service:

- *talking about her health*

- *complaining about the volume of the music*

- *whining about the lack of hymns in church*

- *failing to congratulate younger women for victories won*

- *not attending conferences, dinners, etc. (see money issue above)*

- *going off on tangents—the latest whiff of doctrine—in order to feel that she is on the cutting edge*

- *becoming controlling with intercession*

- *constantly talking about and defending the past while criticizing what is happening now*

- *allowing her social skills to diminish*

- *only talking to other older women at church*

- *allowing the younger men and women in leadership to dismiss her as a "pray-er" when she is still a party animal at heart*

45

*Everyone wants to finish his or her days with dignity. Both Moses' and Joseph's final hours were spent blessing the next generations **who hung around to be blessed!***

Mother, thank you for remembering to live.

The world needs our 21st-century Naomis to think about living, not dying.

ASSOCIATING WITH MATURE PEOPLE

Orpah's return to the familiar may, perhaps, shut the lid on her progress.

Ruth, on the other hand, produces an impassioned speech that carries the air of abandonment to the cause of Christ that typifies the approach to ministry of so many women who equip believers to do the work of the ministry today.

Ruth now stands before Naomi, pleading for association. She is a young woman who, although no longer a virgin, is still to experience any conception, awakening or birthing of her own life-flow. She looks around at the possibilities that the world is offering and chooses to walk in the footsteps of one who is older, even though it means walking into the unknown. She wants more out of life, and she sees that an older woman can take her toward the intangible glory of God. Instead of a girly and proud approach to the aged one, Ruth demonstrates a maturity of choice that will become the very attribute that partners her with God's divine plan for mankind.

Before moving on, I want to pause at this stage in Ruth's life...no longer a virgin, but without ever experiencing a conception, let alone a birth. At the risk of laboring the point, so many young men and women are at this place in the church. They are being used to satisfy the ambition of more senior ministries and have not been brought to any place where their own call is being fertilized. The world calls these people "clones."

I have heard senior ministry men state enthusiastically from the pulpit that it is possible to tell the young men whom they have influenced because everything about their leadership style mirrors the senior man. Part of this is natural. I have curly hair. One of our sons has inherited my curls. I have a crooked little finger. One of our sons has inherited that characteristic. But part of this is so unnatural. It is as though, in the younger man or woman, any potential adulthood in ideologies, creativity, decision-making, discernment, or even theology has been pruned back to the stark level of the trunk, thus producing a stunted growth.

If the church is to move forward in a strong and healthy way, our emerging leaders must be initiated into the ministry and then released to their own ability to conceive, incubate and birth things from their own life-flow.

What Ruth is offering is loyalty in association, not blind loyalty. She is not saying, "I will never have any opinion but yours," or "Whatever you think, I will think." Utter loyalty must exist. The need to walk in step requires a high level of loyalty. However, loyalties must never be blind. Charismatic leaders will often draw blind loyalty, even demand it. But to give it is to give away one's soul. Despots rise when their decision-making is never questioned and when the opinions of others are not sought for and valued.

Ruth is following, but it is not because Naomi has demanded this allegiance. This makes the friendship safe, with room for fruitful developments.

In the context of a younger Ruth with an older Naomi, it is worth mentioning a post-war sociological phenomenon. Although adolescence has been recognized by appropriate rites of passage in many cultures, our western post-war culture has developed a lengthy and, perhaps sometimes, inappropriate rite of passage called "the teen years." (These teen years can last for decades in some people!) An unfortunate by-product of the worship of youth and the expensive pursuit of youthfulness by those who should know better is a disdain of anything old.

When foundation stones are thrown away; when ancient landmarks are jettisoned; when a creed loses its language—these are "when's" that result in insecurity and uncertainty followed by legalism. Legalism is man's consistent response to a famine, or a spiritual vacuum.

Along with millions of others, I sat glued to the TV screen on 11 and 12 September 2001. As the horror and magnitude of the attack was becoming known, face after face spoke into cameras—fire chiefs, security agents, politicians, city fathers, emergency service workers and so on. Over those two days, dozens of people were interviewed. Their words carried comfort, reassurance and conviction as they spoke of strategies for rebuilding what had been destroyed. Amidst all of this, I was forcibly hit by the fact that every single face belonged to a mature-aged person. They knew stuff. Anyone under 50 was not yet ready for that level of leadership. But, if accurately recognized and released, they will be ready for the next crisis.

The late Julia Finlay, a senior lecturer at a Christian university in my city, said this: "Children are equal in intelligence; just not equal in experience."

This maxim holds true in the recognition, development and release of young people for ministry in the church. They can have an observable capacity and calling, but until they have experience under their belt, they are too dangerous. They need to serve an Elisha-sized apprenticeship beside a mature leader.

BURYING YOURSELF IN GOD'S WORK

Before moving on, there is one other point to be made about Ruth's commitment to Naomi. The flavor of romantic abandonment that accompanies Ruth's magnificent commitment to Naomi can flavor ministry marriages. Here is what I mean.

Ruth's "where you go I will go" is the story of many women who have chosen to put their own call aside in order to be more culturally acceptable as helpers for their pastor-husbands.

There are extraordinary pastors' wives, vicars' wives, rectors' wives and ministers' wives all over the world who are buried wherever their husbands' level of ability has taken them.

They are in obscure towns, suburbs of big cities and remote rural areas. They are in churches of 10's, 50's or 100's. They often hold down secular jobs so that the family can eat. It is not uncommon for their husbands to do the same.

On stipend, negotiated salary or personal funds, these couples faithfully and lovingly care for the sheep. Sacrifices of money, proximity to extended family and social contacts are willingly made for the work of God.

These men and women are heroes. There is no doubt about this. How does their journey begin? Here is a typical scenario (one of many).

They recognize and respond to the voice of God calling them to devote their lives to the task of equipping the saints to do the work of the ministry. They save hard, make appropriate sacrifices, and head off to Bible college or seminary. (They arrive married, or fall in love and marry around the time of their college experience.)

Often, the wife holds down a job or two so that the bills can be paid. She may be able to study a subject or two during the years that they are in training. Maybe she is also a full-time student.

Graduation day arrives, and they receive their first assignment. It is almost always based on the merits of the husband. Although the couple will be interviewed together, the comments heard are "she is a good asset to his ministry" or "she is prepared to get a job to set them up."

This is only acceptable, and will only work, if she has not been called to equip the saints to do the work of the ministry. If she has, problems are already brewing below the surface.

In fact, some frustrated ministry marriages are not much more than two people who are wearing ill-fitting yokes or who are on the wrong side of the marital yoke.

While he sits at his computer, or stays closeted in the office trying to figure out where and how to lead the church or getting next Sunday's message, she is visiting the sick, counseling the distressed, balancing their non-existent bank account and running the "outreach" playgroup.

What if she has the vision? What if she is the preacher? What if she has an enabling to equip the saints? What if she has the creative flow and a wide-ranging thought process that speaks of vision, direction and facilitation? What if her husband is also fully devoted to the cause of Christ, but without the dynamism that will see the church grow? Perhaps they should swap sides of the yoke.

These couples are working hard for God without the progress that could and should be the fruit of their level of dedication and skill.

Yet for the sake of their marriages, and because of the prevailing culture, these wives choose to walk the way Naomi walked with Elimelech, the way Ruth walked with Naomi. In effect, they say, "Where you go, husband, there I will go, and there will I be buried."

These burials are not just taking place in marriages. Single women are buried in churches everywhere. Their devotion to their churches or their pastors is often blanketing a hidden yearning to be in the pulpit themselves. They are secretaries or prayer coordinators clomping about the flat and low elevation of the building on feet that are shod for mountain-climbing. Their victories *and* their defeats are meant to be part of the vista of leadership. They are not meant to be engaged in tussles over the color of the new carpet or in the bustle of matching table napkins with the floral arrangements for the next church event.

51

Their utter devotion—perhaps their blind devotion—is burying them instead of placing them where God places all His Naomis and Ruths: in the middle of the harvest fields and the threshing floors.

Then there is the burial that is less frustrating for the individual, but perhaps just as ignominious for the story of the body of Christ. It is the burial of the single woman on the mission field. Although she is somewhat free from the questioning of her obvious apostolic mantle by various governmental bodies, she may be forced to function without the peer mentoring that every leader desperately needs.

Having observed so many of these scenarios, and having spoken with so many leadership women who are paying a big price to make their marriages work, it is a great relief to be able to attest that, at least, they buried themselves in the ministry instead of anywhere else. These lives of dedication and devotion—of both men and women—have produced fruit in season and out of season.

It has been the status quo until now. A new breeze has been blowing for nearly a generation. It is gaining momentum. Now, we are watching it sweep into a mighty wind.

WHERE THINGS ARE RIGHT NOW

However we look at it, the strongest message, which must ring louder than any injustices or frustrations, is that Naomi and Ruth are on the right road and are getting closer to their intended destination where they will find life. Ruth is carrying a banner that bears the most powerful message of commitment that any leader can make: "Your people, Father God, will be my people."

Responding to Opportunity

For Naomis, Psalm 18:35-36 says, *"You give me your shield of victory, and your right hand sustains me; you stoop down to make me great. You broaden the path beneath me, so that my ankles do not turn."*

For Ruths, Psalm 16:5-6 says, *"LORD, you have assigned me my portion and my cup; you have made my lot secure. The boundary lines have fallen for me in pleasant places; surely I have a delightful inheritance."*

❧

RESPONSES TO OPPORTUNITY

- Carry your own load.
- Resist second best.
- Own pain without bitterness.
- Think about living, not dying.
- Associate with mature people.
- Bury yourself in God's work.
- Own God's people as your people.

Chapter 3

RESPONDING TO DISAPPOINTMENT

꙲

Naomi and Ruth have arrived back in the place where the best food for them is grown.

For Naomi, it is a return to the familiar. The streets and lanes are familiar. The taste of the food jolts memories of times past when the feasting produced utter contentedness. The styles of clothing are familiar. She understands the language. Oh, the bliss of being where she belongs.

For Ruth, it is another story altogether. Where Naomi has returned, Ruth has merely turned up. Without the guidance of a mentor, Ruth is going to quake under the threat of mistakes made out of inexperience. She doesn't know her way around the church. Everything she tastes requires an adjustment. Her clothing, which worked back in Moab, doesn't hang quite right in Bethlehem. And she can't understand a word that is being said. Oh, the terror of being out of place.

Ruth will be okay, though. She has committed herself to an older woman; she has pledged an allegiance to this woman's God; and she wants to belong amongst the people of this woman.

ALLOWING SPACE FOR "FAILURE"

Their arrival is not unnoticed. It is a similar stir that comes in church life when someone new is in the building, or when a long-departed but treasured parishioner returns. This time, however, some of the welcoming greetings and smiles become frozen as the people of Bethlehem look into the face of the worn-down Naomi.

Naomi's previously pleasant disposition has been replaced by something so strong that it has altered her appearance. Every step from Moab to her hometown should have seen a lifting of her soul. Instead, she nurses a bad attitude toward God, fed by disappointment from broken dreams. Her perspective is so clouded by her circumstances that she hauls herself down the main street wearing an invisible neon sign that reads, "God has let me down." The return journey should have changed her confession. Instead, the opposite happens, and every step closer to intended victory reinforces her belief that God has done her wrong.

Now, just ten years after leaving Bethlehem, she has returned, nearly unrecognizable. Fortunately, Naomi doesn't succumb to the malaise of 21st-century culture by wearing a mask. "Naomi, it's good to see you again. How are you?" "I'm fine, really. Love what you have done with the decor." Instead she responds like the psalmist in Psalm 38:9-10: *"All my longings lie open before you, O Lord; my sighing is not hidden from you. My heart pounds, my strength fails me; even the light has gone from my eyes."*

Of course the risk in being transparent is succinctly described in the next verse of that psalm: *"My friends and companions avoid me because of my wounds; my neighbors stay far away."*

Oh yes, we can be honest, but it is not long before people avoid us. That is why we sometimes elect the mask-wearing approach to answering questions.

God speaks to us about life, not death, and that dynamic alone must energize us. Nobody wants to turn up after a long absence looking much older and more worn than he or she really is, devoid of any sense of being alive. And that is not an unhealthy desire.

There is nothing quite like the stupid look we can get on our faces when we return from a lost venture of faith. Who wants to wear the look of sorrow and defeat? None of us do. Somehow we have to turn up at the old church and cope with the questions, the looks, the superficial chat which ebbs and flows, adroitly avoiding the fact that the things we have set out to do for the Lord have been a bit of a flop.

One young pastor who went through Bible college under an intolerant leader described the ministry to me like this. He said, "They throw you in at the deep end. If you swim, they take all the credit. If you sink, they say that you never had 'it' in the first place."

This barbaric approach to rearing sons and daughters in the ministry has not served us well.

We must work harder at making it safe for "failures" to return home without being judged by appearance and confession.

57

These drooping disciples are struggling enough with their own feelings of defeat without having to cope with a critical or quizzical community of believers.

Ray and I strode out in God, quite purposefully, many years ago. We were moving away from friends and from full-time church work to another of our states. We were quite sure that God would open a door of employment in our new community. As the weeks and then months went by, accompanied by a resounding silence from heaven and an airless atmosphere of inactivity, we faced the weird fact that things were not going to turn out as we thought. In fact, 20 years later, we still have no idea what it was all about.

The church where we were in fellowship in this new city stands in my mind as the perfect example of a loving community. We were never subjected to quizzing, nor was doubt cast upon our capacity to hear from God.

Moreover, during many of the months of unemployment and wagelessness, an envelope was placed in every Sunday morning's offering bag with our name on it, containing $50. At that time, with two little babies, this amount of money fed us well week by week. We ate lots of bread and corn fritters, but we ate.

Our faces may have portrayed bewilderment, anguish and even concern. I don't really know if they did or not. And why don't I know? Because the only reflection that we ever saw of ourselves in the faces of our church family was of an acceptable man and woman who loved the Lord and who belonged.

Now that is how it is meant to be. Whether we succeed or fail by earthly standards, whether we succeed or fail by our own standards, the church must provide a place of acceptance that contains and covers our frailty, not run the highlighter of judgment or ridicule over it.

SEEKING GOD'S PERSPECTIVE ON YOUR CIRCUMSTANCES

Naomi is seeing her life from the perspective of her facts—that she has no husband and no sons and that the whole Moab venture has failed. For her to move on with her life, facts have to be outweighed by truth. Fact: She's back without husband or children, which looks like failure. Truth: The kindness and faithfulness of God's promises contain more life-giving properties than her apparent failure.

Her sons are dead and, yes, the Lord gives and removes the breath of life. At that point, she is right to mention the involvement of Almighty God. But to hold to the belief that she went to Moab full and returned to Bethlehem empty because God has judged her—that is where she gets it wrong. She was never full on her way to Moab. She and her family were out of season. They were quite empty. Her sons didn't reproduce and her husband died young. Quite empty. Not full at all.

Naomi, your emptiness going out, despite having husband and sons, was more hollow and less capable of reproducing life than the emptiness you think you feel now. You haven't come back empty. You have come back to the place you belong with someone who is looking to you for mentoring. You have just become a generational leader in the body of Christ. A God-induced misfortune, Naomi? Oh no. You are on the brink of a God-ordained opportunity that will result in the arrival of a Savior on this frail earth.

EVALUATING THE SEASONS OF YOUR LIFE AS "HARD," NOT "BAD"

Before moving to the next stage of the story, it must remain in our conscious thought that we miss out on the breath-taking majesty of life and its outcome of productivity if the seasons of famine/escape/return are not endured. Oh, sure, we may still produce Obeds, but the stories that he tells his children will lack the color and jaw-dropping awe that will otherwise be told.

Ecclesiastes 3 is the template for the seasons of life. *"There is a time for...."* No one willingly subjects him or herself to the dying, uprooting, tearing down, weeping, silent, hating times of life. They are hard seasons. But the faithfulness of God ensures that they are followed by seasons of incredible richness—of living, planting, building, laughing, communicating and loving.

It is not in our best interest to always know what God is doing. In fact, there can be a spiritual elitism in always knowing "what God is doing now." Often, it is in our best interest to remain adorned with attitudes of humility during the seasons of His divine silence and with attitudes of responsive obedience when He does speak. The *"men of Issachar, who understood the times and knew what Israel should do"* (1 Chronicles 12:32a) were remarkable men, and we must have these people in the body. But, for most, it is okay to say, "*I* haven't got a clue what God is doing." Remembering that *He* does stands us in good form.

The ancient prayer doesn't say, "God, grant me the serenity to accept what I have managed to change; the courage to take the credit for doing so, and the wisdom to know, well, everything."

WHERE THINGS ARE RIGHT NOW

For now, for Mara, bitter one, there is a harvest, and it is just beginning. By the time it is completed, this self-description will be dropped—for the rest of her life.

RESPONSES TO DISAPPOINTMENT

- Allow space for "failure."
- Seek God's perspective on your circumstances.
- Evaluate the seasons of your life as "hard," not "bad."

Part Two

WHOSE YOUNG WOMAN IS THAT?

Ruth 2 (KJV)

And Naomi had a kinsman of her husband's, a mighty man of wealth, of the family of Elimelech; and his name was Boaz. And Ruth the Moabitess said unto Naomi, Let me now go to the field, and glean ears of corn after him in whose sight I shall find grace. And she said unto her, Go, my daughter. And she went, and came, and gleaned in the field after the reapers: and her hap was to light on a part of the field belonging unto Boaz, who was of the kindred of Elimelech.

And, behold, Boaz came from Bethlehem, and said unto the reapers, The LORD be with you. And they answered him, The LORD bless thee. Then said Boaz unto his servant that was set over the reapers, Whose damsel is this? And the servant that was set over the reapers answered and said, It is the Moabitish damsel that came back with Naomi out of the country of Moab: and she said, I pray you, let me glean and gather after the reapers among the sheaves: so she came, and hath continued even from the morning until now, that she tarried a little in the house. Then said Boaz unto Ruth, Hearest thou not, my daughter? Go not to glean in another field, neither go from hence, but abide here fast by my maidens: let thine eyes be on the field that they do reap, and go thou after them: have I not charged the young men that they shall not touch thee? and when thou art athirst, go unto the vessels, and drink of that which the young men have drawn. Then she fell on her face, and bowed herself to the ground, and said unto him, Why have I found grace in thine eyes, that thou shouldest take knowledge of me, seeing I am a stranger? And Boaz answered and said unto her, It hath fully been showed me, all that thou hast done unto thy mother in law since the death of thine husband: and how thou hast left thy father and thy mother, and the land of thy nativity, and art come unto a people which thou knewest not heretofore. The LORD recompense thy work, and a full reward be given thee of the LORD God of Israel, under whose wings thou art come to trust. Then she said, Let me find favour in thy sight, my lord; for that thou hast comforted me, and for that thou hast spoken friendly unto thine handmaid, though I be not like unto one of thine handmaidens. And Boaz said unto her, At mealtime come thou hither, and eat of the bread, and dip thy morsel in the vinegar. And she sat beside the reapers: and he reached her parched corn, and she did eat, and was sufficed, and left. And when she was risen up to glean, Boaz commanded his young men, saying, Let her glean even among the sheaves, and reproach her not: and let fall also some of the handfuls of purpose for her, and leave them, that she may glean them, and rebuke her not.

So she gleaned in the field until even, and beat out that she had gleaned: and it was about an ephah of barley. And she took it up, and went into the city: and her mother in law saw what she had gleaned: and she brought forth, and gave to her that she had reserved after she was sufficed. And her mother in law said unto her, Where hast thou gleaned to day? and where wroughtest thou? blessed be he that did take knowledge of thee. And she showed her mother in law with whom she had wrought, and said, The man's name with whom I wrought to day is Boaz. And Naomi said unto her daughter in law, Blessed be he of the LORD, who hath not left off his kindness to the living and to the dead. And Naomi said unto her, The man is near of kin unto us, one of our next kinsmen. And Ruth the Moabitess said, He said unto me also, Thou shalt keep fast by my young men, until they have ended all my harvest. And Naomi said unto Ruth her daughter in law, It is good, my daughter, that thou go out with his maidens, that they meet thee not in any other field. So she kept fast by the maidens of Boaz to glean unto the end of barley harvest and of wheat harvest; and dwelt with her mother in law.

Chapter 4

COMING OUT OF ISOLATION

᪥

Naomi is back. She has had a brief, painful conversation with some old friends and it looks as if she has withdrawn to a very private place with no company other than Ruth. Her great need for healing from the sickness in her soul and from the physical exhaustion of her long trek can't be met by the community, partly because she is not engaging with that community. As outsiders looking in, we are quietly chanting, "Go back to church; go back to church," for we know that healing through love and compassion and without judgment is one of the most potent elements of the community of believers.

Fascinatingly, Naomi does little or nothing to activate any old associations. It seems that she prefers to live in isolation than enjoy the comfort and hospitality of her relatives.

Naomi has returned from a somewhat despised land, visibly changed and bad-mouthing God. Perhaps it is just as well that she keeps to herself, but the tragedy is that she is meant to find acceptance and healing in the company of her family.

Instead, it seems, she chooses to keep aloof from those who remember her from old times. What is she afraid of? That they will keep reminding her about her husband's bad decision-making? That she will find out about God's sustaining grace toward her old neighbors during the famine, thus rubbing salt in her woundedness?

Perhaps her isolation is caused by an increase, not a decrease, in sorrow. As her feet heal from the long trek home, the dull ache in her heart of lost expectations worsens. Being with people is something she can't handle just yet. She is too sad.

She is so numb that she doesn't even pursue some of the obvious answers to their immediate needs. Not only does she avoid her relatives, but she also doesn't even arrange for Ruth to work on the staff of one of their properties. This is self-absorbed behavior, to say the least.

This is all made into a tragedy of deeper significance when we realize that her people's God is completely relational. Furthermore, relationships within the household of faith are His intended provision for people like her. In a few generations, David will express it like this: *"A father to the fatherless, a defender of widows, is God in his holy dwelling. God sets the lonely in families, he leads forth the prisoners with singing..."* (Psalm 68:5-6).

Both Naomi's past and present point toward a prosperous future or, at the very least, a provided-for future. Historically, her late husband had property. Currently, her extended family through marriage still has property. In the town of Bethlehem, this particular clan has substance. Because her head hangs down as she nurses her sorrows, Naomi fails to see any of these possibilities.

So we have an impasse. Naomi doesn't seem to know how to re-enter her community and her community doesn't know how to say or do whatever it takes to draw her toward them. The result is that she stays huddled in her hunger and isolation, unable to meet her own needs, let alone those of the younger Ruth.

FREEING OTHERS TO LOVE YOU

It is a distortion of mature thinking to make assumptions about the responses of others to our plight. We can chew over, analyze and deduce all manner of complications in relationships when the winds of change are blowing around our transitional feet. There is probably good reason for this. When the challenges of life create pain, others read it on our countenance and don't always know how to respond.

Many years ago, Ray and I moved back to our previous state and began to attend the church that is still our home. Although we had never been to this church as parishioners, I knew a small number of people who attended there from past friendships. These people knew that, when we were last in this city, we had both been in ministry but now we weren't. In a church culture that often portrays "the ministry" as being the ultimate point of arrival, to have walked away from it can carry a stigma. It can be seen as putting one's hand to the plow and then turning aside to a less spiritual life. It isn't necessarily so, of course. But it can be seen that way.

A few weeks after our arrival, I met one of these old friends for the first time. She looked unsmilingly at me and said scathingly, "What are you doing here?" Feeling as embraced as a pimple on a prom queen, I muttered some kind of answer and walked away wondering why I had bothered to reach out to her at all.

Although this happened nearly two decades ago, I can still recall how it felt to receive the sting on my cheek of an unwelcoming moment when what I should have felt was the warmth of a sisterly kiss.

If this happened now, I would react differently, but as a young mother with three little children, I allowed that rudeness to create an emotional distance between me and those few acquaintances. What a waste of time and of life. It is all water under the bridge now—well and truly—but my story serves to illustrate the importance of love and friendship at all levels of person-to-person interchange in the church. We rarely know all the story of anyone's walk, and looking to the high side of life is almost always going to reflect the relational heart of God.

BELIEVING THAT GOD HAS SOLUTIONS TO YOUR DILEMMA

All manner of unfortunate human behaviors can keep us locked in isolation. Our good news is that God, in His mercy, and in His commitment to building His church, has solutions to which He gives form, placing and positioning people and events with an eye for possible future developments.

For Naomi and Ruth, the solution is a man named Boaz...Boaz who is, of himself and by himself, unable to reproduce. His fertility is in potential form only. On his own, he has no capacity for generational growth. As things stand, at best, all he achieves in his lifetime will be handed over to a distant relative; at worst, it will all be handed to someone who won't have been tutored and mentored by him in land development or staff relations or investment of capital and so on.

Moreover, without intervention, all our heroes are going to end up alone and dying with unfulfilled dreams of bringing to birth the potential that is lying within.

For the sake of the call of God that rests on the lives of Naomi, Ruth and Boaz, and for the sake of keeping the message of salvation alive, circumstances have to change and Naomi will have to re-engage with life for it to do so.

SETTING YOURSELF BACK IN THE FAMILY OF BELIEVERS

Here is more evidence that isolation never really helps. The Israelites are schooled by God about their requirement to care for widows in their distress.[1] Does it strike you as weird that a Moabite who has never heard that teaching is the only one who bothers to provide for the widow Naomi? Something isn't right.

Whether the fault lies with Naomi or her family is not being questioned. What does stand out is the futility of withdrawing from the very people who just might be able to provide what is most needed: sustenance. Is it any wonder that David challenged us to set those who are on their own into families—a value in the church reinforced by the Lord when He and His mother, also by then a widow, were together on the hill of Golgotha. *"Dear woman, here is your son...Here is your mother"* (John 19:26-27).

It is never in the providence of God for widows to be without provision. It *is*, however, a smart thing for all of us, whether widows, unemployed youth, laid-off professionals or the like, to do something to attract provision.

Naomi, get with the living.

BEING GRATEFUL FOR WHAT IS AVAILABLE

Adding to the poignancy of this principle in their story, "Coming Out of Isolation," is the low level of expectation in which Ruth is now living. With Naomi setting an example of misery and morbidity, Ruth's vision of the life God intended for her is as yet unformed. She describes (probably gratefully) her food source as *"leftover grain"* (Ruth 2:2).

God's intention for Ruth's daily food is far above leftover grain. She is destined to sit at the head of the feasting table, eating the best cuts of meats and the finest delicacies. But her sense of destiny is fairly ground down right now, and her expectations rise to leftovers.

Well, at least it is grain. It has value. It is not to be despised. Leftovers will feed us; they have some nutritional value. Leftovers will ease the gnawing hunger for finer food.

Jesus was born in a cave—a dugout—behind a hotel, euphemistically called a manger. It was the place where animals were given shelter and food. These animals would eat from the feeding trough of the manger. With each mouthful, drool spilled back into the trough, but at least the animals were fed.

Although most preachers draw inspiration, quotes and ideas from other ministries, any time we preach someone else's food it will contain drool. There is such a danger in that. Our salvation contains the promise of new wine for each day. We don't need to survive exclusively on someone else's leftover messages ourselves, and we don't need to feed them to those in our care habitually.

Yet, I have been a little amused, and rather encouraged, that God dignified the plight of desperate preachers by including a sloppy feeding trough in the earthly things that His Son's life first touched—in Bethlehem—two millennia ago. No fancy office lined with reference material for quiet and contemplative solitude...just a drooled-in trough where every living thing lined up for a munch and a slurp.

TAKING INITIATIVE TO MEET YOUR OWN NEEDS

Ruth's plan is to find *"anyone in whose eyes I find favor"* (Ruth 2:2). Just anyone will do. She wants to pick up a bit of leftover food from just anyone. Naomi, who has the contacts, is failing to take any initiative; thus leaving Ruth to the potentially perilous task of finding just anyone.

Space will only be made for her on the field of work if the man she approaches makes room for her. He won't know if she is a worker or not. He really has to go out on a limb here. He has to give an unknown—and a woman at that—a chance.

In fact, there is a case for suggesting that she is not very physically attractive. After all, her own family couldn't marry her off to one of their own race. They gave her in marriage to some strangers who came empty-handed to their town.

Whether gorgeous or plain, this young widow has lost any sense of her own winsomeness, and she is looking for any kind of work with any kind of landowner who will give her some miserable leftovers.

It must be a long time since Naomi has spoken to Ruth of the hope and the future that the Almighty has in store for her.

Older people must speak those truths fervently and often to those whose prime ministry years are still ahead. Naomis must be so careful to speak well of the church, of possibilities and of the times and seasons. Notice, I did not say "glowingly," just "well." I did not say "untruthfully," just "well." There is a lack of integrity and a frightening level of stupidity in speaking glowingly of things that are not so. It verges on dishonesty to label something as brilliant when it is, in fact, mediocre. This is not "speaking well of." I think the world calls this behavior, "putting a spin on things."

Many years ago, I was involved in an organization that had some great strengths and some glaring weaknesses. Organizationally, it was haphazard. The person to whom I was answerable used a stockpile of clichés to most searching questions. For this person, everything needed to be in all ways and at all times right, regardless of the evident chaos around us. I was frustrated by the lack of progress that I was able to make in my designated task, but I was also conscious that God was speaking to me, through that frustration, about His ways. After a time of meditation, I have realized that the pop-doctrine of "speaking well of" is in need of wise tempering.

What a mess there would have been if the watchmen on the walls of the ancient cities had called out such things as, "There is a glorious sight approaching the city. I see a large number of trained and disciplined men whose buckles and buttons are gleaming in the sunlight." If we are not careful, the spin that is put on things can provide a smoke screen for threatening situations that might improve quickly if they are handled with higher levels of mature honesty.

The job of the Naomis is to call things honestly while still maintaining wise and appropriate levels of hope and possibility in all communications with the emerging Ruths.

The job of the Naomis is to call things honestly while still maintaining wise and appropriate levels of hope and possibility in all communications with the emerging Ruths.

While the foreman she approaches is deciding if he will allow Ruth to glean or not, let's remind ourselves about a very important matter. The call of God is on Ruth's life. Whether this man sees it or not, she is already chosen by God for an extraordinary ministry.

God chooses to place large destinies in the hands of our frail and finite understanding. If only He would maneuver everything Himself. But, no, He relies on the foreman, the overseer of the field, whom Ruth approaches to hire or fire her. Oh my. This is risky. What if this man doesn't see her worth? She won't get leftover bits for her own meager

needs, much less an opportunity to oversee the whole oper-
ation with her husband later on.

It is my personal belief that we rarely need to ask God to
put us in tricky positions so that we can grow in faith and
trust. Life does a good job of that all by itself.

Ruth goes out anyway, despite the uncertainty of the
response of the men she approaches.

EXPECTING ACCEPTANCE IN THE FIELD

Now comes a glorious coincidence. Even the narrator of
Ruth's story doesn't spiritualize this moment. He writes, *"As
it turned out..."* (Ruth 2:3).

My learned friend, Margaret, introduced me to this quote:
"Coincidence is the name we give things that God does
when He wants to remain anonymous." I love that.

"As it turned out," God is orchestrating an intersection of
a childless man and a childless woman, each of whom carry
the hope of being mentioned in the genealogy of Christ, but
neither of whom will get onto the list without each other.

What happens to women who can't find acceptance from
men whom they approach for ministry opportunities? Do
they just go from field to field, perhaps moving further and
further away from the place they are meant to be?
Generally, at this time in the church, women still need men
to open doors of opportunity so that they can participate,
rather than spectate, in leadership.

It can be a shaky moment...that moment when a woman
decides to get out into the field instead of staying indoors
doing "women's stuff."

If she is owned, honored and allowed in, the harvest is gathered more thoroughly and in less time.

If she is disowned, dishonored and not allowed in, well, at least men can still do "men's stuff" without having to worry about offending female sensibilities, but the harvest will take longer and lots of details will probably be left undone, leaving an unnecessary mess in the church.

Although we never find out the name of the good foreman who gave Ruth a chance to be involved, we can give him honor because his action is a crucial link in the chain of circumstances that give an Obed to the world. A worthy man, for sure.

And Ruth, you have broken the cycle of isolationism that wasn't helping either Naomi or yourself.

ANTICIPATING A DIVINELY DESIGNED INTERSECTION

Now things start to heat up. Boaz arrives from Bethlehem and greets the harvesters. A man with his people, he knows what they are doing; he knows where to find them; he knows their names; he is in enough of a relationship with them that both landowner and land worker are at ease in their greetings one to another.

I love and revere this gentle, older man. He is careful with the resources that God has given him. He doesn't expect to be waited on, so much so that he happily serves lunch to his staff. He knows what is going on, and what he doesn't know, he asks about. To find things out, he goes to the field where his staff people are working. He doesn't wait for the workers to come to him. Now that is leadership.

WORKING FOR A LEADER WHO LOVES PEOPLE

Before talking about Boaz in relation to women who are called to equip the believers, let's talk about Boaz in relation to churches today.

He does everything right. He gets out with the people. He oversees what they do. He knows them by the fruit of their labors, by their attitude, by their aspirations.

The directions he gives are the result of his research. He doesn't sit in a remote office, making decisions about what his workers will and won't do without first seeing what they are currently doing.

His instructions carry authority that demands respect…and earns response.

Once the harvest has been gathered and the hard work of forming the results of the harvest into useable produce has begun, he is still there. He has not delegated the job of working on the threshing floor to others, but chooses instead to work with his team.

A veteran pastor told me this encouraging story. He had made a habit of leaving the task of praying for those who responded to the message to skilled and godly people in his church. One day, the Holy Spirit challenged him to remain involved in that process. As a result, he joins the ministry team at the conclusion of each meeting and prays with people until the process is completed. He is not replacing the workers. He is joining the workers. It is a wonderful act of humility and inclusion for a leader to be with the people in this way.

Some of the frustrations in church life are found amongst believers who have a shepherd who just doesn't connect.

78

Decisions are made without research. Believers work hard but without the understanding and knowledge of the ones who direct the church. And, just sometimes, the pastor stands in the pulpit, urging people to work harder—at outreach, at relationships, at filling in the job-blanks in the church structure—when he really doesn't know how hard they are already working.

Someone who stands out as a Christ-like pastor is my friend James. He was my pastor many years ago. Prior to taking on a pastorate, James was in management. He told me that every time he moved into a new job, he would spend a short time with all his staff, doing their work with them. This, he said, gave him an understanding of their value as well as the value of the work they did. It also meant that he became a safe delegator because of that understanding.

Before moving off this point of relational leadership, there is one other marvelous piece of wisdom that I have learned from my mother. During the years that my parents operated Bible colleges, at some point in her teaching of prospective pastors' wives, she would say, "Never use your congregation to fulfill your ambition."

It is quite un-Boaz to do so!

WORKING WITHOUT NEEDING TO BE NOTICED

Boaz is in the field. It is after the greeting that Boaz notices a subtle change in the landscape of his field. Because he knows all the people in his care, he quickly ascertains that an unfamiliar form is bent low over the fallen stalks of barley. Promptly, he calls to his foreman, *"Whose young woman is that?"* (Ruth 2:5)

This is not an inappropriate question. To us, it can sound as if Ruth is just another chattel. Whose plow is that? Whose garment is that? Whose woman is that? In the context of the culture of the day, it is not so terrible. In fact, it is rather lovely.

You see, the Hebrew word that Boaz uses is a word that indicates, at the most, an adolescent.[2] In a park, watching many children play, we might say to a nearby adult, pointing to a particular child, "Whose child is that?"

Boaz, probably in his 80's[3] and of a caring, fatherly disposition, sees a young girl, unattached, and wants to make sure that she is cared for by someone.

Observing this care from the balcony of heaven, God knows to whom He can entrust not only the precious life of this capable young woman, but also the precious lives that, together, they will produce.

The foreman now relates to Boaz the details of the brief encounter he has already had with Ruth.

And what does Ruth know about all of this? Absolutely nothing. She may not even know that she is laboring in a field over which she should have had some familial privileges by marriage.

Her head is down, and she is focused on the job at hand.

Oh, the quiet delight of meeting another ministry who starts the sentence of greeting with, "I've heard great things about your ministry." Our head has been down, and we have been doing what we know must be done. Our head hasn't been held high so that we can cast our eyes all over the paddock trying to see if we are being noticed or not. Then, when something is said that suggests that a Boaz and his foreman have mentioned us favorably, it is quite nice.

There is something unattractive, even off-putting, about ministries that are consumed with their own importance. Proverbs 27:2 says, *"Let another praise you, and not your own mouth; someone else, and not your own lips."* When the skill of marketing raises ministries beyond their anointing, there is a risk that we can start to believe our own press. It is better to keep one's head down and leave elevation to God.

The foreman is very particular in the detail he shares with Boaz. He says, *"She said, 'Please let me glean and gather among the sheaves behind the harvesters.' She went into the field and has worked steadily from morning till now, except for a short rest in the shelter"* (Ruth 2:7).

Hard-working women, called by God to gather produce to provide for sheep, are committed and tireless despite the heat of the noonday sun, despite the itchiness of the stalk-filled atmosphere and despite any feelings of being unwatched and unknown. Churches, mission societies and welfare organizations have been the barley harvest field for women throughout all times.

Women have already proven themselves—generation after generation—as willing workers in the church. We have done everything asked of us...run the nursery, led the choir, taught the Sunday school, visited the sick, catered for the supper, cleaned the building and worked in the office.

Be encouraged that a report about our attitude, our industry and our skill has been noticed by God. And the One who both hears and sees all, in His faithfulness, will bring us to that which He has assigned us.

WHERE THINGS ARE RIGHT NOW

Naomi is still hidden, out of range. Her trust in the goodness of God is still in disarray, and her trust of people appears to be beyond repair. Her isolation is not serving her well. She is failing to take her place as a mature woman amongst God's people.

Ruth may have broken the isolation barrier, but she is still a stranger in a strange land. She has no awareness of any connection with anyone of influence who will give her the attention that will reveal her true calling. It is going to take more than a conversation with a foreman to get these women into the center of the action.

※

KEYS TO COMING OUT OF ISOLATION

- Free others to love you.
- Believe that God has solutions to your dilemma.
- Set yourself back in the family of believers.
- Be grateful for what is available.
- Take initiative to meet your own needs.
- Expect acceptance in the field.
- Anticipate a divinely designed intersection.
- Work for a leader who loves people.
- Work without needing to be noticed.

ENDNOTES

1. *Be joyful at your Feast—you, your sons and daughters, your menservants and maidservants, and the Levites, the aliens, the fatherless and the widows who live in your towns* (Deuteronomy 16:14; see also Deuteronomy 14:29; 16:11).

2. "Young woman = na'arah (nah-ar-aw'); feminine of OT:5288; a girl (from infancy to adolescence): KJV - damsel, maid (-en), young (woman)." (*Biblesoft's New Exhaustive Strong's Numbers and Concordance with Expanded Greek-Hebrew Dictionary* [copyright © 1994 by Biblesoft and International Bible Translators, Inc.]).

3. A tradition states that Boaz was 80 years old when he married Ruth. (*The Wycliffe Bible Commentary,* electronic database [copyright © 1962 by Moody Press]).

Chapter 5

RECEIVING FAVOR

꧁꧂

Although my romantic heart skips a beat with the first encounter between Boaz and Ruth, the truth is that it is very unromantic. Boaz sees Ruth as a young girl and Ruth bends so low to the ground that she is nearly eating dirt. Hardly the stuff of romantic fiction.

The first view that Boaz has of Ruth's face is possibly quite unflattering. She has plant life in her hair, dust and dirt on her face and the smell of empty-stomach breath coming out of her mouth.

KEEPING THE ISSUE OF OUTWARD APPEARANCES IN BALANCE

In today's church culture, we tend to be very influenced by outward appearance. I make this comment without censure. We are designed by God—men and women alike—to see with our physical eyes. We do look on outward appearance and we make value judgments accordingly. Naomi knows this. After the barley and wheat harvests are gathered, she will take care to see that Ruth is favorably presented in the threshing floor scene. Looks matter. Therefore, I don't bring the matter up to judge it harshly.

I do, however, want to make the point that the very act of service has taken the edge off the enticing quality of some women. Perhaps the first time they are seen by the senior pastor is cleaning the church, preparing food or lugging furniture. The beads of moisture on their lips, the dirt under their fingernails, the stains of perspiration—these are the outward signs of an industrious woman that may keep her type-cast as a servant. We must be so careful about quick and unwise dismissal of people based on appearance.

I was with a group of very capable women where a few at the table looked, metaphorically, like field workers. One woman, on the contrary, was totally gorgeous. Really, she was. I watched with morbid fascination as she deftly avoided doing anything that looked like work. By the time this meeting was over, the rest of the table of women were fully engaged in the matter at hand, volunteering where necessary. The beautiful woman remained totally poised and uninvolved. Because the leader at the table was also self-absorbed, guess with which member of the group she connected.

Yes, appearances matter. No, appearances must not arbitrate decisions about who is and who is not worthy of attention. In our image-conscious western society, this is a truth that should be sounded out more loudly than it is.

WILLING TO BE NOTICED IN AN OUT-OF-SEASON ROLE WITHOUT BECOMING DEFENSIVE

It is now a very pastoral thing that Boaz does. He encourages Ruth to see her immediate future in his employ and assures her that there is plenty to do while she is there. He then tells her to stay in the company of his servant girls.

Well, this is going to work, Boaz, but only for a while. You see, Ruth was never destined to be noticed as a servant. Her destiny is to be noticed as a wife.

Much is now being said about the desirability of serving another ministry in order to eventually have one's own. Ruth's story puts a question mark beside that teaching. Boaz is only seeing her as a peripheral addition to his flock of servants. He is not seeing her as a possible equal at all. Left to his devices, she will be gleaning beside other servants till she dies. That is not God's plan for her, but Naomi, it seems, is still disengaged, consumed with her own distress, so there is no one to walk with Ruth in a mentoring way. It is how things have to be for now.

There are cases when the serving of another ministry has so quenched the life-flow of an emerging leader that he or she becomes nearly useless for anything but a near-doormat position in his or her particular church.

It is quite sad to recognize a potentially prestigious gifting on the life of a young person, only to watch its edge tarnish through the relentless pressure of serving inappropriately. I have seen this happen in the lives of people serving an incompetent pastor, serving an autocrat or serving a "career" pastor.

In the "serve another" teaching, if "another" doesn't see what is on your life, it won't happen—unless God gloriously intervenes. Thankfully, in Ruth's life that is exactly what is soon to take place.

Boaz tells Ruth to watch the field where the men are harvesting.

Thousands of years have passed, and that is still about as high as women can rise in many church systems and many cultures. "Watch the field where the men do the work." Women are called, equipped and eager to help in the governing of the field and its regular harvest. They want to do more than just watch men at work!

I have heard the phrase quite often, spoken by pastors about worthy women in their church, "She makes me look good." Although this has always been spoken in a kindly and acclaiming manner, I have never heard those same pastors say, "It is my privilege to do what I can to make her look good."

Boaz tells Ruth to follow after the girls. These servant girls were to stretch out the binding ties, lay the fallen piles of barley across the ties, and then secure them into sheaves. It was hot, dusty, dirty work and it was relentless. Boaz wants Ruth to put herself in the position of possibly being just a pest. Her presence in the harvest is going to interfere with the established rhythm of the paid staff.

As we have observed before, this isn't going to work forever.

RESPONDING TO ACTS OF LOVE
AND CARE APPROPRIATELY

Boaz now reveals a sensitivity to Ruth's womanliness, which we will see on three other occasions as well. He tells her that the men in the field have been told that they are not to touch her...that they are not to reduce her gender to the meeting of their needs. Oh my, this is just so magnificent.

It is not easy to extend grace toward men in the ministry who have been predators on the women in their congregations. Women have arrived at churches everywhere to work alongside men in gender-appropriate tasks only to find that, instead of protection, they are devoured. Instead of flourishing in their churches, they are left with the burning shame of illicit encounters. Of course, there are instances where women are just as guilty as the minister of creating the climate of lust. How sad for them that their churches are not led by Boazs.

Boaz finishes this, his first ever communication with her, by saying an amazing thing. He says that every time she is thirsty, she is to get a drink from the water jars that the men in the field have filled.

This is such a lovely picture of the genders working together. The water pots are heavy. God has built men with the physiology to lift heavy things. And Boaz is saying that even the lowliest woman in his organization can quench her thirst from the water that men have collected. The necessary sustenance for working in the field is provided best when everyone works according to their capacity, capability and availability.

Ruth bows low, responding to these great acts of kindness. Wise lady. With a flick of her hair, she could have eye-balled Boaz, downloading a blistering speech to him about the way Elimelech's extended family have ignored them, leaving her to work hard when they have so much money, for goodness' sake. Instead, I get the feeling that Ruth doesn't even think like this, but lives instead out of a genuine heart of gratitude for the least act of kindness that comes her way.

Boaz does one of those "I've been hearing good things about your ministry" speeches, and concludes with a rich prayer of blessing.

He asks the Lord to repay her.

He asks the Lord to richly reward her.

He reminds her that she has a right to refuge and shelter under the protecting wings of the God of Israel.

Hmm. Boaz, you are a sitting duck. You don't know it yet, but God is going to use you to answer your own prayers for Ruth.

When fine women prepare themselves for ministry and begin to take their place at the coalface of ministry life, it is a marvelous thing to find men in leadership who are just as keen to see those women attain every level of maturity, experience and responsibility possible.

WAITING SWEETLY FOR OTHERS TO SEE YOU AS GOD SEES YOU

Ruth's hard work has been noticed, and her initiative is now being rewarded. Even so, it is still in the context of a hard worker in the field. She is not being noticed as a potential co-landowner. Never mind, first things first. Hard work is an inevitable by-product of the call of God. And that is just a fact. The many Proverbs scriptures about the sluggard and the lazy stand before us as confirmation of the nobility that God has invested in hard work. For a woman, the culmination of these

Proverbs is undoubtedly Proverbs 31. It is my somewhat wry thought that this lady is a composite of several of Solomon's wives. And it is a personal perspective that Proverbs 31 is a salute to women who function in business, professional and governmental roles as much as anything else.

In order to ensure that hard work doesn't drift into slavery, the Ephesians 2:8-10 scripture must be woven into our ethic about work: *"For it is by grace you have been saved, through faith—and this not from yourselves, it is the gift of God—not by works, so that no one can boast. For we are God's workmanship, created in Christ Jesus to do good works, which God prepared in advance for us to do."* It is the last phrase that ensures that we don't burn out. If God has prepared the work for us to do, He has equally prepared us to do it.

Lois Burkett says, "God is faithful to us in our calling."

This moment in Ruth's life is saturated in God's faithfulness, and in that she can rest. If she doesn't rest, she will be caught in a performance trap that will demand reward. And that is not God's highest way.

Is hard work enough to attract the attention of the kinsman-redeemer who will change her status from worker to co-owner? Yes and no. He is noticing her. Everyone is noticing her, but she is still bent low doing menial work in the heat and dust of the day. Something has to happen for a strong wind of change to blow so that she becomes noticed as a landowner. The landowner also may work in the field. Boaz demonstrates that superbly. And when Ruth becomes a landowner, she also may continue to work in the field. But until she comes into another level of status—until she is with Boaz behind closed doors—being noticed in the field is getting her nowhere.

For now, Ruth continues to pay her dues.

SPEAKING UP FOR YOURSELF WHEN THE OCCASION REQUIRES IT

With the blessing of the beautiful prayer still washing through her mind, Ruth rises to a new boldness. She lets Boaz know that, even though she is working just as hard as the other workers, she doesn't even have the status of the most humble laborer.

Women with the call of God on their lives to equip believers have often been seen in a lesser light than the "hired help." In fact, it is not uncommon for women working in church administration to be paid—and paid more—than women who are pastors.

If women stay at the level of willing workers and never speak up appropriately to the right people in the right places, the pot isn't stirred. Praise God for the times He strategically places a non-servant woman into the scene where women are busy doing women's things. This new breed of woman needs to demonstrate a capacity beyond that of the hired hand. She is ready to rise to positions of leadership, ministry and strategic oversight.

Some pastors in my circle of friendship are longing for women to emerge onto the platform of preaching, leading and governing. They recognize the vitality and *dunamis* in certain ladies in their congregations, including their wives and daughters. One such man, a very confident and secure man, told me that he loves to hear his wife preach and that her tapes sell faster than his. She serves on the church leadership with him, and the "yoke that is easy and the burden that is light"[1] is a good fit for this couple.

By contrast, stories abound of pastors who have no female leadership on their staff. One pastor said to me, "I don't believe that women's leaders should be paid." Yet another said, "There will never be a woman preaching in my pulpit." Other pastors assert that "women only need events." Well, gentlemen, your cars only need a wash; your yards only need a mow. If the women in your congregation are items which "only need," you have lowered the ceiling on the strength of redemptive life that can be harvested by you in your community.

A worrying observation is that younger men who allow themselves to be influenced by any pastor with a history of sexual exploitation of women will inevitably have a "women only need" mentality. For them, women provide services that men need done.

As a women's leader and a leader of women who equip believers, I have wept with too many hurt, bewildered and betrayed women to have much patience with those who perpetrate the hurt and betrayal.

To overcome my crankiness, I remind myself that the Mediator between God and men intercedes for these predators who are entrapped in their own anguishing misery. I try to be nice, but it is a grim task. Oh, how we all need His mercy.

Psalm 44:3 says, *"It was not by their sword that they won the land, nor did their arm bring them victory; it was your right hand, your arm, and the light of your face, for you loved them."*

Back to Ruth and her dignified stand...although she is speaking out in an appropriate manner about her status, there is still an underlying humility and gratitude that stands in sharp contrast to an attitude of "it's about time you noticed me." By the next harvest, she will be a mother who, instead of being bent over the dry ground in the heat of summer, will be surveying the field of workers beside her husband Boaz. Right now, every move, every word, every sincere communication is paving the way for that to happen. Well done, Ruth.

TAKING YOUR PLACE CONFIDENTLY BESIDE OTHER WORKERS

Wonderful Boaz, serving his servants, makes sure that Ruth has plenty to eat, even some delicacies. In his mind, she is not yet a possible lover. She is still a young damsel. However, something about her winning way is attracting his attention.

For her part, instead of handing the leftovers back, which would have been a cordial, even courteous, thing to do, Ruth's natural thoughtfulness for the well-being of another puts her in the role of provider.

Boaz provides for Ruth; Ruth provides for Naomi. And somewhere in this flow of provision, Naomi is going to awaken from her self-centered stupor and realize that the hand of God is at work.

When Boaz calls to Ruth, *"Come over here"* (Ruth 2:14), we see another magnificent facet of this man. Boaz is eating what the people are eating, and he is eating it with them. Is he different to them? Yes. Does he have better food in a more comfortable setting at his disposal? Absolutely. But there is a time and a place when he lingers with the workers.

Boaz tells the men to deliberately drop barley for Ruth to pick up. This is totally an act of kindness, not an act of condescension.

Bring this to our current church. Women who have been called to equip believers have been able to satisfy their own need to be fulfilled in the work of the ministry by doing the jobs left them by men. In fact, the dropping of tasks for women to pick up is seen, not entirely wrongly, as a fine and noble thing for men to do.

I have felt the raw concern of pastors who, in conversations with me about their approach to the gender issues in their churches, have listed the many opportunities and jobs that are done by capable women in their churches. Out of my own heart has come such a love and honor for these men, overlaid with an awareness of frustration in them created by the ceiling that is over their churches because there are no women in their leadership structure.

So, seeing it from the perspective of this narrative puts a rather cruel twist on what is probably seen as the good thing that Boaz is doing in making a way for her. You see, the more jobs that are dropped, the harder the women work and the less time they will have for straightening up and renewing a vision of where they are meant to be.

And the Boaz leaders of our churches have come by and seen the diligence of these women, their appropriate demeanor and their pleasant attitude. They have liked what they have seen, so they have arranged for more jobs to be left behind for the women to do. Pastors genuinely believe this is meritorious. And it is. But God is calling for a new level of shared leadership and government between genders, so the dropping of wheat will need to be given further thought.

...God is calling for a new level of shared leadership and government between genders...

One Ruth I know began her life as one who equips believers doing one job, which she did very well. It was a job that none of the men wanted to do—or could have done. The women's pastor. She did this so well that, deservedly, she was noticed by her pastor. After she had worked unrelentingly for a couple of years, I asked her what she was now responsible for in her church. I was silently horrified as she listed four major portfolios. Her pastor's spoken attitude is, "If she wants to be in a man's world, she must keep up with men." Aside from his grievous lack of understanding about the ministry being a world for both men and women whom God appoints and places, he had allotted each man on his staff no more than two portfolios.

Another Ruth I know carries the duties in her church that require the most manual labor.

Dropping more wheat may feel like a gesture of recognition, but it is only keeping Ruths bent over, unable to straighten up to assist with the governing of the field. Such containment is very draining and backbreaking.

At this time in the church, women recognized as ones who equip can frequently be left with the jobs that no one else wants *and* then be sidetracked in doing these jobs to the point that they may not be released to function according to their Holy Spirit enabling.

Their backs are bent under the noonday sun, but they are still unable to provide significant influence in the policy-making, vision-seeking and strategic thinking that steers the direction of their local church.

It's been okay, but a change is coming.

TRUSTING GOD WITH YOUR REPUTATION

Now we come to the second sighting of Boaz's sensitivity to the nobility and worth of a woman. He addresses the men in the field with an order. Not a suggestion. An order. He tells them that if they notice that she moves outside of the limited range of privilege that she has been allowed, they are not to draw that to her attention. In fact, they are to make it easy for her to become oblivious of any mistakes that she might make.

Oh, kind and noble Boaz. Your courtesy and consideration in all your dealings with this emerging leader speak of dignity and care.

Boaz never uses opportunities (of which there are a few) to debase, humiliate or poke fun at Ruth.

I wonder if God was holding His breath at that moment of human interplay. The plan that He is going to suggest to Naomi's conscious thought processes will depend upon the way Boaz holds the life and reputation of this young woman in his hands.

So if this particular moment in the narrative is a test, Boaz comes through with flying colors.

WHERE THINGS ARE RIGHT NOW

Ruth, your yieldedness to the circumstances of life are so free of demand and assumed rights that favor is coming your way from the only man who can bring long-lasting change to your ministry status.

RECEIVING FAVOR AS A RUTH

- Keep the issue of outward appearances in balance.
- Be willing to be noticed in an out-of-season role without becoming defensive.
- Respond to acts of love and care appropriately.
- Wait sweetly for others to see you as God sees you.
- Speak up for yourself when the occasion requires it.
- Take your place confidently beside other workers.
- Trust God with your reputation.

ENDNOTE

1. *For my yoke is easy and my burden is light* (Matthew 11:30).

Chapter 6

MAKING WAY FOR PROVISION

꧁꧂

Ruth's first day of the rest of her life is coming to an end. It began with the same needs that every day of her life has contained: the need for fresh air, the need for food, the need for water. All three needs have been met within this strange day, a demonstration of God's provision for all of us. Psalm 65:9 says, *"You care for the land and water it; you enrich it abundantly. The streams of God are filled with water to provide the people with grain, for so you have ordained it."*

Now she bends over for one final moment and threshes the barley she has gathered. She is doing the lot.

FINISHING WHAT YOU BEGIN

I commented earlier about the somewhat disparate worlds of men and women who equip believers to do the work of the ministry. Now, rather than talk about differences, I want to pay homage to both men and women God has placed in the church who do it all. Whether planting and pioneering a new church or a new ministry, or maintaining one in its infancy, there is something noble and healthy about taking the process from start to finish.

My father pioneered many churches in his early years. When he had retired, he planted one last church, at 73 years of age. We were with him in that venture. There was sheer joy in arriving early to put out seats, set up the little Sunday school room and plug in the keyboard. The sense of camaraderie amongst the team and the ownership that each of us had to the process still remains with me.

Although growth and expansion of influence eventually require the divestment of some responsibilities, there is something energizing about starting in the morning and finishing in the evening, hands-on with all that one's life demands.

For Ruth, this moment in her life is not to become the pattern. Hunting and gathering food amongst castoffs is only a stage in her unfolding life. And yet she does it so well. By the end of just her first day on the job, she walks away with about 20 to 25 pounds of solid food. Not bad, Ruth, not bad at all. It is the wisdom that she displays in pausing to process the food that is worthy of comment.

If she doesn't process the food, she will be carrying stalks of barley on her head for the long trek to the humble lodgings that she and Naomi share. Thus the load will be far heavier than need be. Plus, neither of them can eat those stalks without a great deal of discomfort and very little digestion.

DIGGING DEEPER THAN THE OBVIOUS

A woman who is going to rise to positions of ministry and/or government needs to be able to preach and speak beyond the obvious. Many congregations choke and splutter, trying to digest and make spiritual muscle out of unprepared food.

Preachers who stand and share the obvious do okay, but those who thresh out the Word, unlocking its mysteries, are the ones who soon have compelling ministries.

WALKING UPRIGHT AS YOU CARRY THE MESSAGE

Ruth brings the job for the day to its completion by carrying the food back to town. In doing so, she is reproducing the pattern that she had seen established by the older Naomi. In the same way that Naomi had to manage her own bags from Moab, so now Ruth is also managing her own goods. Any assistance from servants is yet to come.

All over the planet, men and women walk into the sheds, lounge rooms, auditoriums and chapels of the world, carrying the prepared word of the Lord upon their heads. It is their honor. It is their joy. It is not a chore. It doesn't kill them. It keeps them upright because they are careful and keen to avoid spillage of the message.

Ruth also brings out, as if from a pocket, the leftovers from lunch. Comment has already been made on the place that leftovers can reasonably take in our diet of divine manna. They are not to be despised.

Boaz's kindness has allowed Ruth to feed herself and another. This genuine act of enabling—allowing Ruth to thresh wheat for just two—is seen in churches everywhere. Women can run small home groups for other women. They can feed the children. Just themselves and another or two.

However, there is seed inside Ruth that will provide the world, not just a little home group, with the message of redemption. It is time for her to move from the backbreaking work of repetitive labor (in which her faithfulness, loyalty and bravery have been well-proven) to the place where life can be reproduced.

BEING ACCOUNTABLE FOR WHAT YOU ALREADY KNOW

Ruth mentions a name—Boaz—and bells of stalled memory start to ring in Naomi's tuneless heart. She shakes herself out of her sorrowful stupor. She may even begin to feel like she is needed again.

"Oh, Ruth, he is more than just a kind man; he is one of our kinsman-redeemers."

Why Ruth didn't grab Naomi by the shoulders and give her a good shaking will forever be a mystery to me. I can imagine her standing in front of Naomi with her legs astride and hands on hips saying, "You could have thought of this before I had to get out there today, job hunting in the heat and dirt of the harvest."

God's timing, God's timing, God's timing. Ruth needed to get a reputation as a worthy worker in the field before life took on greater levels of provision. She needed to do what every called man or woman must do today—that is, pay appropriate dues or serve an honorable apprenticeship.

Making Way for Provision

FACING THE FRUITLESSNESS OF MINISTERING ALONE

What about Boaz? Ruth goes home to Naomi. Boaz goes home to an empty house. Hey, any pulpit that does not have women standing in leadership beside men is a lonely pulpit.

Boaz doesn't know it yet, but his magnanimous gesture is going to get him two things he doesn't have: the love of a wife and the joy of an heir.

But before that happens, Ruth is about to be a regular part of his day. He will see her often—at his request! He may hear her voice during the lunch break (because he joins his staff for that event). He will get to know the bend of her back, the swing of her hair, her smile of satisfaction as she leaves the field each evening with her threshed-out provision. Why? Because he has given her the great gesture of ownership by saying, "Keep with my people, the people of my house."

Sending women away to other vineyards because of the trouble and inconvenience of their anointing will remove the irksomeness of the situation, but it may keep the local church childless. By all means, take time. Prove the ministry, but keep these women with "my people."

STAYING IN A SAFE FIELD

Naomi tells Ruth that it will be good for her to do what Boaz has suggested because in someone else's field she might get hurt. If anyone should know this, Naomi does. She has just come back from ten years in the wrong field, and she is hurting like crazy.

103

Not every vineyard is safe for the Ruths of the Christian community. Not every vineyard will provide for its Naomis. Many women with the call and capacity to equip the saints sit unnourished and even abused in vineyards that could have benefited from their threshed-out wisdom.

It takes kindness and cooperation from both men and women who are called to equip for things to work out as God intends.

It takes kindness and cooperation from both men and women who are called to equip for things to work out as God intends.

So Ruth stays close to the servant girls of Boaz until the barley and wheat harvests are finished, gleaning, gleaning, gleaning. She is still living with Naomi, and there is still no suggestion of moving to the next level of influence.

This period of time gives Boaz longer to watch her and get to know her. There is no evidence, up to this moment, of anything but paternal care, but God is seeing a higher level of relationship and productivity, and God always perfects those things that concern His people.

Up until now, Ruth has gleaned stalk by stalk, ear by ear. The men ahead of her have been reaping faster, bundle by bundle. Each swoop of the scythe has produced more and produced it more quickly than Ruth has had a hope of doing. Yet there is no evidence of frustration, but rather satisfaction at what she has been able to produce—her 20 to 25 pounds a day.

LABORING FAITHFULLY UNTIL YOUR MINISTRY IS RECOGNIZED BY A KINSMAN-REDEEMER

Ruth, a day is coming when you will not just gather your handfuls, but you will co-own the fields. The day is coming when you will preside over the affairs of the field by the side of the man who is your kinsman.

Women who equip believers to do the work of the ministry are looking for like-spirited men—kinsmen—who will buy back their God-ordained right to be "chosen, royal and priestly" and to stand under their God-placed mantle of pastor/teacher or apostle or prophet or evangelist.

Ruth wasn't elevated too soon. She saw one season to its conclusion before another began. By working tirelessly and willingly, Ruth partnered with God, thus effecting the daily provision of need.

WHERE THINGS ARE RIGHT NOW

"Whose young woman is that?" Well, Boaz, it isn't easy to answer that question. Is she Moab's woman? Is she Mahlon's woman? Is she Naomi's woman?

Perhaps the best answer is that she is her own woman, partnering with a holy God, in readiness for the day when she will stand with you, covered by your mantle.

MAKING WAY FOR PROVISION AS A RUTH

- Finish what you begin.

- Dig deeper than the obvious.

- Walk upright as you carry the message.

- Be accountable for what you already know.

- Face the fruitlessness of ministering alone.

- Stay in a safe field.

- Labor faithfully until your ministry is recognized by a kinsman-redeemer.

Part Three

EXTEND THE BORDER OF YOUR MANTLE OVER ME

Ruth 3 (KJV)

Then Naomi her mother in law said unto her, My daughter, shall I not seek rest for thee, that it may be well with thee? And now is not Boaz of our kindred, with whose maidens thou wast? Behold, he winnoweth barley to night in the threshingfloor. Wash thyself therefore, and anoint thee, and put thy raiment upon thee, and get thee down to the floor: but make not thyself known unto the man, until he shall have done eating and drinking. And it shall be, when he lieth down, that thou shalt mark the place where he shall lie, and thou shalt go in, and uncover his feet, and lay thee down; and he will tell thee what thou shalt do. And she said unto her, All that thou sayest unto me I will do.

And she went down unto the floor, and did according to all that her mother in law bade her. And when Boaz had eaten and drunk, and his heart was merry, he went to lie down at the end of the heap of corn: and she came softly, and uncovered his feet, and laid her down. And it came to pass at midnight, that the man was afraid, and turned himself: and, behold, a woman lay at his feet. And he said, Who art thou? And she answered, I am Ruth thine handmaid: spread therefore thy skirt over thine handmaid; for thou art a near kinsman. And he said, Blessed be thou of the LORD, my daughter: for thou hast showed more kindness in the latter end than at the beginning, inasmuch as thou followedst not young men, whether poor or rich. And now, my daughter, fear not; I will do to thee all that thou requirest: for all the city of my people doth know that thou art a virtuous woman. And now it is true that I am thy near kinsman: howbeit there is a kinsman nearer than I. Tarry this night, and it shall be in the morning, that if he will perform unto thee the part of a kinsman, well; let him do the kinsman's part: but if he will not do the part of a kinsman to thee, then will I do the part of a kinsman to thee, as the LORD liveth: lie down until the morning.

And she lay at his feet until the morning: and she rose up before one could know another. And he said, Let it not be known that a woman came into the floor. Also he said, Bring the veil that thou hast upon thee, and hold it. And when she held it, he measured six measures of barley, and laid it on her: and she went into the city. And when she came to her mother in law, she said, Who art thou, my daughter? And she told her all that the man had done to her. And she said, These six measures of barley gave he me; for he said to me, Go not empty unto thy mother in law. Then said she, Sit still, my daughter, until thou know how the matter will fall: for the man will not be in rest, until he have finished the thing this day.

Chapter 7

WAKING NAOMI

꧁꧂

There has been an expected rhythm to each day from the time Ruth has been working in the field until the end of the harvest. Everyone knows the part that he or she is to play.

- Naomi is recovering and becoming involved in life again—still without a defined future.

- Ruth is working hard and gaining a reputation—still without a husband or child.

- Boaz is in charge—still without a wife or heir.

Now it is time for action to slip into the next gear. God nudges the older woman into an emergence from her broken dreams so that she can begin to create dreams for the younger.

ADVOCATING FOR THE NEXT GENERATION

During a season of ministry, I was the women's leader of our church system in our state. At the outset of that appointment,

I met with the leadership team and, together, we examined what we had. It was the old story of working out where we were, then where we wanted to go, and then planning how to get there.

We identified four strategic actions that, if worked through, would keep us ahead of the game. One of the threats that we saw ahead was the lack of younger women rising in levels of leadership within their churches and within our church system. Their churches were their Boaz-owned fields, but they needed to be identified and readied for placement both in and over those fields.

- We needed to encourage younger women into the field.

- We needed to enable those women to be noticed by an overseer/foreman (often the pastor's wife).

- We needed to make it easy for the Boaz owners to observe, eat with and spend time with these young women.

To assist both the churches and these young women, we hosted Preachers' Clinics for them, where they sat under the skilled training of Dr. Lois Burkett. We also encouraged one-to-one mentoring of these young women by our seasoned leaders. We spoke well of them to pastors. Where it was appropriate to do so, we created opportunities for them to find their pulpit voice.

Why?

Because, as older women, we wanted to advocate for these outstanding Ruths in our state.

Or, to use the narrator's language, we wanted to find homes for them where they would be provided for. A few years after beginning this deliberate strategy, three of these young women addressed a room of leaders. Their insight, their anointing, their articulate and well-constructed content left us open-mouthed. Each of those young women are blessed to be in fields owned by good Boazs, and they are all well on their way toward their big futures.

COMMUNICATING GUIDANCE AND STRATEGY

Naomi, now thinking like the leader she was always meant to be, begins to add strategy and facilitation to the vision she has received from the Lord.

Without strategy and facilitation, the would-be visionary is reduced to the level of being a mere ideas person. In fact, a little further on in the history of God's people from the times of Ruth and the judges, God speaks through Habakkuk, fine-tuning the way a visionary is meant to live. He says, *"Write down the revelation and make it plain on tablets so that a herald may run with it. For the revelation awaits an appointed time; it speaks of the end and will not prove false. Though it linger, wait for it; it will certainly come and will not delay"* (Habakkuk 2:2-3.)

"So that a herald may run with it." A herald is not someone who sits at the table where the decisions for the implementation of the vision are made. The vision has to be so accessibly portrayed, and so transportable, that a herald who is a few positions removed from the genuine visionary is in no uncertainty about the vision.

When asked to do a job, the first questions must be, "What is the vision?" "Where is the written mandate?" Once you know what is required, work it into a strategic plan.

There have been times in my life when I have been asked to do jobs by various governing bodies and there has been no mandate, let alone a written mandate. Natural giftings and personal tenacity have gotten me through, but it has been much harder work than it should be.

Moreover, I have seen the devastation in the lives of friends and acquaintances where they have asked for written mandates that have never arrived. This smacks of negligence and carelessness, both of which are below the waterline for all church leadership, male or female.

A crucial element in ensuring progress in the church is the writing of vision, mandate, criteria for employment, strategy and method of resourcing the vision. Of course, any earthly document must be organic. It is only the Bible that must never be meddled with. Everything else is fallible and open for improvement. Nonetheless, we are wise to write the vision, refer back to it, modify it and work it. Without the tabling of such documents, we drift, and that's a fact.

One thing that can't be put on paper or defined is the choosing of those called to equip the church. How would a strategist have laid down the criteria that called each of the 12 disciples? Aside from the issues of character and moral rectitude listed in 1 Timothy 3 and Titus 1, God breaks through socio-economic, racial, academic, age and personality ceilings. Who does He call? This is the business of heaven.

No, we can't define the reason God chooses whom He chooses, but we can, and must, define the task that the called one is to perform.

I have taken note of the rough treatment that men and women receive in this area of church life. It tends to be the way that decision-making is done behind closed doors (usually male-only).

Let's put aside the fact that a lopsided plan will be produced if half of the way God thinks is not represented in the room. (God's female side—His capacity to nourish and adorn, for starters—is significantly contained within women.)

After the doors of the decision-making rooms are opened, it is too often that inadequate care is taken to convey enough information to those who are meant to flesh out the decisions. And we wonder why things run amok.

We must be diligent with our writing and maintaining of vision.

USING WISDOM IN THE WAY SECURE MEN ARE APPROACHED

So Naomi shares her plan. It is a good plan. An amazing plan, even. It just requires two things: a compliant young leader-in-the-making and an open-hearted man who won't be threatened by the presence of a woman on his turf.

"Tonight," Naomi tells Ruth, "Boaz will be where the work is being done. You can rely on Boaz to be involved with the ministry and the people who work in it. He'll be on the threshing floor. You won't miss him."

Boaz will be on the threshing floor in part because he will be protecting the livelihood and source of nourishment for his people.

Vigilance is required by those in authority in any church system to see that the quality of food is not being affected by preachers and teachers who fail to attend to their own threshing floor.

The strategy is further explained. *"Wash and perfume yourself, and put on your best clothes. Then go down to the threshing floor, but don't let him know you are there until he has finished eating and drinking"* (Ruth 3:3).

For women who have been highlighted by God to stand in any pulpit—in any place of government—this is outstanding advice. I cannot bring to mind a mental image of any woman I know who doesn't go into the pulpit looking as good as she can.

A dainty, exquisitely dressed Naomi from my childhood, Meg Wallace, used to say that when she was asked to speak, she would first figure out what she was going to wear, and then she could focus on hearing from God for her message. She always arrived on her threshing floor looking wonderful.

Referring again to my time as the women's leader in our state, one investment that we made was to invite one of Australia's leading style and image consultants, Anne Reinten, to speak to female equippers about many aspects of their personal presentation. Right colors, shapes, styles, etc. Why? Because when we go down to the threshing floor, we need to attract a different kind of attention than the kind we attract when we are dressed like everyone else down there.

Ruth, don't go to the threshing floor, the place of process, unless you are looking completely womanly. Don't go looking, sounding and smelling like a man. Be a woman!

And, Ruth, don't make a move until Boaz is at rest.

On a couple of occasions, I have observed women box in unsuspecting men in church foyers and office doors.

Agony. These men are elsewhere in their heads (as they should be). They are about the business of the church. For them to be required to stop and deal with what will inevitably be a vexing issue—this women-who-equip-believers-to-do-the-work-of-the-ministry-but-are-not-being-released-to-do-so business—is not going to work.

> *A word of wisdom to pastors and leaders is to create safe places and times where women in your sphere of influence can talk freely.*

A word of wisdom to pastors and leaders is to create safe places and times where women in your sphere of influence can talk freely. These times will only work if the men and women involved are free of defenses and cover-ups. Insecurities and immaturities put the full-stop into any dialogue about gender issues and church leadership and/or government...not to mention stale faith, polarization, etc., etc.

As we have already highlighted, Boaz doesn't lie down to sleep until he, himself, has been nourished. Moreover, Naomi knows that this is his pattern. Perhaps the whole town knows that this is his pattern. How secure the staff must feel, and how trustworthy is his leadership.

DOING WHAT YOU CAN AND ALLOWING BOAZ THE FREEDOM TO RESPOND

Now comes the final part to Naomi's plan. She says, *"When he lies down, note the place where he is lying. Then go and uncover his feet and lie down. He will tell you what to do"* (Ruth 3:4).

In a very small way, this sounds like a certain moment, some centuries later, when a young maiden is going to be approached by an angel about taking part in another plan birthed in heaven. It, too, will carry the possibility of social stigma and that young woman's obedience, too, will produce an extraordinary child.

Never would I suggest that there is a racy side to scripture with attached titillations. It is just a point of great interest that, within 24 hours, a likeness is going to be drawn between Ruth and Tamar. Also, Boaz may have cause to think about the outrageous story of his own mother's life, the prostitute Rahab.

With the lives Tamar and Rahab mentioned, what point can be sensitively yet deliberately made? Perhaps it is enough to suggest that the breakthrough from the limitations to the release of women who equip believers may take more than cold, objective study. It is all about life and flesh and blood and people and mistakes and sin, not just a clinical study on rights and wrongs.

How black and white was Tamar's trickery on Judah? Considering the disgraceful abuse by her two brothers-in-law, do we regard her as wily and sly, or as a courageous woman who is committed to the preservation of God's promises?

How black and white was Rahab's willingness to bring yet still more men into her house of sin? Considering the probable reasons that put her into that ancient "profession," do we regard her as an adulterer or as a woman of great bravery?

And now we have Ruth, instructed by Naomi to step into a gray area of behavior. (I am assuming that this instruction was "gray" because, if it was absolutely, unquestioningly appropriate for Ruth to be with Boaz in his bed during the night as a woman yet unbetrothed, Boaz would not have needed to be so careful to have her leave before dawn fully broke.)

It leads me to feel that the heart of the Father is for men and women to be willing to talk and work through issues of call, beyond emphatic beliefs about who can and who can't do certain things. There are times when life takes us beyond absolutes—when life requires us to deal with blurred lines. Paul described it like this in 1 Corinthians 13:11-12: *"When I was a child, I talked like a child, I thought like a child, I reasoned like a child. When I became a man, I put childish ways behind me. Now we see but a poor reflection as in a mirror* [blurred lines]*; then we shall see face to face. Now I know in part* [no longer needing to have emphatic answers on all issues]*; then I shall know fully, even as I am fully known."*

The older we get, the more we face the truth that we will only ever *"know in part."* God asks us to be accountable to Him for the part we know, and then to give ourselves the freedom to recognize how much we don't know.

APPEALING FOR SHARED LEADERSHIP AND GOVERNMENT; NOT DEMANDING IT

The next part of the strategy requires careful examination. *"Uncover his feet and lie down."*

I am treating the book of Ruth as a type. So often women rudely or naively or aggressively attempt to get into the ministry by showing men up. They don't uncover feet and lie down. Their approach is more one of whipping the blanket right off and scoffing at what they see. Crude jokes are made. Insidious asides are thrown into the conference floors that garner only forced ha-ha's from the women and uncomfortable shuffling from men.

Derision of women by men or men by women is the worst kind of behavior in the church. The gender imbalance in church leadership has caused us to face each other with a standoff instead of turning, as one, and facing the real enemy of our faith.

Many years ago, although the flame of feminism was beginning to burn out in the western world, frustrated called women were saying things like, "Anything he can do, I can do." Well, lady, that is only partly true, and any attempt by you to do more than make an advance toward shared life and leadership graciously, quietly and wisely will strip that man of his manhood. Everyone will be the loser if that happens.

Naomi's method is still the best.

- Wait till he is rested and his work for the day is done.

- You go to him. It is not even in his thinking to come to you. He still sees you as a servant and always will. Probably he will never come to you.

- Uncover a part of him that won't be threatening or humiliating.

- Lie down. This attitude of submission is not an intimidated cowering; it is an attitude of rest.

It is a cautionary comment that must now be made. There are some men who have been elevated to levels of leadership that are either outside of their gifting or ahead of where their maturity levels lie. (Ditto for women, for sure; but we are talking about the Boaz/Ruth situation, so my comment is about men in this instance.)

What am I saying? Simply and sadly this: It may never be the right time for some men to be approached. There are men whose insecurities and defenses are so deep that they can't see or hear what is happening in those moments of honest beseeching. (Again, ditto for women leaders, but worse! When women are dealing with women in leadership who are insecure and defensive, they usually have to add jealousy into the mix.)

Do I have an answer for you, dear Ruth? No. Perhaps you can receive courage and comfort just through the knowledge that, within the church, there is a growing awareness of the dilemma. I encourage you to think and discern with a generational perspective. What may not be for your generation within your church or church system may become a reality for a future generation.

RECOGNIZING THAT OLDER WOMEN KNOW MORE THAN YOUNGER WOMEN ABOUT SOME THINGS IN LIFE

Now comes a moment in the conversation between Naomi and Ruth that is a perfect picture of the yielded heart.

Naomi's mental picture of what might happen seems to become foggy. Either she thinks things and is not saying them, or she hasn't got a clue. Wisely, she doesn't try to have all the answers—a smart move for any older woman in ministry. She simply encourages Ruth to be as obedient to Boaz as she has always been to Naomi.

Ruth's response is consistent with the way she is living her life. It is willing, gracious and compliant.

Before we see the strategy come alive, let's remind ourselves of the wisdom of Naomi's instructions. Boaz is probably 80. Ruth is probably in her early 30's.[1] Naomi has to change Ruth's thinking from girlishness to womanliness. Instead of instructing Ruth to enter the threshing floor with bowing and scraping—meaningless, obsequious gestures—she instructs her to enter like an available woman.

And the reason Ruth readily agrees is because she is not a virgin. She knows exactly what might happen, and she is not alarmed at the prospect.

Likewise, there is a readiness amongst worthy and experienced women, at this time in the journey of the church, to take their place beside men, not as daughters, nor hard workers, nor servants, nor virgins, but as equals in positions of shared leadership and/or government.

These women are not of a mind to expose and make ludicrous the inadequacies of single-gender leadership. Instead, they voice honor and recognize greatness. They know the ministry. They know what is involved.

WHERE THINGS ARE RIGHT NOW

Thank you, Naomi, for waking up and activating the brain and the leadership gift on your life that has been dormant since you left your land over ten years ago. Your wake-up call has come at the right time.

༄༅

THINGS THAT HAPPEN WHEN NAOMIS WAKE UP

- They advocate for the next generation.

- They communicate guidance and strategy to young Ruths.

- They encourage the use of wisdom in the way secure men are approached.

- They teach Ruths to do what they can and to allow Boazs the freedom to respond.

- They appeal for shared leadership and government; they don't demand it.

- They know more than younger women about some things in life.

ENDNOTE

1. This assumption comes through three points of deduction. First, she was married for less than ten years. Second, her journey from Moab to Bethlehem and her duration of work being only two harvests would not have taken more than a total of two or three years. Third, from Boaz's own mouth in Ruth 2:5 and in Ruth 3:10, he sees her as significantly younger than himself.

Chapter 8

WAKING BOAZ

꒰ꕤ꒱

It is Boaz's wake-up call that puts the greatest smile on my face, not because it is ha-ha funny, but because of its sheer serendipity.

The precision with which Ruth follows the instructions of the older woman has never mattered more. If she had notified Boaz of her presence at any time that night other than when he was in repose, he would have dealt with her as a cleaned-up servant girl.

But Ruth is not, and never has been, a servant girl. She has been a regal landowner who needed to spend quite a bit of her life looking like a servant girl and doing what servant girls do. Her time of fieldwork has been nothing more than her preparation for placement.

Prior to the evening meal, Boaz would have washed his hands because that was the custom, and now he is lying in his work clothes with the rest of him still unwashed. But he is well fed and that is rather fantastic.

When leaders in the church take the posture of repose before attending to their own nourishment, they sleep fitfully because their stomachs are rumbling with hunger. They wake up feeling less than an overcoming giant of the faith, and they proceed to take out their own lack on everyone else.

Perhaps the most alarming illustration of this for me was the performance of a visiting preacher to our church many years ago. Our pastor was diligent in the care of his sheep, to say the least and, during an absence, had entrusted the pulpit to the visiting speaker in good faith. The man took his place at the lectern, looked at us quite coldly, suggested that we were a fairly second-rate crowd, and then roundly accused us of failing to pray for him as the reason for why he had nothing to preach to us that morning. Sadly, instead of sitting down, he proceeded to preach nothing for over an hour. He turned up with an empty stomach and it growled at us all morning!

I applaud men who, though often faithfully pastoring small churches with moderate incomes, manage to get to conferences and take correspondence courses. They demonstrate a valiant effort to stay personally fed and groomed. And I doubly applaud men who seek counsel before personal problems overtake them, in their passion to stand before the Lord as clean vessels fit for His use.

Back to our story. It is quite impossible for me to imagine what Ruth thinks as she lies meekly at the feet of this older man who is, frankly, not at all fresh in his body odor. He has been winnowing in the breezy dusk. Throwing the grain in the air and allowing the rubbish to fly away has resulted in some of the rubbish landing on his hair, his beard, his clothes. Smelly, dirty, grainy.

Ruth is probably less than half his age. Was she self-talking, "Ruth, just keep thinking about the many acts of kindness this noble man has shown." "Ruth, he's rich." "Ruth, he needs children just as much as you do." "Ruth, stop twitching." "Ruth, stay put."

STARTLING BOAZ WITH A FRESH TOUCH AND A FRESH AROMA

The narrator now employs a glorious use of understatement. In the middle of the night, he writes, the man is *"startled"* (Ruth 3:8). Really? What might awaken him? The touch of skin that is softer than he has ever felt so closely before? The awakening of his nostrils to an aroma that his now-deadened body smells are no longer overpowering? The indefinable sense that someone else is in the room?

Having watched the steady release of women who equip believers to do the work of the ministry in my own church system and comparing it with the lack of release in another significant church system, I affirm Naomi's strategy.

In my own church system, the women are coming to the pulpit well presented, feminine, womanly and, of course, "washed, perfumed and in their best clothes."

In the other church system I am thinking of, the dismissal or suppression of women has created in those same women (the ones called to equip) a manliness in walk, style and speech. It looks as if those women have taken the only road available to them, which is the if-we-want-to-do-what-men-do-we-need-to-look-and-talk-like-men road.

If one of them had been at Boaz's feet, he might have gotten a bit cranky and we would never have gotten our Obed!

KNOWING WHAT IS AND
WHAT IS NOT BEING ASKED FOR

When a woman approaches a pastor and shares her passion and burden for ministry, here is what she is *not* asking:

- To be the token woman at any event or position of leadership

- To be given lots of responsibilities because she is a capable woman

- To be able to share vision and strategy but not be part of the decision-making

- To have her willing loyalty abused just because, in order to walk fully in her call in the highest way she knows how, she will do anything he asks

- To be tested about her commitment by having more jobs added to her portfolio than others on staff

- To be typecast according to the model of woman who preceded her

- To be typecast according to the model of the pastor's wife

- To be required to look, sound, talk and reason like a man

Instead, here is what she *is* asking:

- To be allowed to be a channel of Holy Spirit instruction to her church

- To be given time to gather and express her thoughts (This may take longer than it does with men—although the reverse is also common—but the depth and intensity of what she sees and perceives will add color and texture to the decision-making.)

- To be given ministry positions in her church only if she is the very best person for that ministry position, regardless of her gender (except where gender *does* matter, such as a minister or leader for women or a young mothers' counselor)

Pulpits deserve our careful and finest presentation. It might attract a careful and fine response.

GIVING BOAZ TIME TO ADJUST TO A NEW WAY OF THINKING ABOUT YOU

Still confused, and because of the darkness of night, Boaz doesn't recognize Ruth. He can't see her face. She hasn't yet spoken so he can't tell from her voice. All that he has to go on is the most pleasant smell that he has ever smelled. And that isn't helping him at all. It is new; it is different; it is a bit confusing.

If his olfactory sense had stored the memory of Ruth's smell up till this moment, it would have been the smell of a hard worker out in the field. But that smell is gone. Ruth has not come to him in the cover of night to seek employment. She has already proven that capacity through the course of two harvests.

In reply to his startled question, *"Who are you?"* Ruth introduces herself in a way that he will recognize. She says, *"I am your servant Ruth"* (Ruth 3:9). Any other description will keep Boaz in confusion. She wisely doesn't answer with "I am your next best move" or "I am meant to be in charge just like you are." He is already dealing with the headiness of an unfamiliar aroma. To have given his senses any more to handle would have been overload. I do not say this to demean Boaz in any way, but he is in unfamiliar territory, and Ruth's discretionary approach is allowing for this.

RESPONDING APPROPRIATELY TO THE WOMAN APPROACHING HIM

Now Ruth makes the statement that will make or break her future as well as make or break Boaz's future, or at least his chance for having his own children. She says, *"Spread the corner of your garment over me, since you are a kinsman-redeemer"* (Ruth 3:9).

Although there is an intimacy in this setting that defies any prudish and legalistic approach to Bible interpretation, her request is not for a lover but a redeemer.

God is going to give her both.

Many wonderful men of God are making wise and refreshing decisions about the identification and release of women who equip believers to do the work of the ministry. In effect, they are saying, "There is a perfume that is unlike the perfume of the place where I work so hard. I know my own smells and this isn't one of them. In the midst of my man-smell must come another aroma altogether...the aroma of a woman." The clean and fresh aroma has awakened possibilities in good men.

Unfortunately, a common response from insecure men has been, "I don't like that smell. Get it out of here. Quickly, could someone produce a few scriptures that will dismiss the value and the quality of that aroma? We just want the man-smell in here."

Boaz reacts with a much higher response. He says, "Even though I am startled, I will find out what is going on before I dismiss something that may solve my dilemma of aloneness and childlessness."

ACKNOWLEDGING YOUR OWN INADEQUACIES

His next comment is about as gut-wrenching and humble as it could possibly be. *"This kindness is greater than that which you showed earlier: You have not run after the younger men, whether rich or poor"* (Ruth 3:10).

In effect, he is saying, "You have had plenty of time to scope out the fitter, younger, more muscled men, but you have chosen me. Ruth, without wanting to brag, I want you to know that you have chosen well because I have the capacity to redeem you within a relationship that I want us to have."

By now, the change in his thinking has neared completion. He has gone from regarding Ruth as someone he can provide for by being her boss, to being her redeemer. And it doesn't stop there. Now, for the first time in his life, he is embracing the thought that he could be her lover.

PARTNERING TOGETHER AT A LEVEL OF GENUINE AND HONEST RELATIONSHIP

There is a level of connection between the pastors of churches and the women called to ministry that includes so many shades of genuine relationship. There must be room for disagreement; for the sighting of the ugly along with the beautiful; for iron to sharpen iron and so advance the kingdom.

I speak regularly to many pastors who are younger than I am. One in particular will often sign off a phone call with

"I love you." There is an amazing freedom when the focus of the Ruths and Naomis is not "how can I get ahead" or "who will get me into the ministry" but "who will love me as a woman as well as a fellow minister?"

SPEAKING REASSURANCE ABOUT THE FUTURE

Boaz quickly reassures Ruth that there is nothing to fear. I think that this is rather sweet. It is Ruth who should be assuring Boaz. She is the one who knows exactly what might take place. Boaz doesn't. He is, by all accounts, still a virgin.

This is such an important lesson at this stage in the journey of recognition and release of women. There are times when wise women let men do and say manly things, just for the sheer enjoyment of doing so. In this there is no condescension and no patronizing attitude but rather the delight of men being men and women being women.

Something a little weird happens now.

Boaz also promises Ruth that he will take care of the closer kinsmen-redeemer. What, Boaz? What do you mean, "a closer kinsmen-redeemer"?

Should Ruth be feeling a little duped by Naomi right now? Has Naomi set her up without all the facts being laid on the table? Well, yes. Naomi's strategy-forming skills aren't revealing everything to the younger sister.

Why hasn't Naomi gone to this closer relative herself? It is believed that this man was Elimelech's brother. Surely Naomi hasn't forgotten he exists. Perhaps he has made no attempt to contact her, even though all of Bethlehem knows the plight of these two women. Perhaps, as a result, she has recognized a man who is so concerned about his own well-being that he probably won't do the right thing by this emerging leader. So she has turned to one whose whole life demonstrates a desire to care well for others.

Grown-up woman of God, deal with this. There are probably men who equip who should be caring for you. They should be showing you courtesies and kindnesses. They should be allowing you to work in their field. But they are not doing so. What are you going to do about that? Perhaps you must find a noble man whose strength of character and whose generosity will recognize that he can release you to ministry without endangering his own hold on leadership.

It says so much about the strength and brilliance of Boaz that he is able to handle a brief encounter that has just tipped his whole life upside down and still manage to think rationally about possible outcomes. Of great significance is the shift in Boaz's thinking toward Ruth. Up until now, she has been *bath*, the Hebrew word for "daughter." As the threshing floor conversation unfolds, he begins to use another term: *ishshah*, the Hebrew word for fully woman. Has Ruth changed? No. It is Boaz's perspective about her that has changed.

My friend Sue says, "God is looking for a bride for Christ, not a girlfriend."

WHERE THINGS ARE RIGHT NOW

Boaz, you have handled your wake-up call magnificently. We kind of knew you would!

※

THINGS THAT HAPPEN WHEN BOAZS WAKE UP

- You might be startled by a fresh touch and a fresh aroma.

- Be sure you know what is and what is not being asked for.

- Give yourself time to adjust to a new way of thinking.

- Respond appropriately to the woman approaching you.

- Acknowledge your own inadequacies.

- Partner with Ruth at a level of genuine and honest relationship.

- Speak reassuringly about the future.

Chapter 9

WAITING RUTH

༄༄

Boaz now gives Ruth one of the most ridiculous instructions by any human logic. He suggests that they both lie down again and stay there till morning!

Surely you don't think we can both nod off to sleep, Boaz. I am closer to a man than I have been in quite a while. You are alive to my presence. You want us to sleep. Hardly. Okay, you don't mean sleep. You just want us to lie quietly. What, no self-conscious giggling? No chitchat? No sorting out which bit of the threshing floor is yours and which bit is mine? Just lie and rest, Boaz? You're dreaming!

But rest they did. Let us remind ourselves again that Ruth is not a virgin. She is not a silly, affected, inexperienced woman. Also, she has been selected by God for this assignment based on His call and her obedience. In other words, she has been selected on merit, not because of who she is married to or who her circle of friends are. In fact, God has declared His hand by placing it upon a socially undesirable woman yet again: Tamar, Rahab and now Ruth.

As she lies there physically still but electrically charged by the events of the evening, surely thoughts of "who, me?" or "why me?" are pounding through her mind. In His benevolent love, Father quiets those thoughts by overlaying them with the great truth that He selects whom He will select and, tonight, Ruth, it is you.

HANDLING THE KNIFE-EDGE OF TENSION-FILLED WAITING

The women who are emerging on to the threshing floors of our church systems are saying, "Please, sir, cover me. There is a call and a capacity on my life for leadership, but I am not recognized as anything other than a hard worker, unless you extend a different right to me." These are not faint-hearted, juvenile princesses. These are mature, experienced and queenly women who lack the very thing that their chosen kinsman-redeemers lack: offspring conceived through the loving commitment of men and women together in ministry.

They are often discounted or dismissed because they aren't married at all or aren't married to the right men. This is only the result of imprudent insecurity. Let that insecurity be redeemed and then the church will securely cover generation after generation of Ruths for the building of the house of Israel.

BEHAVING PRUDENTLY

That splendid moment in any 24-hour period now arrives when there is the suggestion of light. It is no longer dark, but the sun is not yet rising. There is the promise of easier vision, but it is still a little way off. Boaz again thinks of Ruth protectively. He covers her dignity and shields her from any possible embarrassment. For the sake of the whole situation, he doesn't want the news of a possible liaison between Ruth and himself to become known before its appointed time. Oh, the wisdom of guarding both his reputation and hers from those who run to assumptions and invent both motive and action.

ACCEPTING FRUSTRATING DELAYS

He places yet more food upon her head, this Ephrathite owner of land in the fertile house of bread. He puts on her head what he enjoys so freely himself. He is saying to her, "Even though we know that a change is coming, you still need food now, but instead of the small portions that you have been carrying, I am placing a larger portion on your head." (I have been told that women who have been trained correctly—probably by their mothers or aunts—can carry up to 20 percent of their body weight on their heads.)

TRUSTING AND RESTING IN THE NOBLE HEART OF BOAZ

Now Boaz leaves his property and hurries back up the escarpment into Bethlehem. What on earth is on his mind as he moves quickly into the unknown? He is in his 80's and has just been offered an opportunity to move from being Ruth's father-figure to being her lover. It is easy for me to imagine that he is chuckling quietly and saying, "You old character, Boaz, she chose you."

Now, although she is carrying the weight of provision upon her head, Ruth returns to Naomi in the mode of rest that Boaz created for her. Together they note and enjoy the fact that, yet again, Boaz has shown that he is a big-picture man.

He doesn't just plan to release Ruth to her great future in God. He plans to include the older Naomi with every possible blessing.

And Naomi's trust in the goodness of God begins to rise. "Wait, my daughter."[1] The Hebrew word for this "wait" contains the fullest sense of resting, abiding and waiting. It is not an anxious, worrying wait. It is a sit-still-and-let-someone-else-do-the-worrying wait.

Perhaps as Ruth rests during this dramatic morning, she thinks about her life:

- Ten years before, she is single, which is bad, but she manages to marry a foreigner.

- He dies, which is bad, but she still has a good mother-in-law.

- They arrive in Bethlehem and have no food, which is bad, but she receives favor from Boaz.

- She still has no children and no husband, which is bad, but there is now a chance that she might marry Boaz.

- If she has a child to Boaz, she will have to give him up to Naomi, which is bad, but...

Yes, it is easier and wiser to rest than to try to figure out what is coming next.

WHERE THINGS ARE RIGHT NOW

Ruth, while you are resting, Boaz is busy—on your behalf and his.

I believe that this is the prophetic call to godly and noble men who are tired of governing a diminishing church. "Do not rest until the matter is settled today."

THINGS FOR RUTHS TO DO WHILE THEY WAIT

- Handle the knife-edge of tension-filled waiting.

- Behave prudently.

- Accept frustrating delays.

- Trust and rest in the noble heart of Boaz.

ENDNOTE

1. "Wait = yashab (yaw-shab'); a primitive root; properly, to sit down (specifically as judge. in ambush, in quiet); by implication, to dwell, to remain; causatively, to settle, to marry." (*Biblesoft's New Exhaustive Strong's Numbers and Concordance with Expanded Greek-Hebrew Dictionary* [copyright © 1994 by Biblesoft and International Bible Translators, Inc.]).

Part Four

BUILDING UP THE HOUSE OF ISRAEL

Ruth 4 (KJV)

Then went Boaz up to the gate, and sat him down there: and, behold, the kinsman of whom Boaz spake came by; unto whom he said, Ho, such a one! turn aside, sit down here. And he turned aside, and sat down. And he took ten men of the elders of the city, and said, Sit ye down here. And they sat down. And he said unto the kinsman, Naomi, that is come again out of the country of Moab, selleth a parcel of land, which was our brother Elimelech's: and I thought to advertise thee, saying, Buy it before the inhabitants, and before the elders of my people. If thou wilt redeem it, redeem it: but if thou wilt not redeem it, then tell me, that I may know: for there is none to redeem it beside thee; and I am after thee. And he said, I will redeem it. Then said Boaz, What day thou buyest the field of the hand of Naomi, thou must buy it also of Ruth the Moabitess, the wife of the dead, to raise up the name of the dead upon his inheritance. And the kinsman said, I cannot redeem it for myself, lest I mar mine own inheritance: redeem thou my right to thyself; for I cannot redeem it. Now this was the manner in former time in Israel concerning redeeming and concerning changing, for to confirm all things; a man plucked off his shoe, and gave it to his neighbour: and this was a testimony in Israel. Therefore the kinsman said unto Boaz, Buy it for thee. So he drew off his shoe.

And Boaz said unto the elders, and unto all the people, Ye are witnesses this day, that I have bought all that was Elimelech's, and all that was Chilion's and Mahlon's, of the hand of Naomi. Moreover Ruth the Moabitess, the wife of Mahlon, have I purchased to be my wife, to raise up the name of the dead upon his inheritance, that the name of the dead be not cut off from among his brethren, and from the gate of his place: ye are witnesses this day. And all the people that were in the gate, and the elders, said, We are witnesses. The LORD make the woman that is come into thine house like Rachel and like Leah, which two did build the house of Israel: and do thou worthily in Ephratah, and be famous in Bethlehem: and let thy house be like the house of Pharez, whom Tamar bare unto Judah, of the seed which the LORD shall give thee of this young woman.

So Boaz took Ruth, and she was his wife: and when he went in unto her, the LORD gave her conception, and she bare a son. And the women said unto Naomi, Blessed be the LORD, which hath not left thee this day without a kinsman, that his name may be famous in Israel. And he shall be unto thee a restorer of thy life, and a nourisher of thine old age: for thy daughter in law, which loveth thee, which is better to thee than seven sons, hath born him. And Naomi took the child, and laid it in her bosom, and became nurse unto it. And the women her neighbours gave it a name, saying, There is a son born to Naomi; and they called his name Obed: he is the father of Jesse, the father of David. Now these are the generations of Pharez: Pharez begat Hezron, and Hezron begat Ram, and Ram begat Amminadab, and Amminadab begat Nahshon, and Nahshon begat Salmon, and Salmon begat Boaz, and Boaz begat Obed, and Obed begat Jesse, and Jesse begat David.

Chapter 10

BUILDING THROUGH LAW FULFILLED

❧

"*M*eanwhile*" this chapter begins in the New International Version. It is such a picture-painting word. While Naomi and Ruth are doing one thing, simultaneously Boaz is doing another. He is at the town gate, waiting to beckon certain people to join him.

CHOOSING THE RIGHT MAN FOR REPRESENTATION

First to arrive is the kinsman-redeemer, this nameless man who is consumed with his own world. His awareness of the world around him is limited, and his head is bare. There is no crown of kingliness or authority on his head. What an enormous sorrow this is. He is a member of a clan named "my God is King." There should have been an anointing on his life for thinking like a leader almost by osmosis. Instead, he is known by billions of people as the nameless man who didn't offer to help a widow in distress. This ignominy is to be avoided by all in the body of Christ. Galatians 6:10 sets the benchmark for these situations: *"Therefore, as we have opportunity, let us do good to all people, especially to those who belong to the family of believers."*

If this man was going to help out his brother's little family, he would have done so by now. Just as well Naomi never wastes her time trying to make a connection with this fellow. His head is always going to be elsewhere.

I wonder if he responded to the beckoning call of Boaz with a defensive air.

Most of us know when we are surfing under the bridge that we should be crossing.

Sorry, sir. We will never know you by name. You will always be the man who didn't reach out to women who needed support. Furthermore, a woman can waste a lot of her time and potency hoping to be noticed by a man in leadership who either ignores her or who finds ways to dismiss the weight of food on her head.

CHOOSING THE RIGHT PLACE
FOR REPRESENTATION

The city gate is the place where justice is dispensed. Although one can imagine heated debate or, at least, lively discussion about the rights and wrongs of the matters attended to at the gate, its intended purpose is to be the site of discourse and then resolution. It is an open place, a public forum.

So often decisions about the role of women in the church or the role of women who equip believers to do the work of the ministry or women in leadership are made behind closed doors without adequate discussion and sought-out information. Consequently, there have been aborted dreams and plans by uninformed or, worse still, wrongly informed decision-makers, all for the lack of carefully (safely) constructed forums.

This is not limited to the world of men deciding what is best for women. It is also endemic in the administration of some church systems. Conferences have begun to take on a triumphal air created by reduced times in business sessions. Although we are all mighty glad to be free of the painful and objectionable behaviors of times past, we have lost something with the removal of the public forum.

Applying this general observation about church leadership and church government to the specific world of women who equip believers to do the work of the ministry, the Proverbs 15:22 scripture says it perfectly: *"Plans fail for lack of counsel, but with many advisers they succeed."*

DIGNIFYING DISCUSSION WITH A REGAL BEARING

If we needed any more proof of the stature of Boaz in the town, we certainly see it now in the nearly imperious action recorded in verse 2 of Ruth 4: *"Boaz took ten of the elders of the town and said, 'Sit here,' and they did so."*

These men are going to pay close attention to anything Boaz says. If we lay the template of the parable of the trees from Judges 9 over this narrative, Boaz is definitely the olive tree of the neighborhood, not the self-absorbed and dangerous thorn bush.

If there is ever a need for a man to appeal to men on behalf of women, may it always be one who is already head and shoulders above other elders...a man who is readily obeyed by other men.

ADVOCATING FOR WOMEN WITHOUT GUILE

Before returning to the narrative, I want to look at the way Boaz consistently covers Ruth's dignity. This is the fourth opportunity that he has had to ridicule her or point out how pushy and inappropriate she is. "Guess who visited me in the middle of last night, asking for a relationship?" "Guess who came into my office today thinking she has a ministry?" Rather, there is no dark insecurity creating cruel jest. Boaz advocates on her behalf without ever mentioning the fact that, by her own actions and through the vision and strategy of an older woman, she stepped up from servant in the field to co-laborer on the threshing floor.

USING EXISTING ASSETS TO AMPLIFY THE REPRESENTATION

A fascinating piece of information now surfaces. Boaz uses a present tense verb to inform them that Naomi is selling Elimelech's land that is hers through the death of her husband and sons.

Land for sale? Why did she wait until now?

In the Israelites' theology, all land belonged to God. What was sold as real estate was the yearly produce from the land—or possibly even just the potential for produce. We would call this "goodwill." Then, in the year of jubilee, the land was returned to its traditional owner. Therefore, what was being sold was the right to the yearly produce of Naomi's field.

Naomi, why did you forget to maximize what was yours to claim? Have you forgotten that God's intention for you is that you be a productive member in His church? Were you deliberately uninterested in this grown-over, uninspiring block of land because your eyes had become focused on the larger, lush fields owned by Boaz?

One of the great mistakes that any called people can make is to wait for the big break.

Although I can see no obvious answer to any of my posed questions, let us take that last one and work with it for a while. Naomi, once you woke up to the truth of your own ministry, did you get your eyes off what you had because of an enticement to own what you didn't have? Although this question nearly insults the character of pleasant/bitter/re-engaged Naomi, there is a lesson contained in it.

One of the great mistakes that any called people can make is to wait for the big break. We can become so consumed with getting known by the right people, with staying in the right accommodations, with sitting in the right seats, with speaking at the right events, that we miss all manner of rich experiences.

Many years ago I determined that, no matter where I was and how many people I was preaching to, I would use my best message with the best illustrations. I decided that I would never hold back the flow of Spirit within me, waiting for a decent-sized crowd or a well-known church. That simple decision has gathered for me some of the richest memories of God's faithfulness to His people.

As called ones, we must maximize every resource and asset at our disposal and, as has been said by many preachers and writers, perform earnestly before an audience of One.

I have read and researched this part of the narrative—the part about Elimelech's land—because it just doesn't hang together well enough for me. Let's use this as a template for the tragedy of the containment of women in ministry, whether single, married to non-pastors, married to pastors, or whatever.

God gives the gifts. None of us go shopping for them. He watches as we awaken to His largesse. And then He watches as we administer what we are finding.

In the spirit of the narrative, we—men and women—have land that can be "sold."

One of the greatest sorrows in the body of Christ for me is the independence that men and women have from each other. Somewhere after the establishment of the New Testament church (where men and women led together) men and women drifted apart into gender exclusivity.

The "us and them" mentality colors so many things that would do better if it was just "us." All of us together. However, right now, in the church, the story is generally one of paternally led government.

I am still talking in the context of Naomi and the land that Elimelech owned and that she can now sell.

An attitude by women that says, "if men won't let me, I'll just do it anyway" has been the only course open to many women for so long. At least it has kept women recognizing and administering the pastor/teacher, prophet, evangelist, apostle mantles that have been on their lives (their "land").

Is a new day dawning? Are we ready to say, "We need each other if we are going to get the job done"? Then, lady, if you have land and if you have recognized your Boaz (kinsman-redeemer), wait for God's timing. It is your inheritance and the correct governing of your land that will create an inheritance for your children and your children's children, one that you may only know about fully when all is revealed on the other side.

COMMUNICATING IN A LANGUAGE THAT THE HEARER UNDERSTANDS

It is now Boaz's turn to use strategy. He starts to present the case to this nearer kinsman-redeemer, beginning with the real estate issue. Why does Boaz talk about the land before talking about the woman? There is a known weakness in the unnamed relative. His integrity is questionable and his vision is so tunneled to what is good for self that, if Boaz had begun presenting the case for Ruth, this man may have responded differently.

We can breathe easily. A master at negotiation is advocating for Naomi and Ruth amongst the city fathers. It does not take long for the relative to relinquish any rights or responsibilities regarding these two women.

There are times when women just have to come to grips with the fact that some men won't stand up for them.

Cowardly men will stand up *to* women when their positions are threatened, but it takes a man of courage to stand up and speak *on behalf of* women. Ladies, should it ever be necessary to do so, choose your advocate carefully.

Here is the reason. Any time that there is a rise amongst women to claim a new level of effectiveness, there will be some men who forget the harvest and think only of their own standing. "I have too much to lose." It seems as if they forget that there are billions of people going to hell and, instead, grab their status as if it is more sacred than the great commission.

WALKING AWAY FROM THE LEGAL TRANSACTION WITH AN EVEN TREAD

The relative removes his sandal and says to Boaz, "Buy all of this yourself." He is saying, "There is some territory that I forfeit the right to walk upon." He will walk unevenly from now on. One sandal is missing. By contrast, Boaz has created circumstances that have given him the right to tread on the soil that his forthright action has bought him.

To be utterly sure that the sweet and unexpected moment of offered relationship on the threshing floor several hours ago can be lawfully consummated, Boaz goes over everything once again, loudly and in public. *"Today,"* he says, *"you are witnesses that I have bought from Naomi all the property of Elimelech, Kilion and Mahlon. I have also acquired Ruth the Moabitess, Mahlon's widow, as my wife, in order to maintain the name of the dead with his property, so that his name will not disappear from among his family or from the town records. Today you are witnesses!"* (Ruth 4:9)

The word *acquired* is also translated as "redeem."[1] Something in Ruth's life that was hers got lost along the way, and Boaz has bought it back.

Togetherness is the very thing that the Christian heart continually strains toward. We hanker for that wonderful communion between man and woman and God. In the Garden, Adam governed...Adam meaning "they." It was to "they Adam" that authority for dominion was given (Genesis 1:26).

Now Boaz wants to spend the rest of his life as a "they." And for that to happen, he must acquire, or redeem, Ruth for himself. What an amazing, heart-stopping picture of the lengths that Christ goes to in order to capture His bride lawfully and lovingly.

RECEIVING ACKNOWLEDGMENT AND AFFIRMATION FROM OTHERS

The men at the gate get into the spirit of the moment, pronounce acceptance of the transaction and declare blessing. Instead of speaking of health, wealth, social standing or political gain, these men speak of the building up and growth of Boaz's house.

When the leaders of the church follow this pattern of advocacy, it is not so that women can flaunt some hideous power or so that men become suppressed shadows of their former ministries. It is so the kingdom will grow. That...is...the...only...reason!

Their final words redden Boaz's weathered cheeks. They speak of a consummated and virile marriage. There will be children, and the fact that Boaz is no longer a young man is dismissed in a kindly manner by the comparison made to one of his ancestors. Judah was much older than Tamar. And brave Ruth has reminded everyone of brave Tamar. Boaz, Judah was virile. Remember that as you lay down tonight. And Boaz, one more thing. *"A kind man benefits himself..."* (Proverbs 11:17).

WHERE THINGS ARE RIGHT NOW

All in all, it has been a good day's work. Boaz, there is a pretty good night's work up ahead during which you are going to move from a cerebral commitment to a consummated connection with this woman who is becoming an integral part of your ministry. The entire process of identifying and releasing Ruth to her new season of life has been handled wisely instead of ignorantly, overtly instead of secretively and with honor instead of shame.

✿

WHEN LEGAL REPRESENTATION NEEDS TO BE MADE...

- Ruth, choose the right man for representation.

- Boaz, choose the right place for representation.

- Dignify the discussion with a regal bearing.

- Advocate for women without guile.

- Use existing assets to amplify the representation.

- Communicate in a language that the hearer understands.

- Walk away from the legal transaction with an even tread.

- Receive acknowledgment and affirmation from others.

ENDNOTE

1. "Acquired = qanah (kaw-naw'); a primitive root; to erect, i.e. create; by extension, to procure, especially by purchase (causatively, sell); by implication to own: KJV - attain, buy (-er), teach to keep cattle, get, provoke to jealousy, possess (-or), purchase, recover, redeem, X surely, X verily." (*Biblesoft's New Exhaustive Strong's Numbers and Concordance with Expanded Greek-Hebrew Dictionary* [copyright © 1994 by Biblesoft and International Bible Translators, Inc.]).

Chapter 11

BUILDING THROUGH LOVE FULFILLED

✦

For Boaz, 80 years of waiting are over. I remind you that, as far as we can tell, Boaz has spent most of his adult life assuming that he will never be a husband or a father. Now he has something that is wildly beyond his dreams: a wife and the hope of a son.

For Ruth, around ten years of waiting are over. And this time, she can dare to hope that the monthly proof of infertility will never again be seen.

RELEASING WOMEN TO LEADERSHIP AS AN ACT OF LOVE BRINGS OBSERVABLE GROWTH

It is a tragedy for the kingdom and for women who are called to be unable to function as pastor/teacher, prophet, apostle or evangelist simply because there is no supporting culture and no supporting city father. Month after month and year after year passes by, and the yearning for spiritual progeny never goes away.

There are Ruths galore waiting to be included in the work of the Lord so they can anticipate a level of fruitfulness that they will never feel while they are arranging the church suppers or running little groups. (Doing those things is not bad or less than best—unless the call is elsewhere.)

There are Ruths galore waiting to be included in the work of the Lord....

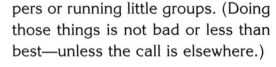

A woman whom I describe accurately, but rather unkindly, as "weathered," has sought inclusion in several church scenarios. She has not just moved in and out of churches; she has moved in and out of church systems. Although it is fairly easy to point out reasons for why she is unable to form lasting attachments, I get a strong sense that heaven travails with her as she faces a lifetime of infertile ministry expression.

A woman comes to mind who has been a member of a church staff for many years. She is petite, stylish, gracious, appropriate and capable. Talk to her about the work she does in the church, and she can respond effortlessly, drawing on extensive experience as a servant in the field. Talk to her about her passion to equip the believers in her church, something she has been prevented from doing, and her eyes fill with tears as she stumbles to express the pain of unfulfilled longing. Contained in her heart has been a ministry of greater potency than stalk-gathering.

Some women will make it to the threshing floors and pulpits that are their assignment. Some women probably won't—mostly because of the human element.

CONCEIVING OFFSPRING WHO ALSO CARRY THE SEED OF REDEMPTION TAKES PLACE WHEN MEN BRING WOMEN TO A PLACE OF EQUALITY

Ruth receives seed that she cannot produce on her own and the result is the conception of life. This speedy conception stands in vivid contrast to the lack of conception during Ruth's marriage to Mahlon. God is revealing to her His benevolent plan for her posterity. Psalm 45:16-17 says, *"Your sons will take the place of your fathers; you will make them princes throughout the land. I will perpetuate your memory through all generations; therefore the nations will praise you for ever and ever."*

Without bringing Ruth into the place of sharing life, Boaz will have made no connection; there will be no conception and therefore no generational provision.

Moreover, and as an utter tragedy, Ruth will go back to the field to glean.

One church comes to mind that has leadership that steadfastly refuses to acknowledge the possibility that the women of that church can be trusted to do anything at a leadership level. Not only are the relationships between men and women strained, the relationships between the women are strained and take a *lot* of work. Finally, the events that the women run are of a high standard of excellence through sheer hard work, but lack the drive of the Holy Spirit that those same women crave. (In the time it has taken to write this paragraph, another three churches have come to mind, aspects of whose journeys match the illustration just given!)

In another church, a fine woman is functioning pastorally alongside men in leadership. The men are called "pastor." She is called "p.a." It is the only label that the church eldership will allow. Comfortingly for her, the leader of that church is as frustrated and sorrowful as she is about this incongruity.

These scenarios or variations on these scenarios are repeated with frustrating frequency in churches and church systems that contain rather than release women.

This is the time and season for churches and church systems to be places of equality. Not tokenism. Not equal numbers. But recognition and release of equal callings, capabilities and capacities.

BEING KNOWN BY A NEW NAME

Ruth now has something that is an indicator of her new status. It is a new name. Upon her arrival in Bethlehem, she is known as a Moabite. By the time Boaz has been her advocate, her husband and her lover, that title has disappeared into oblivion.

I was 27 years of age before I married. Singleness wasn't a huge problem, but there were times when I was introduced as "Joy who isn't married yet." In fact, I recall meeting a woman who hadn't seen me for a while and, with her gaze never wavering from my face, she slid her hand along my left arm until she found my ringless ring finger. Although her audacity amazed me, it was a moment that reinforced my aloneness.

When Ray appeared unexpectedly in my life and I in his, it was a rather lovely thing to need to practice a new signature. I wasn't going to be Joy Averill anymore. I was going to be Joy Graetz. I loved my new name right from the start and was delighted to walk away from the old name. The new name carried a stronger and richer message about my life than the old name. It said that I was now grafted into my husband's life.

Ruth, you are Moabite no longer. You are now regarded as a blessed woman—as blessed as the Rachels and Leahs who also took their place in the genealogy of God's people. You can start to practice your new signature.

For women who are being omitted from significant leadership circles because of a gender bias, there must come a change. "Those women" must become "our leadership team members." "Her" must become "one who equips." This is not a token attempt to give women equal rights. In fact, such a thought makes one gag.

Rather, it must be what automatically happens when release to leadership is based on identification and recognition of anointing rather than gender (or race or socio-economic status).

WHERE THINGS ARE RIGHT NOW

Boaz, it's been a long day. It's been a great night. And now you are facing an extraordinary life. You will never again walk onto that threshing floor without remembering the moment when Jehovah introduced you to a new touch, a new aroma and a new love. A smile will play across your face and you will be so glad for the courage you found to allow a woman onto your platform.

WHEN LOVE IS INVOLVED

- Releasing women to leadership as an act of love brings observable growth.

- Conceiving offspring who also carry the message of redemption takes place.

- Women are known by a new name.

Chapter 12

BUILDING THROUGH PROMISE FULFILLED

~※~

This narrative is drawing to a close and the spotlight turns toward Naomi. This senior woman whose ragged sorrow has prevented her from functioning in life is now on the most wonderful roller coaster ride of recognition and release.

GIVING NAOMI AN OPPORTUNITY TO HOLD HER OWN MINISTRY IN HER ARMS

The town is buzzing with the white-hot news. Naomi has a child once more.

Too old to bear her own child, she is handed the little man Obed to rear as her own. Although she is a dry nurse, she has the joy of feeling the warmth of a baby in her arms. Although it is not breast milk, something of her own supply returns. She is hands-on with the development of a young life. She can claim him as her own and has the legal right to do so.

163

Are we surprised? Psalm 113:7-9 could be describing Naomi's life and ministry thus: *"He raises the poor from the dust and lifts the needy from the ash heap; he seats them with princes, with the princes of their people. **He settles the barren woman in her home as a happy mother of children.**"* He is truly God!

ENJOYING EACH OTHERS' BLESSING

As readers of a great story, we delight in the sheer pleasure that Naomi's newfound blessing provides for her friends. The women of the local church who had failed to reach into Naomi's pain and bring relief are now on fairly safe ground. They can rejoice—and they do so exuberantly. There is not even a veiled hint at jealousy or envy or any other dark sin. Rather, the coming together of Boaz and Ruth is creating a church in which everyone wins.

An amazing element of the character of God is bubbly joy. There is nothing quite like meeting a woman who has just been released to a leadership function which is "her." The twinkling of light in her eyes; the way she bounces from one foot to another; the way she forgoes grammatically correct sentences in her lunging from one ecstatic fact to another. Ah, the sheer bliss of receiving an assignment and being blessed for its beginnings and resourced for its unfolding.

DARING TO DREAM AGAIN

Yet another splendid moment in God's redemptive plan is before us. In these early years of the new millennium, there are wonderful older women everywhere who are watching, mostly from the sidelines, as younger women get opportunities for education, ministry, position and some power. I urge you, fine woman of God, to jump back into the game.

May there be Boazs and Ruths who are wise and selfless enough to give you your own projects and opportunities—things that you can take from infancy to maturity.

One such woman was removed from active service in a most ungracious manner. After years of loyal and faithful work, she was sidelined without any recognition. Rather than whine and spread the wrong aroma, she looked to the Lord as the author and perfecter of her faith. He proceeded to open a door of ministry for her that has placed into her lap a project that she is now taking from birth to full development.

Senior women—called ones—it can happen for you just as it happened for Naomi.

He has preserved our lives and kept our feet from slipping. For you, O God, tested us; you refined us like silver. You brought us into prison and laid burdens on our backs. You let men ride over our heads; we went through fire and water, but you brought us to a place of abundance (Psalm 66:9-12).

Do not cast me away when I am old; do not forsake me when my strength is gone (Psalm 71:9).

Even when I am old and gray, do not forsake me, O God, till I declare your power to the next generation, your might to all who are to come (Psalm 71:18).

WHERE THINGS ARE RIGHT NOW

Boaz, Naomi and Ruth are right where God wants them to be. He takes the posture of repose in the throne room, comforted that those who are the carriers of His Son's redemptive life are fully engaged in living.

***

WHEN THE NAOMIS ARE AGAIN SIGNIFICANT PLAYERS IN THE WORK OF GOD

- They are given an opportunity to hold their own ministry in their arms.

- Their friends enjoy observing God's blessing.

- They dare to dream again.

Chapter 13

BUILDING UP THE HOUSE OF ISRAEL

༄

The narrative closes with a small genealogy. Having already mentioned Judah and Tamar, the narrator picks up the families from their son Perez and does not stop until King David is mentioned.

If Ruth had never stepped onto that threshing floor under Naomi's mentoring, this genealogy would have stalled, or would have needed to move around the times of Boaz or into other clans.

We are running out of time. The church is threatened and menaced at every hand by forces outside of itself—morally, governmentally, politically, religiously. Unless we experience something beyond anything we have ever known before, we are in big trouble.

We have no idea how many times the heavenly timetable has been stalled during the past 2,000 years. Historians and theologians say that the Dark Ages were an ugly time of suppression of called women and, in fact, women in general. So perhaps we have had at least one giant hiccup.

We can't have, we mustn't have, another now.

Let women onto the threshing floor and into the strategy rooms because we really need an Obed right now—an Obed who will keep the line going until the time is ripe for the coming, once again, of the Savior. The house of Israel must be built.

But for now, in the story of Ruth, the genealogy hasn't stalled, and David, that mighty king, is only two generations away.

Um, Mr. Narrator, there are no women's names in that list. And he replies, "Does that really matter?" To which women respond, "No, not at all."

WHERE THINGS ARE RIGHT NOW

It is the theme of this book to allow all those who are called into pulpits or into government of the church to have free access to either, whether they are men or women.

CONCLUSION

My credential papers sat on my desk for over 18 months before I filled them in. The defining moment that precipitated that act was the funeral of a woman who was around my age. She and her husband had been missionaries for many years. In his eulogy, her husband said, "A soldier has fallen. Will anyone stand in the gap?" That night, I began to fill out the papers.

There were three reasons for that delay of 18 months.

The least reason was that I was in a season of life in which I was having to make double the bricks without much straw. God's faithfulness to the call on my life enabled me, but it was a demanding time.

The next reason was a concern that I wouldn't know enough.

It was the third reason that created the greatest pause, and here it is. I knew that I would stand before God both as a believer and as one who equips—a called one. Having observed my parents' life of devotion to God and to His people, I had no illusions about the yoke of the ministry. When it fits, it is joyfully and surprisingly light, but it *is* a yoke. Did I want to wear one? Was I up for that?

Well, the pull of God's heart for His people was compelling. And the papers were completed.

I tell you that story to say this. If every man had a chance to say why he accepted God's call to the ministry, his story would probably contain a sense of feeling compelled.

And if every woman had a chance to say why she accepted God's call, that would be her story also.

These women, precisely the same as their male counterparts, are called to positions of leadership, influence and government. Sadly, and as a loss to the growth of the church, their voice has been silenced and their influence limited in so many church systems or local churches.

The days of infertility in the church must be ended.

The days of the aborted call in women must come to an end.

The days of the call and vision being carried so far beyond its gestation that it dies in the womb must come to end.

That's where things are right now.

For the cause of Christ,

Amen.

ABOUT THE AUTHOR

❦

J oy Graetz is an international conference speaker as well
as a credentialed minister with the Assemblies of God in
Australia. A former school teacher and speech pathologist,
for the past three decades Joy has been preaching in
churches, conferences, seminars and colleges. Many of her
hearers have been blessed by her warmth, humor and
prophetic insight as she ministers. Joy credits her husband
and three adult children with her capacity to be relevant and
relational.

raising our
children's
children

raising our children's children

ROOM in the HEART

Second Edition

DEBORAH DOUCETTE

with Dr. Jeffrey R. LaCure

Taylor Trade Publishing

Lanham • Boulder • New York • Toronto • Plymouth, UK

Published by Taylor Trade Publishing
An imprint of Rowman & Littlefield
4501 Forbes Boulevard, Suite 200, Lanham, Maryland 20706
www.rowman.com

10 Thornbury Road, Plymouth PL6 7PP, United Kingdom

Distributed by NATIONAL BOOK NETWORK

Epigraphs: Chapter 1, excerpt of poem "The Bad Mother," from *Unremembered Country* by Susan Griffin, copyright © 1987 by Susan Griffin, is reprinted with the permission of The Permissions Company, Inc., on behalf of Copper Canyon Press, www.coppercanyonpress.org; chapter 5, excerpt of poem "Crazy Quilt," in *Quilt Pieces* by Jane Wilson Joyce is reprinted by permission of Gnomon Press; chapter 9, excerpt of *I Know Why the Caged Bird Sings* by Maya Angelou is reprinted by permission of Random House.

British Library Cataloguing in Publication Information Available

Library of Congress Cataloging-in-Publication Data
Doucette-Dudman, Deborah, 1948–
  Raising our children's children : room in the heart / Deborah Doucette, with Dr. Jeffrey R. LaCure. — Second edition.
    pages cm
  Revised edition of the author's Raising our children's children, published in 1996.
  Includes bibliographical references and index.
  ISBN 978-1-58979-926-4 (pbk. : alk. paper) — ISBN 978-1-58979-927-1 (electronic) 1. Grandparenting. 2. Grandparent and child. I. LaCure, Jeffrey R., 1964– II. Title.
  HQ759.9.D68 2014
  306.874'5—dc23
                                                                2014004543

Printed in the United States of America

For my Nana

Contents

Preface

There are 2.7 million grandparents raising 5.4 million grandchildren in the United States alone.[1] Other countries such as Canada, the UK, Australia, New Zealand, and Africa are also struggling with this growing trend. Situations in which grandparents have informal custody of grandchildren remain grossly underreported. Some grandparents conceal the fact that they have children in their care, fearing the loss of their "elderly housing." Some dread interference by social service agencies that may take their grandchildren from them. Some fear reprisals from drug-involved children and keep a low profile while doing their best to keep their grandchildren out of harm's way. Grandparents who don't want to rock the boat don't tell.

Grandparents stepping in to help take care of grandchildren when parents cannot is nothing new. However, the exploding epidemic of drug and alcohol abuse in our society has forced more and more grandparents to rescue their grandchildren from the devastation of a life poisoned by addicted parents. Factors emanating from a home ruled by addicts such as poverty, chaos, neglect, abuse, and incarceration add to the problems the grandchildren bring with them. Other factors include divorce, illness, the economic downturn, mental or emotional issues, irresponsibility, teen pregnancy, and death of one or more birth parents.[2] In the case of African grandmothers, "With almost no support, they have stepped forward to care for millions of children orphaned by AIDS."[3]

Many grandchildren coming into the care of our elders are hurt, deprived, and needy. They may be affected by attention deficit disorder, fetal alcohol syndrome, attachment disorders, learning disabilities, or hyperactivity. They have suffered the mind-numbing wounds of neglect and a terrifying array of abuses—physical, sexual, and emotional.

Frequently grandparents are forced to struggle with birth parents, the court system, and/or social service departments in costly and protracted custody battles. Too often social service systems under the mandate of "family unification" squander the childhoods of the children involved, condemning them to years of being jerked from foster care to failed birth parents and back into foster care again. All this shuffling is done for the sake of "parental rights" and a narrowly defined policy of reunification of the family.

Sometimes a family is *not* a family when birth parents cannot, do not, or will not parent. Obviously the function of giving birth does not automatically lead to healthy child rearing; many obstacles may stand in the way. Meanwhile the concept of family reunification, so strictly adhered to, may prevent children from living with loving members of that same *extended* family.

Social service agencies need to redirect their "prime directive" to read, "in the best interests of the child." The mandate toward family reunification must be secondary to what is best for the child, always. That mandate should be altered to fall under the broader heading of "family preservation," while expanded to include extended family such as grandparents and the strengthening of those preexisting bonds. It takes work to preserve a family in the larger sense, to *strengthen* families. And it will take a more encompassing outlook by society at large as well as social service agencies and the judiciary in particular. "It takes a village to raise a child" is an old proverb that rings especially true today.

I heard about a boy whom I will call Jimmy who had been bounced around between foster care and group homes. When he was thirteen, Jimmy was finally placed with his grandmother, whom he loved. But her poverty, and the rough neighborhood she was consigned to live in because of it, made their situation unworkable. Jimmy was taken from his grandmother and placed in a group home for teens. Group homes and similar institutional care for kids like Jimmy can cost over sixty thousand dollars a year. It would have taken a lot less to allow Jimmy and his grandmother to stay together as a family in a safe environment with an appropriate support system.

The fact is *grandparents do not receive the same services or the same financial assistance as foster care providers.* Although "kinship care" is a concept that is beginning to be considered today, for the most part the prevailing attitude seems to be that extended families should care for their related children solely out of the goodness of their hearts. But one can't eat goodness, or buy clothes with it, or use it to obtain counseling, better housing, medications, or specialized services. Grandparents willing to relinquish hard-won custody to the local departments of social services *may* qualify as foster parents or they may *not*. But these grandparents do not want to relinquish control of their grandchildren back to the social service/foster care systems from which they fought to free them!

Preface

What are the answers? Raising awareness of this escalating trend and the special challenges grandparents and their grandchildren face, defining families to include kin, providing loving family members with the means to care for damaged and needy children, and recognizing grandparents as a resource gold mine!

Grandparents raising their grandchildren, contrary to what most people believe, is not only an urban problem, a minority problem, or a problem restricted to the poor. This is an exploding sociological phenomenon with far-reaching implications for our future. It spans every segment of society—rich and poor, black and white, Asian and Hispanic, urban and suburban. Whenever and wherever drug or alcohol addiction, domestic violence, or child abuse and neglect touch a family, the specter of hurt and abandoned children haunts us all. The measure of a culture is how well it treats its most vulnerable—its children. The strength of a culture is determined by what those children become. How are we measuring up?

This book is home to the stories of many families. Each chapter is a window into the private lives of those grandparents, birth parents, and children who are at the core of this alarming trend. Within each interview are examples of the many challenges that face grandparents who are drawn into the fray to protect their grandchildren. As you read their stories, you will see for yourself how well we, as a society, measure up.

Look in one window and find a court system fumbling its way through a child rape trial; another affords a view into troubled social service systems riddled with inconsistency. Another shows us a drug war focusing on an ineffective cops-and-robbers game while overlooking the children caught in the crossfire and poli-

Preface

ticians who just don't get it. One window clearly shows a prison system ruled by gender politics, and still another shows school systems inadequately prepared to deal with the influx of the special needs of this particular group of children.

For grandparents, these windows offer ways of coping and methods of healing. There are views onto what has worked for others and what has not, as well as a look at the skills used to navigate the minefield of challenges that confront grandparent caregivers.

My hope is that these windows will lead to doors—doors to finding help for grandparents, doors to raising awareness, doors to changing our views about parental rights, the nature of family, and what is in the "best interest of the child." Ultimately, I hope these doors lead to a better understanding of the complex issues involved when we must raise our children's children.

—Deborah Doucette

NOTE FROM THE THERAPIST

While working as a counselor and coordinator for a family services agency in Roxbury, Massachusetts, I learned that while there were many skilled and competent mental health professionals, there were, however, very few who truly understood and appreciated the variety of issues that occur in foster, adoptive, and custodial families. I am an adoptee and know firsthand what it's like to be raised by someone other than a birth parent. I empathize with the struggles and joys of the families highlighted in this book. If a grandparent is willing, loving, and available to parent his or her grandchild, it can be a win-win arrangement for all involved, particularly the child.

Preface

My commentary, liberally sprinkled through the book, offers my professional advice on issues with which each family must contend. I have addressed challenges that face grandparents every day, from dealing with a troubled grown child, to family secrets, to guilt. I hope that the advice I offer, combined with the experiences of the grandparents interviewed, will help others successfully deal with their own family situations as they work together for the sake of their grandchildren. There is no better motivation.

—Dr. Jeffrey R. LaCure

Acknowledgments

First and foremost I would like thank my children for their un-flagging support and encouragement of my work on this book. As always, I am deeply appreciative of my loving family—my source of strength and inspiration.

A special salute goes to the members of the Massachusetts Grandparent Support Group Network and to the Massachusetts Executive Office of Elder Affairs, who have worked so hard and done so much for caregiving grandparents, and to Dr. Jeffrey La-Cure for his expertise.

Finally, I wish to thank and praise each of the grandparents, children, grandchildren, and all those caring individuals who participated in this project. Without their generosity, strength, wisdom, and love, this book could not have been written.

—Deborah Doucette

Introduction

Where there is room in the heart, there is always room
on the hearth.

—Elizabeth Marbury, *My Crystal Ball*

"Mom, I'm pregnant." One of the most dreaded phone calls parents of a teenager can receive.

I was in my office when I got the call. At that time, I was a real estate broker in a country-style suburb about thirty minutes west of Boston, Massachusetts—a bedroom community of daffodil trails and bridle paths, with a one-gas-station, volunteer-fire-department, don't-blink-because-you'll-miss-it center. We settled on this little town for the acre minimum zoning, the best-in-the-state school system, and because maybe, if you pay enough, it won't rain until after sundown.

We had three children: our oldest daughter was nineteen and a sophomore in college, our second daughter was sixteen, and our son—a surprise package—was just three years old. Now, this phone call had brought me more than just another surprise, a mere bump in the road; this was more akin to a cement wall across the highway—a crack in the sky. It was a dizzying shock, the kind that spins you around until you are facing in a totally different direction, forever altered, and the very next step you take is a journey into foreign territories, unfamiliar landscapes.

My daughter's voice held a faint tremor of panic, so unlike her. I pictured her hunched over, sitting on the edge of her bed, gripping the phone as if she could squeeze some comfort from it. My heart hurt for her, and at the same time I was thinking, "Stupid, stupid, stupid!" I blurted out an "Oh my God!" before managing to get a grip on myself. I told her everything would be okay. We would work things out. "Don't worry," I told her—and myself—then drove out to Connecticut to be with her and make some short-term plans.

She was too far along in her pregnancy for a safe termination. She was taking birth control pills but had suffered a bout of bronchitis months ago for which she took antibiotics, never having been informed—and I didn't know—that antibiotics can reduce the efficacy of birth control pills. Having gone through a painful breakup with a boyfriend months before, she was feeling more and more defeated, depressed, and angry. She dropped out of school and came home to have her baby. She talked about putting the child up for adoption.

I let her talk. I knew, though, we would never allow that to happen. At first I hoped, fantasized, that she would become an entirely different person and actually want to raise a child. But I knew her all too well. She never wanted children, never liked babies, never even played with dolls, and never harbored any wish to be a mother. She was super bright and artistic, always marching to the tune of a different drummer. We always accepted that. We accept it—celebrate it—even now. But at that moment, she was feeling so trapped, so sad, that I didn't want to agitate her any further; I kept my thoughts and feelings to myself for a while.

She asked me to find her a female doctor, and I made an appointment with a very well-regarded ob-gyn group in the area. Then I made a call to speak to the doctor personally so that I could explain my daughter's situation to her. I began to tell her that although my daughter might want to talk about adoption with her, we would never allow that to happen. I didn't want any action taken to hook her up with prospective adoptive parents. Among other things, I still held out a small kernel of hope that she might change her mind during the process of pregnancy, and I certainly didn't want that potential severed prematurely.

I no sooner got the words out of my mouth, "She will want to talk about adoption," than she cut in on me, telling me effusively that she had "many wonderful couples in my practice waiting to adopt."

I interrupted her, "Wait a minute. I just wanted to let you know that it will never happen, that my husband and I would adopt the baby before we would allow the child to be adopted out."

"Because that's the way *you* want it to be!" she spat out at me indignantly. I believed I could hear her salivating over the phone lines, licking her chops over my grandchild.

Angered, I replied, "Because that's the way it *will* be."

This baby was already part of our family; to this doctor she was a hot commodity. I wondered then about society's well-meaning rush to sever tenuous bonds with other young women brought to their knees by the uncertainty, fear, and desperation of an unexpected pregnancy. I am uncomfortable with the blanket of moral certitude under which those decisions are made by those in authority. Attaching young pregnant women who are often alone, unhappy, and impoverished to happily married couples who are further along in life and more financially stable may force the beleaguered birth mother's life-altering decision into a too early fait accompli. I wonder about this still.

The doctor made me her adversary from that moment on. She never understood that, for us, this was a *family* decision. My daughter was young, panicked, and confused. At this point, all she wanted was to have her pain erased. We needed time over the next few months to help her sort out her feelings and goals and make plans for the future—hers and the baby's.

I wanted this doctor to be an advocate for the family as a whole, but she couldn't get past her bias. Ironically, society as a whole embraces the concept of traditional adoption, but adoption within families is still regarded as odd. I have come across this attitude time and time again over the years, the attitude that although there is something inherently good and noble about traditional adoption, there is, on the other hand, something unfortunate and confusing about interfamilial adoptions.

When I made a subsequent call to the doctor about my concern that my daughter wasn't eating, she responded, "I'm going to tell her that you called!" She said it like a threat. And while I fully realized that she needed to share this information with my daughter, she couched it in such a way as to portray me as interfering, my call as unacceptable.

Over the next few months, the doctor and her staff managed to convey the idea of grandparents adopting a baby as peculiar. Fortunately, my daughter has never felt the need to be conventional or feared things that were "different." Nonetheless, their attitudes

Introduction

made our family decision-making process that much more difficult at a time when we would have welcomed any constructive input.

In time, my daughter came to see the good in keeping the baby within the family and relaxed into the idea. Their individual relationship did have a slow start. Shortly after the baby was born, my daughter left to go back to school. I spent a lot of time explaining to her that even though she wouldn't be a "mother" to her baby, she needed to establish a relationship with her. She was so traumatized by the whole experience that it took some time to reconnect the bonds of love that were buried under her personal pain. Eventually she did lift herself out of that well of despair, but it took months. It took phone calls and visits and talks and tears. Slowly her negativity evaporated as if a bad fever had finally broken, and she was herself again. Even during those most difficult days, I had confidence that my daughter would work her way through her pain and ambivalence.

During those bad days—the ones I swam through in lethargic slow motion as if in a river of molasses—and after several weeks of sleep deprivation, the endless round of feedings, diapers, naps, and worries, I was feeling quite sorry for myself. We never regretted our decision—not ever! But that never stopped me from rolling in self-pity now and then.

Here was our little girl—all seven and a half pounds of her. I watched her slip quietly into the world—into our family—and I recognized her instantly. She was ours. The fourth in a line of firstborn daughters, connecting us to generations past, leading us into our future. It was inconceivable that our sweet, bald-headed baby girl could be anywhere else. The absence of her—the loss would be unimaginable. I never lost sight of that.

Meanwhile, because of the added workload, I not only left my job at the real estate office, but also totally abandoned any hope of continuing my fledgling career as a freelance journalist. While I am sure there are women out there who are able to combine teenagers, toddlers, and infants with a writing career, I knew that I was not one of them.

In addition, this was the second time in my life that I had to deal with the combination of a teenager in high school (my second daughter) and an infant in diapers. (My oldest daughter was in high school when my son was born.) It seemed a weird and incompatible mix. There I was, again, waiting up at night for one child to come home and getting up an hour later to feed the other. For the second time in my life I was grappling with a teenager over schoolwork, dating, drinking, and birth control, while adjusting formula, worrying about colic, and trying to work out naps with an infant. This time, I also had to navigate nursery school carpools, karate lessons, and play-date arrangements for my three-year-old son. And I was older; too old, I thought, and too tired. A friend pointed out that I must be working out some mighty strange karma. This was not what I had envisioned my forties to be like.

One morning, while sitting on the couch still in my pajamas, my hair uncombed, the baby lying against my chest so she would finally—Please, God!—*sleep*, I tuned in to a local TV talk show. There were two older women talking about their support group, Grandparents as Parents. I remember clearly one of the women saying to the host, "We haven't even had time to roll over." The host didn't have the slightest clue what the woman meant by that, but I knew. No chance to ever think of yourself. No time when you didn't have to get up in the morning for someone else. No time that you could just roll over and go back to sleep if you chose.

Introduction

I managed to write down the telephone number that flashed on the screen without—Thank you, God!—waking the baby. Later that month I traveled thirty miles one rainy night to attend their monthly meeting.

That meeting—with over fifty other grandparents, mostly women—was a tremendous eye-opener for me. At the age of forty-two, I was by far the youngest there. As the others talked, they revealed concerns and problems ranging from custody battles to losing elderly housing because of grandchildren in their home to finding child care while they went into the hospital for hip replacement surgery. Some were so old they had trouble making it down the steep stairs to the basement meeting room of the Council on Aging building. Hearing about their experiences really put things into perspective for me. I stopped feeling sorry for myself and came to see myself and my family as thoroughly blessed.

Yet we still had some kinks to iron out with regard to the newest member of our family. Because my daughter had left so soon after the baby's birth to go back to school, I was deeply concerned that she did not have time to bond. I knew their relationship would need to be encouraged and nurtured for it to grow. It would take patience and time and work.

Their relationship has blossomed. They have grown to love one another and have become connected in a very special way. The birth father and his family are an essential part of my granddaughter's life as well. We have been successful, I think, in integrating both birth parents into her life and ours. It takes a lot of work. It takes a commitment to family—immediate and extended—and to the good of the child. I have always believed that there is room for everyone in a child's life and that it is healthy and in fact quite normal to be so inclusive.

Introduction

Our story is not the norm, however. In most cases many destructive forces have come into play, leading to the necessity of grandparents stepping into the breach to rescue their grandchildren. We have been very, very fortunate. We did not have to deal with any of those negative elements, and so it was relatively easy for us to open our arms in welcome to everyone involved.

Other grandparents do not find their lot so easy. They may be elderly and coping with ill health and fixed incomes. They may have several grandchildren to house, clothe, and feed. They are often dealing with birth parents who are abusing drugs, alcoholic, violent, or in jail. And they may be dealing with grandchildren suffering the effects of years of abuse and neglect, children with serious special needs. Many grandparents must scrape by at poverty level, receiving little or no assistance from state agencies for their grandchildren. Or they may be embroiled in an emotionally and financially draining battle with birth parents over custody of the children.

These are the families for whom this book is written: for the grandparents who hesitate to step forward and ask for help because they are too filled with guilt or shame, for families who feel that their situation is unique, for families who need to know that others have been there too and that there are ways to cope, opportunities to heal, and help available.

In gathering material for this book, I met with family members—grandparents, adult children, and grandchildren—over the course of a year or more. Seasons changed as I got to know each and every one of them, the remarkable people that speak to you now from these pages. Their stories are harrowing, touching, and true. With a few exceptions, names have been changed, and in some cases locations and other identifying markers have been

Introduction

altered to provide some measure of privacy. But I have tried to capture the essence of each person, each family, each experience, and to share with you their feelings and mine in hopes that you can feel you know them as well as I do.

Additionally, family therapist Dr. Jeffrey R. LaCure provides guidelines for coping with the situations described in each chapter. Questions that arise about adoption, birth parents, sibling rivalry, and the like are answered by Dr. LaCure and also by the successful experiences of the grandparents themselves.

The people interviewed for this book came forward out of a desire to help others. They opened their generous hearts to me, often revealing painful wounds and unspeakable hurts. And even though some grandparents' stories have been utilized to show examples of problem areas, they all have one thing in common: they are raising grandchildren who have thrived under their care.

Here now are the intimate portraits of families who have survived cataclysmic rifts in their family structure. Their backgrounds vary; they have differing religions and beliefs, come from various ethnic and socioeconomic groups, and function within a set of circumstances that are, at once, specific to them as well as universal to families everywhere. But at their very core, they share the same goals—children that are healed and families that are whole.

ONE

The "Bad" Parent

She drives with all her magic down a different route to darkness.

—Susan Griffin, "The Bad Mother"

"He hates his mother." A grandmother was telling me about the teenage grandson she was raising. "He told me he'd like to kill her!" Her eyes glittered with self-righteous satisfaction. I winced and thought, here is the next generation of men who hate women.

We were at a monthly meeting of Grandparents as Parents (GAP), a support group for grandparents raising their grandchildren. GAP has chapters nationwide, as do other grassroots organizations formed over the last twenty years to fill the need for information and for connecting with others trying to cope with similar issues and concerns—groups such as Grandparents as Parents in the United States and the UK, CanGrands in Canada, and many others. I began a support group in my area when I realized how many grandparents were struggling in this situation with nowhere to turn.

Clearly, the self-righteous grandmother attending our little group disliked her daughter-in-law, despised her in fact. There are toxic birth parents, to be sure, and perhaps this was one. But we as grandparents must be careful with the delicate balance between what we know and what we convey to the grandchildren involved. We should not conceal truths, but rather explain faults.

Working to preserve a relationship between birth parents and child is one of the caregiving grandparents' most critical tasks. Grandparents need to find ways of dealing with the questions and concerns children have that help them to turn anger into understanding.

Many grandparents harbor hard feelings toward the birth parents who left them struggling with the care of their grandchildren—parents who may even have neglected or abused the children. It's a difficult job to check back that anger and talk about the birth parents calmly with such a bitter taste in your mouth. But the children deserve to see the world with clear eyes, unclouded by hatred.

I wince again every time I think about that teenage boy and how the hatred he harbors will infect his life. I would be willing to bet that he will grow up not just hating his mother; he will hate himself, and he'll feel that he is worth nothing because he believes his own mother is worthless. Perhaps he will be fearful and suspicious of women in general. He will probably have low self-esteem and the poor judgment that grows out of it, and the cycle of addiction, abuse, and neglect will come full circle.

Certainly grandparents do not intentionally plant the seeds of doubt and self-loathing in their grandchildren. They may do it inadvertently, however, with the unchecked remark, the conversation overheard, or the stony silence when the birth parent is mentioned.

The "Bad" Parent

Healthy children are what we grandparents are all after. Sometimes the road to achieving that is so hard that we have to leave all the negative feelings behind—like so much dead weight—or we won't get to that good place.

THE DONALDSONS

Marci and Pete Donaldson are a caring, thoughtful couple in the midst of a custody battle with their daughter. They often talk about her and her boyfriend with angry voices as they churn over and over again the events of the last few months. The challenges they face on a daily basis with the care of their grandsons, the court battles, and their disappointments naturally fuel the fire of their anger. They may believe the boys are too young to understand. But they understand all too well, and they quietly store up their feelings. They will let them out later.

Cranberry Court is quite nice, not what I expected at all. Here the trailers are laid out on comfortable little tracts of land just like any other neighborhood. The small homes, looking very much like ranch houses, sit on landscaped lawns dotted with trees, gardens, and shrubs. At the edges of each of the lawns is a rim of sand that fans into the street, a reminder that the ocean isn't far away, an explanation for the scrub oak and gnarled pine and the flirting breeze that ruffles the leaves in defiance of the white-hot air. Some yards are neat and orderly, and some are scruffier, scattered with flung-down toys, Barbie carcasses, and large plastic turtle-shaped sandboxes. The Donaldsons' yard is clearly the latter variety. Two orange and yellow "crazy coupes" dominate the front walk. A big blue Oldsmobile has been carefully parked across the lower end of the drive so that rambunctious little feet can't paddle into the road.

Matthew is the first to greet me. At five years old, he is close to the same height as his three-year-old brother, Joshua. Matthew has a sweet, pixie look with sparkly blue eyes and a freshly "buzzed" head ready for the summer heat wave we are swimming in. His face has the flattened appearance typical of children with fetal alcohol syndrome. Joshua runs up to me and shouts, "Hi!" He has a sturdy look about him, from his full, round face to his solid shoulders, a direct contrast to his older brother. I become instantly confused as to which is the older and which is the younger brother, a problem that plagues me throughout the interview.

Their speech is difficult to understand. It is essentially still baby talk, but in Matthew's case, the sounds he makes are also affected. They are muffled and monotone, like the speech of someone hard of hearing. Marci and Pete alternate translations.

Marci and Pete are an average couple—middle-class, middle-aged, working Americans, young as grandparents go, forty-something. Pete is compact, wiry, energetic, with a careworn, mustached face and brown eyes underneath expressive dark eyebrows. Marci, a bit taller than Pete, has neatly coifed, short blond hair; flawless alabaster skin; and nearly transparent blue eyes that flash with anger as she speaks.

Matthew and Joshua are the children of Marci's twenty-five-year-old daughter, Jennifer. Pete is Jennifer's step-father. Marci's back goes rigid as we sit around the dining table, and she begins to talk. "From the beginning when they were born, we were very concerned about their well-being," she says. "Jenny's boyfriend, Mark, had always been very abusive with us, very hostile and violent, and it made me wonder what kind of man was this to be around children. And of course we can't prove it, but we think he also abuses her."

The "Bad" Parent

Pete leans forward and adds, "He is abusive to her, but she doesn't admit it—she's battered, but she doesn't recognize it. He has dragged her around by the hair. He has verbally abused her, and he has taken some swats at her, but she excuses it. She says, 'Oh, he's got problems; he's a schizo.'

"We began to see the signs before Matthew was born. Marci had brought vitamins for Jenny to take while she was pregnant. Mark told Jenny, 'You don't need vitamins. My mother never took vitamins, and you don't need them either.'

"Sometimes after we'd spoken to Jenny, and maybe we might have argued with her or told her she should be doing this or that, he would call us up and threaten us, tell us he was going to cut our heads off or put me in cement shoes and drop me into the water." Pete relays this information calmly, leaning forward; his voice is even, his speech slow and measured.

"When I went in to see Jenny while she was in labor with Matthew, there he was slapping her on the thighs and saying, 'It don't hurt. Don't be a baby!'" Pete's eyebrows shoot upward and he shakes his head. "And I mean if you've had a child, you know what the pain is. So I encouraged her and I helped her through it. Mark left. After a while he came back, but he was more out of the room than he was in. Then the doctor came in and said to me, 'You're coming in with her.' Well, I had never done that before, but I went in and the baby was born.

"Two or three days later we went back to the hospital," Pete continues, "and we told her we would come back in the morning and she could come home with us for a few days. We were concerned because she was young and inexperienced, and we wanted to help out. When we came back the next morning, Mark yelled at me, 'You're not taking her anywhere!' and he pushed me against the wall. I tried to calm him down and told him, 'All she wants to do is come down with her mother for a few days. She's never taken care of a little infant before.'

"'That baby's not going anywhere!' Mark said. Well, I got really angry and told him, 'If you are so concerned, why don't you go put your name on the birth certificate.' He wouldn't do it. But a nurse came over to us quietly and said, 'It's best that he doesn't do that. Let that lie. Someday, if you ever want custody of the child, you can just ignore him.'"

Marci is sitting at sharp attention, focusing intensely on Pete's recollections. She jumps in with some memories of her own. "When Matthew was born, and later too, he had all the classic symptoms of fetal alcohol syndrome—not sleeping, hyperactivity, short attention span." She adds, "Of course we didn't realize what it was at the time.

"Things became more and more difficult between Jenny and us. From time to time they would come down here for visits, but mostly they would hold Matthew over our heads, not allowing us to see him. After a while, it got to a point where I just gave up. I didn't call anymore." Marci continues in a thoroughly disgusted tone, "Jenny got pregnant a couple more times and had abortions, and then she finally got pregnant again and had Joshua."

The children have been playing in a screened porch chock full of toys adjacent to the dining area where we sit talking. I look behind me to see wide brown eyes, round as stones, peering back over a huge yellow dump truck.

"Bad-mouthing" birth parents in the presence of grandchildren will only serve to build a false, fragile allegiance between themselves and the children that will, in all probability, backfire down the road. More important, it may cause the children to feel that, if my birth parents are "no good," then I must be "no good." Grandparents need to be mindful of the whereabouts of their grandchildren, no matter how young or old, as they discuss the shortcomings of their birth parents.

At this point Matthew runs over to Pete and says, "Papa, Papa, more," and holds up a sippy cup with a few drops of apple juice still left in it. Pete bends to him and says slowly, patiently, "More? In a little while I can get you more, okay?" Then he asks Matt, "Did you say hi?" and nods in my direction.

"Hello," I say to the little boy. Again I ask Pete, "Which one is this?"

"Matthew," Pete answers in the same patient tone he uses with the boys.

"This Papa Pete!" Matthew says to me proudly, pointing at Pete. Marci and Pete burst out laughing. Pete rubs the spikes of hair at the top of Matt's head, and Matt fairly sizzles with delight at the attention his grandparents are focusing on him.

Pete tells me that after Joshua was born the child had some difficulties breathing. "Well, she smoked real heavy during both of the pregnancies. We didn't see Joshua that much at first. We hadn't seen either of the children for a while. It was difficult. We would try to visit them down there at their apartment, but Mark would turn the music on so loud while we were there that you couldn't even think. We would try to ignore him because we didn't want any fighting or anything like that in front of the kids. Then Jenny started coming here to visit. We noticed that the children had bruises on them. That was just a couple of years ago. Matthew was two and a half and . . ."

"*Matthew* is the oldest?" I interrupt Pete, confused again. "I'm sorry, I have to write this down. I can never keep track of names," I say in apology. In fact I am mortified because I realize that every time I make this mistake I am inadvertently pointing out that there is something very wrong with Matthew, that the reason I cannot keep straight which is the older and which is the younger brother is because Matthew is underdeveloped and so very delayed. I am horrified with myself. I open my notebook, and in large print I write, "MATTHEW IS THE OLDEST = HE JUST TURNED FIVE," and I keep the book open in front of me.

Marci tells me that Jenny started to allow them to take the children for extended visits. "But when we started noticing more bruises on Mattie, we took them both to a doctor here in Plymouth. He said it looked like someone had grabbed Matthew's arm like this," Marci grabs her upper arm and squeezes hard. The doctor said that Matt had failure to thrive and was malnourished. And they both had very high lead levels. That was when we first heard about fetal alcohol syndrome and the shape of Matt's face being abnormal. The doctor reported all this to the Department of Social Services (DSS) where she lives. They went and investigated, but they said they found nothing wrong.

Professionals that work with children, such as doctors, nurses, teachers, counselors, and the police, are mandated to report any suspicions of abuse to the Department of Social Services. This report is referred to as a 51A and is simply a claim alleging abuse or neglect of a child by a caretaker. Anyone can, and should, file a 51A when abuse is suspected.

Although abuse and poor parenting are a significant part of the boys' relationship with their parents, the boys will struggle with loyalty issues between their birth parents and grandparents. Even when children suffer from traumatic abuse at the hands of their parents, most children still want to "protect" their parents and continue a relationship with them.

It is critical that Pete and Marci foster the children's need for connection with their birth parents. Speaking accurately, honestly, and using age-appropriate language with the children when discussing Jenny and Mark will give Pete and Marci great mileage and actually serve to strengthen their own relationship with the boys.

"DSS has done nothing," Marci continues. "The man I spoke to there was very rude to me on the phone. He refused to talk about it with me. I have a file this thick." She spread her index finger and thumb apart about three inches. "All the paperwork, everything. I have the doctor's report that says he spoke to them. They were supposed to look into it but . . ." Marci shrugs and then stares at her hands folded on the table in front of her, shaking her head.

Documentation is critical for grandparents embroiled in custody battles with their children. Keeping a daily journal chronicling the amount of contact, telephone calls, missed visits, and conversations between birth parent and child is important for drawing a clear picture of the kind of relationship the birth parent is capable of sustaining. This information is particularly useful in court if birth parents attempt to portray an entirely different view of events. Written details, dates, and times lend credibility to an account brought forth by grandparents.

Marci looks up and says tightly, "We were supposed to have the kids all that week, but when Jenny found out we took them to the doctor, she called up and said, 'I'm coming down to get those kids.

Don't try to stop me or I'll get the police.' She'd done it before, so I said, 'Well, come down and get them then.' The visits after that were very sporadic."

"Then came last August," Pete says. "We pulled up in front of the office building where Jenny works to pick the kids up. Matthew had no underwear on and pants that were way too big for him, hanging down and filthy. He stank of urine. Joshua stank of urine, and they were very, very dirty. Jenny was inside working. Mark was outside sitting on a truck with a bunch of other people drinking beer. Mark was the one who took care of them while Jenny was working."

Marci interrupted, "We have a reason to believe that the children were left alone. We can't prove it but . . ."

"That's right," Pete continues. "When we moved the kids into their bedroom, I had to take the door off the hinges before they would go inside, they were so afraid. They are terrified of closed doors. After I took the door off, they were so happy about their new room, and they laughed. But it's funny, they have a laugh that has a cry in it too—it's a laugh with a cry . . . ," Pete trails off pensively.

"Anyway, when we were at the office building to pick up the children that day, Mark picked up Joshua and threw him, literally threw him at me, saying, 'Here, take 'em!'"

When Matthew and Joshua begin to ask questions, such as why they are not with their birth father, I would suggest the grandparents respond with something as follows: "Your father left you alone a lot, and sometimes he didn't treat you as well as a father should treat his sons, as well as you deserve to be treated."

I would encourage Pete and Marci, when talking to the children about their mother, to use clear, age-appropriate language, such as, "Your mother drank too much, and she did not take as good care of you as she could have," rather than something like, "Your mother is a drunk who isn't worth a damn." While many grandparents may be tempted to go with the latter, they will find that their grandchildren's self-esteem will benefit from the former.

Sharing information needs to be at age-appropriate times. As the children approach the ages of nine or ten, they will be old enough to hear and understand the specific details of their father's behaviors and lack of parenting skills. Before the children are teenagers, they will need to know the rest of their story, including their parents' chaotic past.

"They smelled so bad, and they were so dirty. We had to take them somewhere and get clothes for them and wash them up before we could even continue on."

Marci adds, "Matthew had a gash right here." She rubs her finger across a spot over her eyebrow.

Pete says, "I asked Matthew, 'What happened?' He said, 'Daddy boo-boo.' I said to Marci, 'These kids are not going back.' She said, 'Well, what are we going to do?' I said, 'We'll just stall for time.' So we kept them.

"I said, 'Come on, we are going up to the courthouse, and we will get in front of a judge today, because these children aren't going back.' Jenny called us and said, 'Are you bringing the children back?' and I said, 'Oh yes, we'll be up there.' I lied to her. Then I called back and said, 'The car broke down; we won't be there until later.'

"So we went to the courthouse and waited there with the children from nine o'clock in the morning until five o'clock in the afternoon to get in to see the judge. We finally saw the judge, and he granted us temporary custody for one week until we could get Jenny into court. The judge told us we had to go serve her with a paper that explained it.

"We drove back up to Saugus, and Jenny started off, 'Okay, c'mon, kids.' I told her, 'Wait a minute, Jenny, we went and got custody of the children today because you're not taking care of them.' She said, 'You can't do that!' then she ran back into the building and came back out with Mark's mother, who works in the same building.

"I told her again, 'These children aren't being taken care of, they are neglected, and until we get this straightened out, we will keep them.' She said, 'You can't do that.' I said to her, 'Jennifer, get in the car and come home with us if you don't want to be separated from them.' She said, 'You can't control my life; you're not telling me what to do!' I said, 'But you aren't taking care of these children, and we have a right.'"

"We got into court a week later," Pete goes on. "We saw Mark come in. He had gotten a haircut, he was all cleaned up, and he said to us, 'We'll see what goes on today.' While we were sitting there, he kept taunting me, and his father, who was also there, kept going like this." Pete slices his fingers across his throat. "I just ignored it.

"We all went into an office with the court officer who was trying to straighten things out. We sat down, and Mark started ranting and raving. Finally the court officer said, 'Wait a minute, I am getting a little nervous sitting here with you. I can imagine how these kids feel living with you.' Mark went off the wall. Then the court officer said, 'I ran your rap sheet, and you have quite a few warrants out for your arrest. I have called, and they are coming to arrest you right now.'

The "Bad" Parent

"One of the warrants was for rape. They came and arrested him, took him away, and we didn't have to deal with him that day; we had to deal with Jennifer."

Matthew comes running full tilt up to Pete again.

"Wan more!" he says and plunks his juice cup down on the table.

"You want more?" Pete says, looking fondly into Matthew's eyes. "How would you like me to put the sprinkler on?"

"Yay!" shouts Matthew.

Pete smiles into Matt's face, pleased at the delight he sees there. The heat has steadily risen and is well over ninety degrees now, humid and stifling.

"These trailers really hold the heat," Marci admits. A fine veil of perspiration glistens on her upper lip.

The boys have been very patient, and we take a break so Pete can turn on the hose and help Matt and Josh into their bathing suits. Marci and I chat a while with the tape recorder off as we sip on tall glasses of ice water. She grows quiet, at loose ends without Pete by her side.

Their home is very small but comfortable, neatly kept and jam-packed with mementos, photos, and knickknacks carefully arranged about the room. A waist-high stack of children's videos fills one corner near the TV. Another corner holds a bookcase overflowing with books—Danielle Steele is featured heavily. Marci tells me they really need more space now and are looking for a larger home.

Marci asks me about my own situation and how I came to be writing a book about grandparents. She seems to relax as I talk on, and I realize how tense she's been, not from nervousness, not because of the tape recorder, but from the angry feelings she harbors for her daughter, the situation, and the reliving of it.

She begins to tell me that early on when they were having difficulty obtaining access to their grandchildren, she went to court to petition for visitation rights. At probate court she was given forms to fill out, but her situation did not fit any of the categories required for completion of the form. There were provisions for divorced birth parents, or a parent with a deceased partner, or couples who have moved out of state, but none of that fit their particular situation. Grandparents' rights are sketchily drawn and vary from state to state. For the most part, when there is an intact marriage and one or both partners feel the need to exclude grandparents from the children's lives, they have that right and ultimate power. In other words, grandparents have little or no legal recourse. Marci asked if she could just fill in "other" and leave it at that, but the clerk said, "You better get a lawyer." "But I don't want a lawyer," Marci replied. "I can't afford a lawyer, and I shouldn't have to have one to fill out a paper!"

Marci says that Pete eventually went back to probate court to see the lawyer they have on hand to answer questions. He waited all day, but there were so many people still ahead of him he finally left. "It was just a month later that this other stuff came up, and we didn't need to go that route," Marci confides.

Pete comes back out of breath, settles into his chair, and picks up where he left off. "Mark had been scheduled for a rape trial and had never shown up. The rape supposedly took place just before he started seeing my daughter. So that was hanging over his head, and they arrested him right there. But he only got fined and then let out on the street."

"Ha!" Marci blurts out angrily. "That didn't surprise me."

Pete talks a little more about Mark. "He is a very nice-looking young man, very well spoken. But he is like Jekyll and Hyde. He collects SSI (Supplemental Security Income) because he is supposedly an epileptic. And that's the reason for being the way he is, according to my daughter. 'He can't help it; he's an epileptic,' she would say, or 'It's a reaction from his drugs.'

"Anyway, when we got back into court with Jenny after the week of temporary custody was up, the judge told Jenny to set up day care for the two kids while she worked. But when we went back to court, she hadn't done it. So the judge ordered her to see a psychologist and come back with an evaluation. But when we went back to court again, she hadn't done that either."

"We have a family services court officer that has been working with us," Marci explains. "That court officer was trying to help Jennifer get the children enrolled into day care, but Jenny wanted Mark's sister to take care of them. I told the court officer, 'Do you think I'm crazy? I don't want them around anyone in that family, because I don't want Mark around the children. If they are with his sister, I don't trust the situation.' The first piece of paper we got from the court says that he is not supposed to have any contact with the children.

"The court has been very good to us. We did this totally without lawyers. The family services investigator has been very cooperative; we can call her at a moment's notice."

In a custody dispute, a judge may assign a court officer to assist in the investigation process. The court-assigned investigator is not an advocate for any of the parties involved. He or she is required to be an impartial finder of facts only. In some cases, a judge may assign a guardian ad litem (GAL) to assist in the investigatory process, or attorneys for either side may also request a GAL for that purpose.

A GAL may also be enlisted by the court to represent the interests of a child involved in a difficult custody dispute. The level of commitment and care each GAL brings to a case varies from person to person. However, in the vast majority of cases about which I have heard, when there has been a GAL advocate to stand up for the child, the GAL has been an invaluable help in determining what is best for the child. Sometimes the only voice to speak for the child is that of the GAL.

"When the case worker came here to do a home study, she was here almost all day talking," Marci continues. "We had a very nice visit. She went that very same week to Jen and Mark's apartment. He threatened her; he was going to throw her down the stairs. And when we went back to court in October, the court officer told the judge, 'I refuse to go anywhere near him. I refuse to go to the apartment, and if I have to meet with her [Jennifer], it will be in my office.' And every time she would ask Mattie about his daddy, he would go like this." Marci balls up one of her fists and strikes her outstretched palm with it with a loud smack. "She said to the judge, 'Mark Harrold is abusive and violent with me. Imagine what he is like with little children.'

"I don't know whether it's because of drinking or she just wasn't cut out to be a mother. She [Jennifer] has only been here five times to see the kids since last August when this whole thing began. She is supposed to come every Monday on her day off, but she doesn't. We'll tell her, 'Come down and spend the weekend with them.' She'll come down and spend one night or one afternoon, and then she'll call one of them [Mark's family] and say she has to go right back. It's like someone who is in a cult and her brain is programmed and they are controlling her. She hardly talks to the kids on the phone."

"She talks to Mattie," Pete says. "She'll always talk to Mattie. But if Josh doesn't speak to her first, she doesn't care. Jenny would call on the phone, and Josh would say, 'I huv you, I huv you.' And she would say, 'What's he saying? I don't understand what he's talking about.' I would tell her, he's saying, 'I love you.'"

> The children will need to receive support and information about the disease of alcoholism to help them understand that their mother has an illness that she cannot, at this point, control. At some point, Al-Anon or Alateen will be a useful resource for the children when they are older to help them understand that they are not alone and to validate that they did not cause their mother's drinking problem.

"It bothers me," says Pete, "and I think it bothers me more than it bothers Marci, that Jenny is not a mother to these kids. As time goes on, it bothers her less and less that she doesn't have them.

"Both of the children are going to a special-needs school where they get occupational therapy, counseling, and speech therapy. They could barely speak at all when we first got them. The only thing they could tell us was who gave them the boo-boo. When Matthew can't say something, and he gets frustrated and slaps himself in the face."

> Anger is a very normal emotional response for children who have been abandoned, abused, and neglected. This anger will be released in the only place the children feel safe, in this case, with their grandparents. Understanding that this anger may sometimes surface in inappropriate ways allows caregivers to be more patient and consistent with the children. If grandparents can provide an environment that doesn't attempt to take away a child's anger and instead allows the anger to unfold in a safe

way, they will be providing an environment that encourages healing.

Pete says, "Mark now claims that we 'ripped Matthew off' and that we only wanted the children because Matthew was collecting SSI because of his learning disability."

Jennifer and Mark had received a retroactive SSI check in the amount of approximately two thousand dollars for Matt before the monthly checks of nearly four hundred dollars began to be rerouted to the Donaldsons. Pete asked Jennifer if she would send some of the money for the care of the boys, but she angrily refused.

Jenny and Mark eventually lost their apartment and moved in with Mark's mother. Jenny became pregnant again. Pete says, "My heart goes out to the child." But Pete and Marci feel they cannot take in another child. "Because next year she's going to have another one, and then she's going to have another one," Pete laments. He has offered to pay for birth control, but "she won't do that. She says we are trying to control her," he tells me. "I have told her, anytime you want to get your act straightened out and you want to come down here, we will help you with these children to straighten out your life, but until you do, you will never get them back."

Marci adds, "Not while he is in the picture. A while ago, when my other daughter, Judi, was living here temporarily, Jenny called, and Judi put Mattie on the phone to talk with her. Next thing Judi knows, he's hysterical and crying, so she listened in and Mark was on the phone saying, 'I'm coming down there to get you. You are not going to go to school there.' So Judi told him off. Then he got verbally abusive and threatened to "come down there to wipe all of you out!'

"When I got home and learned about this, we went right up to the District Court to get a restraining order. I was afraid he was going to do something to us. The woman at the court said, 'Is this man related to you?' I said no. She said, 'Well, I can't give you a restraining order.' But we were able to get him on violating his court order to not have contact with the children. Now we always talk on speaker phone so we can hear what's being said to the boys."

"For a while, Matthew wasn't sleeping," Marci says. "He was afraid his father was going to come and take him. His therapist said he had never seen him so upset. And now when you mention "Daddy," he says [here Marci sticks out her tongue and blows raspberries—a short, emphatic blast!]

"The therapist has given a report to the court that says he would be strongly opposed to the children going back to their birth parents and recommends that they stay where they are. He has found evidence of sexual abuse—nothing done directly to them, but they have witnessed things they shouldn't have seen; they know things they shouldn't know. To have that in writing from a man who knows what he is talking about! I would hope a judge would not even *consider* giving them back!"

There is a sharp and desperate edge to Marci's words that escape through clenched teeth as if she's trying to hold them back, swallowing down her fear. This fear seems to be always just beneath the surface as she speaks. A lot of effort is expended to keep it from bubbling up and taking control.

The Donaldsons haven't heard anything from the courts in over nine months, and although Marci says "No news is good news, I guess," she shifts uneasily in her chair. The uncertainty is wearing them down. Thus far, the court has awarded them temporary custody only, and although they are afraid to press for more for fear of "rocking the boat," their real goal is to gain permanent legal custody of Matthew and Joshua.

"During that time when Judi was staying with us," Pete explains, "the kids were sleeping out here." He gestures to a nook beyond the dining area that holds a bookcase and a small table now. "Jenny called DSS on us. She told them it wasn't a suitable place to be sleeping. I said, 'Well, Jennifer, when they were sleeping on a mattress on the floor that was all dirty and there were cockroaches and bugs running all over it, do you think that was suitable for them?' And she replied, 'Material things are nothing; they don't need material things.' I said, 'They don't? They don't need things like clean clothes and food?' She said, 'Everybody's not rich like you!' I told her we were far from rich.

"Another time she called and said, 'I've got a little bit of news for you,' and I said, 'What's that?' She said, 'I am going to court tomorrow, and I'm going to swear out a warrant for your arrest.' I said, 'Why?' and she said, 'You sexually abused me.' I said, 'I did? Well, let me tell you something. I will get a lawyer, and when they find out you are lying, I will sue you and you will end up in jail.' Well, I never heard anything more about that. It was just a threat to try and scare me into giving up the children.

"I told her that if I thought I had to go to jail or give up these children, I would go to jail, but I wouldn't give them up. We still love Jenny, and we pray that she straightens out. But I'm afraid that's not going to happen."

"Not yet," Marci interjects. "She is really going to have to hit bottom first. We thought that when her grandfather died—she was very close to him—that would maybe do it. That was just a month ago.

"He was my father, and I was very close to him too. Jenny is the first grandchild in the family, and almost every picture I have of her when she was little has my father in it too. He was so heartbroken when she hooked up with this guy. The day that Jenny went over to my parents' house to show them the baby, Mark started some argument and almost hit my father. My father stood right up to him, and Jenny stood right there and watched him nearly strike the grandfather that she loved so much!"

Marci shakes her head with a mixture of anger and sadness and becomes quiet, lost in thought. When she continues, she looks over to Pete for encouragement. "Pete and I are going to marriage counseling. About three years ago we got a divorce. We are not married now. Jenny brought that up in court, but we had already told them. I told them they could have the records from our counselor; we have nothing to hide."

I wonder out loud if the stress of this unfolding situation was a contributing factor in their breakup.

"It didn't help," Marci exclaims. "All the tension! That was on my mind all the time. You get stressed out. Now we are getting just a little back to normal."

Pete says quietly, almost inaudibly, "I'll always wonder if we waited too long to get the children. So many things have happened to them."

"But when they're babies you can't prove anything," Marci bursts in frantically, her voice rising. "I didn't want Mattie to go home with him [Mark] the very day he was born! If I could've kidnapped that child and gone away with him I would have. Because I could see it!" The desperation is clear and present on her face. Her lips tighten as she continues, "There is something wrong with that guy. I don't know what this child is going to grow up to be like. Every day of my waking hours until he came to live with me, I was petrified that something was going to happen to him."

"We went up to visit them, and there were no screens on the windows on a third-floor apartment," Pete adds in disbelief. "Even though it is very stressful to raise children at this age, at least you know they are taken care of and you can go to sleep at night and not worry, Are they falling out of a window? Are they being abused?"

Marci agrees, "Exactly. I'd rather have them under my roof."

"And as much as it would be rough for Jenny to come here to live and straighten out her life, it would be well worth it," Pete adds.

"My advice," says Marci, choosing her words carefully, "to anybody who is going to do this is: Make sure you have help. If Pete were still working, I don't know how we would be able to take care of them." Pete is a fireman with a permanent disability. He takes care of the children while Marci works full time. "I have often thought of switching to something more part time to be home with them more, but we need the money and they are on my insurance."

The boys run in soaking wet from the sprinkler. Matthew runs off to the bathroom with Marci. Joshua begins climbing on Pete, monkey fashion, clamoring for attention. Pete says playfully, "You're soaking wet! What are you doing in here? Moo-Moo will be mad." They laugh together, knowing he's just kidding. "Whose baby are you?" says Pete with great affection as he strokes the side of the little boy's round face. Joshua answers, "Papa's!" happily.

"What happened to your face?" asks Pete, concerned about some minor scratches. Josh, of course, doesn't know what he's talking about and just replies, "I all wet!"

Pete excuses himself to help Marci. They tend to the children together, drying them off and dressing them. The boys come charging back into the room, whooping and laughing. They are dressed in shorts, T-shirts, and blue-and-white jacquard towels flying behind them, secured around their shoulders with wooden clothespins—two tiny Batmen.

Marci, the disciplinarian, marches behind them. "Get your sandals. No puzzles now. Get off the couch. No jumping!" she orders. She settles them down at the table with us. They are kept busy with individual plastic bowls of animal crackers.

Meanwhile, Pete continues on. "There has been no mention from Jenny of straightening out her life to get her children all under one roof. We had told the court we wanted Mark to get some psychiatric help or just be evaluated, but the court can't force him to do that unless he wants to be adjudicated the father. And I'll bet you when this next baby is born, the birth record will read, 'Father Unknown.'

"I didn't know men were that scarce in this world that a woman would have to put up with what she puts up with from him. She is a perfect example of a battered woman. We called a battered women's hotline, and someone called her from there. Jenny told them to mind their own business. She says to me, 'I'm fat. Who would want me?' And I tell her, 'Someone who would see the good in you.' But you can't get that through to her.

"Now here is a girl that was very kindhearted. She used to cry at *Little House on the Prairie*. Marci and I married when the girls were quite small, and I am the only father they have ever known. They never went without. I don't know where she went wrong."

"She started drinking—sneaking from a liquor cabinet we kept locked—at around fourteen. She hit a certain age and she went bananas, climbing out the window, staying out all night, smoking. At fifteen she stole some stuff out of the house.

Marci explains it this way: "She's a follower. She hooked up with the wrong crowd, and that was it.

"She still, to this day, will not admit the damage that has been done to him," and she points to Matthew. He lifts his eyes from his bowl of crackers briefly—his long eyelashes flick up, then down—aware that he is being discussed. Marci plows forward, "With Joshua it's not too bad; it's been mostly aimed at Matthew. I don't know why. And yet Matthew is the one they want to talk to on the phone; he is the favorite. I think if I told them [Jenny and Mark] that I am keeping Josh and sending Matt back, she wouldn't care." The two boys stand like little sentries by the table, biting off zebra heads and elephant legs, munching away quietly.

> It is a mistake to state in front of children that parents have a "favorite" child. This can be very damaging to both children's self-esteem. The favorite child may believe that he has to live up to the expectations of being the favorite, while his sibling may feel that he must "live down" to the lowered expectations. A self-fulfilling prophecy may develop for the less-than-favorite child and may, as often happens, result in difficult-to-manage behaviors, tantrums, and poor self-esteem.

Pete says, "Jennifer says to us all the time, 'You can't run my life!' and I say to her, 'But you can't abuse these children,' and she answers, 'But they are *my* children!'"

"I just want this settled through the courts, so I know she can't come and take them out of here," says Marci.

"It's a horrible feeling to know it might happen. What would it *do* to them?" Pete says.

Marci adds, "If someone came in today and said I had to send them back, I couldn't live with it, knowing the life they had. If that life changed and things got better, it would be different. How could she stand back and allow her children to be abused? They are terrified of having a door closed. They are terrified of having bathwater run into a tub. Why? Jenny's response is, "Oh well, that can't be anything too serious." It took a long time before I could put them into a tub to bathe them!" Marci is leaning forward in her chair. Her eyes are locked onto mine. They are wide and questioning, alarmed.

On the wall across from the dining area where we have been sitting is a large framed picture that stands out from the many others arranged around the room. There is a girl of about nine years old, wearing a crew-neck sweater and looking like she just came in from picking apples—pink cheeks, a slight smile, and a direct, firm gaze from clear blue eyes. She shares those eyes with her mother and has passed them on to Matthew. Her face is lovely, full of promise—perfectly formed.

Just then, Matthew, who now has his towel draped over his head and pinned under his chin like a little sheik, or saint, stands beside his Moo-Moo, points a tiny finger at me, and says, "You go home? You go home?" Marci and Pete laugh, slightly embarrassed by his directness.

I take hold of his little extended finger and repeat, "Am I going home? Yes! Are you sick of me being here? I don't blame you." I have taken up most of this blazing hot and humid afternoon monopolizing the attention of his grandparents, and he has had enough. There are games to be played, toy stores to visit, and ice cream to be licked. It's time to go.

As I am leaving, Marci shows me an old black-and-white snapshot that had been blown up to eight-by-ten size. It is a grainy photograph of her father as a young boy of about six or seven. Familiar dark eyes look out of a full, round face.

"Look at that," Marci exclaims. "Doesn't Josh look just like my father?" she says with pride and full of hope.

Matthew and Joshua will need support and guidance to understand why their parents made the decisions they did and to be reassured that those decisions are the parents' responsibility and not their fault. As they continue to help their grandchildren understand their birth parents' behavior and help Matt and Josh feel good about who they are, Pete and Marci need to work on feeling good about who they are as well.

If grandparents can overcome the temptation to talk negatively about the birth parents in front of the children, they will strengthen the relationship with their grandchildren while moving toward the healing and recovery process.

TWO

Family Secrets

Shame needs three things to grow in our lives: secrecy, silence, and judgment.

— Brené Brown

Secrecy is seductive. It can creep up on you, and before you know it you're caught in its web. Or it can be comforting, like a big blanket that can be pulled up over your head—a hiding place. It can have a life of its own. Secrecy requires the layering of more and more secrets upon itself to maintain its existence, and so it grows, fragile but suffocating, like a house of sand.

Grandparents are driven to keep secrets out of the desire to protect their grandchildren. They fear their grandchildren will be hurt or damaged by the knowledge of the frequently painful details of their former lives and/or separation from birth parents, even from knowing who those birth parents are.

The younger the children are when they come to live with their grandparents, the easier it is to slide them under a blanket of concealment. Most often the cover-up is not planned or even thought about at all. Secrecy can be a passive thing, an omission of telling.

At first it may seem that the child is just too young to understand. Stories of abandonment, neglect, or abuse seem too complex and awful to broach to a little one. Grandparents are loath to allow even the hint of the former turmoil from which the child has come to disrupt the hard-won, peaceful existence they have painstakingly fashioned for him or her. Later it may become more and more difficult to open up such an enormous can of worms. Where does one begin? What age is the *right* age?

An abundance of literature deals with questions such as these for the traditional adoptive parent. But for caregiving grandparents, whether adoptive parents or not, these questions take on a wholly different spin.

Family dynamics come into play. This makes for an array of variables not charted in the adoption manuals. Hurt feelings, betrayals, disappointment, anger, frustration, bitterness, shame, and resentment—the list goes on—all play a part in making a difficult situation seem overwhelming.

Grandparents deal with a mass of conflicting emotions always. The task of weeding out their bad feelings to bring up the subject of birth parents with a small child is daunting. Just as difficult is talking with an older child or adolescent about the weaknesses of their birth parents that have caused him or her such distress and upheaval.

Caregiving grandparents, in fact, rarely see themselves in the traditional adoptive parent role even when they have legally adopted. They seldom seek out adoption literature to help them deal with issues that come up while raising grandchildren. They simply see themselves in an entirely different role, one for which there is no definition, and for which there are no hard and fast rules—and little help.

Grandparents need to know that there are methods of dealing with questions children ask about their past, about birth parents, and about their place in the family. Grandparents should be mindful of explaining faults without assessing blame when talking about birth parents. They should give simple, age-appropriate answers in much the same way one does when asked "Where do babies come from?" Obviously, how much you tell children depends on their age and maturity level. Often they are looking for only the simplest of answers. And like the answer to the "babies" question, appropriate information should be spooned out over time. Waiting to have that "big talk" when the child is "older" is a mistake. Very often the child will have formulated his or her own distorted theories by then.

Although I often recommend author Lois Melina's book, *Making Sense of Adoption*, to grandparents, they seldom take up my suggestion, and when they do, they have difficulty correlating the author's advice with their specific situations, particularly when they have not adopted. Additionally, negative feelings toward birth parents ultimately cloud the picture. While it is true that each grandparent caregiver does function with a set of fairly unique circumstances, much of the advice given to adoptive parents can be extrapolated to fit grandparents in most caregiving situations.

I often hear, "Why does he have to know *now*?" The answers to that question are many: because children have a right to know how they came to be there; because even though they aren't asking the questions, they are wondering; because when children wonder, they imagine all sorts of things; because the longer you wait, the more difficult the telling and the more telling the blow.

When our little one was barely three years old, she muttered something to me as I was dressing her. I couldn't hear or understand what she was saying, but she was looking at me out of the corners of her eyes with her head down while she said it. She was definitely waiting for my response to what she had just whispered. I bent my head near to hers and asked her to repeat what she had said.

"The princess was adopted," she said a little louder, while keeping her head low and looking up at me through her lashes.

Where did *that* come from? It was as if she had made up a story in her head and just told me the punch line. We had not as yet directed talk of "adoption" toward her. I was astonished that she knew the word. And yet she clearly knew that it had something to do with her—something important. What must she have been thinking? What baby fantasy had she concocted in her head until she had the courage to blurt out the word to me and watch carefully for my reaction?

We talked a bit that day about what it means to be adopted. It wasn't too difficult because she already knew that her birth mother was the one who had "carried her in her tummy" before she was born. She already knew her birth story and how she came to live with us. But I had neglected to bring her up to snuff on the legal formalities. Who could have guessed that this child, barely out of diapers, would need to know more?

It gives me chills when grandparents tell me that their grandchildren haven't asked questions, so they don't offer answers—grandchildren who are five, eight, or ten years old. Who knows what may be churning around in their imaginations?

Additionally, family secrets are nearly impossible to keep. Someone usually spills the beans. When this happens in adolescence or young adulthood, the results can be disastrous. Children of any age are better able to cope with the story of how they came to join their grandparents than they are able to recover from years of deception by those they trust. Adults who have inadvertently discovered the truth about their adoption, or who have been told late in life that their sister is really their mother, invariably feel that the very foundation on which they have built their lives is not solid but rather like a house of sand.

THE WINETRAUBS

The Winetraubs have been bitterly disappointed by their daughter's abandonment of her young son, as well as what they refer to as her "lifestyle."

They are a solidly upper-middle-class couple just entering retirement age and living within a pencil's throw of a prestigious college. They are deeply religious, kind, intelligent people who have spent a lifetime teaching and helping others.

Irene welcomes me to their home between pale admonitions to their cocker spaniel who barks maniacally, skittering backward, nails scratching against the polished oak floors.

Irene Winetraub is pleasant, gray haired, and grandmotherly. She leads me to the kitchen, (where I always seem to wind up) and introduces me to her husband, Bernard. Bernie is a short bear of a man wearing a yarmulke and working in the midst of a pile of papers.

There are birds in a covered cage by the window and a very old and coddled cat sleeping under a square of sunlight. He has diabetes, they tell me, and is given daily injections by the Winetraubs. The ancient, gray-black tabby is lying on the kitchen table. Irene laughs, a little embarrassed, while proclaiming, "You do not see a cat on the kitchen table!" He stands up from his indulged spot—no doubt realizing he is the subject of conversation—and hobbles stiffly across the table to greet me. When he nearly reaches my nose, Irene scolds him mildly and scoops him down.

They begin to tell me a rather typical story of a troubled young woman, their middle child out of three daughters. They try to be positive at first. Irene begins, "She was very vivacious, and she had everything going for her." But as a teenager, things began to change. "There was tremendous dissension always. As far as we know, she was never on drugs. Alcohol was never a question. Just the idea of any kind of responsibility was completely overwhelming to her. She was extremely, extremely rebellious. My husband and I went through a tremendous period of tension and stress. Nightly phone calls . . . different worries . . . where is she? Is she coming home? Three months before she was to graduate, she left school." As their daughter Susan got older, Irene tells me, "we took her in several times back into the house. We tried everything possible. We tried counseling. She would stop going." When Susan was in her mid-twenties she came back into their lives. "She begged us and promised that everything would be fine, and we took her back into the house. Then we found out she had a boyfriend and she was pregnant."

The Winetraubs supported them both, "financially, emotionally, every which way," says Irene. But eventually the boyfriend "wanted out," and Susan followed suit. She left her infant son with her parents and disappeared.

Irene continues, "She knew the child would be taken care of and there would be no problems. We gave her every opportunity;

we gave her everything. Everything you could possibly do for a child, we tried to do. We decided, when she did leave, to obtain legal custody."

"Someone said, when we were going through the adoption, it was like a divorce, a bad divorce," Bernie tells me, head in hand. There is a hint of his old New York neighborhood in his speech.

"She contested it," Irene says. "By this time she was already living with another man. She didn't want the adoption, and yet she didn't want the child. So what do you do?" she shrugs. "We fought it. It cost us a fortune, both emotionally and financially."

In a contested action, the birth parent is usually eligible for free legal assistance. In fact, the more troubled, down and out, and destitute they are, the more likely they are to be assured of free counsel. Grandparents fighting for the welfare of grandchildren must go into debt, lay down life savings, and secure second mortgages on their homes in order to gain legal custody. And even then, they are not always successful. As in other types of legal battles over the best interests of a child, the rights of the birth parent are paramount and often conflict with what is in the child's best interests. Grandparents have few rights; children have none.

"She didn't want to assume any responsibility; she wanted to be like the divorced father," Irene tells me heatedly. "And finally I said, 'Forget this! I don't want it!' Why should the child be so completely confused? She doesn't want any part of his upbringing."

Aaron is now nine years old. At the time adoption proceedings began, he was two, and he became three before it was finalized.

"She has visitation rights which she stopped on her own," Bernie tells me. "She hasn't seen him for over three years."

Irene's eyebrows arch high above her wide eyes. Her hand lightly cradles her coffee cup as she sits, turned sideways on her chair, her feet locked side by side in front of her, so she fully faces me as she talks. We munch on homemade oatmeal raisin cookies big enough for a meal and coffee too strong for me. The gallon of milk is on the table where the cat was sitting a few minutes before. Mitzy, the cocker spaniel, barks loudly at the mailman, the neighbor's cat, the wind. She has a pretty face, puckered with anxiety, and a shrieking bark. We all do our best to ignore her, and Irene continues, her voice weighted with concern, "Maybe it sounds as if we are portraying her—especially me—as an ogre. She isn't. You say a million times, 'Where did we go wrong?' and yet we feel we didn't do anything wrong.

"I don't know what kind of life she leads; I really don't want to know. I appreciate the fact, for whatever reason, that she does not come around. Because I don't feel that the child should . . . I think it would be confusing for the child."

Bernie interrupts, "It was her responsibility—if she was not coming—to tell him. Or sometimes she was late. Or she would leave with him, and bang, within an hour she was back. And then the tension that we would build up—you could see it, feel it."

"Until I saw him back in the house, it was just awful," Irene says.

"We were waiting—waiting for her to come and get him, and then waiting till he came home," Bernie recalls.

"When she did come," Irene adds, "she came very erratically. This went on for a year and a half."

"When he was having contact with her, what did he call her?" I ask.

Family Secrets

"By her name," Irene replies dryly.

"But how did he know her?" I ask.

"As a sister" slips out. Then, "Well, he does talk about her . . . he does *remember* her . . . he *absolutely* does . . . *absolutely*. He does remember her." Irene rambles as she picks at the tablecloth in front of her.

"How do those conversations go?" I ask.

"He loves animals, and she has a couple of cats. Just a couple of weeks ago, he came out with, 'Susie has Buttons.' It's a cat named Buttons. I bristle. I can't help myself. . . . I, I just ignore it. I don't continue the conversation at all."

"And you bristle because . . . ," I prompt.

"Because I don't want her involved at all in our lives. I appreciate the fact that for whatever reason she doesn't come. I am thankful. I don't want any contact with her. It's very difficult for me to admit that. But that's the way I feel. I don't want to have anything to do with her ever again. I want her completely out of our lives." Her voice is very tight when she tells me these things, but she remains composed.

"I don't know how that's going to be later on. Right now he doesn't ask any questions. He knows he's adopted."

When adoptive parents or other primary caregivers such as grandparents intentionally keep information about the birth family from children, generally those children view the "hidden" information as a secret and, in turn, assume the secret is something to feel ashamed about.

Regardless of the intensity or severity of the information, at some point during childhood, children need to be told. It is not only helpful, but also necessary for children to have a clear picture of their past, specifically their biological past, and the events that led up to their separation from their birth parents.

"How did you approach that?" I ask.

"We had never really said anything one way or the other. He was going to a Jewish day school. He was about four. And they learned among other things that God produces miracles. And there is a story of Abraham and Sara. Sara was in her old age when she had a child. And this is how we refer to it. We tell him how loved he is and that God made a miracle—that I wanted a little boy so badly and 'You're my miracle!' And he just let it go. That was enough for him at the time.

"He never seemed to ask about being born . . . and it just went on because he's not lacking love or attention or anything from any of us. In fact, sometimes I think we're a little excessive," she laughs. "We're the parent *and* the grandparent. We're the spoiling grandparent," she laughs again.

"And then about a couple of years ago, he had some buddies. And the parents were the kind of people that felt their children should know everything, everything about everything! And these children were extremely bright children. However, as bright as you are, when you are eight years old, there is only so much you can absorb and understand. And these parents would tell them everything about how a child is born, how a child is conceived—I mean things that are completely unnecessary. He came running in one day screaming hysterically. We got really frightened and said, "What happened?" It just so happened that my oldest daughter was here that day too. We all ran to him, and he started to cry and scream until he could get it out of him. 'So-and-so told me that

Family Secrets

you're not my mommy. That I'm adopted and my mommy didn't want me!' I said, 'Just a minute . . . calm down,' and I said to myself, 'Uh-oh, here it is.'"

> When Aaron comes home frantic because neighbors have told him he is adopted and that his "mommy didn't want him," he demonstrates profoundly how desperately he needs to hear the truth and how much he needs to hear it from his family. All children need to know that they have birth parents. They are ready to hear and understand this information as early as four or five.

"All the wheels started turning . . . what do you do? All the books, what do they say? So I said to him, 'Now Aaron, you know that Mommy did not have you.' And he started banging me in the stomach. 'Was I in here? Was I in here?' And I kept saying, 'No. In a woman's life she can only carry a child for so many years. You weren't carried in my tummy, but you were carried here in my heart. Now, who was the first one to hold you?' My daughter quickly ran to get the picture albums to show him. 'You know that you're adopted, and that means that I did not have you in my tummy, but that does not mean that you are not my child.' And that was fine, and that was it. He never asked who his real mother was. He never asked why she didn't want him."

"You say he knows he's adopted. How does he know he's adopted? When did he first hear that he was adopted?" I ask.

"I think that was the first time that it really sank in," Irene replies.

"Although we had been talking about it and brought books home from the children's library at school," Bernie chimes in.

"There were some terrific books. We talked about it and read them with him. He was a *little* boy!"

"He was a *little* boy!" Irene repeats almost in unison. "I don't know how much he absorbed."

Irena and Bernie are one of those couples who talk simultaneously, so you're forced to either choose one over the other or flip eye contact between them as if watching a fast-moving tennis match. When they are not doing that, they finish each other's sentences. Neither one seems to mind.

"So whatever you initially told him around the time he was adopted when he was around three years old, he somehow absorbed enough of that?" I ask. "And you didn't talk about it again?"

"No," Irene replies, and Bernie shakes his head no.

"And he never brought it up?" I ask.

"No, and he's never questioned," Irene tells me. "We give him so much love and attention that right now he doesn't require anything else."

Many adoptive families believe that love and love alone is all children need. They believe that love will make everything all right and heal all wounds. However, children need the truth too. All children thrive when they are loved; all adopted children thrive when they have love and the truth about their past. They need their information. They need to know why their birth parents abandoned them or why they are unable to take care of them; they need to know why they are living with their grandparents. They need to know that they didn't do anything to cause their birth parents to fail at parenting. They need to know the truth.

Family Secrets

"The more he's with us, the more we're Dad and Mom," Bernie says. "We are constantly here as his dad and mom, and that's the way he talks about us."

"What do you plan to do when the question comes up?" I ask.

"I don't know," Irene answers. "I think it would be much easier, as far as I'm concerned, if it were a completely strange person or an agency that we got him from. I think it would be easy to tell a child in that instance. How do you tell a child that his mother is . . . you know . . . my daughter? I don't know how I will deal with it. I hope that it will never happen. Maybe that's wrong also. Depriving him of . . . I don't *know* what. But right now, I want him exclusively in our family. Maybe it's also wrong to try to shelter him so much. But life is tough, and he'll have other problems to deal with. I just hope that it'll never come for him that he has to deal with it."

Irene sighs heavily and looks away. "What will happen, I really don't know. And then I say that maybe we should tell him because I don't want it to ever happen when we're gone. Then the girls are going to have to tell him, and that'll be difficult also. It's not fair to put the burden on them, and it *is* a burden."

"Do you worry that she will come back into his life?" I ask.

"Yes, constantly." There is a long pause before Irene continues. "I don't know what she could do . . ."

"I didn't mean that she would try to take him from you," I explain. "I mean just show up at the door."

"Yes, she could, she could. I know she wants to come back into the family. I know she does want to come back—just the fact that she calls every now and then. She has the right to call and to speak to the child. She calls constantly, knowing that it's like a stone in my heart," she says, placing her fist under her bosom, pressing it there, her voice tightening. "She calls me knowing he isn't home from school yet."

Bernie joins in. "She calls asking for menus and recipes," he says, waving his hands in the air over his head as if brushing away flies.

Irene adds, "She calls up out of the blue to ask for the most bizarre things that you just wouldn't believe. The last time I spoke with her when she called—she was pregnant again—and she called because she wanted the Hebrew names. In the Jewish religion you name the children after deceased people." The Winetraubs are Orthodox. "So I told them to her.

"From what I understand, she had the baby," Irene continues. "And I don't know anything about it. My husband spoke to her the last time. I don't know what that conversation was. I don't want to know.

"If she came back at all, she would only come back on her terms, I feel. It would be the same nonsense all over again. Promising him to come, promising she'll buy him this or she'll do that, or take him there, and then disappoint him. You can't do that to a child. You just can't do it!"

"But now he has a half brother or sister," I point out.

"I guess," Irene replies curtly.

"We don't know anything about them," Bernie breaks in quietly.

It is very common for birth parents of adopted children to have subsequent children; thus, many adoptees have biological siblings. Hiding this fact from a child may make him distrustful of his grandparents. The reality is children eventually find out about having siblings. If the existence of biological brothers and sisters has been purposefully hidden from them, they may wonder what

Family Secrets

else was hidden from them. This may place a wedge in their relationship with their grandparents.

"You read about these extended families and say, 'Oh my goodness!' Irene says. "I think they are horror stories. This one is married to this one, and that one is married to that one. My husband was a schoolteacher for so many years, and the kids didn't know which end was up."

"The last ten years in school, I never saw such needy children in my whole life," Bernie adds. "And it was getting worse and worse. I don't know what the reason was. . . . If I knew, boy . . ."

"You could write a book and make a fortune!" I kid him.

"A fortune! A fortune!" he laughs.

"So you feel like you want to avoid that kind of mess?" I ask.

"Right," Irene answers emphatically. "It *is* a mess! The children have a hard enough time just coping with what they're going to do tomorrow. You have to provide stability. This is the way it has to be," Irene says finally.

When I leave, Irene walks me to the door. She asks me if she can be of any help. If I need anything, please call, she says sincerely. She's always willing to help.

THE RANDALLS

Another couple, the Randalls, have also adopted their granddaughter. But while the Winetraubs fear contact from the birth parent, the Randalls long for it. While the Winetraubs actively conceal the true familial relationships, one might describe the Randalls as sidestepping the issue. They both pray for more time and inwardly hope that the time never comes when they will have to face facts with their grandchildren. Both couples, as do most other grandparents, deal with issues like resentment and loss, sibling rivalry, and the "name game."

Betsy Randall and I are members of the Grandparent Support Group Network in Massachusetts, which is an offshoot of the Massachusetts Executive Office of Elder Affairs. She is energetic and talkative, a tireless worker. She has told me that in her little town, she knows of several other grandparent caregivers in Sara's kindergarten class alone.

She promises me lunch if I drive the two and a half hours out to meet with her and bring donuts. I happily stop at Dunkin' Donuts for a dozen mixed and head out for the afternoon.

It's only the first of December, but it's flat, dead cold, and Christmas is already in full swing at the Randall house. Plastic evergreens and red holly berries wind around the lamppost, while Santa looks out each first-floor window.

Millpond is small-town by anybody's standards. Only about two thousand people live in this former mill town deep in western Massachusetts. There are homes that seem etched into the densely wooded landscape and farmhouses that appear to have landed in fields lining the scenic route that meanders through this neck of the woods.

Then there are the houses—village colonials we called them when I worked in real estate—that remain clustered around the town's sparse center and old mill factories; sharply peaked roofs top the narrow-shouldered girls circled by porches that droop in spots like uneven petticoats. The Randalls' gray clapboard home sits neat and at attention, virtually in the back yard of what was once a thriving paper mill and now is home to Mother's Mincemeat.

Family Secrets

Six-year-old Sara bounces out of the kitchen door like an eager puppy, excited to have a visitor. I'm glad she's still home; I like to meet the grandchildren when I can.

She is getting ready for afternoon kindergarten, putting on her winter jacket and thick, homemade purple mittens attached by long strings that loop through her sleeves. She keeps up a running dialogue as she dresses—silly talk about her dog Boots and her favorite hat, which is in the shape of a cat's face, whiskers and all. She dearly loves the hat. It looks at least a year too small, and the white fur has taken on a yellowed cast, but to Sara it's perfect.

Sara is not precocious or demanding; she is simply chatting as she would with any friend. She is truly friendly; in fact, and her openness is remarkable. Her plain little face tilts upward to look into mine as she sits on the floor and slides her legs into puffy pink snow pants. When she speaks to me, she doesn't fidget but looks directly into my eyes. "My name is Sara. What's your name?"

I don't think it's just a thing to say. I think she really wants to know. She stops struggling with her pants, waiting for my answer. "Deborah," I reply, and Betsy simultaneously answers, "That's Mrs. Doucette, Sara," as she fixes lunch for us and her husband, unexpectedly home on his lunch hour.

Dan Randall looks exactly like a drill sergeant; perhaps it's because of all those years he spent in the Marine Corps. He is stocky, barrel-chested, and has a wiffle, or is it called a flattop? His old warrior stance belies the quiet, caring attention he shows to both Betsy and Sara.

The grownups sit at the kitchen table for soup and salad. The Randalls have raised four children here, and I try to picture four boisterous teenagers, three of them boys, sitting around this table and thundering through the tiny house. We exchange small talk while Sara concentrates on dressing. It's serious business getting into her cold-weather gear; there are straps, buckles, snaps, *and* zippers to tend to and a lot of slippery fabric. Sara, smallish for her age, has chin-length, dark blond hair and glasses. Her eyes swim overly large and earnest behind pale, tortoise-shell, child-sized frames. Her bangs flop over the tops. She looks a lot like Betsy.

Sara is finally into her entire outdoor ensemble—snowsuit, boots, cat hat, and mittens-on-a-string. She walks stiff-legged over to me, her bulky nylon pants swishing noisily with each step. She brings her face close to mine as she looks up at me with a serious expression to ask me a little question—I don't remember what. I only remember the utterly unself-conscious trust in her eyes. It touches me, and I think of it sometimes still.

I answer her question, and she maneuvers around the chairs to sit next to her "Dad." She asks him politely if she may have a cucumber slice from his salad. He picks one out, then another, and we both watch in fascination as she deftly, delicately sprinkles the tiniest bit of salt and the teensiest bit of pepper on each green sliver before popping it into her mouth whole. The school bus arrives at last, and she springs from the chair, runs over to me, and gives me a hug—spontaneous, huge, and loving—tucking her head into my shoulder as if she really will miss me. I am touched again by her sweet intensity. I wish she didn't have to go.

After the others leave, Betsy and I settle onto the couch by the woodstove with donuts and mulled cider, and I listen to another tale of irresponsible parents, a drug-abusing mother, and an infant with failure to thrive. Betsy has horror stories to tell about the Department of Social Services—incompetency, inconsistencies, and rules and regulations interpreted differently by whomever she spoke to last. In addition, there seemed to be little or no cooperation between states regarding the placement of children with out-of-state relatives—a complaint I've heard frequently. A bureaucratic mire for grandparents to wade through.

Sara was two months old when their son Donnie arrived at their doorstep with her.

"It was Halloween," Betsy recalls. "We always joke that she came for trick or treat and she never left." She lets out a bubbly laugh and her eyes crinkle up. Betsy is short and, she would admit, somewhat overweight. She has curly, light brown hair—short in the front, long in the back—and big glasses. She talks a mile a minute and takes in deep breaths of air or lets out long sighs in between. Betsy has that soft, motherly look that fairly oozes of baking big batches of chocolate chip cookies for PTA meetings, knitting fuzzy wool mittens for church fairs, and having several useful craft projects made from common household items going on at once—sort of a down-home Martha Stewart.

But Betsy thought she was done with the cookies and school thing, and like most grandparents thrust into parenting again, she struggles with bouts of resentment. Indeed, as Irene Winetraub remarked to me hotly, "Anyone who says they don't feel resentment is lying." Fueling that resentment is the loss of friendships with peers who no longer have the extra baggage of small children to complicate dinner plans, visits, and vacations. Betsy tells me, "There were times that I wanted to say, 'Forget it, I'm not going to do this. I want to go on with my life—I want my life back!'"

When Donnie first brought Sara to them, the Randalls thought that their new situation was temporary. "We really believed—for years—that one or the other of them would get their life organized and get straightened out." She half laughs and half sighs. "And I think that was one of the saddest things, the hardest thing as a parent, was to finally realize that it really wasn't going to happen. And then in ninety days we got permanent custody. Neither parent cared enough to even find out what was going on. They never asked." She takes a big breath and continues, "A day never went by that I didn't look up to see if the mother was coming down the street. Not in fear—I didn't live in fear at that point. I really hoped that some way, somehow, she would find her way from Texas out here and want to be a mother to this child. You know, I imagined that—because I was a mother myself—that this girl would just beg, borrow, steal, hitchhike, whatever, to find a way to be with her child.

"By the time Sara was a year old, the mother was pregnant with another child by another boyfriend. She was still back in her old lifestyle. And with her and my son, it was one of these on again, off again type things. Donnie would call us, but not that often. He didn't really call to find out how the baby was. They *would* want pictures of the child. I was very, very good about it. I lived in a little dreamworld, so to speak. I would send letters, and I would send pictures to both of them. I really wanted them to be part of her life.

"And then she would call, 'Well, how come Don got two pictures and I only got one?' So then I resorted to writing a note to each of them, each one saying the same thing and each of them getting the exactly same snapshot." Her voice rises to a high pitch, which it invariably does when she becomes agitated.

"When I found out she was pregnant, I thought, 'Oh God! She's going to come and want this baby. She's going to have maternal instincts.'" Her voice zings skyward. "Well, it never happened, and that child was in and out of foster care and in and out of DSS.

"So another year later, she had another child by another boyfriend. Now understand, she and my son were, and still are, legally married. She traipsed around Texas, the whole nine yards, and the two kids are on again, off again, taken back and forth. In the meantime, we're raising Sara. Nobody seems to care what's happening to her.

"When she was two, my son came to see her. I was really excited that he was coming because I thought that he really wanted to become part of her life. Well, he came here, and the first thing, the absolute first thing he did when he walked in the house was open the refrigerator and take out a beer." There is a long pause as she looks at me wide eyed. She is smiling, but it's a smile that says, Can you believe it?

I can picture Betsy busying herself in the kitchen, hovering nearby, giving him sidelong glances and waiting for her son to ask for Sara. Waiting for the moment when he would scoop her up in his arms and give her a hug or tousle her hair affectionately. Surely any minute now, she would be thinking, he's going to want to see her, hold her.

I had seen a photograph of Sara at two. In it, her hair is platinum blond and falls around her face in happy disarray. She is dressed in yellow. Babyhood clings to her still, and in the sunlight she appears incandescent. She is golden and delicious, sweet as a lemon drop. But her father never asked to see her.

"Before he went, he used the telephone, and he called his wife and he said, 'I'm in Massachusetts and I'm getting to see Sara and you're not. Ha, ha! He wanted absolutely nothing to do with her. Nothing.

"Sara, to this day, does not have one material thing that either one of her parents have given her. Which is very sad because someday I can't even say to her, 'Your mom or dad gave you this.'"

The Randalls' three other children dote on Sara. One son, who is in the Marines, sent her a map so she can keep track of where he travels. It is posted to the pantry door in the kitchen at child's height. He makes sure to send her a little something—postcards or a picture—from every place he goes.

Donnie came home again once more when Sara was four and didn't stay long enough to even look at her.

"I cleaned everything in sight while he was here! That's what I do when I get nervous; I either eat or clean. Most of the time I eat," she laughs.

He would not leave an address with them. "I know where you are; you don't need to know where I am," he told them. This is one of the things that hurt Betsy the most. Her son has "walked away from everything he had been born and brought up with all those years." They have a very large and close family. Her husband Dan is one of eight children. But Donnie hasn't stayed in touch with anyone or anything from his past.

"The family traditions, the holidays, the community traditions— not a holiday goes by that I don't wonder, 'I wonder if he thinks about us.' I look at Sara, and all the things that she can do, and I think, 'You've missed all this.'"

While in most families grandparents continue to have a very positive relationship with their grown children, sadly, in others, relationships are strained at best. For some, the lack of contact with their adult children is a loss akin to a death. Grandparents must accept and grieve the loss of the adult child and make peace with them in order to move forward.

Betsy tells me, "At one point during Donnie's visit, we were having an argument, and he said to me, 'I don't know what you're crabbing about. I let you have her!' I think she's more of a possession to him. I could never make him understand that, at this point, she was a little person. When she was six months old or a year old, if they wanted to pick her up and take her, that would be one thing. But when she got to be two, three, and beyond, she was a little person. You don't uproot her from her life.

"Nothing would have made me any happier than for one or both of them to come here and be a part of her life and really share in her life. I used to hesitate to buy clothes from one season to the next because I always imagined they were coming for her. I lived kind of in a dreamworld. I guess I was really hoping." Her cheeks are flushed and her eyes fill, but the tears don't spill over. She smiles through her tears as if to say, Aren't I foolish?

"And to be very honest, it wasn't until a week before we went to court to adopt Sara . . ." She talks slowly now and chooses her words carefully, very uncharacteristically. "She had got bit by a bee and spent all night in the hospital. I was driving home with her and she was in the car seat, and I looked back at her and I literally burst into tears. And I said out loud, 'They really aren't coming for her.' It wasn't until then that I realized *they really weren't coming for her!*

"And that was the hardest. . . . I looked at her, and I thought, 'Look at what they're missing!'" Betsy takes a deep breath. Her face has pinked up again, and the tears are filming her eyes behind her glasses. But she continues to smile through her tears as she talks. "I really have a lot of mixed feelings. I think that when you have a decent relationship with the parent, you can at least talk to them about the child and share some of the things. But when they literally, literally don't want anything to do with her . . ." A tear finally starts to escape, and she places a finger behind her glasses and lifts it from the edge of her eye. "It's very hard." Betsy swallows back the lump in her throat and says dejectedly, "I don't know which is worse, to have the parent of these children that you're raising in and out of their lives and disappointing them, or one that never sees them at all.

"What's happened now with Sara in our situation is that all that hurt and all that heartache is ours and not hers for the time being. Because she doesn't know the disappointment. She doesn't know as yet what she's missed. She doesn't know that they haven't had anything to do with her."

> Many times it is assumed that because children ask very few questions about being adopted or about their birth parents, they aren't thinking about it. However, I have seen in countless adoptive families that many children will not ask their parents any adoption questions because they sense their parents' discomfort with or fear of the subject. Children may remain cautious because they are concerned that if they ask too many questions, their caregivers may become hurt or angry. They fear that this anger could lead to rejection, a situation few adopted children are willing to risk.

"Tell me, what does she know?" I ask.

Betsy reflects, "What does she know? She knows she came from Texas. She knows she came on a big airplane. She knew that we were her Gram and Gramp.

"When she first started to talk, it was Mom, because that's what children say first. And we would say G-G-G-Gram. And she would say, 'G-G-G-Mom!' It would break my heart. She would say, 'I'm going to keep you forever. Are you going to keep me forever, Gram?' And I would never, ever say yes to her, 'Yes, I will keep you forever.' All I would ever say to her was, "I'll always be here for you.' Because that's about the time that that "Baby Jessica" thing was going on [a news story involving a three-year-old who had been living with her adopted family and subsequently had to be returned to her birth parent], and all I could envision was me promising I would keep her forever and them coming and taking her and her screaming at me, saying, 'But you promised you'd keep me forever!' So in my own mind, I just could not tell her I'd keep her forever.

"But then she got so that she would ask the question more and more and more. Even though we literally stopped talking about her situation whenever she was around or in the house or anywhere within earshot. So we knew that it was bothering her.

"Well, when she was five, my husband said, 'We're going to go for broke. You find an attorney; we're going to go for broke. We're going to go for adoption.'"

It was then that the Randalls ran up against a roadblock of incompetence within their local DSS district. The local social workers could not figure out how to comply with the requirement of the "home study" because Sara had not been in their system. Normally, when a couple files with the probate court for adoption, the court requires a home study to be completed by a licensed social worker for the state or a private agency. The Randalls could not afford to hire a private agency, and the DSS in their area would not do it; they just couldn't figure it out. It took months of wrangling with officials, both high and low, before Social Services were able to sort out this simple procedure.

"There were many, many times when I just wanted to put her in the car and put her on DSS's doorstep and say, 'Here you go. Now you figure out what to do. And when you finish, let me know.'" She tells me this in a shrill falsetto.

Betsy went on to say that some days she would feel so frustrated and tired and down that she would want to give up. But fortunately her husband was able to buoy her spirits. And when he was discouraged and wondered if it was worth the endless struggle, she was able to keep him going. "Luckily," she tells me, neither one was down at the same time.

"I'll be honest, there were a few times when I thought, do I really want to do this? Do I really want this for the rest of my life? Maybe I should just try to find her parents and just say, 'Hey, this is your job, now you do it!' But of course I didn't, because I love her."

I ask Betsy if Sara knows she has birth parents.

"Well, yes . . ." She hesitates. "My husband would show her pictures. I couldn't do it. I'll be honest. I could not do it! But she loved to look at family albums and pictures, and my husband would get them out and they would look at them together. I couldn't even stay in the room."

"Because . . . ?" I prompt.

"Because I didn't really know what I felt," she expels in a big breath. The words burst out of her as if she'd been holding them in for a long time. "I—I wasn't comfortable with what I was feeling.

"We had pictures in the album of her first couple of weeks of life in Texas—snapshots that her [maternal] grandmother had sent of Sara and her mother and her father. My husband would show them to her and say, 'This is you when you were a baby, and this is your mom and this is your dad.'"

"Did she ever question it beyond that?" I ask.

"No. Because I think she was young enough that it was only a name to her. It was like saying this is your brother, this is your uncle, this is your sister. It didn't really click in her mind. So she didn't really know.

Family Secrets

"Then it got to be that she was almost five. I had very strongly told my husband, and he went along with it—I'm not sure he agreed with me, but he honored my wishes—I told him that if by any chance the mother or father should ever arrive on our doorstep, Sara was at an age where I didn't want to confuse her, and I would not refer to them, or tell her at that point, that they were her mother or father.

"Because I didn't really know how to explain . . . I didn't know how I *felt*! And I couldn't deal with my emotions about it, and I didn't know how I could explain it to her. I didn't want her to think of them as some kind of 'knight in shining armor,' these wonderful people that have come, and confuse her. I said, until she's old enough to realize, I don't want her to know who they are."

It is important for the adults to separate their fear and anxiety about sharing information from the child's right to know. I am not suggesting that this is an easy balance or that one could expect to be always comfortable about discussing the past, but the child's need to know takes precedence over the adults' need to protect themselves from anxiety. Grandparents may need to speak with a counselor or family therapist to work through their own discomfort.

Betsy falters and takes several deep breaths. "If either one of them came into her life right now, I would not tell her, at this point, this is your mother or this is your father. She hasn't asked.

"Nobody's told her, and it hasn't dawned on her yet. And I just . . . I haven't . . ." She falters again and struggles to give voice to her feelings. "The opportunity has not come up to explain this to her," she says, finally and emphatically.

Grandparents need to recognize that opportunities are always there, and they must not allow their insecurity and anxiety to prevent them from finding them or, if need be, creating them. Grandparents must take the opportunity to explain to their grandchildren the different people, situations, and experiences that have made up their grandchildren's lives. If they wait too long, they risk having someone other than themselves let the cat out of the bag. As previously mentioned, this can set up a potentially devastating breach of trust no matter how well intentioned.

"Have you fashioned an answer in your head for when it does come up?" I ask.

Her voice rises a notch. I think she is annoyed with me. She exhales loudly and says, "Well, yeah. Depending on what the situation is, I would probably tell her, well, you were born in Texas, you had a mom and you had a dad when you were born, but when you were only two months old, a little, tiny baby, they just couldn't take care of you, so you came here to live with us. And I guess that's about all I would tell her for now.

"I always said I would never, never bad-mouth them. I don't want them to sound like dirtbags. But yet I also refuse to make them sound like some kind of heroes, that because they loved her so much, they sent her to live with us." She looks at me steadily, a little defiant and with a lot of conviction.

Sometimes what is said is not as important as how it is said. I never recommend that adoptive parents tell their children, "Your birth parents loved you so much they gave you to us," because the implications can be confusing and even painful. For example, an adopted child may be confused as to how someone who "loves" them so much can give them away. Also, the adopted child may wonder, "If you love me, will you give me away too?" It is far more useful for grandparents to share with their grandchildren that "your birth parents made a decision because they cared about what happened to you. Our love and commitment means you are staying with us. Our decision means you will always stay."

Betsy continues, "And I guess what I am thankful for is that each day that goes by that she doesn't ask any questions, she's that much older and a little bit more mature so that I can explain it to her. And she would have to be quite old, or quite mature, before I would explain it to her. I don't want to go into the whole story with her of what I explained to you today, of how she came to be here and all that. Sara doesn't need to know that.

"I'm sure I'll know how to handle it when the time comes. But to try to fabricate a story, to try to figure it out? I guess my only answer would be, 'They just couldn't take care of you.'

"We never hid the fact of where Sara has come from [in the community]. It's no secret. Everybody in the area knows who she is; they know that she belongs to my son. So I mean it's no deep, dark secret. And I don't want it to be a secret from *her*. It's just something that, because I feel that at this age they can be so . . ."

Betsy begins to tell me a story about one of her support group members to illustrate the point she is trying to make.

"We have one woman in the support group whose child is four or five years old. And the mother is probably never going to be able to take care of this child. The father left the mother when he found out she was pregnant and has never been back. He just blew the area. And yet they've told the child about this father, and so the child sits there and fantasizes that her father is going to come for her one day.

"So I mean Sara at this point is a very well-adjusted, loving child. I guess I've been through enough with raising four kids of my own to realize that you'll know what to tell them and what not to tell them when the time comes.

"I'll tell her when she's old enough, and I mean *old* enough, that I feel that she can really handle this and she really honestly wants to know. By that point, if you feel that she can handle it, then you can tell her the whole story as to what has happened and why she came and everything. But it's going to be a long time from now before she's ever ready for something like that.

"It's always very hard because they have never had anything to do with her, and because it was always very one-sided on our part. How long can you keep up the charade of 'This is your mom and this is your dad?' If we had told her earlier, by now she'd be saying, 'Well, where are they?'"

"But your husband has done that," I point out.

"He doesn't do it anymore. He hasn't done it for a long time. I don't think she remembers.

"When the adoption was getting ready to go through . . . I'll be honest, I probably have a dozen photos of Sara and her mother or father up until she was about two months old. And I'll be honest, I took them out of the picture album and put them away. I put them with her adoption stuff, and I put them away. I guess I'll know when the time is right to show them to her.

"I just don't want this little child fantasizing, thinking that they are going to come rushing down the street and make this wonderful happy family for her. On the other hand, I don't want her to think, 'How come they don't want me?'"

Family Secrets

All adopted children experience sadness and loss because they were not kept. My advice to adoptive parents is to not attempt to take away this sadness and loss, but instead create a family environment that allows it to occur and be worked through.

"So I just don't say anything for now. It may be right, it may be wrong. I don't know." Betsy's voice is rising again. "I guess there's really no right way and no wrong way. You just have to do what you feel, and you know the child well enough to know. That's the way you do it."

"But she knows she's adopted," I confirm.

"Oh yes! She was almost six years old when we went to court and she was adopted. And when you ask her what does 'adopted' mean, she says, 'It means I am going to live here forever and ever and I never have to leave you.'"

"Before the adoption went through she had an inkling that her place wasn't permanent?" I ask.

"Right. She had the feeling that she wasn't going to be able to stay here forever. She didn't know why; she only knew that there was some reason why she might not stay here forever."

"And now she doesn't feel that way?" I ask.

"No!"

"The solution to that feeling was the adoption? And she never questioned beyond that?" I ask.

"No. She used to say it all the time—it was an obsession with her—'I'm going to keep you forever; are you going to keep me forever?' And now only very occasionally she'll say, 'I'm going to keep you forever, Mom. I love you so much.' And now I'll say, 'I'm going to keep you forever.'"

Raising Our Children's Children

Children hunger for open, honest, accurate information, even if it isn't always joyful or easy to hear. It is far more painful not knowing the truth than it is to know why the pain exists. Most important, children need to hear the information from loving caregivers. The facts need to be presented lovingly and truthfully, not sugarcoated or with some information strategically removed.

By the age of five, children should be given an age-appropriate family history by their caregivers. Grandparents should then begin to discuss the grown child who is also their grandchild's birth parent. They should start by talking about the adult child's history and then ease into the fact that he or she is, in fact, the child's birth parent. Then, briefly, describe why the birth parent was unable to take care of the child and how the child came to be in the care of the grandparents. *This is a discussion that will need to be revisited all during childhood and into young adulthood.*

When caregivers do not share important information with children and the information is discovered as a teen or adult, a huge break in trust occurs from which some families never fully recover. In a healthy environment based on truth and trust, issues can be resolved and children can make peace with their past.

THREE

When Couples Don't Agree

When those closest to us respond to events differently than we do, when they seem to see the same scene as part of a different play, when they say things that we could not imagine saying in the same circumstances, the ground on which we stand seems to tremble and our footing is suddenly unsure.

—Deborah Tannen, PhD, *You Just Don't Understand*

Throughout my daughter's pregnancy, there were times when I mentally walked myself through the adoption scenario—giving our grandchild up for adoption. I would get to the end of the scenes playing like a loop over and over in my head and find a brick wall. I knew these were scenes I would never actually be in, places I could never really go.

My husband at that time never considered it as an alternative for us even for a moment. He would not play out the imaginary adoption scenes with me. Whenever I would point out the difficulties ahead of us, he would merely listen quietly and say, "We'll manage." I knew that was true. We would manage; we *could* manage. Financially we would struggle but probably stay afloat. For many grandparents in similar circumstances faced with a daunting array of decisions, whether or not they will be able to manage is far from certain, even doubtful. Disagreements are common. Allowing a baby to be put up for adoption or standing by while a child is placed in foster care may be a viable alternative for some. For us and others like us, it simply is not.

Our personal feelings about whether or not we could cope with raising another child were not the only challenges we faced. Outside our family circle, what we encountered was shock and disapproval. Friends, acquaintances, doctors, and therapists became divided into two camps, those who didn't "get it" and those who did.

A very dear friend, during a conversation in which she listed all the ways that adopting my granddaughter would be fraught with problems and just plain "odd," finally announced, "The child will grow up warped!" One person called me "selfish." Many people told us we were crazy. A therapist I was seeing at the time to help me sort things out remarked, "You're trying to sabotage your life." I stopped seeing him.

My physician, the man who delivered all my children, told me he understood completely and said that "of course" he would do the very same thing. He used words like "family," "heritage," and "flesh and blood." He got it.

My former husband and I had the luxury of having all our puzzle pieces fit as far as this decision went. We were in agreement and saw things the same way. Nearly all our large and extended family saw things the same way. But what happens when husband and wife don't agree?

When Couples Don't Agree

Decisions are not always black and white, the way they are not always crystal clear. Are the children in danger? Can we *do* this? Can we afford it? Is this temporary or permanent? Guardianship or adoption? How will we manage? Where shall we turn?

THE HARRISES

I met Laurie Harris through the Massachusetts Executive Office of Elder Affairs. She attended a couple of Grandparents' Network meetings before she had to drop out because of her busy work schedule as a nurse. She spoke with me one afternoon by phone, taking time out of a crammed-full day to tell me about the conflict pricking at the fabric of her marriage like a thorn on silk.

Laurie and her husband Bob are grandparents in their mid-forties. Their daughter put her baby into foster care when she felt overwhelmed by motherhood. When Laurie discovered what had happened, she intervened, waged a short but intense battle with Social Services in another state, and finally took the baby home. Working on what she describes as "gut instinct," she did not discuss the issue with anyone, not even her husband, Bob. "I did what I had to do," she told me.

Laurie and Bob have been married for twenty-four years and have raised five children; the youngest is nineteen and in college. They had just begun to take vacations alone together, to go out on weekends to dinner or a movie, to enjoy themselves as a couple.

"We did without a lot when we had our own kids, sacrificed a lot," Laurie told me.

When the dust settled and temporary custody was awarded by the courts, three months extended to six months, and it became clear that this was more than a short-term situation. Laurie filed for permanent custody. Bob said, "I don't want this. Put her up for adoption." Laurie's reply, "No one is going to keep her from me!"

Laurie told me, "Most of the burden, the responsibility of her care, is mine. He wants to love her as his grandchild, but he doesn't want her to be here. He says, 'I don't want this. I don't want to give my freedom up, to raise another child.' My answer is, 'There's the door.'"

They still see this as a temporary situation, although more long term than they would like. Their daughter is in the service and trying to pull her life together. Laurie believes that within a few years her daughter will be able to shoulder the responsibility and have her child returned to her. She hangs on to that hope. Laurie works hard at preserving the connections between mother and child. She shows her granddaughter pictures and letters, all the while talking about how much her mother loves her. "When she slips and calls me Mommy, I correct her," Laurie tells me.

Laurie is trying to juggle her granddaughter's well-being and a marriage while holding on to the fragile tightrope of faith she has in her daughter. She is doing everything she can to shore up the relationship with her husband without sacrificing her grand-child. At the moment, she seems to have all the balls suspended in midair.

Laurie and Bob sought counseling and are trying to work to-gether to keep the marriage going. Laurie tells me, "We have to come to terms with how we are going to have a relationship for ourselves—what can we do to make things better for us?"

Laurie believes they will make it.

Parenting can test the strength of any marriage. Parenting your grandchild, however, adds the burden of unexpected stressors to couples ready for an entirely different stage in life. Parenting attempted, at any stage, without mutual support and respect can break a marriage. Caregivers need to make their marriage a priority. They need to do this for themselves, and they need to do it for their grandchildren. Children sense the tension in a marriage, and they may assume that the tension and stress are because of them.

Bob may feel that he wasn't given a choice and thus may feel some resentment toward both his wife and his grandchild. Laurie and Bob need to be in this together. They need to spend a significant amount of time actively discussing the pros and cons of raising their grandchild. They need to respect and listen to each other's feelings and opinions. Clearly they cannot be successful as caregivers if they approach parenting as adversaries instead of as partners. In fairness to each other and their grandchild, Bob and Laurie need to continue to address these concerns with the help of ongoing counseling.

PART ONE OF THE PARKS FAMILY TRILOGY

The story of the Parks is one of rescue and redemption, a life-and-death struggle. Ben and Elisabeth Parks' marriage hangs on by threads. But those threads are strong, like the warp and woof that remain when the nap wears away on a carpet.

Ben and Elisabeth's story is a good example of what happens to marriages when couples don't agree on the issue of raising grandchildren. As their story unfolds, many other important issues surface as well—anger, denial, grief, and loss. First, Elisabeth and Ben tell their story together, then Ben alone, and finally Elisabeth alone, as I fully chronicle their journey. In a later chapter, which focuses on making room for birth parents in their children's lives, Marion—Ben and Elisabeth's daughter and the mother of the children in their care—also reveals her story.

For the Parks family, the road to gaining custody of their two grandchildren was murky, confusing, and perilous. Ben and Elisabeth viewed the picture laid out before them with starkly pronounced differences. It was as if they were looking through the same kaleidoscope of fractured pieces and colors and interpreting what they saw in totally different ways. They became frustrated and angry when the other could not see the patterns adding up to the same whole.

Their methods of coping, of expressing their feelings, and their approach to the unfolding drama were at opposing ends of the spectrum. They struggled and fought, split and came together. But the fracture went deep. It has not yet healed. Perhaps someday it will.

Ben and Elisabeth

When I finally find it, the buff-colored contemporary waits on a narrow lane surrounded by 1930s and 1940s Capes and cottages. This area was once a vacation retreat complete with big band dance halls and an amusement park. Now the curvy little roads that wind around this lake and a few others like it are flanked by modest but updated older homes as well as pricey newer contemporaries like this one, which take advantage of the spectacular views that the lake affords.

The house is just as pretty on the inside as it is outside. Enormous expanses of glass bring the idyllic setting into every room of the house. There is an eclectic mixture of comfortable contemporary seating combined with formal antique furnishings handed down through the close-knit family. Homey treasures touch down everywhere—porcelain butterflies, pictures of children and grand-children, and handmade dried flower arrangements. There is a white bisque angel sitting on the woodstove. She has a mauve French ribbon edged in gold around her neck. She is blowing kisses.

Elisabeth tells me this was to be their retirement home—they are both in their late fifties—until their lives were turned upside down shortly after they moved here. Marion, their oldest daughter, had gotten pregnant at the age of sixteen. With the birth of their grandson, Craig, their story begins.

"Marion was home with us," Elisabeth begins, "and he [Thomas Connor] was coming over bringing diapers, baby food, providing support—you know, this wonderful charming guy."

"Did you think he was wonderful and charming at the time?" I ask.

"Well, I didn't, because he got her pregnant, and I didn't think that was wonderful and charming. I was pretty angry that she had gotten pregnant. But let's just say that we were trying to make the best of the situation, not knowing . . . Who was I to judge? She was too young, but he was wanting to help. She made the decision to marry him when Craig was a year old. She was close to eighteen by then, wasn't she?" Elisabeth turns to Ben for confirmation.

Ben has a rugged, deeply tanned, craggy face covered by a trimmed-short mustache and beard. His hair, slightly balding, is neat and evenly cross-cropped. His voice is cavern deep and loud. The air vibrates when he speaks. He talks quickly, pushing his words out machine-gun fast with force, as if he's in a rush to get it out and over with.

"Yup," Ben barks.

"They were going to move right around here and they would be close by, so we just figured we would give them a lot of support. But what started happening was she was starting to drink. And the more I tried to get close to her, she was holding me away. But she was also deathly afraid of him. It had started very early on with him hitting her."

"You were not aware?" I ask.

They both answer at once.

Elisabeth exclaims, "I had no idea!"

"We were not aware," Ben mumbles.

"Absolutely none!" Elisabeth finishes.

"And her brothers didn't," she continues. "I have *big* boys. One is a police officer. But they had no idea at the beginning."

Their sons eventually became aware of the problems Thomas and Marion were having, but they never told Elisabeth and Ben what they knew or suspected.

"They were all doing the drinking. But at that time, it wasn't unusual for high school or college-age kids to be having a beer, right?" she asks, looking at me for affirmation. "But we were totally in the dark about how much drinking might have been going on, and how much pain they were in. We did not see. I was beginning to see the dangers of too much partying—that I saw. And I was worried about it, concerned about it. I tried to talk to them about it, but it was, 'Oh, Ma! Everybody drinks!'

"They were starting to party in a house over there," Elisabeth gestures to the other side of the lake. "Right where you parked your car, as a matter of fact," she laughs. I had become lost on the way there in the maze of streets that weave around the lake. I had called her on my cell phone, and she had to drive over to lead me to the house.

"That place has a lot of horrible memories for me. There was a barroom there that they've taken down."

"Really?" I say in surprise. The place I had stopped was a lovely residential neighborhood of brand new homes overlooking the lake—swing sets, people in sweat pants walking dogs, flower boxes overflowing with impatiens.

"This is a small town, but there are a lot of barrooms in it. Not a lot of parks or things to do, but . . ." Elisabeth fades off.

"There are more barrooms and liquor licenses in this town than Las Vegas has, per ratio of people—how's that!" Ben interrupts, his deep voice reverberating through the dining room. "Twenty-seven liquor licenses—the town has only four thousand people—there's supposed to be only one," he says. Ben seldom meets my eyes when he talks. He looks over my head, or across the room to some faraway point beyond.

Elisabeth sits quietly with her hands gripping her teacup. She has an elegant, almost patrician look about her, with a shock of short, thick, gray-white hair brushed back from her face. She wears no makeup, not even lipstick, which gives her a somewhat weary, washed-out appearance. She looks out from enormous brown eyes, through glasses with delicate, rose-colored frames that sit on her aquiline nose.

Her usually pale face is flushed, and her eyes are filling. "I didn't realize how much emotion I still had about that house." Elisabeth pauses, tries to compose herself, then continues, but her voice is full of pain. She talks with difficulty as if she's choking on her words. "But that's where the children got hurt so bad, and she did. A lot of suffering went on there.

"I was always on her [Marion's] back about getting help—going down, checking on the kids, checking on her. I was going to Al-Anon to see what I could do to help. I talked to counselors. I did everything I could to try to help. I couldn't get her in [to counseling]. And I would approach him [Thomas] and his lovely family and say, 'Would you help me with it?' And he'd say, 'Ugh. Your daughter is disgusting, she drinks!' Like he was this wonderful guy. It's amazing how these guys can con everybody! In this town I am sure everybody thought he was the nice guy and she was the slut."

"Well, they did! Ben interjects."

"And the school system . . . by the time I got into the school system with my grandchildren . . . I could just feel it!" Elisabeth bursts in.

"We had just moved into this house, our retirement house, about ten years ago," Elisabeth continues. "We had a wonderful summer. This place is so beautiful. Our dream home. This peaceful place by the water. She [Marion] came to us, and I was so grateful; I was really so grateful. By that point, I was out of my mind with worry about the drinking and what was going on over there at that house."

"She hit bottom, but she came here," Ben adds. "She did it on her own."

"She brought the two children and said, 'Please help me,'" Elisabeth says.

"Not financial help, but help to get into the recovery unit," Ben explains.

"So she went into the hospital for rehabilitation for alcohol and drug abuse," Elisabeth continues. "She wasn't even in there a day or two before the counselors called to say, 'Please do not have Mr. Connor come with the children. Could you please bring the children, Mrs. Parks?' Now, right up to this point I was almost alienated from her because all I could see was the externals, like she was hurting these kids by the drinking and the neglecting. And I was really angry at her, but I was still trying to appeal to her, to tell her I would help her and support her."

> It is good that Elisabeth is able to admit that she is angry at her daughter. It is very common for grandparents to be angry with their children for their failure to parent adequately. Admitting the anger is a healthy first step toward mending strained relationships.

At this time Marion was in her mid-twenties. Craig was seven and Christine was two years old.

"Whenever they [the counselors] would try to talk about her marriage, she would get hysterical—hysterical! And they would back off. But evidently they got enough to know that it was okay for us to come [to visit], but it was not okay for him [Thomas] to come.

"So the first day we were supposed to go—it was visiting day— we had to tell him to please not come until she was ready. But he said he was definitely going down to see his wife. He had roses.

"All I can remember is getting off the elevator with the children, walking into her room, and saying, 'Hi, you're looking good!' and she went cowering back in the corner screaming, and I didn't even know at *what*, until I turned around and saw *him* in the doorway. That was the first time I had any idea of what my daughter was going through. She ran down the corridor, didn't she, Ben?"

"Yup."

"And screamed hysterically. They [the staff] ordered him out of the hospital. And even during the rest of the thirty days of counseling, not a lot came out. They said she had posttraumatic stress syndrome and also amnesia to severe abuse that caused her to either blank it out or she couldn't talk about it. That was the first hospitalization."

> Posttraumatic stress disorder (PTSD) is frequently seen in survivors of violent crime, physical or sexual abuse, battering, or any other physically and emotionally traumatic event. Symptoms frequently include powerful and vividly frightening nightmares, flashbacks, difficulty trusting others, withdrawing, mood swings, insomnia, and paranoia.

After the first hospitalization, Marion had begun to pull away from Thomas Connor. She wanted a divorce. During that period of time, the children were being coached to put pressure on their mother to stay with him. Marion started drinking again. Also, although no one was aware of it at the time, Thomas was going to her while she was working as a waitress at the local country club and threatening that if she wouldn't go back to him, he would kill her parents and the children.

"She knew he was capable of it," Elisabeth tells me. "He also offered her booze and drugs to go back."

> Batterers use fear and pain as their tools of control. Children who witness the cruelty found within a violent relationship will need long-term, intensive treatment to help them understand what they saw and why they saw it. The children may suffer from fragile self-images, and their caregivers will need to provide safe, consistent surroundings and boundaries for these children to heal.

When Couples Don't Agree

Children will benefit from caregivers who are united and mutually supportive of one another; otherwise they may feel vulnerable or fear that their new home isn't stable either.

Elisabeth continues, "After she went back to him, it was a horrible time—nothing but beatings. She left him again and came here again, and went into the hospital again for drinking.

"It was during that second hospitalization that I noticed that Christine was being hurt. I was giving her a bath, and I noticed that her vagina was all red. I knew that something was terribly wrong . . . as a grandmother . . . as a nurse. I just talked to her, as I washed her, about her private parts and how you never let people touch, and it just kind of went into this kind of conversation, because I was dumbfounded. She spit right out that day, 'My cousin always hurts me there, Nana.' This was his [Thomas's] sister's son. He was eleven, but very big for his age."

"My grandson, Craig, was seven, very small for his age—slim, tiny, a little bit of a thing, never ate. But Alan [the cousin] was a very big boy for his age, big-boned, heavyset. I did not like that child. That's a terrible thing to say, and I don't usually say that type of thing about kids, but he had a terrible mouth. He once swore at Ben's mother. That was a real eye-opener! That concerned me about my grandchildren going to their house at that point. What kind of people were these? What's going on here? So we began to have a lot of concerns, but until that day in the bathtub, I had no idea of the violence . . ."

Ben interrupts, "It continued into the summer because they would go camping. What we didn't realize was that he was going to New Hampshire and dropping them off at his sister's so that he could go do his thing, play golf or whatever. And she ended up babysitting for the weekend, and they [Craig and Christine] would go through this torment.

"To make a long story miserable, that boy today has already been convicted of rape, armed robbery, assault, and battery. He has broken out of jail twice. This all started with [what happened to] Christine."

"Christine started talking," Elisabeth interrupts.

Ben interrupts back. "Worse things were going on with Craig, but she didn't know at the time. He wouldn't come near me; I couldn't talk to him. To this day he shies away from men. And he is not gay either. He's a normal boy, but he does not trust . . ."

Elisabeth interrupts, "Well . . . he's a boy with a lot of problems."

Ben continues, "He does not trust men at all. Even myself, to this day. But he went through hell with those guys!"

Elisabeth says, "With Christine's story, I immediately went to DYS (Department of Youth Services) in New Hampshire. I was working for Franklin Pierce Medical Center in New Hampshire at that time as an LPN, and when I first became aware of Christine's problem, I immediately took her to a pediatrician there to document it. But she was a new doctor, and at that time I don't think she was aware—she says so now—she was not aware of abuse. Even [later] when the therapists would call her and say, 'Christine's telling us she's being touched. You say she has vaginitis,' she would say, 'Well, she hasn't told *me*.' So this thing dragged on for a while.

"I tried to talk to the doctor about Christine's manifestation of the fourteen danger signs, the red flags of sexual abuse—migraine headaches, stomachaches—that she was starting to exhibit around this time. We thought Craig had Tourette's syndrome—he was doing this when he would come back weekends [she throws her head back and twitches her face]. Angry. He couldn't concentrate in school. Then they would start to calm down a little during the week.

"I tried to approach my daughter on a visit and asked her if she had any idea [what was happening to Christine], and she went hysterical, screaming about migraines and, 'How dare you? Don't you talk to me! That's not true! What are you doing?' And then the counselors asked me to stay away, that I was upsetting her. They didn't know the whole story.

"It was kind of looking like I was this interfering, crazy mother. So what I decided then was I had to help the children and just let that piece go. I couldn't get any help from her. She was obviously much sicker than I realized.

"At that point I filed a 51A in the state of New Hampshire. One of the counselors at the hospital also filed a 51A (naming Thomas Connor's nephew, Alan, as the perpetrator). Marion did accompany me, even though she couldn't seem to get involved or to handle any more than that. And then they brought the children in and asked the children. "And . . ." she drops her voice to a whisper and leans across the table, past the basket of apples, past the squeeze bottle of honey, past the child-made napkin holder, toward me, ". . . that information all disappeared. The woman social worker who did the intake left her job. Nothing was ever followed through. It fell through the cracks—whatever. *Nothing ever happened!*

"At this point, they [Thomas Connor's family] started putting a lot of pressure and violence on the children. Unbelievable pressure. They [the children] started presenting with a lot of symptoms." By then Craig was eight and Christine was three.

"He [Craig] was totally falling apart. This was when my daughter totally separated from Thomas, during her second hospitalization. He was taking them to his apartment in Dorset, or to his mother's in Lakeville, or the sister's house in New Hampshire. The children were touched in all those houses.

"Oh boy!" Ben expels loudly, shaking his head. This is so painful for them to dredge up.

"That man was insane!" says Elisabeth. "He's insulin diabetic and he drank. He was this seemingly quiet guy."

"A weight lifter," Ben recalls.

"As we look back," Elisabeth says, "when he would come in with the children, the children never reacted with him like my father and us growing up, or Ben and the children—you know . . . affectionate. They would come in the room and stand like little toy soldiers."

"They would just stay against the wall and look at you," says Ben.

"I was always thinking it was the drugs and alcohol [that Marion was abusing]," Elisabeth says. "They would often be angry at *me*."

The fury the children are unleashing on Elisabeth is, of course, misplaced rage at their abusers. They feel comfortable enough with Elisabeth to vent their anger. They feel rage toward their abusers and at the world for allowing this to happen. These bottled-up emotions can only be released where and when they feel safe. Although Elisabeth and Ben may have been confused by the children's behavior, it is a normal reaction to abnormal circumstances.

"That was very early on when my friend Maryann Alden started helping me." Elisabeth says. "I was helping her with her mother who had Alzheimer's. And what happened was a gift from God."

At this point Ben becomes irritable. His body language changes. He tries to interrupt Elisabeth several times and finally succeeds. "Tell her about the boys," Ben urges.

"Let me do this piece," she says to Ben, glancing at him from the corner of her eye. "I was helping her with her mother . . ."

"Wait a minute," interrupts Ben.

Elisabeth whips her head around to him, and he laughs a little nervously, saying, "I'm not saying you're wrong. But the most important thing that took place is that we went to Social Services over the abuse thing," he turns to face me now, holding the floor, "and Thomas's best friend's wife is the receptionist!"

Elisabeth raises her voice to him as she says, "I haven't even got that far yet!"

Elisabeth and Ben begin to lock horns over the best way to tell the story. Elisabeth clearly has a sharper command of all the facts, but it seems that Ben wants more control over the interview. Elisabeth won't give it up. Ben is becoming agitated in his chair, impatient.

Elisabeth raises her voice again, saying, "But it's a very important piece! Because Maryann is a very important factor in my rescuing the children. She was starting to prepare me that there was a lot more going on here, and whatever was going on with my daughter and her children was not because of me. The whole world was beginning to look in here and say I was this bad mother and that we did a terrible job. It was awful. I guess I was very low and depressed at the time because I felt that I was being 'pooped' on by everyone!"

"Who do you feel was blaming you for your daughter's behavior?" I ask.

"Even my own family, my sister, my parents," Elisabeth says.

"To this day," Ben interjects.

"They were just looking and saying, 'God, what a troubled family!'" Elisabeth says.

"Yeah, we're the black sheep of the whole group," Ben mutters. He has turned around in his chair with his back to Elisabeth, facing sideways, bent over at the waist, his arms resting on his knees, his hands clasped between his legs. From where she sits, all Elisabeth can see is the expanse of red plaid flannel that stretches over the cold curve of his back like a dull rebuke.

Elisabeth continues, "Well, they didn't understand what was going on. And it certainly looked like we did this lousy job. And I was feeling I didn't think I could help anybody.

"My friend Maryann is the one that started giving me the support and made me strong, helped me get stronger. I wasn't strong at the time I started realizing what was going on with my daughter and my grandchildren. It was mind-blowing! Then when my grandchildren started telling me stories little by little, it was . . ." Elisabeth drops her voice to a whisper again and leans forward. The whites of her eyes are showing all around her round brown irises. She grips her teacup, and her lips tighten to white lines. ". . . *mind-blowing!*

"I don't know, I grew up in a family—my mother's Italian, my father's Irish—that was, shall I say, protected? Naive? I mean, you knew things happened. But not to us. My parents weren't educated; my mother only went to the sixth grade. So college for their oldest daughter was not something they encouraged. You know, your boys went, but . . ."

Elisabeth blames herself for not recognizing the extent of what was happening to her grandchildren and her daughter, Marion.

Like many women of her generation, she feels uneducated and perhaps not very smart after a lifetime of deferring to the better-educated males both within her family and without. In the absence of any real support from Ben, she grew to rely on her friend Maryann, who has a master's in early child care and whom Elisabeth admires and respects.

Elisabeth continues, "She was a tremendous help to me by pointing out the mannerisms of the children that pointed to more than just alcohol and drugs, that I was not this lousy mother. She could see what I was feeling. 'You did the best you could. You're going to buck up! And we are going to do this thing together.' She made that promise.

"I was helping her with her father who was dying of cancer and her mother who had Alzheimer's. But I had all this going on too. When they were both buried, she walked into this house and never left. She had a computer at home that she helped me put the chronology on. Terribly important! She told me all the time, 'Write it down! Write down everything! Document! Call the doctor! Tell her how they came home, whether they want to hear it or not! Tell the lawyer this! Tell DSS this! Don't tell DSS that! She was an unbelievable help to me."

At this point, Ben leaves without a word. The door slams shut behind him as he goes outside.

I try to lead Elisabeth back to the events in chronological order, and she tells me that after her daughter left Thomas for good, after her second hospitalization, he had sole custody of the children.

"Those children started going downhill fast; they couldn't even function in school. I finally got my foot in the door by calling the school to say that I had concerns about how my grandson was doing in school. I explained to them about the drugs and alcohol and my daughter's hospitalization. I told them I thought they were not getting the support from their father that I felt they needed.

"Then my daughter finally went for the divorce. We helped her put the down payment on her lawyer to get the divorce started."

I ask her if there was any follow-up with the 51A that had been filed initially in New Hampshire.

"No," she said. "We didn't have anything. They couldn't even find the papers. When we went into court, all we talked about was the divorce. She wanted to get away from him. We didn't know that much then either. Christine had just told us about her cousin touching her, so at that time that's all we knew about for certain.

"So when we went into court—I say *we* because the children were going between us and Thomas Connor—so when we were mediating, it was sort of like a three-way divorce. So when she filed for the divorce, what of course happens is they [the court] say they want the best interests of the children."

"Yup. That's what they say," I mutter.

"That's what they say! I say pfft!" She makes a dry spitting sound and laughs mirthlessly. "As far as the courts helping them, pfft!" We both laugh, but we don't really think it's funny.

"But what the courts tried to work out was where the children were going to go—how many days here, how many days there, what school.

"Now, as I was going to the school, I was more able to—not have control—but I was more able to represent my daughter, shall we say. So that's what I would do. I started taking that role on, calling the school and saying I was concerned. 'How can I help the children in any way?' So then they started telling me things. 'This little guy seems to be going through a lot. He's falling asleep. He

When Couples Don't Agree

doesn't have lunch money. He's unkempt, dirty.' Oh God! I would be so upset. So I would call the court person.

"Maryann would give me some good advice. She would say, 'Make sure you ask them how you can help them. Maybe you can ask if they can go to the Lakeville school system.'"

Ben has come back in and is moving about in the kitchen right next to where we are sitting.

"We were going to a family therapist who was helping the whole family," Elisabeth says. "Marion was out of the hospital. Ben and I didn't know if we were going to do this piece."

"The therapist was working with you and Ben on whether or not you were going to do this '*piece*'?" I ask.

"Well, um . . . this was putting pressure on . . . um . . . everybody . . ." Elisabeth falters.

She is obviously uncomfortable. I try to help her clarify. Ben is moving around busily, but silently, in the kitchen. Elisabeth is trying to be cautious. Tact is choking her.

"So, in other words . . . ," I prompt.

"There were a whole bunch of pieces here that were kind of pulling apart; all the family was falling apart," Elisabeth blurts out finally. "The children would not talk to my husband and tell him the things they were telling me. He was having a hard time believing it. I was having a hard time with all of it. So in other words, we were going to counseling for *all* the pieces!"

She doesn't tell me about the piece that is lurking in the air, unspoken but present—the gulf between her and Ben, the damage done to their marriage.

It really appears that Ben let Elisabeth down. She needed his support and guidance, but most of all, she needed him to believe.

She needed him to be part of the "team," the team that put the children's best interests first.

I recommend that Elisabeth share with Ben her disappointment that he had to struggle to believe the magnitude of the abuse. If this issue does not get resolved, Elisabeth's feelings of disappointment and hurt may continue to act as a wedge in their marital relationship. Relationships need not be perfect, but children will heal more thoroughly in an environment in which their caregivers are respectful of one another. If hurt feelings are left unattended, those feelings will continue to grow, and so too will the distance in their relationship.

"The pieces of my daughter falling apart and how we could help her . . . ," Elisabeth falters again.

"And whether or not you should get so involved in helping your grandchildren?" I ask. "Was that one of the pieces?"

"Right," Elisabeth answers.

"Taking on another burden?" I continue. I watch Ben in the kitchen, but he does not acknowledge this conversation; he does not look our way.

"Yes! Because, you know, it looked like it was going to be a long fight," Elisabeth says hotly.

That they sought counseling is critical, but it is fairly obvious that Elisabeth was more invested in the process than Ben allowed himself to be. Even though Ben does not appear open to any long-term therapy, he might benefit greatly from some individual short-term counseling to address his feelings of ambivalence and frustration.

"Marion was also going to counseling. They were telling her to stay away from *me*. She wasn't telling them everything that went on. She couldn't bear it I guess, or her mind covered it up and she was denying it.

"It was very, very difficult. I was walking a terrible road, because my daughter would be denying it. When Christine would tell me something horrendous, it would blow my mind. It would take me off my feet for a couple of days."

"Like what?" I ask gently. Up to this point she has been tentative about giving details of the sexual abuse. She makes references to being "touched" and "hurt," words that are easier to say but that mask the true nature of the violation, damage, and suffering that occur when children are sexually abused. Although I don't wish to make these revelations any more painful for her than they already are, I want the real version of events, not the polite one.

"Well, I'm trying to think when she started telling us about her father touching her," Elisabeth begins. It was a long route. "It was the cousin, then an uncle that touched her over at 'Grammy's house.' He was starting to hurt her upstairs in the bedroom."

Ben calls out, "There are nine brothers and sisters!"

"And the grandmother went up and tried to interfere, and he hit the grandmother," Elisabeth continues. "And all this whole time, this other grandmother never told us what went on, because obviously this has been a family of generations of abuse and a weak lady that was hurt too, a battered woman I am sure. I compare her to Marion.

"My daughter was frightened, so frozen with fear and the threats that she couldn't . . . He knew what to do, I think, to keep her that little, weak girl that she was. Maybe I made excuses for her. I don't know. But I hear battered women . . . I have gone to seminars, I've taken a rape crisis counselor course—anything I could take that I could learn about what I was dealing with and who I needed to deal with and how to handle it as best I could."

"At that time, your daughter didn't want to hear these things. Craig was denying it. So you were looking like the 'crazy lady?'" I ask.

"Yes! They [the therapists] thought I had this vivid imagination. Even when we started therapy, we had terrible experiences with therapists for the children, terrible experiences.

"We went to court at the end of the school year because I had been calling the court person and telling her, 'Look, I can't help these children! I can't take them to the doctor. I can't take them to the dentist. They need help! This father is doing nothing. I need a piece of paper saying I can help these children legally.

"So we went to court, and every time we went it was sort of like a little neglect charge was being thrown in. He had been taking them to his sister's where we *knew* they were being hurt. I told the court this, and they ordered him not to take them there, because by that time we had a little proof. Teachers. A doctor. Counselors."

"I thought that was when we were going to the DSS," Ben calls from across the room where he stands, arms folded across his chest, listening now to what is being said.

"No, no, no, no . . . they weren't even involved yet," Elisabeth cuts him off. "So at that point, I got a piece of paper that we signed, Marion signed, and he [Thomas Connor] was supposed to sign, giving me authority to be able to take them to the doctor, give them medicine, etcetera. During the course of the summer they were supposed to go on a ten-day camping trip. I told the court, 'They are supposed to go on this camping trip with the sister, and we know her son hurts them all the time.' Craig would admit to being punched and hurt that way. 'And they are supposed to be in a camper with them for ten days for God's sake! The court told him he couldn't go with his sister camping.

"You know what he said when he came out [of court]? He came right to the door and said, 'No one is going to tell me what to do with my kids! Get the kids and get them in the camper!'

"They left for ten horrible days. They were sexually abused by all of them! Because Christine had opened her mouth." Elisabeth has welled up and can't continue. Ben has come back to the table and is sitting with us. He tries to say something a couple of times and then gives up. We are all trying to compose ourselves. Its several minutes before anyone can continue.

Ben finally says, "And a lot worse than that!"

"That was the beginning of the nightmare," Elisabeth says, her lips quivering and looking away from me. "When I started finding out how bad it was, I was hoping it wasn't as bad as it looked?" She says this as a question, blinking as if to hold back the nagging guilt along with the tears.

"When they came back from that camping trip, they were in horrendous shape. They couldn't play . . . they didn't care about anything . . . they were in terrible shape." Elisabeth's voice is low and full of pain. "Christine could barely sit down."

"I called the abuse hotline for some advice, and they said, 'Take her to Saint Joseph's Hospital.' They had a nurse there that dealt with abused children. God bless that nurse.

"She told me she had worked with abused children and she knew how I felt. She was wonderful. She let me go in with her and had Christine sit on my lap when she examined her, first of all with the dolls. And when Christine told her with the dolls what had happened to her on that camping trip, I asked her if there was anybody else who could document it. This was going to count finally! But I wanted someone else too, and she suggested a social worker. I asked if it was a woman, because she wouldn't let a male near her, and it was. So twice that day they documented what had happened to her through the dolls and by Christine telling them.

"When the doctor came in to examine her, she started screaming. Didn't want to go anywhere near him. He was very cold. Christine wouldn't even talk to him. He examined her and just wrote down 'vaginitis,' even though we told him what she told us. 'Well, it could have happened on her bicycle,' he replied.

"A 51A was filed, one by the social worker and one by the nurse, and it was documented in the hospital records that day. And then I told our pediatrician about it, and she again hesitated to file a 51A. She either didn't know much about abuse or didn't want to get involved. I could never quite figure that out.

"Back then we still thought it was only Alan that was hurting her."

"The story she was telling with the dolls was just about Alan?" I ask.

"Right. She was too fearful of him," Elisabeth begins.

"Too fearful of her father," I clarify.

"Yes! Too fearful of him to say any more. But what she was doing when she would draw pictures of the family at preschool—and I took those pictures to the therapists—the whole page was a picture of her father's face, and in the corner over here . . ." (Elisabeth hunches over to make herself small and bends over to a little corner of the tablecloth to show me what it was like) "was a little picture of her mother, and even tinier than that was her brother,

Craig, and tinier than that—almost like a dot—was Christine. I was keeping track of all those things.

"I started doing a complete work-up on Craig. I hooked up with a pediatric neurologist. They were presenting with so many physical problems, medical problems. Maryann had suggested a complete work-up at Children's Hospital."

"You did not suspect that Craig was also being sexually abused?" I ask.

"No, because we thought it was the cousin touching a little girl," Elisabeth explains. "I can honestly say no. I think Maryann did. She started saying things to me, getting me ready, I think. 'It may be more than this,' she said at the time. But I had so much going on then."

"We were taking care of my mother," says Ben.

"Yeah, I'm a great caretaker," Elisabeth says dryly.

"We were starting all over again with testing so I could bring all the results to the Lakeville school system when the children started school there. I had him tested the year before, but in the face of all the results, the Dorset school system said he didn't have any problems—this kid who was failing every subject." Her voice rises sharply. "It was a matter of money; they didn't want to give him special ed. So with Maryann's knowledge of the school system, how it worked, she would tell me, 'You get your own work-up done. You get the neurological work-up, the psychological work-up. And when you walk into the school system, they have to help you by law; they can't say no then.' And that's what was done."

Elisabeth told me later that no matter what she described to the schools, they would tell her they'd seen worse, children who were more depressed, more needy. Her grandchildren, even now, are sometimes described by teachers as being "insubordinate" and "not trying hard enough." When Elisabeth explains the children's history once again, she is told, "They look fine in the hallway; they are talking and chatting." Elisabeth's struggles to get the children the services they need and are entitled to are ongoing, and unfortunately the unresponsiveness she has encountered in the schools the children attend is quite common elsewhere as well. Most school systems are overwhelmed and ill prepared for the numbers of special-needs students, particularly those who have been affected by the traumas—physical, emotional, and mental—caused by using and abusing parents.

"A woman—God bless her—a pediatric neurologist from Children's Hospital said to me, 'I think what you need is a guardian ad litem. He [Craig] is not having seizures. There is no brain damage. This is all emotional.' So after that I went full speed ahead with therapy, calling DSS . . ."

"But what was their [DSS's] response to the 51A you filed after that camping trip?" I ask.

"Pfft . . . nothing," Elisabeth says.

"Nothing!" Ben seconds.

"Nothing . . . nothing. I was this 'crazy grandmother' putting ideas in people's heads, and even at Children's Hospital . . . ," Elisabeth lowers her voice to a whisper, "we found out much later . . ."

Ben bursts in with his booming voice—this is the story he has been wanting to tell, "The secretary there was Thomas Connor's best friend's wife. We all had to go to therapy there, and this woman is his closest friend's wife! He was going too, by the way, at different times. Anyway, they all took his side. They didn't believe anything we said, and they believed him." Ben's voice is filled with disgust.

"They believed him when he was saying what?" I ask.

"That he never did anything really wrong," Elisabeth jumps back in. "And that I was the 'crazy grandmother' trying to take his kids away." Ben nods in agreement and says, "We never tried to take the kids away."

"Every time we went to court, it was *never* over my wanting custody of the children. Never!" Elisabeth says. "It was over neglect and abuse of the children."

"Right," Ben agrees.

"His story was that I wanted custody of the children," Elisabeth tells me.

"And that their mother was the unfit parent," Ben adds. "His whole defense was against her [Elisabeth], saying she was a grandmother talking from outer space, wanting to take over the grandchildren."

Although Elisabeth and Ben never sought legal custody of the children, the children were spending a great deal time with their grandparents. Elisabeth was caring for the children during the week on Marion's behalf, and their father, Thomas, was taking them on the weekends.

A report had been filed by a psychologist at Northrop Children's Hospital that characterized Elisabeth as an interfering grandmother and that hinted she was putting a lot of pressure on Craig that was causing many of his problems. Both the court and the school had this report on file, although Elisabeth and Ben were not aware of its contents at the time.

"I *was* calling like a crazy woman after these weekends when they would come back. They were so traumatized. So hurt. Nightmares. Couldn't sleep. I was up all night, getting no sleep. I was getting nuts too. And I was calling up saying I wanted them to know the condition that these children were in. I wanted them to know! I wanted them seen like this! I wanted them seen on a Monday when they'd come back on a Sunday night! I wished they could be seen Sunday night! Or Friday when they were getting ready! They ought to have come out here on Friday when they had to go with him and see what they were like—they were almost killing each other, and angry, and scared!" At times like this she becomes a ramrod of fury—trembling, fists balled up, thin lips like slashes drawn across her tense face, her brown eyes bulging circles, with the whites showing all around behind her glasses.

"So I was calling and making a pest of myself, and that's basically what they thought of me," she says more calmly. "But Maryann was wonderful. She would tell me not to be hysterical. 'Make sure when you call, just calmly give them the information. Only talk facts.' You know, because I would be so upset and I would ramble sometimes. She was giving me all this support and telling me how to stay clear and focused, telling me to write down on a piece of paper what I wanted to say before I made the call. Because she knew me." Elisabeth laughs at her tendency to ramble on. When she smiles, her face takes on an impish quality. Her round eyes narrow a bit as the laugh lines take over.

"But what was happening was that my lawyer was patronizing me, DSS was patronizing me, and even the therapists were. Christine was confirming what I was saying [to the therapists], but then they would take Craig in and he would say we were all lying."

I look over to see Ben leaving again. He does not come back this time. But I can see him through the big windows all afternoon long, hauling lumber, digging stumps, repairing his boat. He never stops working.

Elisabeth confides in me, whispering, "And my husband was not supportive. You can see the anger in me via my frustration. He would go away on business trips."

I ask if he was one of those who thought she was just a crazy lady.

"Yes! And he was almost befriending him [Thomas]. I have a lot of rage—not anger—rage!"

"He was denying that there was a problem and taking Thomas Connor's side?"

"Right. So he would not have to believe it. Usually what he'll do when I am talking about it with anybody is change the subject— defer it onto something else. I get so angry!"

In cases of sexual abuse, sometimes a family member will doubt the truth because if they accept it, they must accept the anger and all the painful consequences that come with it. Ben does not appear to be very comfortable with painful emotions, and to acknowledge that his grandchildren have been sexually tortured may be far too emotionally overwhelming for him. It's as if he feels that, 'If I can't imagine it, then it doesn't exist.' This denial is preventing him from emotionally supporting his wife and grandchildren.

"We had a few problems before this, but what happened when I wasn't getting any support and he was pulling me apart." She drops her voice to a nearly breathless whisper. "I could not walk away from those children. So that's what happened at that time. I couldn't walk away, and he was asking me to. I said, 'No. And if you are asking me to, it's telling me something about who you are as a person.'

"I am not saying my decision was right, but I knew I was the only one who could save the children. They would have been on the streets, using drugs, and thrown from one foster home to another because they were almost like two little animals at the time.

"We are working things out because it's easier for the both of us financially, staying friends, salvaging what pieces we could. There was so much damage, and I keep hoping that someday we can get back to what we had, but I'm afraid . . . so far it hasn't happened."

"Do you think that he is now glad that you kept the children?" I ask.

"I don't know if he is glad. I think accepting might be closer to what we have here. He wouldn't leave me even back when I couldn't deal with him. But even at the end, when I would show him something as concrete as that . . ." She lifts a newspaper clipping bound in plastic reporting on one of the criminal trials for child rape. "He would . . . ," she imitates a dismissive gesture with her hand, a disgusted wave.

"So it took a long time to die. I think that's what it is. Something died in here . . . ," she points to her heart ". . . as far as he and I go, and I feel very sad about that. It's very, very painful. That's another painful piece."

To save their grandchildren, the Parks need to save themselves. Elisabeth is making it very clear that she feels much pain and sadness over the current state of her relationship with her husband. She needs Ben to be her partner. Without his partnership, I am not sure how much more pain their relationship can bear. I would like to see Ben and Elisabeth actively pursue and participate in couples counseling. If Ben will not go, Elisabeth would benefit from therapeutic support to help her either accept Ben as he is or possibly make some very painful—but necessary—changes.

The Parks' story is lengthy and complex, a roller-coaster ride of sharp twists and turns. It contains many highly charged issues: sexual abuse, drug abuse, domestic violence, denial, and damaged children, as well as an ineffective social service system and protracted court battles. All of these elements took their toll on the Parks' marriage.

For now, we will put aside the Parks' struggle to free their grandchildren from devastating abuse (to be concluded in chapter 4, "Healing the Wounds") and focus on their marriage.

Ben's point of view is the final piece of a picture that shows the disastrous effects on a marriage under stress when grandparents don't agree.

Ben

It's a cool early fall day when I travel back out to talk with Ben. The sunlight has taken on a hard, yellow slant. The hydrangeas next to the Parks' front stairs are turning now from creamy white to a deep raspberry pink, and miniature green and gold leaf tornadoes swirl at my feet as I step onto the front walk. I have been sick for days with a relentless intestinal flu, but I have also felt driven to keep this appointment. I was concerned that I had left the last time with a bundle of negative feelings and questions left unanswered for Ben. So, armed with Maalox, crackers, and ginger ale for the long car ride, I set off.

When I first met Ben, I had a sense of déjà vu. He was so familiar to me, very much like many of the men I grew up with—a doer, a builder, a hard worker—uncomfortable with feelings, and possessed of a low tolerance for and about women.

After that first meeting, I called on a psychologist friend of mine, Dr. Kimberly Gatof, and anguished over it. "What's with these guys?" I asked. "Why did Ben have such a hard time believing Elisabeth? Why did he treat her efforts with disdain? Why can't some men value and validate their wives without feeling threatened by them?"

She told me that each time we enter into a dialogue with someone, we carry with us a lifetime of collected experiences and biases. As we drag this heavy baggage into conversations, it weighs on us, influencing how we hear and understand what is being said. I knew that I had a few leftover issues from my childhood, even from my own marriage, that I was hauling around, and I was afraid it was affecting my objectivity regarding Ben.

I do not dislike Ben; quite the contrary. But I have pigeonholed him, I know, and I know I need to free him from that box I've put him in—for both of our sakes. My friend tells me I must meet with him once more, just him and me.

I drive through the town past the American Legion Hall with the "Meet Shoot Saturday Night" sign, past the other small lakes that dot the landscape and are ringed by new home developments, past the little strip malls scattered like matchsticks along the winding roads—uninviting boxes, indistinguishable from one another, strung together like cars on a train. There are stubby dry cleaners, seedy package stores, and the pizza parlors, glowing dead blue with fluorescent lighting and serving as hangouts for the local kids. I stop at the high school and look around—newly built brick buildings, somewhat fortress-like, but crisp and clean, with apple-red trim. I don't know what I'm

When Couples Don't Agree

doing here, what I expect to accomplish. I drive on with the question trailing me.

As I sit with him at their table once more, Ben points out a great blue heron perched on a piece of jagged driftwood at the shoreline. We admire the handsome bird for a while, and then I begin, gingerly, by asking Ben about their home—their dream come true. I know that they had planned for it to be their retirement home—this beautiful sanctuary by the water. Fishing. Boating. Gardening. I try to get him to talk about that period of time just after they finally moved here, when Marion got pregnant.

Ben talks about his mother who lived on this site for many years in an old house that he replaced with this one. He talks about the differences between prefab homes and stick-built construction, between Acorn Homes and Deck. And he talks a lot about his children, his pride in them. "We've been very lucky; we've got a good bunch of kids," he tells me. He does not talk about disappointment or lost dreams.

I chat with him about real estate and building, hoping to make him comfortable enough to open up. "I was a real estate broker for twelve years," I tell him, and talk about the houses I've renovated and the ones I've built. I ramble on a little about being a grandparent and how I feel about raising my granddaughter.

Finally, I stop beating around the bush. "Well, I guess what I'm driving at is that—and I guess it's true for all grandparents who are in this situation—you get to that age when you think that you are going to start to enjoy yourself, and you get pushed back to square one." I watch him as he responds.

"Of course, at that time, when we built the house, all of this hadn't come about," he says.

"Pretty soon after that," I lead.

"A year after," he says.

I wait a few beats. Silence. "So, you sort of feel like you're back in it again . . . and it's hard." I am prodding, dangerously close to putting words in his mouth.

"It was harder back then than it is now, even though I am out of work right now. I don't know what the future's going to bring within the next year when our finances run out. We had a *savings*. You know, I always had a good job. I always had a good-paying job, so financially it was never . . . even with the gang . . . you know, we had six children . . . we got by pretty well.

"I am angry at the lawyer stuff. They did absolutely nothing, and we went through our total life savings. But anyway . . ." He pauses a while. "But see, this thing just built up—I'm sure Elisabeth explained it to you—it just built up and built up. From the nephew abusing them to the point where . . . I had never . . . I couldn't even believe that it was the father."

"Did you have a hard time believing?"

"I *did*, because the boy, to this day, has never . . . in fact he told me that his father never touched him," Ben says. "But he doesn't tell Elisabeth that. He tells her a different story."

"I guess that's typical of boys that have been abused." I am dangerous again. Who do I think I am, Anna Freud?

"We knew that Christine was being abused by the nephew. *That* we knew for a fact. That came out at the time with the examinations she had. It looked like the father was taking her up to the nephew, because they're a close-knit family too. There's chaos in that family; they are a violent family. I've known the whole family long before Elisabeth did. I grew up with his father."

When Couples Don't Agree

I find myself saying, "Mmm. Oh? Uh huh," continuously. I am sitting to his right at the dining room table; he is at the head. I turn my body fully toward him, nodding my head, leaning forward, urging him on. I'm trying too hard.

"But anyway, one thing led to another, and Craig told us about the father abusing him," Ben says. "Plus knocking Christine and Marion around. We didn't even know about that."

"So when it was all happening . . . it probably took years to unravel . . . but there was probably a long period of time when it was really hard to comprehend," I say.

"It was one thing after another. The whole of the seven years, all that was discussed was the abuse thing and the kids." His voice is down to a quiet, gravely mumble. "It got to be old hat after a while. I don't discuss it because I get so sick of it. I never discuss it with people at work. I never did, you know."

"Well, that's understandable."

"It's something, I guess, that will never go away," Ben says. He sounds wistful. "We have everything going here. We have them at home. The kids are healthy. But emotionally they're damaged, the boy more so than Christine. And he shows it. He's very quiet. He's a good kid. It's a shame. He loves sports.

"We are lucky that we had this home to raise the kids in, too. Really! We had a lot of things going for us." Ben pauses again.

"So it put a lot of stress on the marriage—that's true for a lot of grandparents," I say, fishing, fishing.

Ben responds by telling me, "It put a lot of stress on all the kids." Deflecting, deflecting.

I change the subject. "Do you think the Connor family got any fallout from the court trial or anything?"

Ben perks up, becomes animated. "No! That's a good question! All of their kids were big-time athletes in the school. Girls too. I am talking *excelled*. They led everything. If it was a boy, he led in basketball, football, touchdowns. Each kid. And the girls excelled in soccer and girls' basketball. They were always the captains. Nine kids, every one of them excelled.

"Most of the boys have been in all kinds of jams. They always got out of it because of the prestigious name. The town backed them, and all of that. Our kids took a backseat. Like Joanie [their youngest daughter] had to suffer through high school being rejected a lot by teachers who liked *them*."

"No kidding!" I say, truly amazed.

"Oh, she went through a lot of that. Now these two [the grandchildren] are going through a little bit of it."

"Even though he was found guilty?"

"Yup!"

"Why do you think that is?"

"Well, they were very active, like I said, in the sports end of it . . ." Ben drifts off.

"Were they likable?" I'm really trying to understand this myself.

"Oh yeah. They're very personable people. It's like anything else, Deb. If you sat in a room with them, you'd say, hey, no way does he have these types of problems. And they probably all don't. I know for a fact that two of them do. But you can't blame the others either. You know what I mean?"

"You knew their father?

"Oh yeah. I grew up with their father. He was a great athlete too when he was younger. I played ball with him."

"So there was never any real fallout for that family, and in fact there is still some loyalty left around," I confirm.

"Yeah, there's a lot of that. But we got a lot of support from people, people who knew what was going on even before we did."

"Who knew," I ask, surprised.

"Oh, the police, the peer groups all knew what was going on. When it all came out, then they'd all start coming over, saying, 'It's too bad you never knew.' That kind of stuff. But you can't take that to court. It doesn't mean a hill of beans when they start investigating things.

"It's a stigma. We all see them [the Connors]. You have that feeling when you're in a store and you see them or one of their neighbors; you try to go in the other direction," Ben confides.

"That must be very uncomfortable."

"It is . . . I mean, this is a small town."

"So does that bother you to the extent that you wish you lived somewhere else?" I ask.

"No . . ." Ben pauses again. Then he starts and stops a few times before he continues, "I wasn't around here. When I was working, I did a lot of traveling with the job I had. I went overseas. I was on the road an awful lot. So I wasn't involved as much as Elisabeth was. I wasn't involved at *all*, in fact, because I wasn't *here*. I was in and out all during that time. It wasn't until the last three years that I've been home. But up until that time, she was taking the burden, the brunt of everything.

"And there was nothing I could *do*, Deb," Ben says. It sounds like a plea, a bid for understanding.

"Craig never would discuss it with me. Never. No way. Only once I asked him when I thought he'd be comfortable with me, and he went violent. So we never discussed it again. We can discuss sports. We get along fine as far as the sports go. We generally watch it together. And I enjoy watching him play. He's a very good athlete, *very* good. My kids were too. I played a lot of football and baseball when I was younger. So he's got the genes in him—from both sides really, you know."

"Now, as you look back, are you glad that you have them?" I ask.

"Oh yeah! I agreed. I've got no problem with that at all. We both, I think . . . well, I shouldn't talk for Elisabeth because she's not here—but I thought that maybe Marion would've come to the point of taking them. But it never happened. But I don't hold that against her either."

"Well, most grandparents do that," I tell him. "They wait—they hope that their children will get their acts together."

"Which she did! But she just couldn't cope," Ben explains.

"Elisabeth mentioned that you all went to counseling. And one of the things you discussed was whether or not you would continue on that path . . . to keep the children." I am not being direct enough, I know. I find this difficult. I can sense the discomfort in Ben. It rubs against the air between us like sand on glass. I wish I could brush it away.

"We went to so much counseling, with so many different people, you wouldn't believe it. She's into this counseling thing that just blows my mind. No one gets to the root of anything, as far as I'm concerned. And one of the things was . . . uhhh . . ."

The seconds tick by. I really do not want to take him where he does not want to go—perhaps *cannot* go. But I want to give him the opportunity to tell it the way he sees it. Ben sidesteps.

"When it came time for education . . . all I wanted was that this guy was going to pay for their education.

"I already had three girls in college. And Joanie is the last one going. It's a big expense. Anyway, that never came up [in court], and I was a little upset at that. Although Craig may not be college material because of his emotional problems. He's a very good artist, by the way, this boy. And Christine will go; I'm sure Christine will go. But I don't know . . . at our age then . . .

"He did that poster over there." Ben proudly points out a pencil sketch, a woodland scene with a fox, framed in silver and hung on the brick wall behind the woodstove. "He just did that in about ten minutes! He's very good with human figures. My daughter is too. He must take after her in that respect."

"You were trying to secure their education for them." I let him take me where he wants to go. "Was that one of the disappointments you had with the lawyers?"

"I still have a problem with it. Thirty-two thousand dollars so far! And we've got nothing for it as far as I'm concerned."

"Does he [Thomas Connor] pay child support?

"Twenty-five dollars a week per kid. I could care less about that," he harrumphs. "That's not even food money for a week!

"I am more or less on the outside looking in," he reveals suddenly.

"So all this mess was sort of swirling around, and you felt like you were on the outside looking in," I repeat.

"Well, I was. I gave her no support because I was . . . the stories changed every day. I perhaps should have kept a diary of my own. I made a lot of mistakes too, as far as not recording things for my own benefit."

It is good to see Ben acknowledge that he made mistakes too. Sometimes the only way to get on the path of forgiveness and healing is to acknowledge our own mistakes. Sexual abuse impacts every family member, even those not directly suffering the abuse. In many ways, Ben and Elisabeth are victims too. I can tell Ben does not like being a victim, yet he needs to admit he hurts too. The entire family needs to heal from the aftermath and scars of the sexual abuse that occurred. For Ben's healing to begin, he not only needs to acknowledge he has made some mistakes, but he also needs to admit that his grandchildren were sexually abused by their father. Sometimes half of the battle is admitting we have a battle. I don't want to see Ben lose the war.

"How do you think that would have helped you?" I ask Ben.

"It would have helped me because . . . it would have helped me with the wording when I had discussions with the lawyer. Like I say, I wouldn't be here during the day, and I didn't go to some of the meetings that she did have with the lawyer because I was working, so . . ."

"Elisabeth's got a whole file. She's got the file, and she's got names, dates. I have to give her what's due to *her*, and that's 100 percent. She did it all, I did nothing. I was . . . tagging along.

We all need validation. We all need to know that the people we love appreciate what we do. Ben should tell his wife, frequently, that he recognizes she did do it all. He should let his wife know that he recognizes that this time, she was stronger. Partners can get a lot of mileage from validating what the other has done. I'm sure there have been many times that Elisabeth felt unappreciated by Ben and perhaps even doubted herself. She needs to feel appreciated and recognized for her dedication toward her grand-children. She needs this from Ben.

"Obviously you had mixed emotions at the time. It was a great big mess, and you weren't hearing the same things she was hear-ing. So the question for you was, did you want to continue with all of this? The court battles?" I fumble, afraid to shoot the arrow too directly and wound him.

"Oh yes! Because of the fact that I was hoping that the nephew was going to get dragged into this, who was the biggest offender as far as I am concerned, which we know! The kids came right out with *him*!

"I thought it would've finally come to *that*. I figured this guy [Thomas] would *never* take the heat . . . that he was covering . . ." Ben begins this startling revelation, but I cut him off. I don't realize right away the significance of what he is starting to say. He men-tions Alan, and I am off on that tangent.

"He never went to trial, though, did he?" I ask. "Just the father did."

"Never."

"I wonder why not."

"Because he was a juvenile at the time, sixteen. This guy at six-teen years old—I have two sons that are six-footers—and this guy is bigger than them at sixteen. And here is this *baby* . . . Christine was two!" He shakes his head, still in disbelief.

"You must have a lot of anger."

"Oh yeah! Toward both of them! After him [Thomas] going to trial and being found guilty, and I would have bet my *whole life*—I would have laid down my life—that there was no way . . . he is finally going to crack and say, *I* didn't do this, my nephew did. He didn't. He took it!

"Then I figured, well, he *is* guilty then. For him to sit there and take it, being found guilty, and then *plea bargain*, and then come to Massachusetts and plea bargain! I said, 'Oh boy!' That's when it really hit me!"

"Do you think some people think that he was merely covering for his nephew?" I ask, stunned.

"I don't know. I really don't know, Deb.

"I'll tell you something that has something to do with him maybe making that decision. I coached him and all his brothers in softball when he first married my daughter. Then I found out their temperament. Their violent temperament and their decision making—they were stupid. They were really stupid! You had to tell them exactly what to do. These guys had all played high school sports, graduated from high school, and had jobs . . . and they didn't have a brain! They were like Little Leaguers. They were all stupid. I couldn't believe it!

"So I can believe now, after looking at that. The bad decision making just in the sports thing, for him to make a decision of whether he was going to go to bat for his nephew, cover for him . . ." Ben trails off.

"So you think he might have made a stupid decision like covering for his nephew and taking the blame, but was really innocent?" I try to keep my astonishment from showing. Did Ben really harbor a lingering sliver of a thought that Thomas Connor might have made some kind of perversely heroic gesture to protect his nephew? Was this a coping mechanism for Ben? Was nurturing some doubt a way to avoid the horror, the depth of betrayal?

When Couples Don't Agree

"Probably. I don't know. One thing led to another at the trial in New Hampshire. And the repercussions we were getting from the police department about his nephew and his sister, who was in all kinds of trouble. We were getting this feedback, and I said, 'Oh man, this family is more whacked up than I thought.' We thought there were just stupid things, but there were serious things they were involved in. Then it wasn't hard for me to make a decision—okay, this guy is a loser! He didn't seem like it. He seemed a little different from the others. But maybe I was just trying to make excuses in my own head about it."

"It was a long process for you to come to that point," I confirm.

"It was! This was very confusing, this whole thing."

There is another long pause. The seconds stretch out into the silent room. I think Ben is done with talking. He is looking out the big glass slider, past the deck and over the water. I can actually see the choppy lake reflected in his glasses. He has been remarkably patient with me. I recall something he said, with his dry sense of humor, the day I met Craig. This trait also seems to apply to Ben: "That boy only says nine words a year, and he said eight of them today." I like Ben. I ask him one last question. "Do you think that you and Elisabeth might get back to the point where you were before . . . before all of this began?"

"I don't know. I really don't know. It doesn't look too good. Too much damage. We get along but . . . we're just existing here . . ." Ben drifts off, staring out the window with a faraway look in his eyes.

One of the important questions here is, can Ben allow himself to grieve the loss of his grandchildren's innocence? Events have unalterably changed the nature of the Parks' relationship. That is not to say they cannot have a very mutually satisfying relationship together. They can. However, the sexual abuse has claimed Ben and Elisabeth as victims too. Because of this, they both must learn how to grieve the loss and pain that sexual abuse creates.

I don't believe that there is "too much damage," although it's plain to see the extent of the damage caused by this ordeal. However, if Ben and Elisabeth want their relationship to succeed, they must put a substantial amount of time and energy into it. To that end, Ben must allow himself the opportunity to heal, which can only begin by admitting the need for healing and moving forward from there.

For both families presented in this chapter, we see what happens when there is a substantial breakdown in communication or even no communication at all. For couples contemplating the important, life-altering decision of parenting their grandchildren, much heartfelt, thoughtful, mutually respectful discussion needs to take place with each other before, during, and after the arrival of the grandchildren.

Even though grandparents may not have much time to discuss new living arrangements beforehand, they do need to take a great deal of time after the fact, to discuss openly with each other the potential for stress on their marriage and, together, make plans for dealing with it.

FOUR

Healing the Wounds

If you have faith as small as a mustard seed . . . nothing will be impossible for you.

—Matthew 17:20

After you have swallowed your bitterness and dismantled the secrets, after you have rearranged the parameters of your life, taken stock, and assessed the littered landscape of family relationships, where do you go from there? It's time for healing.

Many grandparents move instinctively toward methods of healing in the same manner that for eons grandmothers have provided chicken soup and chamomile tea laced with honey to soothe the little hurts and fevers of their loved ones. Some rely on their faith for inspiration and guidance, but that alone is not always enough.

Support groups are often a good first step toward healing. Sharing experiences and information, breaking the isolation barrier, and connecting on a personal level with those in similar circumstances can serve as a powerful balm for families in conflict as well as offering much-needed information on navigating the "system." Each time grandparents are thrown into the melee, they must reinvent the wheel. Where do I go? What do I do? Is there help for me? Very often the one place they can get the information they need is from their local support group and the people who have already been through it.

Some of the grassroots organizations that have sprung up throughout the country are connected to local Councils on Aging or with Departments of Elder Affairs, but most have formed through word of mouth among grandparents in crisis. Some have the benefit of professional facilitators, but most are run by grandparents just like you and me. Grandparents use their support groups to help them over rough spots or to garner information about legal rights, aid, and the like. Some just like knowing that others are out there going through the same things and take enough comfort from that to keep going.

Additionally, groups such as Alcoholics Anonymous and Parents Anonymous can be useful resources. These groups offer helpful tools for coming to grips with issues such as substance abuse, codependency, and family relationships.

Stress is the little black cloud that can be found following grandparents around, hovering overhead, raining droplets of resentment and guilt, self-doubt, and depression. Stress management seminars and literature on relaxation techniques can be helpful to those open to new ideas and remedies. Stress is the one universal element to parenting your grandchildren, whether grandparents are young or old, financially secure or scraping by, in a custody battle or one big happy family. Stress is the natural by-product of caring for children all over again, just when you thought it was time to think of yourself for a change. Learning how to overcome or manage the stress in your life, to prioritize and put events into perspective, to value yourself and your efforts, and to work toward attainable goals while letting go of things you cannot change—these are the lessons essential to healing.

Another component to healing is empowerment. Sometimes grandparents, specifically grand*mothers*, feel as if they are in a black hole of events over which they have no control and which they are powerless to alter. This feeling of powerlessness often leads to depression. Women are usually the keepers of the peace in families. To achieve that, they learn early on to sublimate their own needs and desires for the good of the family as a whole. They are unfamiliar with the power that is theirs and do not know how to use it to effect positive change for themselves.

One of the grandmothers that attended my support group was caring for her teenage granddaughter. Her own daughter, the child's birth mother, was an alcoholic. Although the grandmother was having some difficulty dealing with the angst of an emerging teenager obsessed with cars, boys, and parties, her life was on a pretty even keel. Then her daughter lost yet another job and apartment and asked if she could live, temporarily, at her home. It wasn't long before she was wreaking havoc on the household, and the grandmother was slipping into a vortex of helplessness and depression.

The daughter was utterly dependent on her mother, physically and financially, yet for some reason this grandmother had assigned her all the power in the situation and had abdicated her own in the process. I said to her, "But it's *your* home, *your* food, *your* car, *your* gas. You hold all the cards!" But she couldn't see it. She had lived a life of giving her personal power away and didn't know how to reclaim it. She was the lost bird, trapped inside a room, growing weak but within reach of an open window and freedom if she could only see that it was the way out.

Professional therapy and counseling are often necessary before real healing can begin. The complicated circumstances implicit in family dynamics often require outside help for sorting out feelings and managing circumstances that can seem overwhelming. Family therapists can offer help on the issues of family relationships, conflict resolution, and marital stress. For children, issues of abandonment, loss, and grief may be best addressed through the expertise of therapists specializing in adoption issues, whether or not the child has been adopted. Like any other search for professional help, it is always best to seek specialists. Children who have suffered sexual abuse should be taken to therapists specializing in that area. Grandparents whose marriages are under stress should seek couples counseling, and those who are having difficulty dealing with troubled birth parents should look for a family relationship expert. It takes some time to "shop" for the right fit. It is important not only to find the right category of therapy, but also to feel comfortable with the therapist. The special circumstances that lead grandparents to become parents, either temporarily or permanently, usually require some level of expert counseling.

Unfortunately, the older the caregiving grandparent, the less open he or she may be to seeking professional help. Those of the "old school" wouldn't hear of going to counseling or seeking it for their grandchildren. "Psychiatrists are for crazy people," one grandmother told me.

They may be unfamiliar with the symptoms of ADD or hyperactivity (conditions common in neglected and abused children). A grandchild affected by these conditions may appear to elders as merely naughty or willful. A negative triangle can result between an afflicted child, an overburdened teacher, and an uninformed grandparent. These situations and others like them could be ameliorated by education, awareness, and sensitivity on the part of professionals in the fields of education and health care.

Professionals—teachers, school administrators and counselors, pediatricians, health care providers, and social workers—should work together to provide a safety net for these new intergenerational families. But they are generally unaware of or blind to the special circumstances involved when grandparents are primary caregivers. Grandparents may be out of touch and out of step with child-rearing guidelines, health care requirements, nutritional standards, and the teaching practices of today. Positive attention must be focused on the intergenerational families that turn up at school and pediatricians' offices, or that turn for help to social workers and clergy. Professionals must first be made aware of the differences in approach grandparents may bring with them to child rearing. Often they may be dealing with caregivers functioning within a fog of culture shock. Those suffering the worst effects may be raising adolescents across the great divide of decades worth of changes, in some cases half a century or more.

Grandparents need help as they maneuver through the obstacle course before them. Systems in place to help children and families are as yet ill equipped to deal with grandparents' specialized needs and concerns. Grandparents exist in a kind of limbo with regard to social service agencies across the board. They do not fit easily into categories set aside for aid; trying to jury-rig a fit, such as requiring grandparents to become foster parents—like the square peg in a round hole dilemma—just doesn't work. Even when grandparents are entitled to assistance by law, such as medical benefits, the ignorance rampant in bureaucracies results in denial of, or barriers to, receiving what they deserve.

Grandparents will not get the help they need to heal and move forward until the people, places, and organizations from which assistance may be available realize grandparents' importance in the equation of holding families together and decide that it is in the best interests of society to value that importance.

Grandparents have some things going for them that you cannot train into foster care providers or pay residential staff to do. Grandparents love their grandchildren. They offer children connections, roots, devotion, and belonging. They think their grandchildren are the most precious, important, and wonderful people on earth. Ask them. Nowhere else can a child get such things.

It is out of that love and devotion that grandparents look for and find ways to heal themselves and their grandchildren. Some don't know where to look or what questions to ask. Some falter and stumble and may lose their way because they are overburdened and underhelped, but they all try.

REVEREND YARDE

Reverend Eduardo Yarde is what we all hope for in our clergy. Caring, sensitive, and open minded, he struggles to deal with the extreme needs of families in extreme circumstances—families often ripped to the core by bitterness, shame, and grief. Families in need of healing. I visited with Reverend Yarde at his church one cold Sunday this past snowless winter to talk about his philosophy and his methods.

The Morning Star Baptist Church rises up as graceful and important as the Parthenon on a bleak city block. White columns,

Healing the Wounds

brick front, and crisp white trim declare the building's dignity, while sheets of crumpled newspaper and stained coffee cups blow into the shrubbery stretching along the sidewalk. Cars are double- and triple-parked out front all up and down this section of the parkway that runs through the center of the city of Mattapan.

Mattapan Square is a mixed bag. Flourishing establishments like Brother's Deli and Restaurant, Zodiac Domino Sports Club, and Lavinia's Hair Salon press up against hollow-eyed shells like TC's Variety, barely held together by graffitied plywood planks. Other businesses are closed for the day; corrugated gray metal sheets or black grates are pulled over windows and down tight to the sidewalk, like a slap in the face. I rubberneck as I drive through, worried that I'll miss my turn. The city bustles, even on Sunday morning. Groups of boys congregate outside places like Store 24, and men and women stroll with baby carriages or wait in tight clumps for buses.

I pass several churches—St. Angela's, Lily of the Valley Baptist, and another Christian denominations I can't quite catch as I drive by—housed in low-slung buildings that look as if they might have been a garage in a former life. They each seem to be full and busy.

It's too early to be spring, but the unfiltered sunlight, squinty bright, forgets it's only February and builds up strength as the morning moves along. After pushing open the heavy oak doors at Morning Star, it takes a few minutes for my eyes to adjust from the raw daylight to the dimmed, recessed lighting inside. I find myself at the back of a crowd of people yet to be seated. Ushers are helping families to the pews. There are lots of ushers; the men wear neat black suits and white gloves; the women wear white dresses that look like uniforms, white shoes, and white gloves. Some have three-cornered paper caps on, like nurses from another era. Behind me the big doors open with a whoosh of cold air mingled with the scent of perfume as a trio of stylishly dressed women enters, all heels, hats, and color.

I can't find Reverend Yarde, and as more and more people brush past me on the way to their seats, I feel more and more uncomfortable. I tap a nearby usher on the arm to ask if he can direct me to him. The usher, a wiry, smallish man in his fifties with graying hair, turns quickly, and when he sees me he recoils a bit—it's an almost imperceptible hop backward. It shakes me, and I suddenly feel like an intruder here. He doesn't know Reverend Yarde, he tells me, and slides off. But other ushers come by and offer me a seat and help, and I relax and begin to enjoy the service while I wait.

The place is packed. I find out that there is a Jewish group from the Anti-Defamation League here on sort of a cultural exchange. They come for a service on Sunday, and in turn members of the Baptist congregation visit them for Seder. The pastor tells his flock that they are "blessed" to have their Jewish friends there, and he adds in jest, "You are Baptists today!" Then he says, "Hit it!" to the organist and choir, and they begin a joyful, belting hymn to the clapping and laughter of everyone seated under the soft glow of the curved, white ceiling. Fans hanging above rotate in time to the music, and there is a warm feeling of fellowship moving in the air.

One of the ushers motions me to follow him, and I lope along behind, disappointed, like a child taken from a grown-ups' party and led to bed. Music and amens fade as we walk down the side corridor to the back where the offices are.

Reverend Yarde is a big man, bulky in Harris Tweed, with a calm, open face. He is young for a pastor, I think, somewhere in his early thirties. He is soft spoken and smiles broadly and often as he talks.

Healing the Wounds

"Growing up I had a very difficult childhood," he tells me. "There were people who reached out to me. And now that I am grown and look around, I realize that it made a difference. Because someone took the time out to care for me. So rather than be judgmental, I just reach out to the young people. I'll be driving by and see some of them on the street and start talking to them. And I get to know their families. Most of them are living with their grandparents. They are taking on that responsibility all by themselves, so then I offer to help in any capacity I can. I find most of the time that a word of encouragement or just being there helps."

We talk about the younger children and what he does to help them through their times of trouble.

"I thought of the mustard seed according to The Word. I thrive on the saying of Mrs. Rose Kennedy—I'll never forget that, it stays with me forever—she said that if the Lord was to take everything from her and just give her faith, she could thrive. And then I applied that to my own life. That little mustard seed seems so small and insignificant." Reverend Yard extends his arm and holds his thumb and forefinger together as if he held one of the tiny seeds in his thick fingers. "But then you nurse it, and it begins to grow." Each of the children is given a mustard seed pendant to wear as a symbol of hope and faith. A reminder that someone cares.

He speaks with a Panamanian accent—sort of a Panamanian/ Boston drawl—and is sometimes difficult to understand. I lean my head forward and cock my ear toward him, hoping that on tape his words are clearer. But soon I become accustomed to the lilt and cadence of his speech and find it a pleasure to listen to.

"So the idea started from that and transcended to the parents and grandparents and even those who are incarcerated. We try to make a bond between them," he links his fingers together to illustrate, "and find a positive program to help because I feel that the church needs to take a stand, because we have left everything up to the government to provide for us, and the government is really overwhelmed. So I just go into their homes and try to see what their need may be, or I see sometimes that they are so stressed out by everything that's going on. So what I do is try to get them together and sit down with them and start sharing with a word of encouragement and let them know what a wonderful job they're doing. Sometimes I might take their kids and take them to a movie or something and relieve them from that pressure a little. Other grandparents in the same situation have come together, and we've formed a spiritual support group"

When he says "we," he refers to himself and a wonderful African American woman named Vera Lenox. Vera is a social worker, now fifty-eight years old and nearing retirement, who has been working for over twenty-five years with the inmates that come through the Nashua Street Jail in Boston. Several months ago, Reverend Yarde, there to offer healing services, met Vera and forged a bond with her over their mutual concerns for the mothers and fathers of the inmates who were taking over the care of the children left behind.

Vera, too, has made it her personal mission. She takes the grandchildren to Sunday school, has weekly "rap sessions" with them, babysits, and hosts a Sunday afternoon spiritual service for grandparents in her home, with Reverend Yarde presiding. She personally works with the approximately thirteen families and over twenty grandchildren with whom she has connected through her work at the jail.

"We have several grandchildren that we are working with, myself and Mrs. Lenox. One grandmother has seven grandchildren.

Healing the Wounds

With another grandmother, one of the grandchildren began acting up in school, so we suggested to her that he needs to see his dad (who is incarcerated), because he was very close and then that was taken away. So she started doing that.

"They depend on us for so much, so much support and uplifting because sometimes the burden gets *heavy*." He draws this last word out and bends forward as if that weight was pressing down on him. "I always try to give them a shoulder to lean on. Just give me a call and I'll try to be there. I can't be there today and tomorrow find excuses."

"What are the problems you hear of most often?" I ask.

"The problem begins financially. For the grandmother who has six or seven, it's really hard on her. And having to deal with the grandchildren *and* with the children's parent. The problem has divided both at times. It's very difficult, especially when their own child is demanding from them, and they don't know where to turn to."

"Do any of them have anywhere else to turn besides the church?"

"Many of them are not aware of places to turn to, and that's where we come in as sort of a consultant to them. We try to inquire, find out what are the places, what type of need there is. We try to make sure that it's a legitimate need. We try to find out what we can help with, and we connect them with other grandmothers who are in the same situation and then they can communicate. And by listening to them and coming together and sharing, it really helps them a lot. But we find that most of the time we are the only support they have so far. At times it's difficult, very difficult, because we are not funded. Even though I am at Morning Star, most of this I do on my own.

"Most of the grandparents and parents that I work with, their children are in a drug program or incarcerated. Some of them are not ready to open up publicly. So rather than bringing them into church, if they don't feel comfortable coming here, I usually meet with them after service. Or we go to Mrs. Lenox's home. Or if there is a grandmother who is really going through a great deal, or they're depressed, or we haven't seen them for the past few days, we go to that particular person's home and just give them a word of encouragement, so that they know we are still there and they're being thought of. That alone means a lot to them, to know that someone has taken the time out to care. At times, when we listen to their testimony, they say, 'We didn't know someone else cared for us. We thought we were just in this ourselves.'

"And we say, 'We're here for you.'"

I find it remarkable that in the short time that he has been reaching out to grandparents he has been able to put his finger on exactly what their most pressing issues are: finances, support, isolation, and respite. I tell him about a grandmother in a neighboring city who, in her seventies, is caring for five grandchildren from seven months to eight years old, two of whom are HIV positive. She has only her church for support, and although she gains comfort from talking with her pastor, the only other thing they seem to be able to do for her is to bring over food baskets now and then.

"It's so easy to give someone a basket of food and say, 'Well, here,' you know. This is why I try to make a difference. There is more. Because food you can get anywhere, but the thing is that they need someone there for them.

"Sometimes I have people give me tickets to different events. Vera will babysit with their grandkids so their grandparents can get a chance to go out. This past summer I took thirty-three kids to Water Country. Well, at the time I was single," he explains with a smile.

"I feel that the Lord has blessed me. So much goes back to my childhood, because I almost became a dropout from school. But someone took the time to care. A complete stranger. I didn't know her; she was a pastor of the church here. Many times when I thought of walking away from the church, I always thought of her kindness, and that's what kept me there. So I try to apply that.

"It's difficult to complete all the things that I would like to in outreach. A lot of people cannot see your dream unless they live it themselves. Other people really cannot fulfill your dreams. So I try to do things on my own. Then I found Vera, and now we work together as a team."

We talk about how difficult it is sometimes to get the right kinds of help to the grandmothers. "That's where the pastor or minister needs to discern when to seek professional help. Sometimes I see where it's no longer a spiritual need, but a professional is needed, so I refer them. I will follow up and speak to a doctor and give him some feedback."

There have been times that a school official has tried to talk a grandparent into obtaining counseling for her grandchild, but she seeks out Reverend Yarde instead. "Sometimes it's a matter of convincing them to finding a new avenue and to feel comfortable with the idea. I tell them, 'Just try.'

"I'm a servant. I can do nothing else but serve," he says with a wide smile, spreading his arms outward and upward theatrically. "To whom much is given, much is required. And so much has been given to me; I try to return some of that."

We talk about how important the role of the clergy is and lament the fact that there is nothing in place for grandparents in the way of financial aid at the moment.

"We started a spiritual group on our own, and we get no kind of financial support, so what we decided to do is plan a musical at the Strand Theater [to raise funds]. With the welfare reform, this is where the churches are going to play a crucial part. That's one sector that's been neglected. My philosophy is that these grandparents have already raised their kids; they are under no obligation to raise more kids. To me, they are doing us, society, a favor. They are doing the state a favor. They should be rewarded for that. If we can't see that, we surely have lost sight of everything. The state really looks the other way, 'Oh, that's grandparents.'" He gestures a dismissive wave with both hands. "They don't even consider giving them some sort of support, nothing. And it's *hard*.

"These kids are the leaders of tomorrow, and if we don't help them now . . . I don't think building more prisons is the solution. This is a most serious problem, and it's happening right in the home. No one will deal with it. That is why I am committed to this."

Vera Lenox and Reverend Yarde share a dream: to create a day-care center for intergenerational families where grandparents and birth parents alike can come together for the children. They would offer parenting classes and support groups where family members could re-bond. Reverend Yarde says that he and Vera need help from other people who share the same concerns. "The more help I have, the more people I can reach."

Elisabeth Parks, Reverend Yarde, and Vera Lenox all lean heavily on their strong faith, but wisely, they each reach out in other directions as well. However, while Reverend Yarde's story is uplifting, the Parks' story is distressing. While Reverend Yarde ministers to those in the midst of furious turmoil, he has the luxury of stepping back, of floating above it like a guardian angel. The Parks live it. A look into their story is a ride through a storm—jarring, unsettling, gut wrenching.

Concluding this chapter is part two of the Parks family trilogy. In it, Elisabeth's strong determination to both rescue her grandchildren and help them to heal is highlighted. She not only saves the children from their abusers but also from the destructive infection of bitterness and hatred.

Elisabeth is driven, at times obsessive. She is not a saint, nor is Ben a sinner; they are flesh-and-blood people, with failings and flaws, trying to cope with a waking nightmare. Elisabeth uses any and every method possible, from spiritual tapes to karate lessons for the children, to try to keep their lives—so ridden with torment—safe and sane. But her outrage informs everything she does, often giving it a breathless, ragged edge; we can only look on and flinch at times in response.

She enrolls in rape crisis courses, visits shelters for battered women, and advocates for her daughter at every opportunity. Elisabeth's foremost achievement is working toward forgiveness. She first finds it in her heart and then works to nurture it in her grandchildren. It is her greatest gift to them.

Forgiving liberates the spirit and is the key to healing. Yet it is the thing that many grandparents find most difficult to do. Some seem to savor their anger, jealously guarding their resentment for the offending birth parents with a self-righteous piety. They hang on to it for dear life, as if letting go would stop their momentum, their will to go on. The rancor that drags at them becomes a barrier to finding peace for themselves and their grandchildren.

Bitterness is a heavy burden to haul; it requires energy better spent elsewhere. Letting go of anger, learning to forgive, working at forgiving, replaces that dead weight with a lightened heart and enables us to more easily move forward.

In the midst of the tooth-and-nail battles, the emotions rubbed raw, the fiery will to protect, Elisabeth provides her grandchildren with islands of calm, places of peace and healing. Elisabeth is in this chapter not because she is a fighter, but because in the heat of battle she kneels down to kiss away a hurt, to patch a broken heart.

While she is fortunate to have strong allies in her friend Mary-ann, as well as those in her religious community, the "system" fails her at every turn. In many ways she is on her own.

According to Child Help's National Child Abuse Statistics, "Every year more than 3.3 million reports of child abuse are made in the United States. The United States has one of the highest rates among industrialized nations—losing five children a day to abuse-related deaths."[1] Abuse of grandchildren is one of the most frequent precursors to a grandparent's move to gain custody and is the reason the Parks' story is particularly important. Unfortunately, their struggle within the court system is all too common.

At one time, I participated in the Massachusetts League of Women Voters' study on child abuse. Local leagues in each city and town came to a consensus over the issues involved. Here I will share an excerpt of my written presentation given at our league meeting at that time, which was based on research done by me and other local participants in the study, as well as information supplied by the League of Women Voters at the state level.

"The League questionnaire went out to hundreds of professionals at DSS, the police, schools, hospitals, DAs, and judges. Each group had many recommendations, and their concerns reflected an overall consensus on the issues that need to be addressed—education, funding, prevention, changes in attitudes, and judicial reform.

"Severe abuse cases funnel, ultimately, through the court system, and it is the way the judiciary deals with those involved that has the greatest impact on victims' lives. Of all the groups questioned, the judges were, by far, the poorest respondents. 'Some judges declined to participate, stating that they were too busy . . . or that they did not possess the factual information requested.'[2] Of the few judges who did participate, opinions were widely divided on virtually every issue.

"Some judges in the League sample still believe that children's credibility is questionable, that women are either shielding husbands or bringing vindictive, trumped-up charges against innocent men, and that the current system is 'adequate.'"

I ended my presentation with a quote by Justice Francis T. Murphy. In a speech at a Fordham Law School conference on child abuse, he said, "Children have neither power nor property. Voices other than their own must speak for them. If those voices are silent, then children who have been abused may lean their heads against windowpanes and taste the bitter emptiness of violated childhoods.

"Badger every legislator from every county in this state, let no editor or reporter sleep, until the remedy you want is granted. For you are the only voices of the violated child. If you do not speak, there is silence."

Elisabeth Parks was not silent. And while she secured her grandchildren's freedom by relentlessly speaking out, regrettably, she also paid a mighty price for it. Reverend Yarde provided the calm in this chapter, and now we will enter the storm. Through it all, there is much to be learned about healing from Elisabeth Parks, much we can take into our own hearts and in turn share with others in need.

PART TWO OF THE
PARKS FAMILY TRILOGY

Elisabeth

Just beyond the living-room windows, boats scud across the blue-diamond water, their colors reflected on the uneven surface like iridescent scales on a snake. The view is broken only by Ben walking back and forth as he keeps busy outside. Elisabeth continues telling their story without him.

"DSS was very involved, but they were going very gingerly. No matter what happened on weekends, they would come out and say, 'Well, you know, there are two families involved here, and we want to help them. We help fix families.'

"*They don't help protect children; they 'fix families.'* They don't fix families that can't stop themselves and are out of control; there's no *way* that they can." Elisabeth says this angrily, straining forward, pushing her hands against the table.

"The therapists were beginning to believe the children. There was too much there to deny anymore. There were more 51As being filed. Christine went into a play therapy group in the fall, and they did a segment on their bodies. It was an eight-week segment, and by the end of the eight weeks, many of the children that had been sexually abused were able to say it or draw it.

"Christine, for the first time, told that her father had touched her—her father! They told me what she had said . . . but they didn't believe her."

Healing the Wounds

"They didn't?" I am puzzled, shocked.

"No. They said they thought she said that because the other children did. Now remember, I didn't know that the secretary in that office was a friend of the Connors. One of the therapists there later confessed that she had been influenced by this woman. They were still coming from that 'crazy grandmother' place.

"In December, this counseling agency had decided that I was an unfit person, based on the—I call him the 'patsy psychologist' for Mr. Connor that was at this office—based on the therapists all saying that I was coming there very upset all the time, and that they felt I was emotionally upsetting the children, putting ideas in their heads.

"The court was beginning to believe them. The counselors were saying they wanted to take the children away from me and put them in a foster home. I almost went nuts! And I would have lost those children at that point if it wasn't for Maryann Alden.

"She said, 'Like hell!'" She advised me to call my lawyer to see what my rights were. I thought if they had that meeting without us, the children would be gone. Gone for Christmas!

Maryann could not believe it. She was going crazy too.

"By this point, my Community of God's Light was very much invested in these children," Elisabeth tells me, and then asks if we could take a break.

We sip sweetened, milky tea as Elisabeth begins to talk, hesitantly, about a religious community she is very involved with. She makes an offhand remark and gives a sidelong glance to gauge my reaction. I ask her a few gentle questions, fairly sure of where she's heading. "Is this a Catholic group?" I ask knowing she is Catholic.

"Oh, no, we never ask what religion anyone might be—we don't care," she answers.

"Is this group all women?"

"Not necessarily," she answers lightly, coyly, as she spins around the kitchen rummaging in drawers for spoons and bowls, preparing a snack for us.

"Let me put it this way—is the backbone of this group women?" I ask pointedly, holding her gaze.

She laughs, almost girlishly. She checks my tape recorder to make sure it's off and then laughs again in embarrassment. "Yes," she says, and we share a smile of unspoken acknowledgment.

I can see how important this is to her. Through all the private things she has shared with me, she has never been concerned about recording anything on tape. Until now. I am curious about why she is so secretive about it. I think it's because it's not mainstream; it's slightly fringe and—I'm guessing—not officially condoned by the Church. It's also possible she fears being tainted by something some might see as strange, or out of bounds, after her past experiences. I am intrigued by this "women's group," and I press her for more information.

Although she says it's not a Catholic group, there is a priest that guides their Sunday morning service. He "allows" the women to read the liturgy. And therein lies the rub, or one of them: this is not done. They have been investigated by the powers that be within the Church hierarchy. This is one of the things that drives her secrecy.

But as she talks on, I realize that this "community" is much more than Catholic women wanting to read the liturgy at Sunday Mass. This grassroots group is made up of thinking, spiritual women coming together to share their deep sense of spirituality, and empowering each other. Women unbound by the fetters of formal church doctrine, they test their wings. Here is another support group run by women, but with a deeply spiritual base.

She tells me that they have learned the Universal Dances of Peace, and I instantly think of the Salem "witches"—and persecution.

I have been reading a book by Alice Walker, *In Search of Our Mother's Gardens*. Walker uses a phrase in her book that comes back to me as I listen to Elisabeth talk about her group: "*Womanish* . . . i.e., like a woman. Usually referring to outrageous, courageous or *willful* behavior. Wanting to know more and in greater depth than is considered 'good' for one."

That must feel like a threat to many people. Perhaps it is why Elisabeth is hesitant, secretive. But I feel this is too important, this version of a support group. I encourage her to talk freely, and on tape, about it. So she does, and from now on, she mentions the group frequently. I realize that whenever she has spoken of her friend Maryann Alden, there is a wider community of support that connects Elisabeth to Maryann—and beyond.

"By this point, my community was very much invested in these children," Elisabeth says, laughing lightly, as if released, and speaking directly into the tape recorder for emphasis. When she is serious, her mouth is small, her lips thin and pale. But when she smiles, she smiles big. Her eyes twinkle with Irish mischief, and she laughs merrily, girlishly. Her face softens and colors.

"These, like I said, were professional people, many of them—intelligent people. And it was a real eye-opener for all of these professionals to hear where the 'system' was and what was happening. They were all upset too."

Elisabeth speaks again of the meeting that was held to determine her suitability as a caretaker for her grandchildren. "I asked a pediatrician I was working for if he would please be able to be a participant in this meeting. I told him that I would insist upon it so that we would have representation in there as well as they did. It came as a surprise to them [the therapists at Northrup]. I don't think they ever had anybody strong enough that would come with all the 'guns' to a meeting like that.

"At that meeting, representing me was a letter that Maryann wrote about who we were as people, and all the things I was doing and learning to become the best possible parent. Between that and the pediatrician, they decided they wouldn't take the children from me.

"A guardian ad litem was assigned. I hardly ever saw her. We were granted temporary custody by the courts."

The Parks were granted temporary custody because they were the only ones providing child care. They were taking the children to their doctors and therapists. Thomas Connor was doing nothing. He refused to sign the papers relinquishing custody. He was "thumbing his nose at the court," as Elisabeth put it. So the court took matters into its own hands and signed over custody to the Parks. However, Mr. Connor was granted weekend visitation.

Elisabeth rambles on a bit, telling a story about the pediatrician who was so helpful at that meeting.

"Several weeks before that, I was so angry at him because no one was really helping. I had said to him, 'Why do you take an oath to help children, all of you? Why is it that everybody walks around this thing and doesn't do anything concrete that will stand up in court to help these children?' I was furious! This was after I had heard that they were just going around saying they 'weren't sure' what was really going on with the children.

"So I spieled off! And I think that really knocked this doctor into reality. I told him, 'When all you doctors say you take an oath to help children, it's a crock!'" She leans forward, her knuckles

Healing the Wounds

white where she is holding her spoon, and she is wild-eyed with fury. I am reminded that they thought she was a "crazy lady." How else could anyone behave but "crazy" in this situation? This frantic fury, this trembling, eye-popping rage—isn't that normal here?

"I was just so full of anger at that point. Maryann would feel the same way—and these other strong women. Because I was meeting with them and my church, and because of their love for me and my children, some of those women started having memory returns."

"We started what we called a 'parachute group.' It was a group to talk about the book *What Color Is Your Parachute?* It was a book that taught you how to look at your life experiences, how to write resumes, and how to change the direction of your life and all that. It was a course at some of the colleges at the time. It gave us an excuse to get together, and we loved it. Saturday mornings early we would get together for coffee, and we started out discussing the book, but the topic always got around to Christine and Craig. It was almost impossible *not* to talk about it. The women were so supportive.

"So a lot of these women will be my friends until I die because of the connection. Way back, it was a spiritual connection and a church connection, and then it became a connection with people who had 'adult child' things that they were talking about, so that each level that we went into seemed to become a deeper and more trusting level and circle of friends."

Beyond the living room, framed by windows off to one side, is a square flower garden surrounded by knee-high, white pickets. Friends from her "community" came one day with shovels, flats, and fertilizer and planted it as a birthday surprise for Elisabeth. In the center of the garden, surrounded by tall pink and white phlox, blue delphinium, and sturdy magenta dahlias, rests a small stone cherub; sweet alyssum tickles at her toes. She is bent forward with her elbows on her knees, her chin resting on her hands. She looks lost in thought, and her wings are pointing to the sky.

"So all during this, when my days were very dark, I would get help from them. I always have been a woman of strong faith, even when my bottom fell out sometimes. There were times I thought that's all I had.

"When my daughter was starting to drink, and I didn't know what was wrong, I remember falling on my knees one day and asking Our Lady, the Mother of God, who saw her Son hanging on the cross, and saw her Child suffer, would she please help me; I couldn't take any more. That was the Sunday before my daughter came to me. When I was feeling like a total failure as a mother, I laid it in another mother's hands.

"She has enriched me so much, because of that power. And I do believe that every time I thought the worst was coming . . . and it did, it did," Elisabeth laughs ruefully. "There was always a window that opened when a door shut. These women would say to me, 'Hang in there. It will change, and we're going to see that it does!'

"Maryann was wonderful in helping me to get the children re-laxed, to get their minds off what was going on at the time. If they were going in for questioning with a detective or DSS or whatever, she would always be there, first of all, and she would always re-mind me to bring things for the kids. She would say, 'Come and sit with me and play dot-to-dot,' to get their attention so they wouldn't be like this," Elisabeth bunches her shoulders up and stiffens her arms by her sides, "waiting to go in to be asked and having to talk about the most horrendous things. Because of what she would do to help me get them there, they were able to do it."

Healing the Wounds

Elisabeth would call the authorities ahead and say, "If you make these children wait an hour for that meeting, you won't get a damn thing out of them!" Or, "If you say you're going to question them at four o'clock, question them at four o'clock; we'll be there at five of. If those children have to sit there, they fall apart."

Elisabeth is getting a little ahead of herself, I realize, so I push her back chronologically.

"We got the special ed things going at school that year, they got into therapy that year, and they decided they wouldn't take the children from me. But at that time, he was still getting the children every weekend. It was just before Marion went into the hospital for the third time. She was living here, and she had started drinking again. As she started getting worse, I told her I couldn't put up with that. She either had to get help or leave. So she left my house for a while, and her brother, Mitchell, took her in, thank God. She was not in good shape at all, but I couldn't handle her coming in at all hours of the night and upsetting the children."

It is important for parents not to buy into their children's addiction or addictive behaviors. Elisabeth was right to draw the line and tell her daughter to get help or leave. This is not easy, but by giving such an ultimatum, parents demonstrate that they are not buying into the alcoholic's need to be taken care of. It is easy to get sucked into a child's "neediness."

It is common for parents to try to rescue their alcoholic child, but they need to be reminded that only the alcoholic can save himself or herself. Very often these rescue attempts keep the addict from hitting bottom. The substance abuser needs to hit bottom before he or she can begin the climb toward healing.

Raising Our Children's Children

"Then she went into the hospital for the third time. I had a meeting with a counselor up there about putting her in a halfway house completely away from these people that she was around that were getting to her . . . to get her completely away from here."

The disease of alcoholism is a powerful, tragic, gripping illness that afflicts over ten million adults in this country. Millions more are being raised by alcoholics, with disastrous, lifelong effects.

More children feel, at some level, responsible for their parents and their substance abuse. Grandparents need to be aware of this fact and give reassurance to their grandchildren that they are not the cause or in any way responsible for their parents' addictions. Grandparents also need to recognize that many children will not openly admit they feel responsible, frequently because of guilt or shame. However, grandparents will want to approach their grandchildren with the option to discuss their feelings regularly, even if their grandchild gives the impression that all is well. Research proves that for all children with actively abusing parents, all is not well, but with guidance, a sympathetic ear, and a supportive shoulder, things can get better.

We had a little session, Marion and I. She told me to stay out of her business, etcetera, but then she admitted to me that she did want to come back so she could go right back to what she was doing. She thanked me afterward for fighting on her behalf. She said, 'Ma, you know me. I was giving you a crock!' I said, 'I know you were. That's why I was up there doing that.'

"She went up to the Fairfield area to a halfway house. There is a hospital up there that has marvelous programs for women. In the halfway house she got her GED. She went to Fairfield Community

College. She is a wonderful artist; she draws beautiful pictures, as my grandson does.

"Maryann used to say to me, 'This little girl was a victim of this perpetrator as well as the children. He picked on a weak, naive girl that he could use.'"

> Critical for all involved with the alcoholic is the understanding that alcoholism is very much a family disease. No immediate family member is immune to the devastation that alcoholism delivers not only to the alcoholic, but to anyone who loves him or her.
>
> It is common for parents who have watched their child drown in the disease of addiction to question what role they had in their adult child's "need" to drink, and to feel, in some part, responsible. Of course, no one causes someone to drink or abuse drugs. Grandparents may need help processing their feelings about their child's addiction and help in understanding the anger and ambivalence toward their child.

The children were beginning to recant in therapy because their father was sitting in on some of the sessions with them.

"When the children had to go with him to therapy, they would get headaches, sick. I was trying to tell the therapists that they were invading the children's privacy and safety by expecting them to say anything if this perpetration was true. Where were these therapists coming from? A lot of harm was done to the children during that time.

"After Marion went to Fairfield, I tried to reestablish a relationship between her and her son, who was almost completely destroyed by his father telling him that his mother was no good, didn't love him, didn't care about him—all those other pieces.

"Every night we would be saying our prayers that God would help all of us. And as I started explaining to the children that their mother was a victim like them, they completely lost all their anger for her. They were hearing from others that she neglected them and that she was a terrible mother." Elisabeth's voice softens and catches. "She never hurt them. She never hit them. She wasn't there for them because she wasn't there for herself." Her voice breaks as she struggles to continue. "And as they started understanding this, at least it was a piece of healing and repair. No matter what a mother does to a child . . . they need to know, if nothing else . . . even though she can't be there for them . . . they need to know she loves them . . . to survive," she finishes softly. "And that's the piece I wanted to keep going."

> Grandparents should be aware that their grandchildren's sense of self is shaped and developed by their birth parents. By modeling forgiveness, Elisabeth demonstrates to her grandchildren that they can forgive their mother too. For their own emotional well-being and psychological health, at some point children need to forgive their neglectful parents, not only for what they did, but for what they didn't do or were incapable of doing.

"I would be so tired and angry at her sometimes, I wanted to just kill her. But as I became more and more aware that she was a victim, it was okay. I just wanted her to get well. So we would pray every night for what we could be thankful for.

"'What do you mean there is a God? How can there be a God?' my grandson would say, knowing—even though he wasn't telling me then—how bad it was . . . and there was no way there was a God that would allow what was happening to him and his sister."

Healing the Wounds

Elisabeth glances down at her folder of notes, the typed chronology, and reads, "On the fifteenth of February, they returned after a two-day visit [with their father] whining and crying at the drop of a hat. Not hungry, didn't eat all day, takes a few hours to calm down. Christine wants a baby bottle and to be held close, sits in my lap for TV, circles under her eyes, takes some time to fall asleep."

"They were going to karate then. I was trying to get them to feel stronger, that they would learn some power and have something that they could feel that they could hold on to, or learn something that would help them when they didn't feel safe." Elisabeth's voice is dragging heavily over her words as if the weight of them is too great to bear. "Because I was doing everything in my power to try and free them, and it wasn't happening."

Just then, Christine flies in from outdoors, full tilt, her sandy hair flying back from her face. Her cheeks are flushed from bike riding. "Where's the obstacle course?" she demands to know. "Grandpa couldn't put it together," Elisabeth explains apologetically. Christine is huffing and puffing with all the melodrama a twelve-year-old can muster. She swings her arms around as she marches out haughtily to join her friends. When she finally leaves, we have to laugh at this mini-drama. However, Elisabeth feels a need to explain to me why the obstacle course wasn't erected. "I am caring for aging parents too. And we had a birthday party last night. Sometimes you just can't get it all done!"

The "sandwich generation" is a term that describes people who are coping with their own children as well as aging parents. Much has been written about this trend. But a new trend is escalating rapidly to which little attention has been paid and no clever catchphrases have been attached. A new term is needed for grandparents such as Elisabeth, who are wrestling with the added layer of grandchildren on their plates—perhaps the "club sandwich generation," or the "submarine sandwich generation"— extra large, with everything on it, including hots!

Elisabeth takes a deep breath and continues on. "Valentine's Day that year was a horrendous, horrible weekend. Christine's birthday was pure hell. Nothing but abuse went on in that apartment [where her father lived]. They were putting the heat on the kids so bad because people were beginning to suspect and put pressure on Mr. Connor. Counselors were beginning to believe Christine a little bit.

"After what they were seeing in terms of the physical and emotional symptoms in the children—even though the children still couldn't even talk about it—it was beginning to sink in. Things were accelerating; there was more abuse. They were coming home in terrible shape. I was taking them to the doctor almost every week after the weekends.

"Christine was being brutally hurt because she was the one that was talking!" Elisabeth is tensing up again, her whole body stiffening, straining forward as she talks, eyes enormous. "'This is what we do to little people with big mouths,'" Elisabeth quotes.

She slumps back in her chair, her shoulders rounded, and continues in a monotone, staring into her lap. "So during that period . . . her birthday was hell . . . Valentine's Day was hell . . . Easter was the last weekend that he raped her.

"At Easter!" she exclaims, jerking upward, her voice cracking. "Good Friday! Two weeks before Easter she couldn't sit for two weeks!" Elisabeth is crying now. "He was a basket case . . . little Craig. He was humming . . ." She rocks back and forth in her chair to show me, pulling on her ear and saying, "Hmmm . . . hmmm

. . . hmmm. Pulling his ears so bad, like he wanted to rip them off his head! He was twitching like he had Tourette's syndrome . . . migraine headaches every other day . . . stomachaches." She is out of breath from the effort of voicing these terrible memories.

Elisabeth grows quiet. Moments pass, and then she diverges again. I believe she needs this breathing room. She talks about her daughter's current boyfriend to whom she attributes much of Marion's continued recovery. They met in rehab in Fairfield and have been together ever since in support and in friendship. "They do wonderful things together, all healthy things. I believe the reason my daughter is alive today is James. After the year in Fairfield, they moved to Maine, and I'm so grateful. He's big, he's strong, he is a very gentle guy. I believe she would have been hurt if it weren't for James. Thomas stalked her, he stalked us, he stalked the children."

A few moments go by again before she is able to get back on track. "Everything came to a head once the SAIN (Sexual Abuse Investigation Network) team came on board. It is a team of all the agencies in Massachusetts that are connected with abuse cases." The SAIN team is made up of a police officer, a therapist, a DSS social worker and supervisor, a district attorney's office representative, a victim witness advocate, a medical consultant, and a team coordinator. "They come together in a room with a glass in it. They bring the child in the other room—this is supposed to make it easier for the child as far as questioning goes. The point is for all the agencies to get the information at one time. After that, they were able to stop the weekend visits. Thank God for that team—the SAIN team.

"We finally had a court date. But Christine had to be examined by a physician for the upcoming court trial. We did not know if

Christine would be able to endure it. The pediatrician saw how badly she had been hurt and called in a gynecologist. He couldn't even get near her. So then I called the abuse hotline to ask who in God's name, what doctors were experienced in abuse, and they told me Doctor Susan White. Susan had worked with many abused children. She goes to court with them, she fights for them, she *fights* for them. She is my hero!

"We showed Chrissie a picture of Dr. White, and we said, 'This is the wonderful doctor that works with children that you're going to go see. Chrissie. She wants to help you if you let her. Maybe she can help free you. We only want you to tell the truth.

"Maryann would always tell me, 'Don't put words in her mouth. Be careful what you say.' And we were very careful. All I would ever tell both children is, 'All we want you to do is tell the truth. I don't know what you're going to tell them. I can't tell them anything. I don't know; I wasn't there.' So that was wonderful because those pieces helped at the trial.

"By repeating those words over and over again, I was able to spit that out when the lawyer was giving me a bad time about being this grandmother who wanted to take the children." Her voice gets loud and shrill. "I said, 'Ha! At fifty-eight! My retirement? This is what I *want*? Two disturbed children? Like hell!" Her voice levels off. "But keep them safe? Yes! I *do* want them for that reason.

"Susan was wonderful with her. She used the teddy bears and was able to examine Chrissie. She explained how she helps children who have been hurt to get in a safe place, but she has to look and be sure. She said . . ." Elisabeth's voice slows down and softens as if speaking to a child, "'. . . But Christine, I hate to tell you this, but it's only a picture of your bottom that will make a judge pay attention. We have to shock the judge in order to get any attention.

Healing the Wounds

I've been working at this a long time, and my heart's been totally broken at the children that are turned back. So I've learned that that's how much evidence you need.'

"Dr. White took pictures of her bottom, her bruises, and her vagina that was so stretched and hurt! Then she left us to call the DA, screaming and hollering—I heard her from down the hall! 'What the hell is going on here? How long is this going to go on? Do you realize how long these children have been raped?' That's how the SAIN team came on board.

"And still . . . still Craig wouldn't talk. Christine told Dr. White that her father hurt her. It was the first time it was totally documented. That's how we got visits to be supervised."

"They still had to go . . . and they would get sick every time, saying, 'We can't go, I've got a stomachache!' But the court still made them go. My grandson wasn't talking, so they still didn't have enough."

"Enough for *what*?" I ask, shocked and confused.

"Enough to hold up in court for a court case of abuse. Because Craig had denied everything in front of that SAIN team. He said that Christine was lying. So it was just this little girl's word against the father's, and they said it would never hold up. And it was too horrendous a case to risk losing. They felt he would kill them— *kill them*—if he had them much longer. And if they failed, and he got visitation . . . Christine, they said, was very close to being murdered, she had been hurt so badly. And Craig was beginning to be raped as a punishment because he couldn't get his mother to go back; he couldn't get people off his father's back. So he was beginning to do a wicked number on him. He had always hurt him, 'pulled on his pee-pee,' he said, but now . . . he was on the verge of insanity, my grandson.

"Some of the things they told me, I couldn't even bear. I cried myself to sleep. But I couldn't cry in front of them because . . . The first time they told me . . . something so horrendous . . . the tears started coming to my eyes and coming down my cheeks, and my granddaughter said, 'Oh, Nana! It's okay, Nana. We're going to be okay, Nana.' She literally comforted me, and Craig just clammed right up. I learned that I couldn't show my emotions. When they told me something, I had to try to pretend that this was something I heard all the time." She laughs a little through her tears at the absurdity of it.

"Then my grandson started a little bit. I said to him, 'Craig, I know it's there. And I can't push you to talk.' He would start getting hysterical like my daughter would." Elisabeth drops her voice down low, slow and soothing, ". . . when you can, you will. When you want to be safe, you will. We know you've been threatened. It's okay, Craig. I'm not going to put pressure on you.' So I would just spoon-feed him that, and then I'd lay off.

"What I would do is play these spiritual tapes for him at night. 'When I was lost and all alone, you were there to put your arms around me.' And hope that they began to see that maybe there was a God, and there was hope.'

"I had put up a poster in their room of a butterfly, and it said, 'Setting You Free.' I truly regret that they did not give my grandson medication to keep him calm during that time. But what I did have was my spiritual tapes, tapes that my friends would send me: 'When it was black and dark, I cried with you. I was there in the darkness with you, but I am going to send the light.'

"At first they would be angry. 'I don't want to listen to that! Where is He? He's not here!'

Healing the Wounds

I would tell them that I understood that, and it's okay to be angry—that He got angry! He says in the Bible, 'If you hurt a hair on a child's head, I will be stinking mad! I'll take care of those kinds of parents!' And they listened.

"These tapes are what I think kept the children going. And kept me going too. That's how we go to sleep at night. They couldn't close their eyes. They'd scream in the dark. I had to sleep in the room with them until they got to sleep, and their bedroom had to be next to mine; there had to be a light on. It was awful! At that point there was no social life for me whatsoever. And the interesting piece was, I didn't even care!

"It was homework, or I would lie in bed reading them stories. Anything to get their minds on something that a child's mind should be on. I always had a friend over for Christine and a friend in for Craig. They were so fragile. They would fight with each other, bickering. I constantly worked at keeping them calm, keeping the house quiet. I worked *overtime* at it.

"My grandson was a fabulous baseball player. What he was doing was getting the rage out with the baseball. He could pitch a ball so fast when he was in Little League that every coach in town wanted him. He would say things like he could picture his father's face on the pitcher's mitt. Wham!" Elisabeth's mischievous Irish laugh peels out. "That ball would come slamming in, and he would get cheers from everybody! But, they wouldn't know.

"I kept begging the DSS worker, would they please stop doing this to them, making them see their father? And she literally said, 'Until Craig decides to talk, I'm sorry, there's nothing we can do.'

"All of a sudden, Craig started saying some things to me, but then he wouldn't repeat it. He'd say, 'You really know what's going on, Nana. I know you do.' But then he'd back off again and deny.

"At the Christmas visit they were supposed to have, Thomas came laden with gifts. We happened to look out the window and saw him. I guess because it was Christmas, the DSS worker had a tender heart and asked Craig and Chrissie if they wanted to see him. Craig said, 'No! You mean I don't have to? Please, please don't make me see him!' She really felt bad, so she said, 'Okay. I think I can tell the judge that.' So she took us down the back way. Craig was ahead of me. He saw his father coming in and went screaming back up the stairs. 'Oh my God, oh my God, there he is! Don't let him see me!' He didn't want the gifts. He didn't want any part of the man. We went around the other part of the building, and we ran, literally, to our car to leave. And I saw her still looking out the window at their behavior, running for the car like two terrified little animals.

"We had to go see the DSS worker in January. On the way down, Craig asked me, 'Could a judge make me go with my father if we go back to court, Nana?' I said, I'm afraid I don't know that. You never know. You're denying it, so his lawyer can say Nana's lying. We can only try to keep you safe the best way we know how. But judges are crazy. I can't promise that won't happen.' I *didn't* say I'd run from the country before I'd let that happen—I'd go underground. I didn't say that because at this point it sounded to me like he was doing a lot of heavy thinking—and he was.

"We had given him enough safety time now. He had six months of being here, with only supervised visits. He wasn't being raped. He found a safe place. He saw we were fighting for him. He saw people around me that were plugging for him—strong people, caring people. People that didn't want anything to happen to these children or children like them.

"In church on Sunday, he would hear things from these wonderful people from the Community of God's Light. Saying things like, is there anything they can do to help. Playing certain songs that they knew the children liked. They always really put themselves out. And these children knew it. When they were in that liturgy, they knew the liturgy was literally for them. By the things that priest would say gently, not calling attention to them, not embarrassing them, but by praying for justice or by praying for abused children in the world, these kids got the message, strong and clear, that all those people were behind them.

"It took six months of not being with him [his father], and that January he said to me in the car, 'Nana, I know you know he did touch me. Who do I have to tell? Do I have to tell Jane [his therapist]? Will that make me safe?'

"So they had another SAIN meeting. After that, we got the visitation completely stopped. But even then, when you expected something to happen . . . like you'd tell the DA's office—nothing happened. They questioned Craig . . . nothing happened. Nothing was ever happening. When we got to court, we stopped visitation— that's all we got!"

"Did you ask for more?"

"Right. We asked for permanent custody. Nothing ever went anywhere in Massachusetts. Couldn't figure it out, couldn't figure it out," she mutters.

"There was an incident that turned the tide with Craig. Maryann was caring for her mother who had Alzheimer's. She would bring her here because Maryann needed to be helping me. Her mother would be sitting there staring . . . she couldn't see me or Maryann . . . this is Alzheimer's disease, advanced stages . . . but yet, when Christine or Craig would come into the room . . . Christine would bounce into the room and tell her friends, 'Oh, Josephine is here. Come and meet Josephine and watch what she can do. Here, Josephine, put the peg into the pegboard.' And Josephine would put the peg into the pegboard. We couldn't get her to do anything! But this was a woman who always loved children, and in the deep throes of this demoralizing degenerative brain disease, this woman somehow became aware that there was a child in the room. When there was a child in the room, she would turn her head and look at the child, and sometimes she smiled.

"The day that she died, I couldn't get anybody to babysit Craig. I said to him, 'I have to bring you with me. It's not something to be frightened of. I'm going to bring you movies to watch upstairs. You do not have to be down there, but Maryann's mother is dying and is going to die today. I need to be with Maryann.' I was so afraid it was going to traumatize him.

"But Maryann's whole attitude was so incredibly intelligent and compassionate—loving, loving—that the whole dying process was not a frightening thing. The day that she died, he came downstairs literally as she was dying. Right before she died, she opened her eyes. The hospice nurse was looking into her eyes with the flashlight and saying to Maryann, there is no recognition, she is unconscious, and she was giving this whole medical spiel. Maryann and I were looking at each other, and I turned my head. I saw this little boy come into the room and stand at the bottom of the bed. And all of a sudden her eyes went down to the foot of the bed and stayed . . . she was looking at Craig. And Maryann said, 'My God! She knows Craig's here!' She was looking right at this boy."

Healing the Wounds

Both of our eyes have filled with tears. I place my elbows on the table and bring my fists up to my cheeks to try and control the urge to cry. Elisabeth catches her breath, weeping as she continues, "Maryann said, 'Craig, this very day my mother is going to bring you in her heart to Heaven, and God is going to know who you are.' And then she died. And he wasn't frightened. He didn't run." She sobs once and gulps a big breath. "He stayed there. He just held her hand . . . and we hugged each other.

"The next day he told the therapist that he was going to have help with his problems. That was one of the turning points that gave him strength to start talking.

"The other turning point was when, out of the blue, two calls came in one day. It was a DSS worker who said, 'I can't believe all the 51As that we have up here. We are horrified! We just came across this case. Are you still dealing with Mr. Connor?' I said, 'Oh my God, are we!' She said, 'Oh dear! Well, I have a detective here that wants to know if he can help you, Detective Robert O'Hara.'"

Elisabeth tells me that at that time she was also caring for an uncle who was dying of cancer. She says that her strong faith came from the Irish side of her family. Her uncles all "did rosary beads even though they were all big tough guys." She says that he was a "godsend here," even though it added to her workload. He kept the children busy and entertained. "It became a gift to have him, believe it or not." And when she got a call from this Irish detective she started crying, she tells me, laughing out loud, her round eyes crinkling, twinkling. "That's my Irish side. That's my grandmother in Heaven. Hooray!" She raises her fist in salute. "I told Detective O'Hara, 'You better get down here PDQ!'" and she laughs again, shaking her head in wonderment.

"I told him where we were so far in Massachusetts, and he couldn't believe that it had taken that long. He said, 'I really would like to gather some more evidence and get this bugger if we can.' So he came to the therapist's that day and met Craig in the office. He sat there talking to Craig, and he kind of let his coat fall open—it was marvelous the way he did it—and he had a gun in his holster. He said, 'Craig, I am here to help you if you want me to. I hear that you had a really hard time, and so far things aren't where you'd like to see them. Would you let me help you?'

"Craig was looking at the gun with big wide and eyes and said, 'Yeah! Yeah! You sure can!' Detective O'Hara said, 'I've asked your therapist if I can go in with you today if it's okay with you.' They made a tape that day. Craig came out with a lot of things that day."

Elisabeth pauses again, remembering. She is looking down at the table, her mouth turned down, her shoulders sagging. She takes a while before continuing slowly. "Then he asked me the loaded question, 'Did the father ever touch Christine at his sister's house in New Hampshire?' I said, 'I don't know.'" It comes out like a desperate wail.

"He said, 'When you go home, ask that question. Because I don't want to bother with this Alan case. It's too important to rescue them from their father. That's too big. Alan is way down on the list now.' He told me that under New Hampshire law, you have to have dates.

"I'm going, 'Oh my God! How are we going to get a date when it was going on all the time?'" Elisabeth wails again, her tone high pitched and desperate. "Maryann said, 'Oh pfft. We'll get dates! For God's sake, those kids always came back after birthdays and holidays. Don't worry; we're going to nail him. You watch and see. You just ask Craig if he can remember a birthday.'"

Healing the Wounds

Elisabeth leans in toward me, bending her shoulders down low over the table, her eyes boring into mine, and says, "Alan's birthday was on March seventeenth." She continues on in a whisper, hissing out the words as if they burned her lips as they left her mouth, "*Christmasss . . . Christmasss . . .*," a long pause and she breathes out slowly. "If you can abuse a child on Christmas . . . Oh . . . God . . .

"Those were the two dates that got him a guilty verdict," Elisabeth says finally, limp, drained.

But meanwhile there were complications and barriers in the way. Elisabeth tells me that when she and Maryann brought the chronology to New Hampshire, they felt there still wasn't enough evidence. "I don't understand," I say. "If they have both children telling the same story and you have a chronology and doctor's photos . . ."

"No, no they didn't. That was in Massachusetts. The medical records in New Hampshire were weak in comparison to Dr. Susan White's."

"And they couldn't use any information garnered in Massachusetts?" I ask.

"Nothing from Massachusetts! But they decided to go with what they had, which was Craig's say-so of what happened at the sister's house. Christine fell apart on the stand and couldn't be a witness, even though she had been the one talking all along. Craig was now able to speak up. He got empowered by Robert O'Hara and the wonderful victims' advocate up there, Jay Sanders; he was a saint in all this."

Children who are sexual abuse survivors battle so many conflicting emotions. They feel responsible in some way for the abuse, but helpless to stop it. It destroys their self-esteem. For Craig, the day his father was convicted may have been the first time he felt validated and safe.

Because many grandchildren in the care of grandparents may have been abused, grandparents need to be very aware of all the issues that arise for children who are survivors of abuse. Some psychological and emotional effects for children who have been physically or sexually abused are difficulty trusting adults; insomnia, restlessness at night, nightmares, or night terrors; acting out abuse on dolls, animals, or even other children; a preoccupation with body parts and body functions; a preoccupation with their appearance; eating disorders; and problems with self-image, self-esteem, self-worth, and shame.

For grandparents, awareness that these are typical reactions to devastating circumstances will help them understand the child's behavior. Obviously it is critical that grandchildren receive the appropriate treatment and counseling. It is also important for grandparents to receive counseling or support to address their feelings of rage and shock. Sorting out their feelings will make them stronger, more helpful caregivers.

"So he was convicted?" I ask, wanting to be sure.

"He got put immediately in jail that day."

Thomas Connor spent forty days in jail. He appealed. The judge threw out nearly every piece of evidence except for Craig's testimony. A fund-raiser was held for Thomas Connor in his hometown.

The case in Massachusetts had been pending, with continuance after continuance for five years. The Parks family eventually accepted a plea bargain; they finally called it quits. Elisabeth explained that the children had already been through so much she couldn't justify continuing on for an uncertain outcome. It was time to move on, pick up the pieces, and try to heal the wounds. Thomas Connor never spent another day in jail. There are those in this charming, lakeside community who still believe he is innocent and that Elisabeth Parks is just another crazy woman.

> Forgiveness is a two-way street. Grandparents need to forgive their child, and they need to forgive themselves as well; they need to acknowledge what they are unable to do—stop their child's destructive behavior.
>
> Therapy, support groups, and a compassionate ear are all vital tools that can allow grandparents the opportunity to find their path to healing. All of us have times when we need a nonjudgmental, unbiased, non-family member whom we can trust and who will help us help ourselves, someone who is on our side. That is what therapy is all about.
>
> Many people fear therapy or feel that by seeing a therapist they are admitting weakness. This is definitely not the case. Admitting you need help and taking the initiative to find that help demonstrates strength. We all have to recognize we have pain and disappointment that needs healing. For grandchildren to begin their journey toward healing, grandparents need to begin the healing journey first.

FIVE

Integrating the Birth Parents

Dear Lord . . .
patch this work. Quilt us
together, feather-stitching piece
by piece our tag-ends of living,
our individual scraps of love.

—Jane Wilson Joyce, "Crazy Quilt"

"Once upon a time, your birth mommy had a baby growing in her tummy (because that's where babies grow before they're born, in their mommy's tummy). And she said to me, 'You know, I really love this baby, but even though I can do some things really well, like write stories and sing songs, I just don't know how to take care of a baby.' So, I said to your birth mommy, 'Guess what! I really love this baby too, and I do know how to take care of a baby, so when this baby is born, she can be mine!' And she said, 'That's a good idea!'"

My little girl beamed when I told her this story. She called it "my baby story." We told it at bedtime when we snuggled together, and when I got to the end, I'd say, "And who is that baby?" and she said happily, "Me!"

She was three years old when I put together the facts of her birth in what I hoped would be an age-appropriate and positive way. But it wasn't the first step I had made to try to integrate her birth parents in a meaningful way into her life. After she was born, I made a concerted effort to welcome her birth father as well into the family. When she was christened at three months of age, I asked the birth father to be godfather. This gave him a role, a position at a time when he felt like the odd man out. From infancy on, he and his family have been a positive and loving part of her life. We encouraged and supported open-ended visitation. In fact, I always say that I consider that the situation we have is a very, *very* "open adoption." It is not always easy to accommodate the needs of all the individuals in a large and super-extended family, but I think the end results make the effort well worthwhile. I feel that a child cannot have too much love in her life, and anything we can do to strengthen loving family ties can only be of benefit. We have been fortunate in having a wonderful group of people to work with who all have her best interests at heart. Over the years, we have not always been in total agreement and have suffered some growing pains, but in the end we are—all of us—here for her 100 percent.

Although physically including all the players in her life seemed like the natural and right thing to do, confronting the obligation to explain the facts to her hadn't surfaced yet; she was only three. Both my older daughters had been living at home with us. Her birth mom was attending the Boston Conservatory of Music, and my other daughter was taking some time to work before entering college. One icy January, they both left home—my eldest, Chicago bound to try her hand at playwriting and singing professionally, the other, for Westfield State College in the western end of Massachusetts. My little one took it hard. And it threw me for a loop.

Integrating the Birth Parents

She began to have "accidents" night and day. Every day when I picked her up from nursery school, I was handed a plastic bag full of sodden pants, socks, panties, and sometimes even shoes, and a child with a badly mismatched outfit.

To make matters worse, she wouldn't speak to either of them on the phone. I encouraged both my girls to send her little notes and trinkets by mail. But trying to maintain bonds long distance is a frustrating job. Although the effort was important, the results were feeble at best.

I knew something more was needed. I began to have talks with her at night, when the house was quiet and there were no distractions, just the two of us cuddling together. Talks about her birth mother and her "sister." Talks about when they would be coming home and reassurances that *I* would stay. One night I started, "Once upon a time . . ." She became so still and intent; her green eyes grew larger and larger. I knew I was onto something.

A narrative such as the one I finally fashioned can be a valuable tool for beginning the road to healing, for breaking down complex facts into digestible components, and ultimately for initiating the process of fully integrating birth parents into the lives of grandchildren.

I hadn't as yet focused attention on explaining facts to our little one because she was so young and because everyone was *there* for her. It was easy to take that for granted, and we were not prepared for such a powerfully negative reaction when her family situation altered. Her birth mother, even though her role was as more of a sister, was very much a part of her life. When both she and my other daughter left simultaneously, I was astonished and horrified at how deeply she felt the loss. It made poignantly clear to me that she had abandonment issues, and no matter how well we think we have at least tried to handle things, she will always have those issues, and we will always have to help her deal with them.

I have been aware from the beginning of the need to nurture all the relationships at hand. We had always referred to her "birth parents" long before the term would have any real meaning for her because I felt that it would serve to make the transition to other details smoother. I believe it's important to begin in small ways such as these, laying the foundation for the gradual inclusion of more and weightier information.

I was, however, drifting along at that time, blissfully unfocused on the way in which we would actually begin to explain the complexities of interfamily connections to her. Events, as frequently happens, forced us to come to grips with her need to know. She *required* information to deal with issues relating to loss and abandonment, and issues relating to her place in the family.

One of the ways in which grandparents can show a grandchild in a tangible way how important her place is in the family is to keep a journal that would include her baby story, a family tree (this will come up in elementary school, so you'll be ahead of the game), and events and milestones large and small, such as the first time she walked or talked. Talk about how wanted she is and how happy you are to have her with you. A book I recommend for reading to children that have had a tenuous start is *On the Day You Were Born*, by Debra Frasier. It is a book about each child's importance in his own family as well as the family of humanity and nature. The last page reads, "'Welcome to the green Earth,' the people sang. And as they held you close they whispered into your open, curving ear, '*We are so glad you've come!*'"

The story I created obviously was a story designed for a very young child. It was a story that was added to and expanded as she grew older until it became not just a story, but the background of her life—her reality. I like to believe it was a solid background.

One of the mistakes I made as we struggled to make our inter-family adoption work was trying to force a relationship between birth mother and child. I was impatient and controlling. There is a wobbly line between encouraging and controlling, and I often fall down on the wrong side of it. I have learned to release—and am still learning—to let what comes naturally come and not press for more or for something different. They love each other, and they have worked out a relationship between them that defies labels. That's all right. It is enough that they are both content in their hearts when together.

Within the parameters of establishing and/or maintaining a bond between birth parent and child are definite lines that must be drawn. Roles that may have, of necessity, shifted or been replaced altogether must be clearly defined and firmly reinforced. When grandparents accept the parent role in grandchildren's lives, it is important to maintain that role with consistency, particularly in the presence of a birth parent who has, for whatever reason, relinquished that role. Grandparents must learn to say no to the birth parent and say it with confidence and authority. Adult children have to learn to accept the new boundaries, whether temporary or permanent. It is a step they must take before they can connect with their children in a positive and constructive way. If they cannot, it may leave grandchildren open to torn loyalties and confusion.

One of the most difficult circumstances for grandparents is when adult children continue to behave in ways that are disruptive and destructive for the grandchildren. Occasionally, under extreme circumstances, grandparents must let the grown child go to fully protect their grandchild. It is one of the most painful choices grandparents are sometimes forced to make. It comes down to this: Solomon-like, one must weigh the needs of the grandchild against the needs of the adult child. On one hand you have a youngster who is vulnerable, impressionable, and helpless without you, and on the other hand, you have an adult child, frequently needy as well, but for whom you have already done your best and who is old enough to make decisions and choices, who has had his or her chance at life. The decision is wrenching but clear: your grandchild must have *their* chance now. Luckily, I never had to make that desperate choice; sadly, others do.

Under those conditions, it is critical for grandparents to have a palatable explanation for their grandchildren—one that faces facts squarely but gently and leaves room for hope for better days to come. Integrating the birth parent is always an essential part of rearing healthy grandchildren under any circumstances, perhaps especially under those most dire. And if the only means for doing that at your disposal are effective narratives, then make certain that the facts you present neither glorify nor vilify birth parents, but present the facts in a way that makes your grandchildren comfortable with their heritage.

Hopefully most of us will never have to face choosing between grandchild and adult child. Most of us need only to find ways to either maintain or reenergize the bond between birth parent and child. Sometimes doing that means dealing with or putting aside our own anger and disappointments. Frequently, to achieve that, counseling may be the best course of action, but however one goes about coping with bad feelings toward birth parents, it is another essential step toward integrating birth parents and raising whole grandchildren.

Integrating the Birth Parents

For the sake of the child. Let that be your mantra if it is the only way you can get through it: *For the sake of the child.*

ANN

Ann Leonardi, petite and trim as a girl at fifty-three, lives with her grandsons—Douglas, six, and Brad, five—in a sprawling multi-level home in an oceanside community at the northern corner of the state. She sits primly, the tips of her very short dark hair barely brushing the navy blue frames that set off her baby-doll eyes. She is wearing a crisp white shirt that makes the freckles running up her arms and under the rolled-up cuffs stand out like cinnamon sprinkles. She tells me her story in a matter-of-fact, nearly businesslike way.

Her grandsons came to live with her and her husband a couple of years ago. Their son, Nick, discovered them at the home of his estranged wife being looked after by three strange men—"druggies"—and delivered the children to his parents. Ann and her husband, Joseph, acquired temporary legal custody of the boys immediately.

Both parents went into rehab. "I thought she was getting her act together," Ann recalls. "I thought that my son was getting his act together, but as it turned out, she left rehab and started living with another man." Ann's son came to her home to live. "It worked out okay for about three months. He was really good about paying attention to the kids, and then I could see him backsliding. He wanted to get custody of his children back. He wanted to live here, have custody of his children, have me do all the work, and be able to call the shots. And I said that's just not going to happen. So we went to court and we had a custody battle over it. I got custody of the kids, and I asked him to move out because he was drinking, he was not working, he was not showing up when he said he would show up to be with the kids, and then he started gambling."

Meanwhile, Ann explains, the children's birth mother "had gotten into a pattern of calling me and saying, 'Can I come see the kids tomorrow?' and I would say, 'Yes, come at two o'clock.' Well, fortunately, I never told the kids Mom was coming at two o'clock, because Mom wouldn't show up. I never told them until she rang the doorbell; I just handled it like a big surprise. I didn't want them to be disappointed when she didn't come." She would call, make excuses, and then make subsequent appointments that she would not keep. "It was bad enough when she did come and she left. I mean, she would come and spend an hour and be like . . . ," Ann snatches furtive, nervous glances at her watch to illustrate. "'Let's hurry up and do this. Mommy's got to go quick.' And she'd leave them crying. Well, you know how hard it is for kids to separate from their mother." Soon their birth mom stopped coming altogether.

At that same time, the Leonardis' marriage began to disintegrate. Joseph didn't want to raise children again. "He loves them," she shrugs, "but he didn't want them here. He didn't want them in a foster home, but he didn't want them here. He didn't know what he wanted. We always had some problems." That was the wedge that finally drove them apart.

Ann's family situation, as well as her grandsons', had unraveled, and it was up to her to begin to try to knit them all back together as best as she could. Ann's son never severed contact with the boys; he remains bonded to them and visits them regularly and consistently. While his destructive behavior is a source of pain to Ann, she must put her feelings aside to allow her son and grandsons the freedom to remain connected. She has developed a "hands-off" approach to their relationship and his parenting style. That "hands-off" approach can be a difficult one to manage and requires constant maintenance. Weighing when to make suggestions while trying not to be controlling is tricky at best. But, to her credit, Ann feels that she needs to do what she can to allow their relationship to flower without her constant vigilance. While working at all of that, she also works at pointing out to her grandsons which behaviors are acceptable and which are not, an important aspect of raising a grandchild with troubled birth parents. She never denigrates Nick, but rather explains inappropriate behaviors.

She tells me that the boys' relationship with their father "improved since he moved out," but that he "had some not so great things to say about me—that I was this or that because I threw him out. The boys brought it up to me. 'Mimi, Daddy says you're blankety-blank because you threw him out.' And I have to correct them, 'Daddy needed to go live by himself so he could learn to be responsible for himself, so that maybe someday he can be a very good parent.'" Once they asked Ann, "Mimi, when we get to be Daddy's age, are you going to throw us out?" She told them, "'No, honey, you can live with Mimi as long as you want, as long as you follow the rules.' I just let them know that there are expectations."

Most grandparents can expect that, at some point, their grandchildren will test them to some degree. This testing I call "the necessary test," necessary in that these children will feel that they must find out if they will be asked to leave or be removed from their grandparents' care. They will force the caregiver to prove that the child will be kept no matter what. Most times, this testing shows itself through verbal challenges and annoying and manipulative behaviors. Children expect that if they are "good," well behaved and polite, they will be loved and kept. However, they need to know that if they are moody, naughty, or willful, you will still want them around and love them. Children know that it is easy to love someone who is perfect, but they need to know that you will love and accept them, imperfections and all. Being aware of this and expecting the "necessary test" will help you to understand and move through the trying times.

Ann continues, "Even when they've said Daddy said this or that, it's always, 'Well, that wasn't very nice of Daddy.' Or, 'Daddy shouldn't have said that.' I can think what I want, but they need to be taught that there is another way to deal with situations; they don't need to hear the verbal abuse."

This is a very challenging situation to say the least. But Ann is committed to encouraging and supporting the boys' relationship with their father. Their connections with their birth mother, however, are fractured, and Ann has not attempted to put those pieces together. Her face tightens up each time the subject of her daughter-in-law comes up.

"My basic explanation is that 'Mommy's real sick. And Mommy has to stay with the doctors and nurses so she can get better, until she's able to take care of you.'"

Ann believes their birth mother will either end up in jail or dead from drugs. She has heard that the birth mother is "looking to give away" the two children she has had since losing custody of Douglas and Brad.

"I know she is their birth mother, and I know that when they are grown they are going to want to see her, but not now. I have always told them, 'Your Mommy does love you, but she just can't take care of you right now; she's just not well enough.'"

Integrating the Birth Parents

Regardless of when or why the separation occurs, and under what circumstances, children will feel the loss of the birth parent very intensely and very deeply. And, at some very basic level, children will feel like they were not good enough, not good enough to be parented or good enough to be kept. Grandparents will need to provide an environment that allows for and encourages the children to discuss their feelings of disappointment and loss. To do this, grandparents will need to model for their grandchildren that it is good to talk about feelings, and the way to do that is for the grandparents to talk about their sadness and hurts. Grandparents should provide opportunities for quiet time when the sharing can occur. All children look for cues and leads from caregivers as to how and when to express feelings. They need guidance and support to learn how to share their feelings, particularly around abandonment issues.

Ann tells me that although the birth mother "never really bonded" with her younger son, Brad, Douglas was very tied to her. She thinks the reason Douglas has trouble going to sleep at night is because he misses his mother. "I was looking through some pictures the other day, and I found some of him. I could see the sadness in his eyes."

She is also in the position of maintaining a relationship with her ex-husband, their grandfather. "He has never called me on the phone and said, 'Can I see the boys?' I have to take the boys to him. And I do that simply because the boys need to know this is their grandfather, and they need to have a relationship with him."

I point out to her that she makes the effort to take the boys to their grandfather but does not make the same effort to take the boys to their birth mother.

"No, I don't," Ann replies slowly, thoughtfully, "simply because her lifestyle has not changed at all. And now she has two babies. In fact, I don't even know where she's living. But it would only break their hearts to see her with other children."

Ann is probably right, but it sounds as if Douglas's heart is already wounded. She needs to make more of an effort to include his birth mom in his life in some meaningful way. I ask if he has a picture of his mother and suggest that she place a framed photo at his bedside and say a few soft and kind things about her at night before the boys go to sleep, words to have sweet dreams by.

> Group support for children who have experienced abandonment or separation is an excellent resource. They will encounter, probably for the first time, that they are not alone, that other children have experienced similar losses too. This can be a very healing revelation for children at any age.

Ann has a lot to deal with—her son, her grandsons, her ex-husband—she has few emotional reserves for dealing with the added burden of maintaining a positive link with a birth mother that she dislikes. She must dig deep to tap into the forgiveness that will enable her to help her grandsons heal fully.

PART THREE OF THE
PARKS FAMILY TRILOGY

Marion Parks Connor

In the Parks' case, Ben and Elisabeth's daughter, Marion, often rankles at the pressure her mother Elisabeth applies. Elisabeth

Integrating the Birth Parents

Parks hasn't gotten the hang of "hands off," and it may be that in her case, more vigilance is required; it's hard to say. They still constantly bump up against one another—Elisabeth trying to get Marion to be more of a "mother," and Marion trying to find her own speed.

Marion's story, like Ben and Elisabeth's, contains many explosive elements. She was a battered woman and a substance abuser, which made her an unwitting accomplice to her children's abuse. She cannot forgive herself for that, and the turmoil she lives with because of it sometimes threatens to consume her. But Marion loves her children and is constantly trying to overcome the guilt and pain that get in the way of her relationship with them.

While obviously a relationship with their father was out of the question, Marion's children needed to be reintroduced to her once she became clean and sober. The bonds needed to be reestablished and cultivated. Elisabeth had already laid the groundwork for their re-bonding by talking to the children about their mother as a victim, her substance abuse as a sickness, and explaining her behavior to them in ways they could understand and forgive.

Marion's story is the conclusion of the Parks family trilogy. It gives us new perspectives—that of the rebellious daughter, the birth parent, the battered woman, the alcoholic and drug addict— and brings us full circle. "How could this happen?" Marion asks of me during the interview. Perhaps accompanying Marion down the dark path she took will give us some answers to that question.

Marion is a striking young woman, tall and slim with startlingly blue eyes and an enormous, infectious smile. She answers the door of her oceanside condo on this damp fall morning dressed in a turtleneck top, shorts, and sneakers. Her legs are long, tanned, and muscular—runner's legs. Her dark hair is drawn up into a ponytail. She has the slouch that some very tall girls develop in adolescence, trying to look shorter, trying to fit in.

Marion and her son Craig look remarkably alike—the piercing blue eyes, dark hair, and height. But while Marion's face is tanned dark and strongly angular, Craig's is fair and fine boned. I ask her to talk a little bit about her adolescence, the time when she first met the man that would become her abuser, and ultimately their children's tormentor. I am searching for clues, a blueprint for disaster that we can study and learn to avoid, a flowchart of flaws.

She folds herself into an easy chair near the Palladian windows in her living room. There is a golden woodsy stretch beyond. I remark about the lovely setting, and she tells me she likes it here; she likes the quiet. Marion is only a little wary, a little hesitant and nervous as she begins to talk about how it all began.

"I was in high school when I met Thomas. Wow, I haven't thought of all this for so long. It's not very pleasant memories for me, for one thing. And a lot of it I've blocked out." She swings her open hands up, slicing the air at the sides of her head. "A lot of it!"

"Actually, I met him at a party that my brothers were having. My parents used to go camping on the weekend, and I used to go with them all the time and my brothers would always stay home. I remember begging my mother and father, 'Please let me stay home,' because I knew they were having a party." Marion was fourteen years old. One brother was a senior in high school, the other a junior.

"I remember my mother letting me stay home, telling my brothers that they were responsible for me. Of course, they didn't really care what I did. They kept an eye on me, but they were having a party. And that's where I met Thomas Connor.

"I can just remember thinking, 'This guy is actually paying attention to me!' And his family was very popular. All the boys in that family played football; they were all wicked good athletes. I just couldn't understand how come they were paying attention to me, because I really had very low self-esteem.

"At that party I drank. My brothers didn't know that I was drinking. I felt like one of the big kids, you know. I just liked him the minute I met him. He was very funny, he was paying attention to me, and once he paid attention to me, all his brothers paid attention to me. And it was like this really big deal! And I thought that I was crazy about him. Now I realize I was just a kid with a crush.

"So I continued to see him behind my mother's back. I thought that he had just graduated and was maybe a year older than my oldest brother. I didn't have a clue how old he was. He told me he was seventeen, and I believed him. Because when you're fourteen, somebody seventeen is like all grown up. I didn't have a clue he was twenty-two years old.

"I snuck around for a long time. Then I went to a football game . . . begged my mother to let me go. His family was going, and by this point I knew all his sisters in school. Once they knew that he liked me, they became friends with me. His sisters were older, but I played sports with them. All of a sudden they just started paying attention to me and being nice to me and telling me that Thomas liked me, and I got to be really close with them.

"The football team was playing down at Martha's Vineyard, and the whole school was going and they were all going to stay overnight in a hotel. I begged my mother, 'Please let me go!'

"When I went away to that football game, he came, and all his brothers came. I just remember that every single time I was with him, he would always buy me booze. Back then I didn't think anything of it. But today I look at it and think, I never knew him without drinking, ever! I never sat and had a conversation with the guy without him buying me beer, or smoking dope. I think that's when I got pregnant. I do not remember it. It was a complete blackout most of the time I was there because it was all drinking the whole time. Of course I hid it from Mrs. Connor. She was supposed to be watching me. The only reason my mother let me go was because all the girls were going, the Connor girls. And Mrs. Connor was going, and she said she would be responsible for me. Well, of course I snuck out! It wasn't her fault. I don't blame anybody.

"I don't remember exactly where we were, but everybody was drinking. That's all I remember, except that I have a brief flashback of getting out of bed in a hotel room—out of Thomas's bed, and there were a whole bunch of people sleeping around us—and sneaking back to my room, praying that Mrs. Connor wouldn't know that I was sneaking in. She didn't; she was sleeping. I don't even remember having sex with him.

"This is how I found out I was pregnant. I was on the basketball team. I kept getting really sick around Thanksgiving. I kept thinking that I was having appendicitis pains. So here I was playing basketball. My coach kept telling me that it was just aches and pains that I had to work out of my system, and she made me stay an hour after practice and run, run, run and do a thousand sit-ups and a hundred push-ups just to get the pains out.

"My period was really irregular. I think I only got it like once or twice and never got it again. So it was no big deal I didn't get my period. When I didn't have my period for three months, it was no big deal to me. I never in my wildest dreams thought I was pregnant. I didn't even remember having sex for starters.

Integrating the Birth Parents

"I was at home. Everybody was there. It was a Sunday, and I just remember keeling over at the dinner table with pain so bad. My father thought it was an appendicitis attack and took me to the hospital. They did all kinds of exams on me—a pelvic exam, which I had never had before. I'll just never forget I was lying on the bed in the room waiting, waiting it seemed like hours. And a nurse came in and said, 'Are you still here?' and I said, 'I'm just waiting to go home. Can I get dressed?' And she said, "Well, you're pregnant, and the doctor's telling your father now,' and she just closed the curtain and walked out.

"I'll just never forget how devastated and scared to death I was! My father came in and I started crying, and he was crying and just hugged me and said that he would help me through whatever was going to happen and not to worry about it. That's the closest I've ever been to my father. I always loved him to death and strived for his attention, but he was very standoffish, like he couldn't really show affection. I knew he loved me, but he had a really hard time saying 'I love you.' Today it's easier for him—he tells me today—but then he had a hard time with it. Maybe that's why I looked for older people, especially boys. I don't know.

"I remember going home that day, begging my father, 'You can't tell Mom right now.' But he had already told her. I was scared to death. I didn't know what to expect. I got home, and her sisters and everybody were there. When they're all together, they're very Italian; they were crying, and yet they were all excited.

"My mother was trying to get ahold of Thomas and his family because we had to tell them obviously. He had been gone all day with all his friends. I'll never forget it; he was at the brewery in Manchester, New Hampshire. It figures!

"He came with his sister and sat down in the living room. Both of them said, 'Well, you've got to get an abortion.' And I was like, 'Okay.' And I'll never forget agreeing with them and having no idea what I was really saying. Not a clue.

"That night when I went to bed, I was really scared, and my mother got into bed with me. She was really good. Every night she would always come in and talk to us before we went to sleep. I really just loved that part of my life.

"She was hugging me and telling me that she loved me and that we were going to get through this, not to be scared. And I remember repeating, 'I have to get an abortion, Mom.' And she said, 'No. You're not going to get an abortion, Marion. There'll be no abortions in this house. We can talk about, maybe later on, giving the baby up for adoption, or some kind of other options. But no abortions in this house, absolutely not, not under my roof.' And I was like, 'Fine.'

"Anyway, Thomas stuck by me through the whole pregnancy. He brought me clothes, brought me baby stuff. He really put on a show. He said, 'Well, we might as well get married.' Then when we talked about it with my parents, my parents said, 'Oh, no! You're too young. You have to finish school.' Mr. and Mrs. Connor agreed with that even though Thomas had a really good job. For the next year, I lived at home. My mother said, 'In the next eight months, if Thomas proves to us that he's going to be good to you and a good provider, then maybe we'll agree to letting you get married.' Craig was about nine months old when I finally did get married.

"To me marriage was just the wedding; it was going to be a big party. I had no clue what I was getting myself into, and I thought I was in love with him. I really wasn't when I think about it now; it was just the whole glamorization of having my own house, and friends could come over, and I'm going to get away from my mother. Because now, once I had the baby, me and my mother started clashing. A lot of it had to do with the fact that I was into drinking. I was really resentful that I had a baby. I didn't know that then; I realize it now. I was very headstrong. I knew everything; my mother knew nothing. She was telling me that I had to finish school. I didn't want to go to school. So it was a constant butting of heads." Marion slaps her fist into her palm over and over again.

"My sister Joanie was a baby, and my mother got really sick with bursitis in both arms, and she told me I had to stay home from school and take care of Craig. This one day I really wanted to go to school because—this is how selfish I was at the time—I had gone to the beach with my girlfriends and got really tanned, and that was such a big thing. It was all about how I looked on the out-side. I guess when you're a teenager, that's what you go through.

"My mother had a hard time with that, the way I dressed. She was constantly picking at the way I dressed, constantly about the way I looked. She never, ever said a thing to my brothers, but it was always me and Charlene [her younger sister], about the way we dressed, the tight jeans. She used to say to me, 'You already got pregnant. Why do you have to dress like that?' It was a constant butting of the heads every step of the way." Marion strikes her palm with her fist again.

The struggle for teenagers between trying to separate and be-come a responsible young adult and the desperate vulnerable need to still be parented is one that usually turns into a battle within the family. The tried-and-true methods of conflict resolu-tion are the best tools for dealing with this stage of development. First, pick your battles well. Learn how to distinguish which battles are worth fighting over, and which are worth letting go of. Make respect an issue worth fighting over, respect for you, and respect for themselves. Make them responsible at home and make them keep their commitments to themselves and others. Give them consequences for their transgressions.

Have realistic expectations, and hopefully your teen will rise to meet them. Make your teen accountable and set consistent, firm, and fair limits, and with luck you will successfully get through the teen experience.

"When I think back today, there were things she was absolutely right about. Because I find myself saying the same things to my kids when I have them here. It's crazy. Back then, I couldn't wait to get out, away from there, be all grown up and have my own place. We did a lot of fighting in those days." Marion displays a sheepish smile. "We've come a long way since then," she adds.

"Anyway, it started when they finally let me get married. Within two weeks," she says, squinting her eyes, pulling memories from their hiding place, "this man who was such a sweetheart turned into a nightmare. My life turned into a nightmare in two weeks. All of a sudden, he said, 'You can't leave this house. I don't want you going over your mother's house all the time.' He just completely turned, started putting my family down."

"The first time he hit me, I can't even remember really. The first year I was married, I just remember going home and sitting on the back step of the house the first time I had a black eye and telling my mother I fell down. My mother sat down on the steps and said, 'Did *he* do this to you?' and I was petrified. Petrified to tell her. Like she was going to hurt *him* in some way." Marion laughs in disbelief at herself.

Integrating the Birth Parents

"In that year he emotionally put me down so much that I felt like I needed him and I needed to protect him. I got into this syndrome that it was my fault that he hit me. As much as it was inside of me that I was afraid of him, I was quite the people pleaser. I look back today and see I was such a people pleaser; I didn't want anybody to think bad of me. I didn't want to do anything to hurt him, because what was his family going to think if my family was mean to him? I loved Mrs. Connor . . . I *loved* her. She was very much like me. Obviously she was being beaten; I never knew that till years later. I don't know what it was about her that I really loved. I still do to this day. And I feel really bad that I can't have a relationship with her. But I can't." Marion's voice softens. "I'm sure she doesn't want to have it with me," she says sadly.

Marion hunches over, her face draws down, and she is working hard at not crying. Her whole body is bent over as if recoiling. She seems to shrink until she is curled into a small question mark. She manages to say, "I still have a hard time talking about this." Her arms are wrapped protectively around her waist, and she rocks forward.

"I don't want you to talk about anything that you don't want to talk about," I tell her. I mean it. I am not there to cause her more pain. In fact, I am amazed she is willing to talk with me at all, to dredge all this pain up to the surface. Whatever she wants to say to me, I consider a gift.

"I don't actually remember a lot. I remember a lot of . . . stuff; I don't remember a lot of Thomas Connor stuff.

"I remember my friend, Cynthia. I am very close with her. She came over to my house all the time. And it's really weird because I didn't talk to her for many years—like a good six years. I just went to a class reunion and rekindled our friendship. We talked a lot. She was really angry, and she said, 'Thomas was very abusive to you verbally, but I had no clue he was hitting you! Why didn't you tell me?' She was really angry about it. 'Another thing I don't understand is why did you stay in it? The first time he ever laid a hand on you, why did you stay there, Mare? I don't understand that!'

"I have another girlfriend that was living the same nightmare out in Las Vegas. And she's like, 'Look at Dawn. She's doing the same thing, and she's staying in it! It's beyond me.' She was furious." Marion relates this story in an angry, disgusted tone. She's either imitating her friend or feeling anger and disgust herself. I can't tell which.

"I said, 'I don't know. You're just a different person, Cyn. I don't know. There was a lot of guilt, and he always made me feel like it was my fault. For one thing, I was in the midst of my alcoholism. I had a lot of other problems. I felt really guilty. I don't know . . . I can't explain why I stayed in.'"

Marion tries to explain it to me now. "I just had a lot of fear. I had nowhere to go. Look at how old I was; I was sixteen or seventeen. I didn't know how I could raise my kids alone. I knew I could go back to my mother's. Every time I did go back to my mother's, we ended up in a big fight. I just wanted . . . freedom . . . from everything. And yet I knew I couldn't truly have it."

Marion's boyfriend, James, comes in, and we are introduced. He seems uncomfortable with me there. Although pleasant, there is an edge of suspicion. He stands sideways several steps from me and does not come over to shake my hand. He leaves quickly after making a few arrangements with Marion.

She continues, "I was actually a little angry at Cynthia. I don't know how come I got mad at her for saying that to me. It was almost as if in my head I was thinking, 'Didn't you know? Couldn't you *help* me?'"

"You were mad at her for not realizing the trouble you were in at the time," I confirm. "Were you mad at other people? Were you mad at your parents?"

"No. Never. Never ever! Because my mother came down to my house. I remember she stood in the door and said, 'Where is he!' She didn't like him at all. That actually made me kind of feel good. It's really weird. She didn't like him, and she wanted to protect me, and I knew that. You know, I held on to that. I almost expected that someday she's going to save me from him.

"She went downstairs and said something to him like, 'How dare you! If I find out that you laid a hand on my daughter, I'll kill you!' My mother told me he said, 'Don't tell me that Ben doesn't slap you around once in a while when you need it!' And my mother almost flipped.

"I always used to get really nervous because my mother could see right through me. I think that's exactly why . . ." Marion seems to be talking to herself, getting some things out that she hasn't talked or thought about for years and discovering a few things along the way. "She could see right through me, and I was dirt. That's how I felt. I was dirt because I smoked pot and drank, and my self-esteem was low. I really didn't like myself much back then. She always confronted me with stuff that I couldn't . . . didn't like to talk about. I was very resentful because I always thought she was trying to run my life. Really she was trying to help me. But I didn't see it. So I got really, really angry with her a lot. She was always right, and she never listened to me or anything that I had to say.

"She stood in the door and said, 'You and I have a big problem, and he's right downstairs!' I didn't know what she was talking about. I was like, 'What?' She shook her head, and she had tears in her eyes and she just left. When Thomas came up, I asked him, 'What did you say to her?' He said, 'Nothin'! Your mother's a pain in the friggin' ass. I don't want her here. I don't want her coming to this house.' He had a big fight with her—told her not to come to the house. That's why she used to stand outside the door.

"She used to come and check up on me all the time. She knew I was smoking pot, and she was worried about the baby." Marion is lost in thought and memories. She sits hunched over with her head down as she talks. At times it appears that she is in conversation with herself alone.

She tells me that Thomas once locked her outside for hours on a screened balcony in the dead of winter. She was barefoot and wearing nothing but a nightgown. "He told me that would teach me. That would teach me." Her head hangs; her voice is low, worn down. "I don't know what it was teaching me.

"I always had people in my house. I hated the way I lived. I lived in this little, tiny, tiny hole in the wall, and I hated it. We always had people there. All his family, all his brothers were there. My friend Cynthia was there. I had no space whatsoever."

"What were the brothers doing there?"

"They would always come over to get away from their house. They were very close. I was very close to Andy. I don't even know if you want to know this stuff."

"That's up to you," I reply.

"His family was real sick. I was really close to Andy. Sometimes I think I married Thomas so I could stay close to Andy. He was in love with me. He used to tell me that all the time.

"How old was he?"

"Two years older than me. He protected me more than anybody did from Thomas. Andy practically lived with us the five
years we were in that house. I ended up sleeping with him . . .
and it was just a way out. I couldn't stand Thomas, but there was
no way out—I really didn't feel like there was any way out of that
whole thing. How could I leave him? How could I hurt everybody? How could I embarrass myself?

"I really feel that if I didn't have Andy to love, I would have
killed myself. I had tried to kill myself lots of times. Andy used to
get really angry. 'How could you do this to me? How could you
do this to Thomas and me?' I was just really hurting. And I think
I would've if Andy wasn't in my life. I would have killed myself."

Marion's pain begins to consume her now. Her face, which had
been animated, is crumpled, ravaged. She's doubled over. Tears
stream and stream down her face as she talks.

"You really felt there was no escape?" I ask her. She's unable to
speak. She merely nods her head. "Even though you had a family
there that you knew was concerned about you, you didn't see that
as an avenue for escape?"

"The Connors had a lot of power over me. I don't know how
come." She chokes out the words. She cries silently and wipes at
her cheeks. "There's too much stuff!" she manages to say through
the tears and pain—suffocating pain.

"Well, let's change the subject then," I offer. "You know I'm
writing a book, and it's about grandparents raising their grandchildren." I speak to her softly. I believe this interview is too much
for her to bear, and I don't want to leave her like this. I want to try
and lift her out of this pain before I go if I can, leave her with some
positive thoughts. "And the reason I wanted to interview you,

Marion, is because most of the time when grandparents are bringing up grandchildren, it's because their children were involved in drugs and alcohol; it's a common thing. Drug and alcohol abuse touches many, many families, and this is sort of a by-product of that abuse.

"The reason I wanted to interview you is that you've been through it, and survived it, and you've been in recovery. I wanted to talk to somebody that's okay now, that's recovered and come through that awful time into a better place. So if you were talking to people that might be in the same situation, what would you like to say to them?"

"That there is a way out. There is a light at the end of the tunnel, that's for sure." Marion pauses and then, to my surprise, continues on. "I had to go through a lot of pain, but I wanted to get better. I think I wanted to get better for my kids. A lot of my pain has to do with . . . not even Thomas, but my kids. I wasted it. I can't beat myself up for it now, which I still do, but I wasted a lot of time. I don't even remember the first five years. Little Craig—I can't even remember him being in the picture." She says this with horror looking up at me, her blue eyes magnified through the tears.

"I feel grateful that . . . I have a lot of pain today, but I mean I've recovered from alcoholism and drug abuse, and I'm not in an abusive relationship, which really blows my mind. I have a hard time with that one still. I keep waiting for something bad to happen, still to this day. It's really ridiculous. James compliments me all the time about what a beautiful person I am. He likes what's inside, you know? I keep waiting for the slams or the digs or something, and they just don't come.

"I still have a hard relationship with my mother. We don't fight anything like we used to," Marion says with a crooked smile and a short laugh. "But I think it's because I've changed. My mother hasn't changed, but I have. When I first got sober, my counselors told me that I needed to move away from my mother. They said even to move away from my children. 'You have to do it to get better, Marion.'

"My mother is very controlling, very controlling. She wants to dictate my whole life, and I can't live like that. I start to feel a closed-in feeling, and that's the feeling . . . that's when I want to drink and drug to escape.

"It's like she can't understand what I'm saying to her. It's like we're still going to butt heads forever." She smiles that crooked smile again, and I realize there is affection leaking out. "We're the same in a lot of ways. We get along much, much better today. I love my mother to death, and I am so grateful for my parents, that they could be there for my kids when I couldn't be.

"It's not crazy like it used to be way back when I was really sick. It was my disease. But I moved away. It was a very hard decision to make. My mother still, to this day, doesn't understand it, and I can't tell her, 'It's because of you, Ma.' I can't tell her that. She doesn't understand it—she thinks I'm horrible living this far away. No, she *doesn't* think *I'm* horrible—she's proud of me . . . I know she is, I know she is.

"And your father is too," I tell her. "I spoke with your father separately," I share with her. I'm so surprised she's still talking with me.

"You did?" She's amazed.

"Ben talked mostly about you kids—his children—with a lot of pride. He talked about the sports. He knew I was coming to see you, and he said, 'You'll really like Marion. He talked about how beautiful you are. 'She looks like a model,' he said, and 'You wouldn't believe it, but Christine looks just like Marion did at that age.' He talked on like that."

Marion murmurs with surprise and is tickled pink when I tell her about comparisons with Christine.

"I didn't ask him specific questions because I want people to talk about whatever they want," I tell her. "But whenever I tried to guide Ben to talking about those painful times, he mostly talked around it. He would shift the conversation, and it would mostly shift to his children. Positive things. He is very much a family man and very proud of his children."

"I feel really bad for my father sometimes. My mother has so much rage against Thomas Connor, and the fact that she couldn't stop it, and a lot of times she blames my father. 'He should have stepped in and done something! He didn't believe anything was going on!' He couldn't deal with it. Who could deal with hearing that Thomas sexually abused my children? That was a really, really hard, hard time for everybody. It was hard for me to swallow. I didn't believe my mother for a long, long time. How could this happen?" she asks me with her hands outstretched, palms up. "How could this happen?"

The pain is back, if it ever left. She is speaking with difficulty again, struggling to get words out. Tears fall down her cheeks onto her hands, her jersey, and drip down her neck.

"I blamed myself. I still have a hard time with Craig, my relationship with Craig, all the guilt I have. I'm much closer to Christine, but I love Craig to death! I know how much that kid loves me too. But we just can't talk about our feelings. We're both like my father; we beat around the bush and we talk about everything else." Her voice trails off to a whisper.

Marion tells me her mother is constantly encouraging her to talk to Craig about the past. But Marion says, "I can't! It's easy for her to say that, but it's not easy for me to do."

Marion needs to let herself off the hook. She needs to make peace with herself and the fact that she was rendered helpless to protect herself or her children. Years of emotional healing are required to mend the aftershocks of domestic violence. It may take years for her to feel that she can trust others again. It may take years for her to feel that she can trust herself to make mature, responsible choices. It will be difficult for Marion to forgive herself unless she works through all the pain and conflicting emotions that have been part of her for so long. She needs to commit herself to the hard work of therapy to resolve her feelings of guilt and shame.

"Everyone has different approaches to things," I tell Marion, still trying to ease her pain. "I think your mother finds it easy to talk about things. That's great for her; that's very healthy for her. She gets a lot out, and she has a lot of people to talk with. She told me about the community that she's a part of. It's hard to understand, I think, when other people "have totally different approaches and can't deal with things in the same way—they just can't."

"My father can't," Marion concurs. "And my mother blames him wicked, and that makes me so sad. It's over and done with! There's no going back to that time. None of us would want to! Everything that happens to us happens to us for a reason." Marion uses her hand when she talks. She hits her knees with them sometimes for emphasis.

"Do you and Craig go to counseling together?"

"I did a long time ago. I'm almost afraid to—it's really crazy
. . . ," she trails off.

"It would be painful, that's for sure," I prod.

"That's what I'm afraid of. I couldn't deal with it. It's bad
enough that . . . I feel like I have a hard time breathing when I start
thinking about it." She clasps her hands to her chest.

"Maybe it would give you some relief," I offer. "Look at me.
I think I'm a therapist!" I smack my forehead with my palm.
Marion laughs, and I'm happy to hear it. The pain that sits in this
room with us is unbearable. I joke with her a little more. "That's
what happens when you ride for three hours in a car with a *real*
therapist," and we laugh together.

"I went to counseling with him one time way back around the
time he was being abused. They made me watch a tape of him.
Ever since that time, I could never go back. Sometimes I really,
really wish I could be like my mother."

"In what way?"

"Well, she's so strong. She's the strongest person I know. Even
though I know that it's been very hard for her. She blames herself
for a lot of stuff. None of it is her fault. I do not blame my parents
in the least for anything that's happened. My mother blames my
father for a lot . . . not protecting us and blah, blah, blah. She
throws that back at him a lot. That really makes me angry when
she does. But on the other hand, she just stands up for all of us.
She's been such a fighter for my kids most of all."

"So if you see your mother as really strong, how would you
describe your father? What would you say about him?"

"I see my father in a way that I'd rather be. My mother will tell
the whole world everything that's going on, and I don't like that.
She obsesses on things, and she never lets them go. My father, on

the other hand, wants to live in today more. I love that about him. I can go and see him and he's happy to see me, and we can talk about what's going on *now*. With my mother, she is constantly, constantly bringing up these poor kids and everything they've been through. Craig still has all this emotional shit going on because he was abused. And she talks about Thomas Connor like it was all today." Her lips tighten up over her teeth.

"I can't deal with that, and that makes me angry! The part about her being strong and she's brought those kids so far through everything—that's the good part. My father, on the other hand, was always there for us, but in a quieter way. And actually I like that more . . . it's hard to explain.

"I can talk to my father about stuff. I can talk to him more than others can, it seems. More in the past couple of years. Me and my dad have become real close, and I know it's real hard for him to talk about the bad stuff."

"Does he? Does he bring it up?

"Yeah . . . ," Marion hesitates. "*I* have to him. I have *to* him. The day I had to go to my lawyers for my divorce, it took forever. I had to rehash all this stuff again, more so what Thomas did to *me*. I came home and fell apart." Marion is falling apart in the retelling. She is frantic, agitated. "I get headaches. I know I was beat up, but a lot of it I don't remember. All I know is when I get close to it, my whole body starts to hurt. When I had to go to court and my new lawyer wanted to know everything that happened to me, I had a hard time breathing. I had to go into the courtroom with Thomas Connor and say what he did to me. My whole body hurt; every inch of my body started to ache.

"I got so upset. My father was the only one home. And I just lost it! I started crying. I could tell he just got really upset too.

And he just hugged me. I know that he doesn't know how to say anything, but I know that he feels really bad. He said that he really wishes that it never happened and he could have done something.

"There was nothing he could have done! I told him that. But he's so positive to me. 'Marion, it's all over with now! Now you can go on with your life and put it behind you. If your mother will let you!' She laughs through her tears. "My father is wicked funny too. That's another thing I love about him is his sense of humor. I think he has a really good sense of humor, but it's to cover up a lot of pain. But thank God for that."

Marion begins to laugh again. "And it's so true because the minute I see my mother, we don't go through any time or any minute of the day without her bringing up past crap. She's just never going to let it go. That's why I have a hard time going there. Because I can't get through one day without her bringing up something. She doesn't say it to make me feel bad. I can see where it's coming from. But God does it hurt when she says stuff like, 'These kids didn't lose one parent; they lost two.'"

"When she says that, what is she trying to get you to do?"

"Be there more. But I work. I'm trying to make a life for myself so I can have it for my kids if they ever need to come here. I want to be able to give them stuff, so I work my butt off. And I still have this 'my mother telling me what to do' thing. I'd go there as much as I possibly could without her telling me *when* I have to come there, *what* I should do with my kids every time I'm there . . . I don't spend enough time with them when I'm there; I'm 'not giving the right emotional attention to Craig.' It's like—God—I do what I can do! That's constant. And I can't deal with her doing that to me!"

"Do you tell her that?"

"Oh, I've tried to lots and lots of times, but she won't listen. I am just 'selfish' when I say stuff like that. That's why I don't say that stuff to her anymore because it just brings up a big fight, and she doesn't listen to me." She slaps her bare thigh with her hand. "I've done it too many years."

"Here's another thing you hear from therapists," I tell her kiddingly. "You can't change other people; you can only change yourself."

She smiles her dazzling smile. "That's right! I can't change my mother and I never will, and she'll always be like this the rest of my life," she says laughing and slaps her thigh again. "So that's the stuff that I try to avoid.

"My mother had my kids for a good two or three years; then I left Thomas and moved in with my mother and father. But I was really into cocaine and drinking—just had no desire to stay home and take care of kids even though I loved my kids. The alcohol was much more important. And the partying. And I felt sorry for myself that I'd missed out on a lot of stuff. It sounds really sick, I know.

"In those years, my mother had them. Then, when I did get sober, the first year living in that halfway house was very hard. Everything started coming out about Thomas Connor abusing my kids, and that on top of trying to get sober. I really in my heart did not think that I could raise those two kids. I knew that my mother could. At one point, I didn't even think I wanted to," Marion admits and then breaks down again. "I just was scared to death. I still felt like a little kid myself."

"I've heard that the years that you drink and abuse are lost years in terms of growing," I tell her. "So you were still a little kid in your development. You were probably stuck at fourteen." I know that I'm crossing the line with Marion at every turn. I know I shouldn't offer up my opinions to her, but I feel the need to make her feel better somehow, to put a gentler spin on the day's events.

"I'm not very proud of myself," she says sorrowfully.

"Well, when you are able to face your own limitations and make a decision about what's best for your kids, I think that's something to be proud of," I comfort her, crossing lines again. "Tragedies occur when people try and do things that are impossible for them."

"Maybe I could take care of them today. I'd have a hard time adjusting to two teenage kids," she laughs. "The relationship I have with them is that I'm friends with them more than their mother."

"I've always said to my daughter that even though you're not going to be a 'mother,' as long as you have a good relationship—whatever form that takes—that's all that matters," I confide.

"I feel that I have a good one with them. I love when they come here. I want to do everything for them; I want to give them everything. It's hard for me to go into the role of the mother. I say to them, 'Pick up your stuff,' and, 'You have to go to bed at this time.' James watches them a lot. He had a really hard time."

I know where this is headed. "Is his style more strict than yours?"

"Yes. I had a hard time dealing with that. Craig came over and was pissed off about something, and he was stomping around the house and slammed the bedroom door. James was so mad he went into Craig's room and said, 'Nobody is going to talk to her like that for starters. She is your mother. You have to have some respect. And for another thing, nobody is going to come into this house and slam doors!' He was furious. He scared me to death and scared Craig. But he just came out and closed the door quietly.

Integrating the Birth Parents

"I had so many mixed emotions, like, 'How dare you yell at my kid, when it's bad enough I only see him once every couple of weeks! Let him be pissed off if he wants because he never shows any emotion.' It was almost like I was relieved that he was actually getting angry at me for something for the first time in his life. I want the kid to tell me how he feels. And then on the other hand, I was so damned proud of him [James] for standing up for me and telling Craig he can't get away with that.

"Then it was so weird, because Craig, within a half hour, calmed right down. I had never seen him calm down that fast. He used to always be angry, and be angry forever. This was obviously because he had been sexually abused and he had a lot of anger in him. He was a very angry kid.

"What an emotional day that was. Craig calmed right down, though. And I knew from right then and there that this kid was actually going to have respect for James. And James was going to have respect for him."

"So you believe they worked it out in their own way?"

"Yes, but I went totally nuts. I was screaming at James after." James had told her, "Marion you can't spoil them."

Marion sighs, "He's seventeen years old now. He doesn't want to come to Maine. My mother says, 'You don't spend enough time with him when he's home.' I tell her, "Ma, when I'm home, he's out the door. He's going to his friend's house, he's going to play golf, he's going to play hockey. He's not ten years old anymore; he's seventeen. He doesn't want to sit home with his mother.' And that's all right with me. It's not all right with my mother, though. She wants us to bond together and spend all this time together. I don't know what she expects us to do.

"I think we are really close in a way. And we do have a lot of shit to work through, and maybe someday we'll go to counseling and we will get over the hurt and the pain, but right now me and Craig get along great. He talks to me, tells me what he's doing, tells me that he loves me, tells me that he wishes I could be there more and that I could spend more time with him. And then, like I said, when I get there, he's out the door. But so what? I'm not going to make the kid feel bad because he wants to go do what kids do. I refuse to lay guilt trips on my kids. I really try hard not to." Marion laughs a bit. "My mother is wicked good at it."

We break for tea and I dip into a bowl of candy corn as she lets Spike, their black lab, in for a visit. He goes nutty when Marion lets him in; his tail could knock over a small car. I fed him pieces of the chewy candy while Marion reveals that she was bulimic all during the court trials because she couldn't deal with it and was eventually hospitalized because of it. She tells me that she felt guilty because she couldn't be there for her children, but she couldn't deal with being with them either. She tells me that James is very protective of her, but sometimes he goes overboard. He argues with Elisabeth occasionally if he feels she's being too hard on Marion.

Marion begins to tell me about her divorce. She says that she really doesn't know how she finally made the break from her husband. She had been away from him for a year but had begun to drink and drug again. He was able to talk her into going back with him.

"We got a new apartment. My mother was scared to death; she knew I was making a big mistake. But I was just *doing* it! We started fighting immediately. All I remember in that time, the last night I was there—I don't know why I remember this so clearly—

he came and picked me up at work. He had been to a party. He was drunk as a skunk. He wanted to go back to another party, and I was totally exhausted and I wanted to go home. He started a big argument and became really violent.

"He drove to the party. I didn't even get out of the car. He grabbed me by the head and slammed me against the window. I just thought, 'Oh God, here we go again!' He made me get out of the car on the highway; he tried to run me over. I don't know how come I can't remember all the other times, but this night I remember most of it. When we got home, he pushed me down the stairs, kicking me in the gut, kicking me in the face. His niece was babysitting—she was scared to death of him. I loved her. She's my godchild, and I can't even see her either.

"He was screaming at me, but nobody came out. I had a girl-friend that lived across the hall; she never came out. I always thought, 'How come nobody *ever* comes to help me?' I used to think that," she says, sounding weary, drained. She sits round shouldered in her chair, but she's composed and calm. "Except when we used to live in the other house and Andy was there. He used to beat Thomas up all the time."

Andy once told Marion that he was sexually abused as a child by his grandfather. He said she was the only person that he ever told and that he was fairly sure his other brothers had been abused as well. She feels that he told her to warn her.

"I don't believe for a second that Andy was one of them that sexually abused my children," she says, straightening up in her chair, squaring her shoulders, her eyes narrowing defiantly.

"Anyway, I remember lying outside the door—I don't think I could get up—and Sharon, his niece, was talking underneath the door, whispering to me that as soon as Thomas went to sleep she would let me in. That was an awful night because my mother tells me later on that he sexually abused Craig that night.

"I was scared to death to leave because he always told me he would kill me if I left. Always! 'If you ever go with anybody else, I'll kill them. I'll kill you. You'll be nothing! You'll never make it on your own! You'll always go back and live with your mother! I was really scared to leave, and I really, really thought that I'd never be able to do it on my own. He told me that so many times, I really believed him."

But, remarkably, Marion did eventually find the courage to leave. She walked away and literally—for good or bad—never looked back.

"I am really, really grateful for the way my life turned out, in one aspect, that my kids are safe. That's the only way I can close my eyes at night, knowing that my kids are with my parents. And they don't ever have to go with Thomas Connor.

> Ideally, birth parents and grandparents will be able to work to-gether as a team, and in many families that is the case. If they cannot work together, grandparents must recognize that the grandchildren will still feel a connection to their birth parents that needs to be satisfied.
>
> Honesty must always be maintained regarding birth parents. However, the amount of openness and contact between birth parents and children can vary from family to family depend-ing on the situation. If there is concern about the birth parent's appropriateness with children, then a supervised visitation can be arranged. Supervised visitations can be arranged through a human services agency, mental health professional, or even the courts. Over time, if the supervised visits go well, unsupervised

Integrating the Birth Parents

visits and contact can resume. Sometimes even supervised visitation does not go well and can be harmful to the child. If this is the case, all visitations should be suspended until the birth parent can demonstrate appropriate boundaries and behavior.

It is so important to be aware that the needs of the children are constantly evolving and changing. Part of the caregiver's role is to change and adapt to those needs. Meeting the child's need to have a positive connection, in some healthy form, to their birth parents is vital to their emotional well-being and growth.

SIX

What's in a Name?

Mother is a verb. It's something you do. Not just who you are.

— Cheryl Lacey Donovan,
The Ministry of Motherhood

Nana, Grampa, Bubbe, Papa, Mom, or Dad? What to choose, and who chooses? Allowing a grandchild his or her identity whole and unblemished is one of the many reasons we give them truth and avoid secrecy. Their formative identity is also one of the reasons *naming* becomes imbued with such powerful significance. What your grandchild calls you, after all, defines your grandchild as well. It establishes a place, expectations, roles, and indisputable belonging. It is no small thing.

One of the first questions I asked at the first Grandparents as Parents support group meeting I attended when the baby was only a few months old was, "What should she call me?" I really didn't expect that anyone would be able to give me a definitive answer, but it was a place I felt comfortable wondering the nagging thought out loud. A few people kindly shared with me what they had worked out, but I left still wondering. Since that time, many grandparents have asked me the same question, and I have offered this deeply profound insight, "It depends."

An unsatisfactory answer, I know, but true nonetheless. We grandparents come into this experience bewildered, with no frame of reference. But, looking back on that first meeting now, I think my uncertainty about what she should call us was ridiculous. We were adopting her. My son was only four years old. They would obviously be brought up as siblings, and there was no rational—or realistic—way for each child to have called us something different. My uncertainty, I think, was born out of a hesitancy to close that final door to my daughter. I think other grandparents hold out for the same kinds of reasons—a thick and binding soup made up of loyalty and hope, love and denial.

Grandparents wait for their adult children to get their acts together. They wait for them to go into rehab, to come out of rehab, to get an apartment, a job, to begin to show some sense of responsibility, some evidence that they can *be* parents. Sometimes the waiting works; often it doesn't. When it doesn't, grandparents must begin to make a series of judgment calls. Although virtually all grandparents hope their sons and daughters will become the parents their grandchildren need and deserve, failing that, other choices must be made. Those choices include "naming," and what grandparents or grandchildren choose depends on a host of variables such as, How old is the grandchild? How old was the child when he or she came to you? Was the child already accustomed to calling you an affectionate name such as Mimi and Pop-Pop? Are the birth parents still a viable part of the child's life? Does the child know them as parents? How long do you expect the child to be with you? And finally, Who is the child's psychological parent?

I believe it is essential to look to the grandchild for cues. If they were very young when they came to you, even if you started out as Nana and Grampa or Bubbe and Papa, a typical scenario may surface when the children reach school age: they begin to want someone to call Mommy and Daddy. They want to be like the other kids in this most basic way and may make the shift to calling grandparents "Mom" and "Dad" on their own. I have even seen examples—lots of them—of much older children making that shift as well. They make it because of the overriding longing to have that need fulfilled.

I never actually made a choice. I was Mama simply because it was a perfectly natural outcome of my "mothering" and her role as my son's "baby sister." I think now that it was utterly thoughtless of me not to realize how ludicrous, false, and ultimately damaging any other decision made by us would have been. But I can remember well the question ringing in my head at the time, "Am I a mother . . . or a grandmother?" My answer now is, "You mother; therefore you are a mother." And ultimately my answer to other grandparents caring for grandchildren in what appears to be a long-term situation is that children need mommies and daddies, and if there is no one else who can fill that role emotionally, physically, or psychologically, then the obligation—the privilege—falls to the caregiving grandparents, providing they are in it for the long haul.

One would assume that having once experienced such confused thinking myself, I would be more tolerant of others' confusion. I am not. One of my pet peeves is a frequently asked question regarding biological connections versus family roles. For instance,

"Won't it be confusing for the child because her brother is really her uncle?" Usually I answer a short and irritable, "No." I don't believe that question is ever put to traditional adoptive parents. Would anyone dream of asking, "Won't it be confusing for your adopted child because his sibling is really not related to him in any way?" Of course not! Because the unspoken "rules" of traditional adoption are inherently understood and accepted by society. Why this doesn't translate to a commonsense understanding and acceptance of interfamily arrangements, I will never comprehend.

Here's another one that bothers the beans out of me: "Isn't it confusing to have so many people involved in her life?" Excuse me? Haven't you ever heard of divorce? Extended families? I would like to shout into their knitted brows, their foggy questioning faces, "What's the difference?" But instead I say, "The more the merrier," cheerfully, behind clenched teeth.

This is my child's life. She has known no other. She is not confused in any way. We have explained, and will continue to elaborate on, her family connections. We are her parents because we parent. She also has birth parents, just like any other adopted child. She loves them too, but they do not parent; she calls them by their names. Fortunately for her—for everyone—those birth parents are an important part of her life, as is the extended family that loves her deeply. My son is her brother because that is his role; my other daughter is her sister because that is her role. Biological designations are practically irrelevant.

There are grandparents who do not agree with me. I've heard many grandmothers vow, "I am not his mother. He *has* a mother!" Clearly, those sentiments do not allow for a realignment of terms. Although my first instinct would be to follow the lead of the grandchild, for others with such entrenched beliefs, there is little room for flexibility or compromise. Sometimes comfort levels must remain at the baseline of the grandparents' tolerance for change. So the best answer remains, "It depends."

Included in this chapter are examples of what some of the grandparents interviewed for this book have chosen to do, or more accurately in most cases, what their grandchildren have chosen. Ultimately, a balance between the comfort levels of grandparent and grandchild must be reached in some way.

The Donaldsons—the first couple introduced in this book—are called Papa Pete and Moo-Moo by their preschool grandchildren. Their situation is relatively new, and they are still working out the boundaries, both legal and emotional. The boys know and remember their birth parents as Mama and Dadda and continue to refer to them in that way. They may drift toward renaming their grandparents as they reach school age—although the names the boys already call them could be taken for parent nicknames. Much of it depends on whether or not their birth parents develop and maintain strong, positive parenting ties.

The Parks' grandchildren were older when ties to their father were totally severed under horrific circumstances. Through their long struggle, Ben and Elisabeth remained Nana and Grampa, and Marion retained mother status even though she was not doing any mothering. The Parks worked at maintaining the mother bond between their grandchildren and Marion, and work at it still, as Marion works at it herself.

Laurie and Bob Harris represent, for me, one of the most discomfiting situations here. Laurie works hard at maintaining a long-distance mother bond between granddaughter and birth mother, but it appears that the only psychological and emotional parent is Laurie herself. Although I feel deeply saddened by

Laurie's attempt to "correct" her granddaughter when she calls her Mommy, I sympathize with what she's trying to achieve. Hopefully the child's birth mother will emerge as the caregiving, responsible mother Laurie longs for. And if she does take over as Mom, hopefully she works at firmly establishing a real bond between herself and her daughter before removing the child from the only "parent" she has known.

It can be very useful to allow children to take the lead as to how they refer to their grandparents. If the children feel comfortable and receive comfort by calling their grandparents Mom and Dad, and if the grandparents feel comfortable also, then this can be a perfectly workable arrangement. I would never suggest, however, that grandparents initiate the shift in names. I also have strong reservations about making the change if the plan calls for anything less than long-term custody. If a child is being cared for short term and the goal is to have them back with their biological parents, then the terms Grandma and Grandpa and the like are not only very appropriate, but also accurate.

And, most important, clarity is crucial. Clarifying for children is so very important to their overall emotional development. They need to know who all the players are and how long they each will be playing. One of the ways grandparents can foster clarity is through "updates" on the birth parents—where they are, what they're doing, and if there is any movement behind the scenes to reunite the child with his or her birth parent.

No matter what grandchildren decide to call their grandparents, it is essential for the grandparents to be very clear to distinguish themselves from the child's biological parents. While all

What's in a Name?

children need someone to call Mom, most important they need to know who their biological mom is.

For both the Winetraubs and the Randalls, the shift in naming occurred as if on cue when their grandchildren reached nursery school age. I asked each grandparent, "What does your grandchild call you?" and here is what they said.

Irene Winetraub explained, "In the beginning when he started to learn to talk and comprehend, the girls would say something like, 'Go ask Bubbe or Papa,' which are the Yiddish terms for grandmother and grandfather. So that's the way he would refer to us, Bubbe and Papa. Whether he knew that meant grandparents, I don't know. And he would call the girls 'Auntie.'

"And as he became more vocal and more comprehending, and perhaps it had to do with making the connection just around the time of the adoption—I really don't remember—the girls all of a sudden started to say, 'Go ask Mommy and Daddy,' just automatically.

"At his day care, my husband would come into the room to get him, and the other children would say, 'Your Daddy's here.' So we were always here for him as Mommy and Daddy, and that was it.

"So it sort of fell into a pattern. When he would introduce his 'sisters,'" Irene and Bernie chuckle, "he would say, this is my sister Auntie Barbara and my sister Auntie Helen. So that went on for a while, and then on his own, completely on his own, he would say, 'I have two sisters.' He didn't include her [his birth mother]. He hasn't included her in a while."

Irene went on to explain that he did, in fact, remember his birth mother, but it was clear to me that he instinctively sensed that she had a different status than being his sister, even though he wasn't sure what that was. He had no name for it.

One of the side effects of grandchildren entering the family in a sibling role with other much older children is sibling rivalry. It is an issue that often catches grandparents off guard. Their own children are usually at least in their teens, many times much older, and the question of jealousy never occurs to grandparents until it rears its thorny head. Irene talked about her daughters and how they bonded so strongly with Aaron. "You love him too much!" she pretends to scold them. But she then tells me how sibling rivalry affected her youngest daughter, who was in college when Aaron was born.

"She was the baby in the house, and all of a sudden," Irene and Bernie look at each other in amusement, "as smart and as old as she was, how many times did we hear, 'Gee, we never could get away with that!' Or, 'You didn't get that for *us!*'"

Perhaps that previously solid sense of place becomes tenuous for an older sibling, whatever the age, when another child horns in. Whatever the reason, it is clear that age does not much temper the prickles of jealousy that sting the older child when a new child, even a grandchild, arrives on the doorstep.

Most sibling rivalry is normal and to be expected, particularly if the children are somewhat close in age. However, if adult children become overly jealous of grandchildren living with grandparents, there are probably some other issues on the table. Families who have added grandchildren into their homes may be faced with issues of the first generation being displaced by the second.

If your adult children are making life difficult because of their jealousy, then tell them so! They need to hear it, and it needs to be said. Put a mirror up in front of their faces and ask them who is the child and who is the adult. One look in the mirror can provide them with a whole new perspective. If this doesn't work, suggest that they receive some support. Most important, make sure you still have some time left for them; they need you too.

The Randalls' grown children never demonstrated any signs of jealousy over Sara. However, as they began to have children of their own, the differences in approach that Betsy and Dan have toward Sara as opposed to their other grandchildren may cause some conflicts down the road, possibly leading to accusations of favoritism.

Those differences also inhibit the Randalls from being the indulgent, doting grandparents they would like to be to the other grandchildren they don't see as often. As Betsy tells it, "Sara lives here. If I allow the other kids to jump off the couch and get into things while they're here, Sara will want to do the same thing, and she'll want to do it all the time."

A grandmother once advised me to have a family discussion with grown children as soon as possible, ironing out the details of inheritance and wills. This is excellent advice for the obvious legal reasons, and in addition it will serve to sort out and solidify formally any recent twists and additions to the family tree. Including all the immediate family members in such an important and life-altering decision is important in developing a unified front and keeping family ties tight moving forward.

Establishing Sara's particular branch of the Randall family tree happened gradually, over several years. Betsy and Dan started out as Gram and Gramp, but Sara now calls them Mom and Dad. I ask, "When did the switch occur?" Betsy tells me about going to pick up Sara from a birthday party a couple of years ago when Sara was just about four years old. All the children were calling out, "Your mom's here!" as parents arrived to take them home. When Betsy walked in, Sara took her by the hand and said to the birthday girl, "Come here, come here, I want you to meet my mom!"

During the ride home, Betsy gently questioned Sara about it, and she replied, "Everyone else has got a mom." Betsy tells me that because the adoption was under way at that point, she felt secure enough to tell her, "I can be your mom if you want." She went on to say, "And she never, absolutely never, messes up!"

"You mean she never reverts back to Gram and Gramp?" I ask.

"No. If you refer to me as Gram, she'll look at you, but she won't say anything."

Sara found her place. She is secure there, and she refuses to be shaken down from it by reminders that it was once in question.

Vera Lenox works with families leveled by violence, crime, and incarceration—families whose configuration has altered with the force and destruction of shifting tectonic plates. She fortifies them, helps them to rebuild. Vera feels a powerful commitment and connection to caregiving grandparents, in part because she was once one herself. She is one of the millions of grandmothers who offer short-term care to grandchildren whose parents are in trouble or in flux. Grandparents have always been there, from time immemorial, to offer a helping hand, a port in a storm, and a leg up. And like so many others, Vera cared for her baby grand-daughter while her daughter, a young single mom, was going to school, trying to get herself on her feet.

Vera started out as Grandma, and as the little one grew older, she became Mama for a short while and then evolved into Me-Ma.

What's in a Name?

That evolution came about because the child's birth mother, uncomfortable and maybe a little jealous with her own baby calling someone else Mama, corrected her child. She would say, "No, Grandma is *my* Mama," and the child would reply adamantly, "No! *Me* Ma!"

Arrangements vary with each family. There are no set rules for such personal, intricate negotiations. One family I know well has a grandmother who is Mom, a grandfather who is Papa, and a birth father—very much a part of the child's life—who is Dad. When "Dad" and "Mom" are out with the little girl, heads do turn.

Another situation I am familiar with is a family who has custody of a biological nephew. His mother is in and out of mental hospitals, and the boy has been with his alternate family for over ten years. He also made the switch to calling his biological aunt and uncle Mom and Dad during his elementary school years. Although the family has tried repeatedly to adopt the boy, his birth mother will not relinquish her rights. This caregiving aunt, a social worker by profession, agrees wholeheartedly that this child's entire identity is at issue and welcomes, embraces, the change in naming.

Shannon is a young woman introduced in the next chapter, "Mothers in Prison." Her entire family, it seems, calls her grandmother Mama. Children know where the parenting, the mothering, is coming from, and they gravitate to the appropriate terms naturally.

Margaret Walker Jackson's granddaughters also call her Mommy. It's a little startling to hear this coming from a four-year-old, addressing a white-haired woman in her sixties. But there it is—the elemental need and pull to establish that basic linkage to place.

Raising Our Children's Children

The resourcefulness of children is awe inspiring. Left to their own devices, they will affirm their own identity for themselves, as long as no outside forces impose on them. And just like Goldilocks trying out bowls of porridge, the size of chairs, and the softness of bedding, sorting out where her true comfort level lies, the child finally comes home to the inner conviction, You are the parent, I am the child, this is where I belong—everything is just right.

When it's all said and done, when the dust settles—and it will—all children need to know who their birth parents are. So, Mom or Dad, Grandma or Grandpa, it is really up to your grandchild and you. However, whatever you are called, make sure you convey the truth and make sure that any shift in "naming" supports the best interests of the child.

SEVEN

Mothers in Prison

Courage doesn't always roar. Sometimes courage is the little voice at the end of the day that says, "I'll try again tomorrow."

—Mary Anne Radmacher

Maybe you think this chapter shouldn't be a part of this book, that mothers in prison are only a tiny minority of people after all. I wondered about that too. But in the end, I decided that incarcerated mothers provide a condensed version—distilled down to the grit—of the many problems grandmothers, mothers, women, and children sometimes face. In their microcosm, all the inequities are made sharp, and the tragedies become all too clear.

Shannon is a twenty-nine-year-old African American woman. About eight years ago, Shannon's boyfriend Jose, after having inflicted yet another brutal beating on her in which she was punched, kicked, hit on the head with a bottle, and dragged through the streets, promised that he'd come back to kill her. When he was gone, she took his gun out of the bureau drawer where he kept it and hid it under the mattress so he couldn't find it. Later when he came after her and began to beat and threaten her once again, she pulled it out and shot him. Then she called the police to turn herself in. Shannon was pregnant at the time. She was so badly beaten, scraped, and torn that her kneecaps were exposed. Nevertheless, facing a second-degree murder conviction, she pled guilty to manslaughter instead. She served six years in MCI Framingham for killing her batterer.

Shannon is about five feet two in her slippered feet. She has a pronounced overbite that gives her a permanent, seductive pout. Her hair is short, I think; it's hard to tell because she has it tucked up into a denim cap. She's wearing jeans, a soft flannel shirt in a bright turquoise color, and a jangle of silver bracelets and rings. In her ears are tiny gold crosses. Her nails are squared at the tips, frosted white, and long, so long that she holds her fingers apart and tipped up to make room for them. But why does she remind me so of a boy, sort of tough and sort of sweet, unfinished?

She has a deep husky voice and averts her eyes sometimes as she talks. She sits down in a rocking chair across from me and grabs a big royal blue pillow off her bed. She lays it across her knees—a soft wall between us—and uses it for the next two hours during the interview to pat, to hug, to stroke, to hit, and to hang on to. I think she is sincere and straightforward. I think she is brave.

"I have two children," she begins. "My son, he eventually went into a foster home, and my grandmother kept my daughter. She ended up going into a residential home, where she's at now, because it started getting rough for my grandmother. Because not only is she raising mine, but she's also raising my aunt's children and my uncle's children. She has five children now at home.

Mothers in Prison

"I think it's better if you talk to her, because it's been hell for her raising children that are HIV. You know what I'm saying? And running around taking this one to the hospital, that one to the hospital, you know, trying to make ends meet. It's been rough."

Then she stops. She tells me she doesn't want to talk about the death of her boyfriend, or her trial, or her conviction. I tell her she can talk about whatever she wants to talk about. I see the wariness in her; she's beginning to balk. She slides her eyes to the right and left as if looking for an exit. I ask her gently what she'd like to talk about.

"I can talk about what it's like being in prison, and being away from your children, and how substance abuse affects you, my children being taken away from me and then my grandmother raising them, conflicts, and the bureaucracy, the injustices.

"It was rough being in prison away from your children because your head starts to become clear; you're not on any type of drugs or anything. The women in prison, *they* love their children." She says this in such a plaintive way. "But their lives are uncontrollable, you know. They're strung out. There are very little resources in the prison system as far as trying to help us get our lives together and, you know, reunite us back with our children.

"The way I was able to get reunited back with my children was when I went to MCI Lancaster, because they have the Trailer Program there. That's a prerelease center. After five years here, I went there. The Trailer Program is where, they are like regular trailers, and they are set up just like home on the inside, and you're able to spend a weekend or up to two weeks in the trailer and you have your kitchen and everything. The only time its supervised is like when they do the count; they just come down to make sure you're okay or whatever. It helps women to get reunited with their children and build their bond back with them."

The room we're in is pleasant, sunny, and crammed to capacity with a bed, a bureau, a computer, and a couple of chairs. Resting on the bureau, behind a lighted candle, is a small framed photo of a young man. I wonder if it's Jose, but I don't dare ask. On the wall there are posters of Malcolm X, Elijah Muhammad, and Jesus. I tell Shannon she looks so young. Her youthfulness took me by surprise when I first saw her standing in the doorway of the halfway house to greet me.

When I called Shannon to arrange this meeting and she told me she lived in Roxbury, my heart shriveled. I tried limply to change the meeting to a different location, but it didn't work. Roxbury is the roughest part of Boston—crime and drugs, drive-by shootings, carjackings, and gangbanging are all daily activities of, and horrors for, the people that live there.

She told me, "It's behind Sam's Tavern. You can't miss it; the other houses on the street are boarded up." I wanted to ask, "Will I be safe?" Of course I didn't say any such thing, but my stomach churned in lily-white fear that began to seep out from my pores, hot sweat.

A neighbor happened to call after I hung up, and I began to babble on uncontrollably about her directions. "She's telling me to drive down Martin Luther King Avenue, past Malcolm X Park!" I related shrilly. And then, "What am I saying?" I was unhinged by misgivings, made stupid by apprehension.

My daughter brought me up short with a disparaging look, exasperated with my hand-wringing. "It's daytime. You'll be fine." High school football games were sometimes played in Roxbury, she told me, and there was never a problem. She is young and fearless; she was disgusted with me.

I tucked my head, turtle-like, back into my cowardly shell and peered out with hooded skittish eyes as I drove off, stopping short of actually driving into Roxbury, though. I left my car what I considered a safe distance away at a garage near Northeastern University and took a cab the rest of the way. My cabby was nice and had trouble finding the street. He was concerned when we finally arrived and told me he would wait until I got in. I wanted to hug him, kiss him, but I gave him a good tip instead.

The newly restored, peach-and-cream, gingerbread-trimmed halfway house looked as pretty as a Disneyland ride between two burned-out, bombed-out, boarded-up wrecks and a hangdog tavern called Sam's. It appeared as though it might have been sucked up by a twister from the Land of Oz and dropped there by mistake. I was relieved to see Shannon standing in the doorway waving me in, smiling like a young girl and looking friendly.

I ask her how old she was when she first went to prison.

"My first time going in there I was . . . what? Fifteen?" she tells me. "I lied about my age."

"Oh," I say, taken aback. What I meant to ask was how old she was when she went in for killing her batterer; I never thought that she might have been there before. I stammer a little and finally get out, "What were you . . . ?"

"Prostitution," she answers quickly, flatly.

I am embarrassed by the gulf between us. My middle-aged-white-woman-from-the-suburbs self trying to connect with this young black woman who has struggled with demons I can only imagine. And here I sit asking her to give me a piece of herself. Why should she? If I were her, I'd want to slap my face. But Shannon is giving, and I guess forgiving. She continues on in her direct way.

"I was there about three months. And then I didn't go back until what happened to me (her conviction for manslaughter). I went in for eight months. I was pregnant with my son. They gave me three weeks' stay of execution, and I had my son. I left my son when he was like a week old, so I'm just getting to know who he is now. I wrote him letters and sent him cards. The foster home that he's in, that's like my second family. They sent me his first drawings, pictures, and things like that. They let him know that I was his mother, because it was an open adoption and everything."

"His foster parents adopted him?" I ask.

"Mm-hmm. But I see him anytime I want. He was here yesterday. It's real hard. It's real overwhelming for me because he calls me Mommy and everything, but yet I don't *feel* like his mother. Because I was stripped away from him and, you know, having my grandmother raise my daughter, that was hard. You know, because, it would be like I would ask her to do one thing, and she'd say, 'Well, I'm the guardian here. I have to do it this way.'

"It was hard on my grandmother. My grandmother raised three generations. And all due to substance abuse. She's getting old now. She's tired."

"How old is she?"

"My grandmother is in her seventies."

"And she still has children. Did you say she has five? How old are they?"

"Seven months . . . ," Shannon begins, and I roll my eyes reflexively in horror, remembering the physical demands of that age.

"I know," she says to me in acknowledgment. "Seven months to nine," she finishes.

"What help does she get?"

"None. None whatsoever, and I tell her, 'Mommy, you need to get some help.' She gets AFDC and she gets SSI for some of the kids. And that's it. And her church might donate stuff, like during the holidays they'll send clothes, turkey, and food. And CAP [Children's AIDS Program], which has a day care for children that are HIV—that has been involved with my family for a while because of my cousin. They have helped my grandmother with a lot because my cousin was going to CAP, but she got too old to stay there, but they still keep in contact. But that's all the help she gets."

"Are there any groups that give your grandmother respite care so that she can take a break?" I ask, although I really know the answer.

"No. My grandmother is up constantly. And it scares me, it really does, because sometimes I think she's going to lay down and just don't wake up. When I first got out of prison, I remember sitting in the kitchen, and she went to go bend over and she had the baby on this side, bent down to pick up something, and the sharp pains just shot up through her, and we had to rush her to the hospital. She's just worn out from all this, and she doesn't get no help. We go up there and try to help her out. Me and my family members do the best we can. But then, my grandmother is real stubborn," Shannon says affectionately, shaking her head. "She's a West Indian woman, and it's like, 'Don't worry about me. I can handle this. The Lord put me here to take care of these children, and I'll take care of them.' And she has her master's and she has all types of degrees, and we call her the professional babysitter." Shannon laughs out loud.

"So her church organization gives her some help. What church is that?"

"Holy Tabernacle. She needs a break. A lot of my family members think she should give the children up."

"For her sake?" I ask, and Shannon nods yes, rocking silently in her chair, clutching her pillow to her chest.

"My grandmother is like, she's tired of seeing all her grandchildren being placed in foster homes and stuff, and if she can prevent that from happening, she's not going to see them go into foster homes."

She fills me in on some details. Her sentence was eight to fifteen years; she was incarcerated for six before she was released for early parole. Shannon's mother is now dead from "complications of drug abuse." Shannon was bounced around to several foster homes as a child. DSS would not allow her to live with her grandmother because "my mother would keep coming around."

One of the tools that can be used for working through unresolved issues involving a parent who has passed away is journaling. Keeping a journal, writing down thoughts, feelings, and what they wished they could have said while the parent was alive, is a helpful tool for some to begin to come to terms with a troubled past.

"That's how the crazy cycle started, anyways. My mother was in a body cast for two years; her addiction started with legal drugs, and then she turned to substance on the street. And so we were taken from my mother—I have seven brothers and sisters—and placed in various foster homes. Some were placed for adoption. I kept on running back and forth to my grandmother's, running away from the foster homes. There was a lot of things that were happening to me in foster homes. They eventually gave custody to my grandmother. By then I was twelve years old."

Foster care is a horribly underfunded, understaffed, underprioritized, flawed system. The overwhelming numbers of children needing temporary care far outnumber the amount of safe, reliable foster homes. The need for foster families is so great; standards are frequently lowered with the hopes that with social service support and guidance, the foster family will be at least adequate. Having had the opportunity to be involved with the system as a foster parent, the question I found myself constantly asking was, "Of the many foster parents I have met, are there any whom I would feel comfortable with raising my children?" The answer was always no.

Shannon represents another victim of the foster care system, a system that at one time directed foster care parents, "Don't let the child get attached to you." Thus, children were constantly moved so that an attachment did not take place. Foster care professionals now recognize that attachments for children are not only important but necessary for the child's emotional development and well-being. Shannon's emotional well-being diminished with each move, each disappointment.

Although Shannon has been a victim, she is also a survivor. Anyone who has gone through such a painful and abusive childhood will need a great deal of counseling and support. Survivors need to learn to recognize that they are good people with much potential.

"By then, I had already turned to the streets. I was on the streets at the age of eleven. Prostitution, you name it, I was doing it. I rebelled against my grandmother. She tried, she tried to instill the proper morals and everything in me, but I was just so angry about the way things were, and I felt that everything was *my* fault . . . because of what was happening to my mother and everything else . . . me and my brothers and sisters being separated. I would run, run, run."

> So many children, regardless of age, gender, or background, feel deeply responsible for the problems that their parents or family have. Most children are unable to see themselves as victims; instead they see themselves as problems. So many children like Shannon grow up believing they are not good enough, not capable enough, not deserving of love and affection. This may pave the way for an abusive relationship later in life.

"Eventually I came back home [to her grandmother's]. I went back to school. I ended up getting pregnant with my daughter. My grandmother took custody of my daughter because I was still a minor." Shannon is relating this with her head hanging down. The rocking chair creaks slowly, and she falls silent for a while.

I know what happened to her in foster care because I've seen the Academy Award–winning documentary *Defending Our Lives*, about eight women incarcerated at MCI Framingham for killing their batterers. Shannon was one of those women. She doesn't want to discuss it now, but she tells it in the documentary while tears rain down her face and slide into her mouth: "I come from an abusive background. I always thought it was okay to accept this abuse, you know, as a child." Her head cast down low, chin to chest, heavy with grief, burdened with sorrow, just as it is now.

Mothers in Prison

Fully 100 percent of women incarcerated at MCI Framingham have been abused physically or sexually as a child, raped, battered, or forced into prostitution. Women generally commit nonviolent crimes against property. They face a gender-biased judiciary when they come to trial, and when they do fall out of stereotype and commit violent crimes such as the one Shannon committed, they are sentenced more harshly than men. Women are convicted of crimes that men never serve time for, like prostitution. Because there are so few women's prisons, they are remanded to centralized, overcrowded facilities far from home that make it nearly impossible to have contact with legal counsel, family, or most important, their children, and they are detained longer and have longer probationary periods than men. For women like Shannon, incarceration is just another stop on the endless road of victimization. And because most women in prison are single mothers, their children inherit the same potential route and destination.

A few of the more fortunate inmates have the benefit of family members to care for their children while they are incarcerated. But DSS is mandated to place the children of inmates under state care and jurisdiction, and up for adoption after two years. They are supposed to take the length of an inmate's sentence into careful consideration, but that doesn't always happen. They are supposed to notify the women when their children are placed in the adoption pool and counsel them, but that doesn't always happen either. Shannon was lucky to have her grandmother, and she knows it.

To say that it's been terribly difficult for Shannon's grandmother is a gross understatement. After a while, Shannon's daughter started rebelling, and the grandmother decided to place her into a residential facility for teens.

"She comes home for weekends, holidays, and doctor appointments," Shannon tells me, shaking her head. "It's like a crazy, crazy cycle."

Shannon's grandmother relies heavily on her bishop's counsel, but Shannon urges her to seek outside help as well. "My grandmother does not believe in nothing that we believe in, things that might have saved our lives—you know what I'm saying—things that were helpful in our lives. My grandmother is strictly church. 'The Lord will save everything.' And I tell her, 'You know, God works through people. You've got to get some help for yourself.' There are times when she gets real stressed out. Sometimes I might call, and I'll say to her, 'What're you doing?' And she'll say, 'I'm so tired.' And she'll be laying on the bed and all you can hear are the babies."

"*HIV babies*—they must be so demanding and so needy," I remark.

"When my grandmother brought my little cousin home from the hospital, it was just the saddest thing. A baby that's kickin' off of heroin and cocaine, plus on methadone. In so much pain . . . it was like . . . oh my God! And I remember we used to all just cry and cry, and my grandmother would be like, 'Listen, don't worry about it. Everything's going to be all right.' She's all right though; the baby's all right. She's not no baby; she's a big girl.

"All the babies that my grandmother raised, just about . . . only mine and one other, they are the only ones that weren't drug addicted. I was smoking reefer and drinking beer, but when I got pregnant with my daughter, I stopped everything. All the rest of the kids my grandmother brought home, they were crack babies, heroin babies."

"She raised them all on her own," I confirm.

Mothers in Prison

"Me and my oldest brother, we weren't drug-addicted babies. But years later, the rest of them were. My mother couldn't care for them, and we got put into foster homes."

"So what help do you get when you're raising a drug-addicted baby? Is there any organization?"

"No. No." Shannon gives me a look like I'm from another planet, and I have to laugh. "No one helps you. The only help you get is in the hospital when they got all the tubes in the baby, and then they're withdrawing them and stuff. But then they come home, and they've still got the shakes, they cry, they shit all over the place; you know what I'm saying? Nobody helps you." She mutters bitterly.

Shannon calls her grandmother Mommy. She always has a house full of grandkids, and all of them call her Mommy. "She only has a four-room apartment, but it's always been like that, where all her grandkids always came to her." Shannon is the oldest grandchild.

Shannon confides that she is writing her own book about her experiences. I notice a note resting on her computer that reads, "Who I was. Who I am. Who I want to be." I ask her about it, and she says, "I'm working my steps. I go to AA. My counselor gave me those three things, and I'm supposed to write fifteen pages on each one. And I've only gotten to 'Who I *was*.' That's it!" She laughs.

"Going through the Twelve Steps is real hard because you have to take it a little bit at a time. Then I had somebody tell me, 'Well, just think of the small things that happened in your life.' And I'm like, 'Everything was *tragic*! Please!' she harrumphs. "I cannot sit up here and tell you that I am going to take small things when there was never nothing small that happened in my life. Everything was major. It was major and it was a tragedy.

"For the first two years [of her daughter's life], my grandmother showed me how to do some mothering. And I wasn't using it. Then when I started using, it came to a point when I was neglecting myself and my kid. And when you go to jail, you realize that the smallest things mean so much to you. Some people do; some people don't. You've really got to hit rock bottom to realize how much you love your children, how much you miss your children, and how much you want to see them. I mean, that is like the *hardest* thing for women in prison. You know, because you have this system that just doesn't care about anything."

She talks about some of the organizations that come to prison to help the women—groups like Aid to Incarcerated Mothers, Social Justice for Women, and People to People. The last two programs have been "booted" from MCI Framingham.

Shannon says that when DSS places the children of inmates up for adoption, those organizations would be the ones that "give support around that because a lot of the women would have such hard times."

"Hard times?" I question, not quite sure which hard times she's talking about.

"As far as giving your children up. That's hard to do! That's . . . that's *real* hard to do. Some women, they did it because they didn't have no place for their children to go. Some of them, they just didn't have no choice, because they would come back and forth through the prison system. It became a revolving door for some of them."

She tells me that Aid to Incarcerated Mothers provides help and support to women inmates with children. "If your children were from out of state, they would fly your children in, put them up, and have your children come to see you every day. And they gave us [mothers and children] Christmas parties and gifts for our children and Halloween parties. They were just there, you know, for everybody. And I think that program kept us sane. If it wasn't for Aid to Incarcerated Mothers, I don't know what would have happened to me." Shannon says that Social Justice for Women used to provide parenting and self-help programs.

Women's needs in prison center primarily around children and family issues. Men, who are far more litigious and aggressive—and successful—regarding their needs and demands, have issues that center mainly around their personal comfort. Men and women both require drug counseling and rehabilitation, but there are fewer programs for women, the lack of which impacts directly on their children when they are finally released.

I ask if she knows why some of the programs aren't there anymore. She shakes her head no. "It's just like they started coming in and snatching all the programs out.

"It's pitiful!" she relates in a disgusted tone. "There should be other alternatives for women with children, you know, because when women go to prison, most of the times they don't have nobody to take care of them. Men go to prison, they have women at home. If they don't have a woman to take care of them, their cell mate will end up hooking them up with another woman, you know what I'm saying? That's how it happens. So men always . . . they have women that come see them and take care of them and stuff. We don't. We end up losing our children in the process. There's no one there to support us, and hoping on the system to give us the proper programs for us to go to, and that gets taken away from us. When they sentence us, they also convict our children."

I ask her what she would say to another incarcerated mother if she could.

"It's never too late to change. Although it's hard. I've been through the wringer. I've prostituted, I stole, I did whatever it took to get my fix, whatever it took for me to survive. Sleep in a motel for the night, but that would be my home just for the night. I knew I would have to go out and get more money to find that second home and to get that fix. But you know, I mean, for me I would say that what saved me is connecting with the right people. I go to Dimock Community Health Center for my treatment, and dealing with Aid to Incarcerated Mothers, and just getting involved in the community's different organizations. I go to my women's group on Sunday."

I encourage Shannon to tell me about her women's group.

"Women come from all over to this meeting—Boston, Springfield, Lowell, sometimes New York."

"Women who have been drug abusers?"

"Some women have abused, have *been* abused, prostitution—you name it, it's there. We're all in recovery. Women of all colors, and it's a very supportive and powerful group."

"So you empower each other?" I confirm.

"Yeah, we empower each other. And that's what's important. It's about change. Because when I was in prison, I would always see women coming back and forth. And that's just like the cycle of violence. The people ask us why we continue to go back and forth into these relationships. Because we know nothing different. And I'd say, 'Why do these women keep coming back and forth?' Because they know nothing different. If there were more people out there to show them a way to do right and to do different, you know, more programs like the house I'm in here. This is for seven homeless women who are trying to reunify with their children. And I came here because I knew I needed structure in my life. I knew I couldn't go back out on the streets because the streets are going to kill me. So I had a choice, either it was going to be them streets or me getting my life together. Just because I did them six years, that didn't mean my life was together, you know? I still had a lot of old behaviors, and I knew I need some type of structure, counseling, and to be around people who were in recovery and people that I knew that could help me to empower myself. And that's what I did.

"It's hard to get out of that cycle, because I was trapped in it for a long time. And sometimes I mentally get trapped in it, and I might have to pick up the phone and talk to somebody. Because sometimes I feel like, what is my purpose of doing what I am doing? Why do I have to wait for housing? If I go out there and make some fast money, I can get housing. You know what I'm saying? I can go get me my own house and not have to worry about anybody telling me, 'Well, you're number sixty-six on the waiting list.' I know how to get that money real quick, but it's not about that today. It's about me saving my ass.

"I used to say to a lot of the women who came through Framingham, 'Why do you keep coming back here? What is here that you *like*?' I used to get real angry with them. I'd say, 'Jesus! If they'd just give me a chance . . . just give me a chance.' But see, what I did when I was in Framingham, I had a rough time at Framingham at first, but years later I started to realize that I could not continue to be angry and bitter. Because we do become angry and bitter. I had to connect with the women that were coming from the outside communities into the prison that were willing to help us. And that's what I did; I connected with them women and they connected me with different organizations out here, and that's why I am able to stand on my feet and go on. It's about women connecting with women.

"I mean, we can be our greatest inspiration, you know? We don't have to connect with men today; we need to be able to empower ourselves. I remember years ago, you couldn't get me to talk to a woman. Because they were all snakes, and they wanted my man." She laughs. "You know how we think crazy and stuff, right? But today, I have women call me all the time just to tell me that they love me. And not because they might want something from me; it's just because they love me, and that gives me the motive to move on. And when I'm feeling bad, I can pick up the phone and say, 'Listen, I need to talk. Sit up if you in the bed. Sit up and listen to me because I need to talk.' So that's what I do for me, and I see a lot of other women doing it that come from the same places I come from. They've been to Framingham; some of them have been to the Fed's joints, and they've turned their lives around.

"I look at other people's situations and realize that my pain is not unique. My pain is not unique because there's other people that are suffering just like I am, maybe worse than I am. I look at their situations and say that I am more fortunate than this person, so let me reach out to this person and give them what I have to offer. My connections, my connections are your connections. I love fellowshipping with women. We have brunches here and just tell the women, 'Come on over.' We talk recovery, recovery, our children, making connections, and we advocate for each other. It's about everything—children, relationships, not just with men but with our family, and how some of us had to pull away from our family because there are active people in our family."

"There's what?" I ask stupidly.

"Active people, people that are using. And like me, I had to pull away from some of my family because I can't be around them. And, like I said, I have to save my ass.

Mothers in Prison

"Tomorrow I celebrate seven years clean time. And you know, any given day that can be snatched away from me. If I choose to be around people that are active, I become vulnerable, and I end up picking up. That's not what I want to do. I want my children in my life and to try to break the cycle in my family. I don't want my children to become a product of the system. They have been for a little while, but right now I'm working on that. I don't want my grandmother having to raise my children. I want to take care of my children."

"So that's your goal?" I ask.

"That's my goal. We go to family counseling together. For the first time, DSS is on my side. God is like really moving in my life."

Shannon believes the residential program that her daughter attends on weekdays is "basically saving her life. We're in Roxbury. I love Roxbury. I grew up here, but you hear about it every day— teenage homicides, crime, teen pregnancy—it's rising rapidly. At first I was angry when my grandmother put her in the residential school, but today I am grateful for it. The school she was going to wasn't about education. It was more or less about who's bringing the drugs in and who's bringing the guns. Young kids her age getting shot down. So basically my grandmother placed her there so she wouldn't get caught up. She's an honor roll student. She's got a good head on her shoulders, very outspoken. She's able to explore life. Things that she's doing there she wouldn't be doing here because of how screwed up the school system is here in Boston.

"She goes skiing, she goes outdoor adventuring, she goes sky-diving," she tells me smiling. "When she tells me these things, it makes me feel so good that she's able to do these things, because I know damn well she wouldn't be able to do these things here. 'Cause they're not thinking about that here. They're not thinking about educating our kids; that's the least thing on their minds. It's about guns, who's using, who's selling, who's pregnant, and I don't want that to happen to my baby. I don't. I'm trying to break this cycle—this insanity. I'm really trying to break it."

Whenever I think of Shannon, I am reminded of a line in author Maya Angelou's book, *Wouldn't Take Nothing for My Journey Now*. In it, Angelou tells about the grandmother who raised her and who, recalling a time when as a young woman she was faced with difficult choices, said, "I looked up the road I was going and back the way I come, and since I wasn't satisfied, I decided to step off the road, and cut me a new path."[1]

Of all the people one may need to forgive, often the most difficult to forgive is oneself. We need to let ourselves off the hook for decisions and consequences in our lives. To overcome the struggles, memories, and challenges faced by those who have come through traumatic childhoods, it is essential to see yourself in a new light. Like Shannon, you must see yourself as a survivor.

EIGHT

Guardianship—Adoption—Letting Go

Set me as a seal upon your heart.

—Song of Solomon 8:6

The voice on the phone line is incongruously cool, and dry as fallen leaves while saying, "I am in a horrible situation." She found my name and number through the grapevine of caregiving grandparents and called—one of many calls I receive, we all receive. Calls from grandparents, predominantly grandmothers, looking for information, for direction, sometimes just wanting to tell someone their story. I ask this grandmother to tell me hers.

Ever so calmly, she tells me that she had raised her granddaughter for eight years, since infancy, and now the birth mother, her daughter, wants her back. Her daughter is going to court, with "her high-powered lawyers," to dissolve the eight-year-old permanent custody decree. Everyone this grandmother spoke with—every lawyer, every social worker, every counselor—shook their heads and told her there was little that could be done to stop the tide. She asks me for advice, a good lawyer's name, and encouragement.

I give her the name of a good lawyer, but I cannot encourage her, and this is the advice I offer: "You will want to try," I sympathize, "but when it becomes clear you cannot retain custody, step back." There was silence on the other end of the line. I wait for a response and think, of course you will want to fight for your granddaughter, rail against the system, argue for sanity. But it won't work, and when it starts to look like the sun will not rise that day, and you can feel the empty spaces in your heart elbowing for more room, and the bonds you wound so tightly are slipping away like cobwebs on the wind, step away. Step away from the wall and go around and come back at a different angle. Gather your energy, pick up what's left of your heart off the floor, and begin again.

Still, there is silence. I implore, "Look at the larger picture. Put your energy into preserving the bond between you and your granddaughter and keeping your family intact at all cost. Work toward mediation, compromise, and healing. Plead the case that you are the child's psychological parent, that you have her best interests at heart, and that all you want to do is share in her life. Keep the lines of communication open between you and your daughter." Hide your anger, I think to myself, pocket your disappointment, fold away your pain. "Don't rile the birth mother; don't push the judge. Try to patch together a workable arrangement that will include you in your granddaughter's life."

The grandmother says she understands, but she worries that because the daughter is now married, she could prevent her from seeing the child at all, ever. She's right, of course; that could easily happen. Grandparents have no rights. I coax her again, "Try to make some sort of peace with your daughter for your granddaughter's sake."

Guardianship—Adoption—Letting Go

"But my granddaughter doesn't want to go with her mother," she tells me, and my heart sinks, my stomach turns. I think of the battles recently in the news, the headlines—"Baby Jessica," "Baby Richard"—the battles between adoptive parents and birth parents who came forward years after the adoption to assert their rights and claim their child. The battles always ended the same—brokenhearted adoptive parents, traumatized children, and triumphant birth parents. Situations created by a judiciary that considers the best interests of the child "irrelevant" in custody disputes of this nature.

"Work hard," I tell her, "very hard, at making the transition for your granddaughter as smooth as possible, for her sake. Make it a priority; make it your new goal."

Finally, I have to ask her—I shouldn't, I know, but I do. "Why didn't you adopt her when you had the chance?"

"Because I didn't think I had to. I didn't think she would ever want her back. I never believed she would fight to get her back after all these years!" Her voice leaves its even plane and rises with frantic energy. I feel guilty for asking.

I recognize the familiar train of thought—the "grandparent drift," I call it, the "don't rock the boat" syndrome, the "I don't want to muddy the waters" philosophy. I used to become impatient with grandparents at support group meetings who expressed variations of those themes. Sometimes I would ask them—bait them, really; it wasn't very nice of me—"What happens when daughter X or son-in-law Y comes back between rehabs all cleaned up and wants to take your grandchild to live in a tent at a Nazi biker, free-love commune in Alaska?" That usually elicited some laughter, but there was a large grain of gritty, scary truth in that dumb joke. Just enough grit, I had hoped, to force a kernel of recognition to grow, one that might nag at them periodically like a pebble in a shoe and wake them up to the hard potential for disaster before them. While not perfect, as recent much-publicized adoption dissolutions have shown, an adoption is much less likely to be disrupted than a guardianship.

Permanency, stability, and security—these are the reasons grandparents march through courts in droves, with costly attorneys in tow, to win the documents that will keep their grandchildren safe, if only for a little while. Grandparents frequently start off with a temporary guardianship, normally granted for a ninety-day period and then reassessed by the court. If situations with birth parents don't improve, grandparents may move on to permanent guardianship, in which the courts grant sole legal authority for the child until and unless the birth parent feels they can prove the case to the court that they are now capable of parenting. And sometimes grandparents choose to adopt.

We adopted because we believed that our granddaughter deserved a mommy and a daddy to be there for her then, now, and always. We adopted her because she is a part of us. Nothing can change that. But we wanted her place in the family to be firmly secured, inviolable. We wanted her to always feel it to her core, to never feel tentative or vulnerable. We planted her roots as deeply as we could.

Economics plays a major role in determining whether or not grandparents adopt. Grandparents whose grandchildren are in the social service system may receive foster care payments (*if* they qualify as foster care parents) and services such as day care, health care, educational grants, and clothing allowances. But they must relinquish control of the children to DSS in the bargain, a prospect that makes most shudder and is usually avoided at all costs.

Guardianship—Adoption—Letting Go

Those who have legal guardianship and whose grandchildren are not under the foster care umbrella *may* qualify for AFDC (Aid for Families with Dependent Children), but generally at a rate that is approximately one-third of what is available to foster care parents. In addition, there is little or no access to other services provided to foster care parents, such as day care, health care, educational grants, and so forth.

Once a grandparent adopts a child who has never been in the "system," the state washes its bony bureaucratic hands of the arrangement altogether, and intergenerational families are on their own—fixed incomes and all.

The most emotionally fragile children, the ones whose lives have been in constant upheaval or torment, the ones most in need of a permanent, stable, and loving home, are often the ones whose grandparents cannot afford to give up welfare benefits or pursue an adoption through the courts. When families must weigh basic, gut-level needs such as having a roof over their heads and food in their stomachs against the slightly more lofty goals of permanency and security, guess which wins. Once more, grandparents are left with nothing more than a choice between one pain or another, in this case lack of economic security versus the absence of emotional stability.

MARGARET WALKER-JACKSON

Margaret is a woman who has been through it all and has survived with grace and style. She has come full circle with custody arrangements for her grandchildren, from informal physical custody, to temporary legal guardianship, to permanent legal guardianship, and now toward adoption. She once told me about a grandmother in her support group raising six grandchildren, saying, "I'm sure *she* doesn't want to adopt!" The unspoken reason is, of course, financial. Margaret's finances are tenuous, meager, but she has come to a place in her life where she wants more than anything else to give her granddaughters that one final precious gift, security—a legacy of love.

Margaret has all the "Ws" covered: she's wise, warm, and witty. I liked her instantly when we first met at the statehouse. She is another member of the Grandparent Support Group Network panel that meets monthly trying to rally other support groups, connect them with local councils on aging, and keep abreast of and support favorable legislation. We try to find, and in some cases pull together, new services for grandparents, such as respite care, wellness conferences, and stress management seminars. Sometimes there is even time to offer one another much-needed support and sharing. We have come to be friends, and I look forward to seeing them all.

Margaret has a dignified demeanor accompanied by an easy laugh, full and throaty. Her white hair reminds me of milkweed seeds that puff out from dried pods in autumn, spiky soft; it frames her walnut-brown face like a halo. She is partial to very fancy drop earrings.

I've learned a few other things about her. I know she has six children, fourteen grandchildren (including the two she is raising), and three great-grandchildren. I know that she has cared for both her thirteen-year-old granddaughter Tamika and her four-year-old granddaughter Charlotte since they were babies. I know she is sixty-eight years old. She has agreed to meet me at the Dorchester Square Health Center where she works to tell me more.

Guardianship—Adoption—Letting Go

The health center sits like an old queen on the corner of a busy inner-city intersection. Thick Doric columns flank heavy carved oak doors at the front of the red brick former library. Mullioned gable windows trimmed in cream reach out from all corners, giving a faceted, hexagonal impression. Her neighbors are a cubbyhole pizza joint, a dingy drugstore, and a flat-topped beauty parlor; she looks out of place, out of time, here. The building takes up the whole small corner, and I wind up circling and circling the little oasis for a place to land.

I walk up the wide, curved back stairway and meet Margaret, who tries to scare up a quiet room so we can talk. The place is bustling. People are in noisy meetings around large, vintage wooden tables, grouped around desks talking privately, marching through corridors carrying manila folders. A few are toiling alone, bent over typewriters or a stack of papers. There is an incongruous mixing here of Formica and chrome with wainscoting and old oak. She finally finds a tiny cubicle with a very high ceiling; one of those mullioned windows is perched way up at the top. It's a tease; you can see the bright blue sky and the cotton-ball clouds that roll by, but you can't get a breath of fresh air to save your life.

I notice a fairly comfortable-looking upholstered office chair by the lone table in the room and plunk down in it. Too late I realize that the only other chairs available are chrome and electric-blue vinyl, straight-backed things. I curse myself inwardly and quickly try to switch my chair for the one in which Margaret is about to sit, but she will have none of it; she turns me down flat.

Margaret sinks heavily into her chair, rests her elbow on the table beside her and leans her cheek against her open hand—a weary gesture. Her hands are long with narrow fingers—pianist's hands. I notice that her light-brown eyes have a corona of blue—

mysterious and exotic—and that she is wearing snazzy dangle earrings; blue beads dip and swing alongside silver moons and stars. I admire her blouse, a forest print, brown with leaves and ferns, also very exotic. It suits her.

She speaks softly and low, so I turn my recorder up to the max and listen carefully as she begins ever so slowly. "My thirteen-year-old began to come to me in small doses from infancy. Her mother is an addict; she has that problem. I was living in Virginia; had a little catering business there. I received a call from a social worker and was informed I had a beautiful granddaughter. But my daughter still needed help. The social worker was very empathetic toward my daughter. She felt that if I would say that my daughter could come and stay with me, she [the social worker] could prevent the Department of Social Services from taking the child away from her.

"Now, mind you—and I'm being very candid—my daughter has six children. She did not raise them. The paternal grandparents raised her two older boys, and a third boy was adopted out. When he was born, the circumstances weren't good [for Margaret], and he went to a loving, very caring family. When I had an opportunity finally, I just thought it would be too heart wrenching, after he had been there from infancy to three and a half years old, to take him out of that home. So I opted not to and just requested that, from time to time, we stay in touch so that he will always know that he has brothers and sisters. And they allowed that, and it works out fairly well.

"When my daughter came to live with me, I told her, 'Now you have nothing to do but take good care of the baby,' and they were with me until the baby was almost a year old."

Meanwhile, Margaret had a number of personal setbacks. Her father took ill back in Massachusetts, and she left Virginia to tend to him. She closed down her catering service. She and her youngest daughter, Jessie, as well as her baby granddaughter, Tamika, and the baby's birth mother, Rhonda, all had to move back to Boston.

Amid all of this, Margaret's brother was advising against allowing Rhonda and Tamika to continue to live with her. He pointed out that Margaret was (at that time) in her late fifties and had many other responsibilities. He cautioned her about taking on too much. So when Rhonda found an apartment in the South End, Margaret decided that the best thing to do would be to help her out financially and get her on her feet and on her own.

"Everything seemed to be going well for her. Then Rhonda began to say, 'Tamika misses you. Could she come and stay on the weekends?' and I saw no problem with that. But then we would go down and get her on a Friday, and we would go back on a Monday and nobody would be home. Tuesday, nobody would be home. And then it just got to be a week or two would go by. So the handwriting was pretty much on the wall.

By the time the baby was eighteen months old, it became clear that Margaret needed some assistance. "I went over to DSS—this was some years ago—and at that time they had very rigid rules. I would definitely have to go into court and declare that Rhonda was an unfit mother. The language really sounded very bad at that time, it was almost making them sound like a criminal. I said to the social worker, "I can't really do that because she needs help. She is more sick than she is mean or deliberately insensitive.

"I did not pursue it. I just couldn't. So I fell on some pretty hard times. I did bus monitoring, and I would have to take her around with me on the buses early, early in the morning. It was really pretty rough."

Raising Our Children's Children

"Where was Tamika's father?" I finally ask.

Margaret closes her eyes and covers her mouth with her hand for a moment. "We don't know," she answers softly, sadly. "I tried to find out because I think it's so important because there may be a sympathetic relative there. You're not looking for physical support; you're just saying, 'Be there for the child, so the child will know that there are other people out there that care for her.' But I met with no success."

> Girls obtain much of their sense of self from their father figure. That sense of self may go undefined because of feelings of abandonment created by a birth father's lack of involvement. Children will question their own self-worth because of a birth father's lack of commitment or caring. The child may internalize, "If I were good enough, pretty enough, or smart enough, my birth father would want to have a relationship with me." Sometimes, even though children may try to rationalize some of these feelings away by concluding, "He's a bad guy," they will remain vulnerable to believing, at some level, that it's really their own fault. If not addressed, this could leave a lifelong legacy of insecurity, difficulty in relationships with men, and a constant quest for a father figure.

"Eventually I was able to land a fairly decent job and have family health insurance; it makes a big difference. Unfortunately my daughter Rebecca's marriage wasn't working out, so she came out to Boston. She and I took an apartment together and we've been buddies ever since. "We were a *family*," she says joyfully. "There was Rebecca and myself, her daughter Adah, and Tamika; there were the four of us, and we were a unit. It was a godsend for me."

Guardianship—Adoption—Letting Go

Margaret's younger daughter, Jessie, had married and started a family of her own by this time.

"I took many jobs after that because of Tamika's emotional needs. Now I don't want to convey that she's knocking out walls and all that sort of thing. She isn't that kind of person; quite the contrary. She is very sweet and lovable, takes all the world's problems on her shoulders, wants to make sure that anything that goes wrong isn't her fault.

"I took a job out in the town of Sudbury as a teacher's aide and bus monitor because I could get her in a special program out there—it's a very small school setting—to give her the kind of tools that she would need. I stayed out there until she finished the fifth grade. We were up at five o'clock every morning.

"Then I heard there was an opening here at the health center. It was convenient because I only live a block away, and the girls' school buses would stop right here at the corner. I could take five minutes here or there and leave my duties because it was informal here, so I could greet the children. They could come in and stay for a little while, and I could check in with them. It worked out very well."

At that time, Margaret still had not made legal arrangements for custody. She learned that she might be eligible for Aid for Dependent Children. "So that helped and that was fine, and I just saw Tamika and me going down through the years together. I got to be sixty-five, and I thought, I no longer want to be a telephone operator. I would like to go back to school, and I would like to do something part time. I wanted to spend more time with Tamika, and I just wanted some *freedom*." Margaret was accepted into Harvard University's graduate program.

Raising Our Children's Children

"But then I heard my daughter had a set of twins. Tamika and I went to the hospital to see Rhonda and the babies. Six months later, one of the twins died. They determined that the baby died of SIDS.

"Once again, this very good friend of hers that was a social worker and I tried to encourage her to go into full treatment for a year, to let us take the baby, the remaining baby, during that time and give her time to bring her skills back and her self-esteem back—all the necessary things that need to come back after a twenty-year habit, for *yourself*, before you can start child rearing.

"Of course she wouldn't hear of it. She is very dramatic and very bright—very, very bright—and she was very convincing. She could 'do this alone,' there was 'nobody but she and Charlotte,' and 'nobody had ever given her a chance'—all those things. She found another apartment, and things began to go downhill. She wasn't even in the apartment a year, and I could see the signs.

"Just before Christmas two years ago, I had been out shopping, and I received a phone call. It was my son-in-law, and he said, 'I've gone to get your grandbaby. The police gave us twenty minutes to get there, or they were going to turn her over to DSS.' The police had come and arrested Rhonda for something to do with possession or allowing her house to be used for drug trafficking. Doors were kicked in.

"By then I had learned a little something. I went immediately after the Christmas holidays straight to Superior Court to find out what kind of rights I had." Margaret sits bolt upright in her chair and clips the last six words out forcefully.

"I talked with a very good clerk of [probate] court. He said, 'Now, there is a lawyer up here. You go to him—that's what he gets paid for—and he will advise you on how to write your deposition.'

Guardianship—Adoption—Letting Go

So I went to the lawyer. I didn't think he asked me very good questions, but I filled out the paper and took it back to the clerk. He looked at it, and then he looked at me and said, 'You are going back into court in about twenty minutes. Take this paper and go over there and sit, and *you* write why you need temporary custody of this child.' So I did. I just said the mother was a drug abuser and was unable to care for herself and therefore she could not take care of this child. The clerk looked at it and smiled and said, 'Now you just wrote your own deposition, and you didn't make your daughter sound bad and you didn't make yourself sound like too much of a hero.'" Margaret laughs appreciatively.

"This is who you go to! And you win them over and you say, 'Thank you!' And if they look a little harassed, you know they have had a bad day. Say something kind to them, and they respond. They will respond to you in kind. I advise everybody, 'Go to those clerks. Have patience and do not be snappy with them, because they have been there.'"

This has been my experience as well. Very often the most helpful, most knowledgeable people one comes in contact with during these legal custody and adoption proceedings are the clerks at probate court.

"I got immediate temporary custody. The judge just said, 'Thank God for grandmothers.'" Margaret obtained legal custody of both Tamika and Charlotte that day.

"Here is what happened next: I didn't know anything about DSS. You see, I was terribly ignorant about how they worked, except that I was terribly afraid of them, having heard all those tales. My daughter had never told me why she was getting all this free day care. She told me it was because Charlotte was so bright. And I would never have known if the day-care provider hadn't called me and said, 'Mrs. Jackson, I look forward to meeting you because I've heard so much about you. But you know they will no longer be funding Charlotte's day care as of the thirty-first of this month.' And I said, 'Who are *they*?'" She tucks her chin into her chest and laughs at herself, her naïveté. "She said, 'Hasn't the social worker been in touch with you?' and I said, 'Nobody said a word to me.'"

When Margaret finally heard from the social worker, she explains, "He said, 'I understand that nobody in this family should be allowed to take Charlotte!' What happened was that when DSS investigated my daughter, she was saying that the people hanging around the apartment were her sisters and brothers."

It is a common mistake to assume that an entire family is dysfunctional or drug involved because of the behavior of one of its members. In a publication of the Child Welfare League of America, it is stated, "The majority of kinship care families . . . were poor but stable and hardworking families who cared about each other. In many cases, the problem parents appeared to be the only dysfunctional member of the family."[1]

"Well, when he came to meet me, he just parked outside of the house until Charlotte came out of the day-care wagon and then came in, saying, 'Oh, what a nice, loving home.' He went back to his office, hit the computer . . . and I lost everything."

There is a long pause. Margaret just sits looking at me, and I at her. The room is quiet except for the noise of traffic outside the claustrophobic cubicle we are in. "You lost everything?" I repeat, puzzled. Surely that couldn't be the ending to that little story. But it is.

"I *lost*," she says quietly, with finality. "I didn't get a check. I lost the day care. He never sent me a letter advising me what to do. But in the meanwhile . . ."

Guardianship—Adoption—Letting Go

"'Oh, what a nice, loving home,' and you lose everything?" I interrupt her again. Now it's my turn to be naive. What do I expect? The children, now under Margaret's capable care and not their heroin-addicted mother's, were no longer the concern of the Department of Social Services. And they, in all their wisdom, saw no reason or way to help the children further.

"Just like that. He hit the computer and went on vacation! So I went over to the local day-care center up the street, and I said, 'I need help.' They introduced me to a very nice woman, Nora, who was familiar with the case." Nora Niles is a social worker who helps in family placement. "Nora called everybody she knew. And everybody was 'very, very sorry,' but I had 'no recourse.' She even wrote to the commissioner of DSS and told him that 'the appropriate steps were never taken in the case, and that if all grandparents were handled in this fashion, what would become of these children, because many grandparents were on a fixed income, and it was not a matter of being greedy.' They portray you as being greedy to cover their own tracks.

"Nora eventually connected me to people at Family Services of Roxbury, and I was able to get a sliding-scale type fee so I could send Charlotte to day care, because of course I had to work.

"Once I realized that Charlotte was going to be in my life too, I realized I needed to talk to someone about it." Her plans to attend Harvard quashed, Margaret went into depression. "I couldn't get out of my bathrobe," she tells me.

"I came here [the health center] because I had friends here. Someone suggested that probably what I needed to do was start seeking mental health counseling. I said, 'No, I don't!'" She stiffens as she states this indignantly. "I need to talk to people who are doing the same thing.

Raising Our Children's Children

"Because I worked at that clinic, I saw so many grandparents who did this—sometimes with *ease*, sometimes *not* with ease—and I needed to talk with *these* people for help and support. That's actually how Raising Our Children's Children [ROCC] came into being. I just started talking to people. I didn't have any pamphlets. I told them how I felt and asked them how did they feel? And we began to meet by twos and threes, and we are up to sixty-six members now." Margaret beams with satisfaction.

She has perked up. She is sitting up taller and speaking up louder, talking at a fast clip, animated and enthusiastic. "We meet in each other's homes, which is why I met twice a month, so that nobody feels as though they missed anything. One meeting is usually more structured than the other, but all of it is for *ourselves*.

"Many people ask if we involve the children. Only once a year, I tell them. Maybe we'll do a picnic or barbeque. My needs now, as we expand, are to have someone help me with special events like that, or Christmas parties, or preparing Thanksgiving baskets."

"My theory behind ROCC is to bring things *to the people*, as opposed to always bringing them out. That's one of the reasons we meet in the home. The second is confidentiality, particularly for new members. When I know there are two or three people that are going to attend that have never been before, I say to them, "Well, we're going to meet at so-and-so's home," and they will come and they feel warm and they feel welcome and they unburden themselves. We are just *there* for each other.

"The group is dynamic!" Margaret laughs, her eyes twinkling. One of my reasons to have these meetings on Saturdays was to get my own family more involved, to establish the fact that you have got to have your own time to do things for yourself. So that if the

Guardianship—Adoption—Letting Go

children know that grandma is going to be out for these two or three hours, 'please help to make arrangements to see that the rest of the household runs smoothly,' and so far it's been working." She smiles, pleased and proud.

"Some people ask, 'Why don't you provide babysitting services?' I am going to stay as far away from that as I possibly can! If, further down the line, some of the younger grandparents feel as though that is something they would like to do, I will help them in any way I can. I will help them get set up. I will make the contacts. I will network and advise. But no, this is for *ourselves*." Margaret laughs, and we laugh together as if sharing a guilty pleasure.

"Also, the other part of this is, we no longer have the neighborhoods. I was describing to Tamika the other night, as I sat on my back porch, that after supper in the city, you could wash your dishes and turn and say to the kids, 'Let's walk across town to the South End. I think we'll go visit Great-Aunt So-and-So. And you could walk! And get back home at around nine thirty or ten o'clock. It was a neighborhood. Sometimes you wouldn't get to your destination . . . you would meet so many people you knew . . . you'd stop and get an ice-cream cone. I can't recreate the old neighborhood, but I certainly can recreate the atmosphere and some of the feeling. Sometimes members have known each other ten years back from the old neighborhood. So old relationships have been rekindled. That's been really great.

"We serve lunch," Margaret tells me, seriously at first and then slyly with a chortle. "Yes, I always make sure we have a nice lunch." We laugh together again; we both know how good it is to have something to look forward to during those long, same old, same old days of child care. These group times—garden clubs, book clubs, even League of Women Voters, and Friends of the Library—serve this function and play an important role in the lives of women. Connections, a few hours' freedom, small talk or deep talk, taking action, and advocating, but no "little people" talk; food, commiseration, advice, and affection—an occasion. Margaret knew the importance of that and was able to turn her support group meetings into a "good time," a social event with a purpose and sense of community. We laugh together, conspiratorially, because we both inherently understand the need.

"We dress up a little, put on makeup . . . but we tackle issues!" she says adamantly. "I have two retired nurses that are part of the group," Margaret goes on.

"Are they grandparents raising grandchildren?"

"They just come to lend support . . . and because they like the *feeling.*"

"They like the lunches," I tease.

"They like the lunches and the camaraderie," she admits with a warm smile. "I also have a number of good friends who are willing to come out and run seminars for us on Medicare, health issues, our own personal health. There's a young pediatrician who will run a seminar anytime we ask, in terms of advice on children's health and children's issues. And I have just now been approached by someone from the school committee who would like to become a part of our group and talk about school issues. The majority of our children attend the public schools here in Boston, so we need to know these things.

Margaret tells me there is someone who wants to talk on "parenting" issues, but she hesitates. She feels the need to "screen very carefully" what this person has to say. She doesn't want her members to feel preached to, as if there is only one way to do things, or to feel that what they have done may be wrong. She is sensitive to needing to "blend the old with the new" ways of parenting.

"The philosophy of the support group as I see it is that no one person has all the answers; we all have different answers!

"I do a lot of networking, making sure my grandparents who have diabetes, or high blood pressure, or heart problems are all right. I stay in touch with them, and I am in constant touch with the medical community. I have a young nurse from Northeastern University that I call on to come to meetings and talk to people separately."

"You are a true support group," I tell her admiringly, "in a deeper sense of the word than most support groups I come in contact with." Margaret seems a bit surprised at that. "And you really lend a wide range of support," I add. I will find out much later that Margaret, although remarkable, isn't unique. There are others like her—quiet warriors on behalf of grandmothers in the trenches, fighting for their grandchildren, for their lives, for their families, women who lead the way.

I ask her what percentage of her group members have custody, and what percentage adopt.

"That's a mix. The majority of grandparents do have custody. It helps because the mother or father of these children is still your own child. If all else fails, once you have legal custody . . . or if it hurts too much to say no [to the birth parent] . . . or if you don't want them taking the child, it helps. There have been times when I wouldn't allow my daughter to take her girls because it wasn't good for them or her. But I felt much stronger once I knew I had the courts behind me.

"Now I am personally going to file for adoption because I *am* sixty-eight." She laughs and shakes her head as if her age were absurd. "I'll be fortunate if I see the older child come of age to make her own decisions; the odds are that I'm not going to see this four-year-old become twenty-one." She laughs again and then becomes very somber as she continues. "And if I do [live that long], what kind of conditions would I be *in*?" She asks. "So I want to make sure . . . I have *little*, but what I want most to ensure is my Social Security benefits [so that Tamika and Charlotte will be eligible to receive them].

"Family welfare is sometimes not much kinder than public welfare. So the less dependent they have to be . . . that's my reason for adoption. The majority of grandparents do not adopt because you live in hopes—you *live* in hopes—that even if you share the parenting, you just hope that they [the birth parents], ultimately, will be able to heal themselves.

"I have a grandmother [in the support group] who's sixty-five years old and is caring for six grandchildren, and the oldest is ten. And I am sure *she* doesn't want to adopt. She is fortunate that she has a large family herself, so she has a couple of daughters and daughters-in-law who help. One comes in from Springfield and takes over for a week or two. She is a very fortunate person that way. Many of us don't have that kind of support.

"The other pitfall, if you have a good-sized family of your own, is that you have to get beyond the 'sibling rivalry' and jealousy. We all have to live through it and deal with it in some sort of way. Because you're the other children's grandmother also. I have four-teen grandchildren in all.

"But after all these years, I can see some of my daughters-in-law and sons-in-law and some of my own kids starting to say, 'You know, Ma's getting old and didn't have these babies herself.' So I can feel attitudes changing, and they are becoming more helpful as they get older and more understanding. But, you know, it takes a few years to wade through all that!

"My oldest son is a psychologist in the Boston Public Schools, excellent with young people, does crisis intervention, is on television; he is a doctoral candidate at B.C. [Boston College], and he is just *beginning* to . . ." She begins to chuckle, and it overtakes her; she laughs raucously, rocking forward and throwing her hands on her knees, her earrings swinging wildly, ". . . just beginning to understand." She wipes at her eyes with the backs of her fingers and becomes serious again, "This is a unique position; it isn't always easy.

"When I address young women, I say to them, don't ever think that what they do to themselves doesn't have that shock-wave effect. Because it affects everybody.

"When that little one [Charlotte] looks at me and says, 'Mama, can I have a Daddy?' how do I answer that? That's why I get angry with these young women. Whatever their motivation is, whatever their problems are, whatever their rationale, take one unselfish moment and think about the child, about that *life*!

"Tamika has a goal in life, and I think her goal is to be with her mother and take care of her mother. She feels as though the family treated her mother badly. This just began to surface in adolescence.

Children of alcoholics and addicts, because they see their parents so out of control, often attempt to give their parents and themselves stability and control in their lives, even if it means sacrificing their own childhood. They struggle with ambivalence regarding the afflicted parent, torn between anger and disappointment with their parent and their urge to be protective of them. They try to parent the parent.

Conflicting "good parent, bad parent" issues may surface as confusion between loyalty and fear that, "if my mother is bad, then I must be bad too." At times, the child may see both themselves and their parent as "victims" and may feel that they are "united together against the world."

"If Rhonda is broke, and things aren't going right with her personal life—and she is beginning to have health problems now because she is forty-five—then she is in touch with us. Although I know where she is, and I know her phone number, I no longer bother to even encourage the girls to call her. The older girl is now beginning to say, 'Do not give my mother any more money.' I say, 'Well, Tamika, I think I understand why you are saying this, but you have to remember that your mother is my daughter the same as the rest of my children. So I would never see her go hungry. I would never see her in real pain. But you don't have to worry. I'm not going to give her big money.' Tamika says, 'She never calls you and asks how you feel, and I am really getting sick of her.' So I just let her vent her feelings."

As author Hope Edelman explains in her book, *Motherless Daughters*, "Like the child whose mother dies, the abandoned daughter lives with a loss, but she also struggles with the knowledge that her mother is alive yet inaccessible and out of touch. Death has finality to it that abandonment does not. A daughter whose mother chose to leave her or was incapable of mothering may feel like a member of the emotional underclass." [2]

Margaret continues to talk about Tamika. "She is an insecure kind of person, so it's really hard, because you will reach out for her and she'll draw back sometimes. She has her own type of special needs."

Guardianship—Adoption—Letting Go

As they emerge into adolescence, most teens become reluctant to talk openly about feelings. While this is normal, it is important for caregivers to continually provide outlets for sharing feelings.

Abandoned children may formulate that they don't deserve to have people care about them. Moreover, they may also feel that they don't deserve success and therefore don't create any in their lives. They may have doubt about their abilities to succeed, thus only allowing themselves to fail. Caregivers must watch for signs of self-defeating behaviors or words, an inability to give or accept compliments, self-critical behavior, or a reluctance to try something new or join in.

Margaret and I commiserate about raising teenagers again, coping with it as grandparents. She tells me, "It's no longer that you know the boy down the street and you know his parents. You don't know anybody anymore. When do you say yes, and when do you say no? I don't envy you," she teases me, and we laugh. "I used to say that to my children, 'I don't envy you having to raise children in this day and time.' Boy, I never thought it was going to come back and haunt me! Ha!" she laughs and then says wistfully, "That's the least of what I wanted to do."

Margaret's thoughts drift over to her daughter Rhonda, and she begins to talk about a meeting she had with a drug counselor at one of the many rehab facilities her daughter had attended. "I challenged him. I said, 'How dare you indicate that I have had a life of roses! Let me explain something to you. When she decided this was what she was going to do, or was led into it, she was a grown woman and out of my house. And you don't know anything about my life, so you can't make suppositions because I smile on the outside. You can't see the pain on the inside. You don't know what I went without, or what I've done, or what my philosophy of raising children is. She did not have to babysit her brothers and sisters; I didn't believe in that. That was *my* responsibility. But she ultimately has to make up her mind that she's not going to put that needle in her arm. I have nothing to do with that decision. That is her decision.'

"I encouraged her to get out of that program. I told her, 'Until the day you can look yourself in the mirror, for better or for worse, and say, "I am really sorry, but *I* did this," then you can move on.' I don't see how you would have the ability to get well otherwise. We have to forgive ourselves. I can't tell you how many things I have had to forgive myself for in order to move on, in order to be a better person."

Margaret begins to laugh and confides, "They wanted her out of that program after they met me anyway."

"You were too much for them," I kid her.

"Well, I was just shocked that those people didn't talk about responsibilities, that when you make your decisions, there's going to be consequences.

"You know, the government's wasting tons and tons of money. I'm not too sure that they don't try to keep these people addicted so they can keep a certain amount of mediocre people in jobs!" She laughs when she says this, but her eyes are hard as stones.

Former secretary of health, education, and welfare Joseph A. Califano Jr. once said, "Neither party gets it. Crime, poverty, health care costs—America's biggest problems lead back to drug abuse." [3] It is certainly a major contributor to the meteoric rise in numbers of children being raised by grandparents.

What can we do to stem the tide of the next generation of addicts, stopping the cycle of hopelessness, rootlessness, low self-esteem, and the need to medicate dreams into existence or numb nightmares away? Making the children a priority instead of uniforms for drug enforcement teams and pumping endless dollars into a failed drug war—perhaps that will turn tomorrow's tide. Prevention: does anyone out there get it?

Margaret says, "As I get older, do you know what I see? I don't see a country that actually cares about its children. And that has nothing to do with color. The court system, the educational system—where do we stand in the world today? The court system only reflects the mores of the country. And we [grandparents] are being pushed down as if we shouldn't be doing this, as if we shouldn't be saving these children—as if we shouldn't be giving them love and saying that all things are possible. I wonder why I had to get so old to realize that.

"I had ultimate faith that in the long run, if you kept on working and kept on trying to do the right thing and gave your kids a lot of love and always looked out for the advantages, you would get them going in the right direction. But the country, I found out, does not care!"

It has been two hours of sitting in that hard chair for Margaret, and I decide to call it quits. We agree on a time to get together again so I can meet her granddaughters. Margaret chuckles and says she can just imagine how her four-year-old will love that. "She'll just try to take over. She's a professional."

She tells me that Tamika has a weight problem and says, "I try not to say anything [about her eating] because I know why she does it. She does have a lot of emotional needs. For a long time she had attention deficit disorder [ADD], but she seems to have overcome that now."

ADD is present in about 5 percent of the general school-aged population. I would be willing to conjecture, however, that the figure is higher among children who have come into grandparents' care from very rocky beginnings. In the book *Driven to Distraction*, it is pointed out that ADD "remains poorly understood by the general public, often going unrecognized or misdiagnosed. The hallmark symptoms of ADD—distractibility, impulsivity, and high activity—are so commonly associated with children in general that the diagnosis is often not considered. Due to repeated failures, misunderstandings, mislabeling, and all manner of other emotional mishaps, children with ADD usually develop problems with their self-image and self-esteem." The authors go on to say that afflicted children are often "labeled lazy or defiant or odd or bad." [4] There are many ways to deal with this disorder—therapy, counseling, behavior modification, and medication—the latter sometimes overused, but the first step is knowledge and understanding.

"It's all about self-esteem. I've been trying to get some counseling for her, if I could find the right person, someone she can connect with, but that's not always easy, especially for a teen. We were told that we were doing pretty good, so we wouldn't be top priority. That's all very complimentary, but that's not the point. The point is that she's thirteen, and I know that I have limits."

Weight problems, poor eating habits, and, in some instances, eating disorders develop in children who have been abandoned, abused, or neglected. For some children, food becomes a way to "feed the soul," to fill up the emptiness they feel. Food becomes a form of self-nurturance, and children tend to nurture themselves with high-sugar, high-fat foods. For many of these children, food

Guardianship—Adoption—Letting Go

becomes a safe, reliable friend, a friend who never lets them down, never abandons them, and never hurts them.

Children with eating vulnerabilities should receive appropriate psychological support to face and resolve those issues of abandonment, rather than feeding the void they create.

As I pack up to leave, I remind Margaret that we have a Grandparent Support Group Network meeting at the Executive Office of Elder Affairs in a few days.

"I'll be there," she promises. We are expecting several DSS officials to attend. They are going to be filling us in on how the "system" works. But Margaret fears the meeting will turn into nothing more than a "love affair" between EOEA and DSS.

She needn't have worried. The meeting is very well attended. Margaret is there as promised. Most of the panelists are grandparents raising grandchildren, and some have had unpleasant experiences dealing with DSS throughout difficult custody proceedings. They are not won over by the "ombudsman" in attendance along with a couple of her assistants. We are all surprised that this ombudsman exists, that there is a branch of DSS that actually mediates disputes both with and within the system. Is this a highly guarded secret, we wonder? There is a lively discussion. The DSS officials are oddly tentative, somewhat patronizing, and lend no new information or potential help.

Toward the end of the meeting, Margaret speaks up. She implores DSS to "treat the grandparents with respect, give them answers to questions, be patient." And if decisions are made *not* to place children with family, "Please tell us *why!*" She asks for "understanding." She tells them finally, "Because . . . this is flesh of our flesh!"

Margaret and I meet once more a week later at the health center. The plan is for me to pick her up there and drive her home when she's done working so I can meet the children. When I arrive, she meets me at the back stairway again, and we walk up to her tiny office space. Charlotte is there. She dashes around, a little pink-and-blue-plaid blur, a dynamo. She is obviously well known and loved in this place. Flying from one office space to another, she greets people, asking for pencils from one, paper from another. She finally settles down at a large wooden conference table and begins to draw.

Margaret doesn't look quite as sharp today. Her eyes are tired, watery pale. Gone are those wonderful earrings. And she's moving very slowly.

She begins by apologizing in advance for her messy house. I tell her, "Please don't worry about it. Who cares! You should see the condition I left mine in today." But she still frets. She tells me she just can't get going lately; she's been depressed. Money problems.

I squeeze into the cramped space next to Margaret's desk as she fills out time sheets. She talks to me, slowly, mechanically—as if she's reciting a grocery list to herself. She speaks so quietly that I lean forward across a pile of papers and strain to hear. She tells me that between what she makes part time at the health center, her Social Security check, and what they take out of it for Medicaid, it's barely enough to make ends meet. She receives some funds for her two granddaughters, but she would receive far more if she were a foster parent, or if her grandchildren had problems, or if she were a drug addict, or if she didn't work. "Shall I buy Tamika the shoes she wants, or pay the electric bill?"

She tells me she tries to do everything right. She shops at the secondhand stores. She tells me people don't treat her with re-

Guardianship—Adoption—Letting Go

spect; they make her feel like she is begging. I ask her who she is talking about, and she says social workers, people at the welfare office, lawyers, politicians. One politician told her she must not be budgeting properly.

Margaret finishes up her work, and we go hunt for Charlotte. We find her still at the conference table, her head bent over her work. Her long puffy braids, all six of them, are secured at top and bottom by elastics threaded through royal blue beads. They bounce as she colors. She is wearing a too-small but pretty pink-and-blue-plaid dress, pink ruffled socks, and ancient saddle shoes—I haven't seen the likes of them in years—one with a floppy sole. I sit down next to her and look at the bottom of her foot, trying to gauge her shoe size, as she sits cross-legged in her chair, drawing.

"What a little foot," I say.

Charlotte jerks her head up, her braids swinging furiously, and gives me a defiant look. She has creamy, coffee-light skin, and wide-set, watchful eyes set into a soft, baby face.

"No!" she protests, pouting. "I'm a *big* girl."

"You sure are!" I try desperately to redeem myself. She does have a small foot, I think to myself, smaller than my little girl's. Could I hand some shoes down? Some clothes? Or would it cause discomfort between Margaret and me—be awkward?

Charlotte takes a shoe off, and Margaret patiently wiggles it back onto her foot, ties the laces securely, and we are off. Charlotte refuses to put her raincoat on—she is clearly a force to be reckoned with—and we step out into the warm drizzle without an argument.

Margaret's street is only a block or two from the health center. We drive up to a "triple-decker," a turn-of-the-century, wood-frame house built for economy. Dorchester is filled with them.

Raising Our Children's Children

Three levels, three porches, three families. The rule of thumb used to be that when you bought the house, you lived in one apartment, the second apartment covered your mortgage payment, and the third was income you used to maintain the place. It was your home, and you had a vested interest in upkeep, in the neighborhood. Now absentee landlords own them for profit only.

This triple-decker will need a coat of paint soon, but it is solid and in good repair. Most of the modest homes on this street have been kept up fairly well, but the yards remain forgotten, untended. The tall houses stand all lined up like the old guard, somber and plain in dull brown coats, the overgrown grass and hardscrabble weeds taunting them from below. At the end of the street, I can see a playground. Impenetrable chain-link fencing chokes in a dried-up ball field and gunboat-gray metal swing sets. It's midafternoon, but no one is playing.

Inside the apartment on the first floor, the walls are painted off-white, the trim salmon pink. Margaret begins to fuss about as soon as we enter, still apologizing for what turns out to be minor clutter accompanied by dust bunnies. I take my raincoat off and sink into a soft, well-worn terra cotta–colored sofa next to Margaret's overflowing desk.

"This is my Tamika," Margaret introduces her granddaughter to me as she enters the living room. I see with dismay that she is obese. She has a beautiful face, purely dark, with lovely almond-shaped eyes that tilt up at the corners—cat eyes. I tell her so. I ask her if anyone has ever told her what beautiful eyes she has, and she says, "My grandmother tells me that." She is sweet and painfully polite.

"I look like my mother, except my mother's face is skinny and mine is sort of round," she says, drawing her finger around her chin.

Guardianship—Adoption—Letting Go

Margaret tries to shoo Charlotte away, and I tell her she's fine, not to bother. Charlotte brings me a plastic-covered toy that came in the McDonald's kid's meal she had for lunch, and I unwrap it for her while she watches intently. It's a miniature "Ken" doll with egg-yolk-yellow hair. She asks me what he does. "Nothing much," I tell her.

Tamika speaks whisper soft and enunciates with precision. She sounds like Marilyn Monroe. I ask her what it's like to live with her grandmother and think that it's a stupid question the minute it leaves my mouth. She answers, "Sometimes we don't get along, but my grandma says that when I get a little older, it will get better."

"Do you see your mother often?"

"Not really. I sort of get along with my mother. I just didn't understand why she didn't take care of me. But I don't ask her because I really don't know how to say it."

"And she might not know how to answer you."

"She might say she couldn't, but . . . She has always told me that she regrets she didn't, but there are some things I probably wouldn't understand now. When I get older, it will probably be better for me to talk about it then, because I'd probably understand more."

"You're right."

"I don't think I can understand at my age."

"It's hard to understand, even when you're a grown-up, why people do the things they do."

"I know she says she made a lot of mistakes, but I just don't understand why," she repeats with a big sigh.

While a mother's addiction is difficult to understand, with assistance, someone Tamika's age is old enough to begin to process much of the information that will help her put into perspective why her mother is unable to care properly for her.

A teen will need help wading through the maze of passionate, conflicting, and confusing emotions. Once this occurs, she will have the opportunity to deal with her unresolved feelings of loss and abandonment. Children need to have that opportunity so they can understand who their mother is and why she behaves the way she does. These questions, and the need to understand them, make up the very fabric of who that child is and who she will become.

Margaret comes back toward the living room from the kitchen where she's been puttering. "Ken's on the floor," I warn her. "Don't step on him."

"Ha! I'm sure it'll be worse for me than for Ken," Margaret says as Tamika leaves to go back upstairs to her aunt's second-floor apartment to watch a movie with her cousin Adah. She shakes my hand shyly and sidles off.

I ask Margaret how Tamika feels about her plans to go forward with the adoption, and she says that Tamika really loves her mother, and she thinks that Tamika feels "way deep down inside of her that it was her fault that her mother is the way she is, and that maybe no one ever really gave her mother a chance. What I had to do is explain to her that my adoption was out of love and protection. I didn't get into the other reasons."

The other reason is her fear that Rhonda could step in at any time and take the children back. "I think DSS really bore it [her fear] out, believing that the birth mother has the ability to make decisions over someone who has loved and cared for these children. I did explain to Tamika about the Social Security benefits, and that as my children, they would receive that support, and I think she accepted that. And also that it had nothing to do with—after she reached a certain age—being with her mother."

"That's what she wants to do?"

"I think so. I tell her, when you are old enough to make choices, I won't try to stop you—advise you, yes, but not stop you."

Tamika barrels in to tell her grandmother a tale about a broken VCR, and who did it, and when, and why, and what she did to try and fix it. "So did I do something good?" she asks jokingly, but she holds her breath and waits for an answer. Margaret smiles and replies, "Yes—you're always good."

> Although teens may not reveal their emotions, internally they are often overwhelmed by the magnitude of their feelings. Adolescents like Tamika need to receive continued support and guidance both at home and from individual therapy in order to help address unresolved feelings of loss and abandonment. In addition, issues of "fault" and "guilt" must be addressed. Children in this situation need to realize that a child cannot ever cause parents to do harmful things or influence a parent's poor choices, and that they do not have a responsibility to take care of their dysfunctional parent. Children need to learn that they are bystanders in the parade of poor choices and consequences created by dysfunctional parents.
>
> The "Big Sister" and "Big Brother" type of mentoring programs are wonderful assets for children like Tamika. They offer safe, reliable adults with whom children can form a bond, have fun, and share feelings and thoughts.
>
> With help and guidance, children are able to recognize that they are capable of making positive choices, and that they can

orchestrate their lives so that those choices have favorable outcomes.

THE GENARROS

Grandparents long for, pray for, and fight for three things: to keep their grandchildren safe; to see their adult children come through their bad times to emerge as healthy, responsible people; and to come together as a family, healed and whole.

Jeannie and Vincent Genarro are as tenacious and valiant as knights on a crusade. They never gave up on their quest for their grandchild's safety, their daughter's maturity, and their family's preservation. Watching their story unfold provides some guidelines for grandparents embarking on their own harrowing crusades. In the remainder of this chapter, we see an example of developing that vital transition period between birth parent and child, as well as a few potential pitfalls to watch for when dealing with adult children.

It has not been easy for the Genarros to let go of custody and control of their grandson, Alexander. They work at it, agonize over it, and talk about it endlessly. And they grieve. They do it for the sake of their grandson, their daughter, and ultimately their family.

Teenage pregnancy, drugs, rebellion, and irresponsibility—all common ingredients in the simmering pot of turmoil the Genarro family tried desperately to keep the lid on. Inevitably the volatile mix boiled over, and Vincent and Jeannie were left to clean up.

"Her teenage years were really tough," Jeannie Genarro tells me, shaking her head. Rose had been running away, staying out all night, and partying since she was fourteen, and no matter what the Genarros did to curb her wild side, she continued to act out. They anguish over the fact that their son, Gary, a few years younger than Rose, "lost out" because "she took up all the energy and attention." Then at sixteen, she became pregnant.

"This was like one more thing. She did want to keep it. Of course, they think they're toys. So she lived with us. Her pregnancy was great. It seemed like she changed overnight from being rebellious and not coming home and things like that. She seemed to grow up a lot."

It was a short-lived reprieve.

Jeannie is in constant double-time motion. She fiddles with the peaks of her auburn hair, the color of dark-rubbed copper pennies, cut in a shag. It feathers down her neck and around her youthful face. She jumps up and down constantly to check if the tea water is boiling yet, to get milk, sugar, and napkins. She is a bundle of nervous energy—cute, quick, busy—and she talks at Chip-and-Dale speed. Jeannie is a young grandma, in her forties, and is dressed for a jog—pink "Bermuda" sweatshirt, gray leggings, and sneakers. She looks more like a teenager than a grandmother.

"When the baby was about three months old, she [Rose]) started going out, and we would allow it to happen. I don't know . . . my husband and I are very . . . we're enablers I guess. When I think back on it now, I think I would have done things very different in those early months, maybe. I don't know. It was hard to let her make her own mistakes. I think I interfered too much."

Jeannie stepped in to care for the newborn when she felt that Rose wasn't doing things right.

"I think I should've stepped back," she tells me, popping up to get honey from the cupboard, banging doors, shuffling contents to find the right jar.

"We were in close quarters here," she calls out from behind the refrigerator door, still looking for honey. The house is a small Cape, all blues and greens and wicker inside, absolutely pristine, newly built. Squeezed into a tightly packed, motley neighborhood of much older homes, it sits at the end of a cul-de-sac like an exclamation mark. This is an old fishing community, with deep ethnic roots. Stacks of lobster pots are as common here as lawn chairs in backyards, and stone Madonnas bless dark squares of freshly tilled earth that promise lush plots of tomato and pepper plants. You can almost gauge the health of the fishing industry here by the number of homes with peeling paint and the expansion of vegetable gardens.

You can't see the ocean from the Genarro's home, but you can smell it the moment you step out the door. You can feel it in the air and see it in the sky, gray and melancholy, heavy with moisture and salt. It makes the grass extra green and the hydrangeas as blue as the sea.

Rose was so young, Jeannie tells me, "so when she started asking to go out, we felt bad. But she started bringing home friends that were completely different. Then she started saying she would be home at a certain time and she didn't show, and it kept getting later and then not showing up at all. And it just got out of hand, and I didn't know how to stop it. I couldn't stop it."

Jeannie tried to be firm with Rose. She told Rose she would not babysit while she partied. "Then she started to come and take the baby out of the crib, taking him with her wherever she was going, riding around in cars, whatever. I just couldn't let that happen. I probably should've. I don't know. You tell me what the answer is."

She leans toward me with an intensity I hate to disappoint, her brown eyes boring into mine.

Guardianship—Adoption—Letting Go

"I have no idea," I tell her apologetically. I have no answers to give her. I don't know that anyone does. All of us paddle our own way, panting and sweating, down uncharted rivers, trying to avoid the rocks and undertow.

She continues, somewhat deflated, "I lost control of it, and I let her go."

After a few months, Rose heard of an apartment and was determined to live on her own. "In a way, I was sort of relieved. I don't know whether I was dreaming or what."

Jeannie hoped that this would be the start of a new chapter for Rose, that she would get her life together and prove that she was capable of being a mother to her young son. But the evening before the Genarros were to leave for a long-awaited vacation to the Bahamas, Rose came to get the baby in the middle of the night to take him with her to her new apartment.

"There was no furniture there. The baby would have to sleep on the floor with her. Which, I suppose, looking back on it now, is probably not the worst thing in the world. But he had a bed here, and I guess I just couldn't see them coming in and taking him out . . . and I knew she had those friends at the apartment. I got hysterical. I remember calling my girlfriend and saying, how could I leave tomorrow? I was just so stressed out. I cried all night."

"When I came home a week later, she was sitting in the house, and she had all those stray kids in my house—no baby. She had left the baby at my mother-in-law's, thank God! But I could tell the house had been partied in.

"I had to go see the baby. I wanted to get the baby. I swear to God, when that baby saw my face—eight months old—I could see the excitement that I was home." Her voice breaks, and tears flood her eyes. It is the only time she cries during the interview, from the memory of her baby grandson and the joy and recognition that lit up his little face at seeing her. She places her fingertips at her lips and lowers her head a moment to stop the momentum of emotion.

"Don't mind me," she apologizes and then continues with a quavering voice. "I took the baby and went home. It just got worse from there. The partying got worse."

Jeannie had just started a new career, one that she had worked hard to achieve and had put on hold until Rose was settled.

"I would come home from work, go to her house, pick up the baby, and bring the baby home because he slept at my house. I would go back in the morning and drop the baby off. I did all his laundry. If my husband got out from work early, he would pick the baby up. So the baby was only with her three or four hours." Unfortunately, it gave Rose more time to party.

"Somebody filed a 51A on her. I was flipping out because I thought, Oh my God! I've heard about these kids that get taken by the state and get put in foster care." She says "foster care" as if it was prison, or hell.

Jeannie explained to DSS that she had care of the baby at night, so he was not affected by the partying, but that Rose needed help. She needed counseling, she told them.

"I remember going over one day. The baby was about nine months old. He was in the tub, and she was somewhere else. He was standing up naked. He was so happy to see me, and he was jumping up and down. She was nowhere to be found. I said to her, 'Rose! You can't leave a baby in the tub. In one second they can drown!'"

"Did it surprise you that she had no mothering skills?" I ask.

"In a way it surprised me, because I just didn't think it would be possible that somebody could do that from the way I was

Guardianship—Adoption—Letting Go

brought up and the way I brought her up." Jeannie says that it was as if her daughter had "stopped growing" after the age of fifteen when she dropped out of school. She seemed to be perpetually stuck in an adolescent loop of self-absorption and partying.

Then she was arrested.

"One night she called me from the police station. There had been a raid at a party where there was LSD. She wanted me to come and get her. I said to her, 'I will come and get you, but I want you to give me legal custody of Alex. I am not going to take any more chances.'

"I had threatened before that, but I could never do it. I don't know if it was just because I thought that she was going to get her act together. Plus, it was my *daughter*. I didn't think she'd be this way her whole life! But something like this could ruin her whole life, if I was to take the baby. There was just so much going on emotionally—the ties that we had with my daughter, and then the ties we had with Alexander."

When the Genarros began their custody pursuit, the birth father and his parents blocked the proceedings. The paternal grandparents became alarmed because they had become involved in the baby's life by that time and wanted to ensure their visitation rights. They advised their son not to sign over custody until a lawyer looked over the agreement. Their lawyer then drew up an agreement solidifying visitation rights for the birth father and the paternal grandparents. At the time, Jeannie says, she was "so stressed out and needed this to happen quick," before Rose changed her mind. The delay cost them six months of nerve-wracking time, legal fees, and aggravation.

"Any little drawback or stall—I thought, This is it! We're going to lose him! I was like a mental case."

Thankfully, all custody issues were combined and heard during one court hearing. The Genarros were awarded temporary legal custody, and the birth father and paternal grandparents were awarded visitation rights.

The delay was stressful and costly for the Genarros, but the paternal grandparents and birth father did the right thing under the circumstances. Although Jeannie welcomes them into the baby's life and describes them as "nice people," in a more contentious situation, grandparents on the other side could lose visitation rights if they don't take the initiative and step in to secure them.

Jeannie says, "I never thought it was going to be permanent. I was just thinking we would have to do this until she gets her act together. I didn't think I would raise him forever. She did love him, and I knew that she loved him. But she just wasn't ready to give up her lifestyle."

Visitation for the birth mother was left up to the Genarros. "I allowed a lot of things that I shouldn't have allowed. Like she would come with her friends and she'd say, 'I want to take the baby for a walk.' She'd never show up on time, or she would show up in a car full of friends, and we'd have to jam the car seat in between them. I should have been stronger. I should have said, 'Look, if you want to see your son, you come by yourself.' Sometimes I did say no, if I thought it was a dangerous situation. But sometimes I would just let him go, and then worry after. I wasn't making good decisions sometimes . . . in regard to being a strong person and just saying no."

"Why do you think that happened?"

"I think I was just feeling guilty. I think I felt guilty about taking him from her. I felt like I *took* him!"

This grandmother needs to cut herself a break. She needs to recognize and take both pride and satisfaction in the fact that she and her husband made positive decisions for the sake of the grandchild. It is not easy for people to let themselves off the hook. If it remains difficult to do so, caregivers may benefit from short-term, focused counseling to address the unwarranted guilt.

Over the next couple of years, the Genarros grappled with their ambivalence, as well as with their daughter's inability to parent successfully or get her life going on an even keel. "She was going from apartment to apartment, and some of them were lousy. She never had him overnight, never. I wouldn't allow that. She had him two hours at a time. Sometimes she might do something good, like go with friends and walk the baby stroller down the boulevard and have lunch. And I thought, Oh wow! But then the time, even if she took him with one friend, she'd come back in a car with a bunch of other friends—they're all smoking in the car, the baby reeks of smoke, it was like . . . akkk!" Jeannie holds her head in her hands in disbelief and frustration.

I ask how her marriage held up with all that was happening, and she tells me, "We argue a lot. Because if I happened to let Alex go with her and he came back smelling of smoke, he [Vincent] would say things like, 'You shouldn't have let him go!' And I sort of resented that he could go to work every day. He didn't have to do the majority of it. Although if he was here now, he'd argue with me, saying, 'I gave up a lot too.' But if the baby was sick, I called in sick to my job, not him. I was the one, I felt, with more of the stress. I had to deal with Rose more. I was the one who went to court. But he went along with everything I said."

"So you were in agreement," I confirm. "And even though it was stressful, you were at least going in the same direction."

"Yes," she replies. "He was worried about the baby's safety. And he did have to share it while I worked. It was difficult."

Jeannie brings up her disappointment with the court system. "I felt like the court system didn't do anything. After a while, my lawyer said, 'Let's have a plan for the future.' So I said okay, let's have Rose work up to regular visitation. It was all done with mediators or through lawyers. The judge didn't ask anything." Alexander was never assigned a guardian ad litem.

"Of course, Rose's lawyer was free. Every time we went to court or had to draw up papers, I had to pay. I guess she has the rights because she's the mother, but the first time we went to court, she didn't even show up. And I thought, isn't this judge going to look and say, 'If this mother's so concerned that she wanted visitation, where is she?' But they never said anything about it; they just rescheduled.

Rose periodically petitioned the court for longer visitation and overnights, but she never managed to comply with the minimal requests Jeannie and Vincent made, like cleaning up the trash piled up outside the house she and her new boyfriend had rented, and having the electricity turned on. Jeannie tells me that she felt Rose actually liked the status quo. "She could use it to her advantage. She was used to it." Jeannie eventually told the court, "Before she gets the baby, I want her to have a job, to have a safe apartment, and to get counseling." Rose fulfilled those requirements sporadically at best. Meanwhile, whenever she had a personal setback or lost an apartment, she would move back in with her parents.

"As the years went by," Jeannie sighs and slumps in her chair, reliving her exhaustion, "she slowly made some changes." The

Genarros fixed up a bedroom in her new apartment for Alex so that he could start to spend overnights. He was now nearly four years old. "Then one night around Christmastime, I went in the apartment, and there were the people there that she got arrested with. I picked him right up out of the bed, and I wrapped him up, and I took him out of the house.

"When I got home, she called and said, 'Did you see us divvying up our pot on the kitchen table?' I am so naive I didn't even see that, but I said, 'Yeah, I did.' And I thought, all this time she's been fooling me! Me thinking she's doing better, and now she has those same friends there, and the baby is there, so how much is she thinking about him? But that really got to her, when I took the baby.

"How it worked out, finally, was she left that boyfriend and came home to live again." Rose began to show a solid sense of responsibility, and the Genarros felt that she was straightening out and that it was time to place more trust in her. Also, Rose had received counseling on and off over the last few years, which Jeannie felt was finally beginning to pay off.

There are some wonderful prevention and early intervention programs for young mothers and families at risk, programs like the Goodstart Initiative, sponsored by the Massachusetts Society for the Prevention of Cruelty to Children, and mentoring services such as Parent to Parent and Visiting Moms. These programs are designed to offer emotional support, to teach young mothers the skills they need to care for their children, and to hook them up with a supportive network of peers in similar circumstances.

"My husband and I went on a vacation, and she was almost the main one responsible for the baby. Rose did a good job. When I came home, the house was clean, and I felt really good. We started looking for an apartment for her."

"Did you help her out financially?"

"Every apartment that she got, I fixed up the baby's room." We both laugh in recognition of a fellow hypervigilant. "I had to make sure that he had everything he needed. Being the enabler that I was," she laughs at herself again, "I felt like I had to make a home for her. I bought her furniture. I thought it would help her." Most times Rose lost everything. This time at the age of twenty-one years old, after nearly five years of ups and downs, it finally stuck.

After Rose was settled once again, the Genarros allowed Alex overnights during the week. "We were still taking him on the weekends, but he got used to going back and forth. So by the time we did the custody thing, he was ready to go with her."

Jeannie stops to mention again that she felt abandoned by the court. They never "checked to make sure" Rose was fulfilling the requirements that had been set. "I guess they were too busy," Jeannie offers generously, making excuses for them.

"I felt like she was doing well enough that he could go back with her. Besides, I was so sick of dealing with all of this stuff. I didn't know that she was going to get any better. I didn't think that she was going to change that much more. And am I going to keep this child forever? Is that the plan? Am I going to fight with her, because now she wants custody? And she was crying a lot, looking back on all the things she missed. But when I gave custody over, I never really felt she had made all the changes that she needed to. It's just that he was sort of out of danger." She says this as if she's trying to convince us both.

Alexander has been with Rose for two years. "It's been a struggle because I miss him wicked. I'm glad it worked out this way, because I like my freedom now. I never realized how much I missed it. I lost all my friends at that time. They were all at the point that I was, getting new jobs and working. They're going to hang around with somebody who has a baby? I never got back with them.

"Now I don't even know how I did it, because he's a handful when he stays over. And I'm glad, looking at the future, that I am not raising teenagers. But I suppose, if I still had him, I just wouldn't think of that . . ." Jeannie trails off pensively.

"Oh, you would think about it," I interrupt, "and it would be horrible," I joke. "But you would do it."

"But it's been difficult, because I miss him wicked. He's my spirit! And I raised him till he was five, so it's something that I don't think I'll ever get over." Jeannie quotes a remark made by my friend, Margaret Walker-Jackson, who appeared with me on a local television segment about raising grandchildren. "One thing that lady said and I'm hoping that it's going to be true, is if you have them until they're four or five, then they are sort of already what they're going to be. So I hope that that's going to be true, because today's world is so hard. I mean, my daughter has made a tremendous amount of change, but it's not how I would raise children, and it's not what I wanted for Alex.

"There are a lot of struggles between her and Alex, but my husband and I just step away from it." Jeannie tries to be supportive of Rose. Sometimes Rose calls her mother after an argument with her son, "I don't know how you ever did it, Ma." Jeannie comforts her, "I know. You just have to try and get through it."

Vincent Genarro arrives home at this point. He is very Italian— it takes one to know one, I think to myself—black curly hair, hawkish nose cutting through a weathered face, trim and fit looking in his jeans and work shirt. Jeannie leaps up for introductions. After exchanging pleasantries, he sits down with us, pushes his chair away from the table, leans back, and folds his arms across his chest.

"Even now," Jeannie continues, "I have to not say things I really want to say. Sometimes my husband says them, and she'll hang up on him. It's very hard, it's like she's raising *our* child, and I don't know if that feeling is ever going to go."

> A mix of powerful emotions will continue to affect caregivers who, for one reason or another, relinquish custody of their grandchildren back to birth parents. The reality is that only one factor will help to resolve the pain and help to let go—time. I would advise grandparents to take each day as it comes, and face each bout of sadness with the satisfaction that they played an important role in their grandchild's life.

"I don't know what other people do, but if we want him to play baseball, we sign him up. We pay for his tuition at parochial school, so at least he'll get some good morals. Not that she's not a good person. But this generation is just . . . different. She doesn't think like we do as far as what his needs are. Maybe because she didn't have him growing up. It's a struggle for her, and it's a struggle for us to let go. We still say too much, I think, but I don't think that will change. I tell her, 'Even if you don't listen to me, let me say it, please.'"

"How does she take it?" I ask.

"I think she feels that we feel that she can't do a good job. Well, in some ways that's true. It's not that she can't do a good job, but it's not the job that I would do if I were raising him. Now she has a little girl, three months old, and I don't have the same issues with her as I do about Alex. And I think because she didn't have Alex, she's really close with this baby and is enjoying every minute of her, and I like to see that. We try really hard a lot of times to keep our mouths shut."

"I can't keep mine shut," Vincent declares, unrepentant. "She hung up on me the other day, but that's the first time she's hung up on me in a long time. She ended up calling me back, whereas before she would've never called back. I think she felt bad hanging up on me, maybe even thought a little bit about what I had said, and that's all I want to do is get her thinking.

"The issue was karate the other day. He's supposed to be there at four o'clock. She calls up at three and leaves a message, 'Alex is not going to go today; he's being punished.' She can punish him all she wants, but she shouldn't take away constructive things that he's doing. That's not punishment. That's destroying him as far as I'm concerned, all that he's been working for," Vincent proclaims, a hard edge of anger cutting into his voice.

Jeannie continues, "If we were his parents, that's how we should feel, but he shouldn't be our responsibility. It's hard to get away from that, though. In a way, we're still raising him like he's ours." She is talking both to me and Vincent, weighing her feelings, her thoughts. She says quietly, almost in a whisper, almost to herself, "Maybe when he gets older, we'll . . . ," and trails off, lost in thought.

I point out to them that through it all, the ups and downs, the arguments, the tears and years of struggle, they were able to maintain that strong bond, the iron grip of family connectedness.

Vincent responds with a half smile curling up, breaking open his tough-guy exterior, and I can see pride flickering around the edges.

"She's come back, let's put it that way. She was gone, she really was. I think she's done a good job. She made a comeback; she's come back to us." He stops for a moment and says finally, "We worked at it. We fought tooth and nail for it."

Letting go means that the loss needs to be put in perspective, the loss needs to be understood, the loss needs to be felt, and most important, the loss needs to be accepted and resolved.

Certainly the feelings around the loss will come up over and over again, which is healthy and normal. A movie or a similar situation on the evening news, or even a song on the radio could trigger memories and a strong emotional response. Sometimes people try to bury the sting of feelings. However, this denial often surfaces in the form of physical ailments, such as ulcers, later on. The other extreme is for the feelings of loss to loom so large that people find they are consumed by them. They may not be able to function in the present because they are stuck in the past.

Although we cannot always control what we feel, we can control what we do with those feelings. Grandparents should look for a healthy outlet for expressing their feelings and recognize that their care and comfort had a positive effect on their grandchild that will be a constant source of strength from which the child can draw always.

NINE

Grandchildren—Having Their Say

> You be a good girl now. You hear? Don't you make people
> think I didn't raise you right. You hear?
>
> —Maya Angelou, *I Know Why the Caged Bird Sings*

President Barack Obama, Maya Angelou, former president Bill
Clinton, Carol Burnett, Jack Nicholson, Oprah Winfrey, James
McEvoy, Willie Nelson, Eric Clapton—what do these well-known
individuals have in common? They were all raised by grandparents, each under different circumstances and for varying amounts
of time. When I envisioned this last chapter, I saw a series of
glowing, happily-ever-after reports from well-adjusted, successful
individuals like those who just happened to be raised by grandparents. That is not quite what I got.

What I encountered in the process of interviewing grandchildren for this last segment was relatively happy, healthy, but somewhat ambivalent young adults, still working to put the events of
their childhoods into perspective. The stories they tell are full of
loving anecdotes, secure foundations, and family connectedness,

Raising Our Children's Children

but they also contain elements of confusion, disappointments, and unresolved hurt.

What follows are the stories of four grandchildren, each at different stages of life: Kit, a Hispanic teenager; Linda, twenty-one, a biracial college student from the inner city; David, a budding politician of twenty-five; and Paul, thirty-six, with a family of his own. They are a diverse group from different backgrounds and economic strata. They each grew up with various legal statuses, from informal arrangements to legal adoption. But for the most part, their stories unfold in similar ways. Because I give my interviewees the lead, usually letting them take me where they want to go, I often get something other than what I expect. But patterns and truths emerge from their unique, untampered-with perspectives. What becomes clear from these interviews is that the loss, absence, or failure of one's parents is a lifelong legacy that leaves an indelible imprint on even those who have been fortunate enough to have loving family replacements step up to the plate. These adult grandchildren demonstrate how important those replacements are to their development and how the way in which grandparents handle the ebb and flow of family relationships is critical to the health and stability of the children involved.

David's story is the one most unlike the others. I feel compelled to include his set of circumstances because they are so commonplace—the somewhat easier, often part-time versions of raising grandchildren. Also I was talked into including such a story by my friend Ruth.

I sometimes share "the Ride" into Boston with Ruth on our way to the Massachusetts Department of Elder Affairs for meetings. She is in her sixties and has MS. The Ride, a shuttle-bus service for the handicapped, allows her a companion, and if I'm running late, which is rare, much to the consternation of Ruth who is a stickler for punctuality, I join her. I always enjoy this time with her. She is an interesting, salty "old pacifist" from the 1940s and 1950s, when protesting violence and war were dangerously unpopular pursuits. We have wonderful talks on our meandering way into town.

Ruth is a feisty, no-nonsense lady with a killer-diller smile that she flashes while zinging me with her straight-shooter retorts. She gets along very well, thank you, with her two aluminum canes decorated with yellow paper Stars of David taped to the handles by one of her grandchildren. One morning on the Ride, Ruth lambastes me. She asks me how work on my book is going, and when I tell her whom I'm interviewing, she pulls me up short.

"What about us?" she challenges me. She thinks I should include the grandparents who are always there for their grandchildren, the ones called on constantly to be "parents in a pinch." They may not have custody of grandchildren, but they pick up the slack for the busy, overburdened, and overwhelmed parents, running interference with the neglectful, irresponsible, and hurtful school or managing dentist appointments, ballet lessons, and birthday parties. Grandparents who spend their weekdays playing nurse to sick children, and on weekends find themselves on damp, arthritis-inducing soccer fields, or risking heatstroke while sitting on fanny-numbing baseball bleachers. The countless, uncounted, underappreciated grandparents. The glue that quietly holds so many kids' lives, so many families, together.

"Ruth," I plead, "give me a break. That's a whole different book!" But I changed my mind when I found David.

Raising Our Children's Children

DAVID

David's parents were divorced when he was eight years old. But he had always spent most of his time with his grandparents. "It used to be me, my grandmother, and my dog, Onyx. We used to drive all over town doing errands for my grandfather. He owned a grocery store. I used to hang out with them. And then when I started getting involved in sports, baseball, my grandfather was always at the games. We used to play father-son games out there . . . sixty years old . . . running around the bases. I was his son. He had only one daughter, and now finally he had a son that he could go to the games with, talk sports, go fishing, and do all that. He used to go everywhere, driving an hour just to go see baseball tournaments and football games. I'd look out and see him in the stands."

His parents were twenty and in college when they got married and dropped out. His grandparents helped the young couple as much as they could. His father worked at the grocery store the grandfather owned. Once they were able to get back on their feet, they went back to school and completed their education. David was about four years old at the time, and from that point on, his grandparents basically raised him.

"What happened was when my mother got divorced, I moved in with my grandparents just as a temporary thing," David explains. "It started off as temporary, but then after about a year, they ended up putting an addition onto the house and said, 'Move in with us.' It was partly for financial reasons and partly for convenience.

"Well, my mother—she's a schoolteacher—she'd be working. Our relationship is more like my mother is like my sister almost, and my grandparents were my parents. That's the relationship that I have now with my mother."

Grandchildren—Having Their Say

I ask if he remembers the divorce and whether it was upsetting to him. "No, I don't remember it being upsetting. I think it was because I was happy where I was. It wasn't all that messy. To give credit to my dad, he understood what the situation was and didn't try to use me as a pawn. I guess that happens a lot. He probably figured my mother and my grandparents would do the best job raising me; he obviously knew he couldn't do that. He always sent me cards and would call and stuff like that. It's not like he was totally out of the loop."

David is adorable, from his teddy-bear eyes, as round as buttons, to his wavy blond hair and cleft chin. He is every mother's dream for her daughter—what a catch! Oy, if only I were a matchmaker! David works for Congressman Barney Frank and looks as if he fell out of the Brooks Brothers wagon, all oxford cloth—light blue to match his eyes—and penny loafers. He has a gee-whiz enthusiasm that's infectious. I always give David a kiss when I see him; he has that kind of face, the kind of cheeks you either want to kiss or pinch, like a yenta.

His most endearing quality is that he is oh so careful to say good things about his mother. Each time he gets on a roll regarding his grandparents, he stops to say an alternately positive thing about his mother. I think it's both unconscious and conscious. I think his loyalties are just a little bit torn.

"My mother is my hero, the way she was able to go back to school and get her degree, and now she's a schoolteacher. She always gave me everything I needed or wanted. It was always me first. And when I look back on it, I am really thankful."

"What about your father?" I ask.

David just shrugs, "Well . . ."

"You didn't keep in touch?"

"We did, and we didn't, you know? We just . . . for whatever reason . . . I guess I was just a little too young to really know what happened when they got divorced. My mother kind of said, this is our family, me, you, and my grandmother and grandfather. And that was the strength right there.

"It's funny, I never really thought too much about it. I mean my grandparents were so great. The more I look back on it, I am sure that at some point when I was a kid I got upset about it. But I don't think it's affected me that much.

"I remember when it was Father's Day and I was about twelve or thirteen, and instead of saving my allowance for a gift I wrote my grandfather a note—it was all misspelled; it had all the *x*'s where the *a*'s should have been or whatever—basically thanking him, 'You've been a great father to me,' and all that stuff. He still has it."

"I'm sure he does!" I tell him. "It's probably one of his treasures."

His mother never remarried. David says she "made a commitment to me, that I was the most important thing."

I ask if his grandparents had the main parenting role, and he says diplomatically, "It was almost like parenting by committee." Although they had very different parenting styles—David's mother was very laissez-faire, his grandparents' were discipline oriented—they did not clash openly about it. David recalls that his grandparents deferred to his mother for the final word.

We are chatting over pasta and a salad at a little Italian restaurant near Congressman Frank's Massachusetts headquarters, with the clang of dishes and utensils and the noisy drone of lunch-hour clamor competing for attention. David tells me, "I think we've gotten too nuclear. The sense of extended family isn't around anymore." Congressman Frank's mother, Elsie Frank, who was the president of MAOA (Massachusetts Association of Older Americans), has spoken to David about the value of programs that pair children with elders, for instance reading to children at day care or in the elementary schools, or rocking and holding infants at area hospitals. He agrees that elders have much to give.

"I go to the New Bedford Y, and I love hanging out with the old-timers, the guys that have been going to the Y for years. You learn so much just sitting there talking to these guys. It's funny listening them talk about Ted Williams. . . . I'm never afraid to ask them questions because I like to learn from them."

"Well, sure, because you've always had such a positive role model in your grandfather, you don't see them as these aliens with nothing to give," I agree.

A couple of years ago, David's grandfather had a heart attack. "That was really tough. Going through the divorce or any of that stuff growing up was nothing compared to that, and here I was an adult. That was a lot tougher to handle than anything else, to see a guy who's been so strong all his life, to see him in the hospital like that . . ." David trails off shaking his head.

I ask David what he would say to other kids being raised by grandparents.

"Embrace your grandparents; embrace your family because some people don't have that. Growing up, looking back, I was royalty. And I consider myself so lucky to have that. Be happy for what you have."

KIT

Of all the grandchildren I interviewed, a girl I will call Kit was by far the most troubled. Her life had been a series of abusers, disasters, and heartbreaks. She was very fragile emotionally in spite of the safe haven her grandmother had provided for much of her life. She appeared to be vulnerable to repeating the cycle of self-destruction, traveling the same path her drug-addicted mother took. During the course of the interview, she regaled me with wild tales. I had trouble deciphering how much of it was true, how much fabrication, and how much embellishment on basic facts. She was eager to talk to me—so eager, in fact, that I found out later she had lied about her age. Ultimately I was unable to use her interview because she was underage and technically in the custody of her birth mother, though she lived with and was being raised by her grandmother.

Kit was the first of the grandchildren I talked with, and oddly enough she set the pattern I was to see in most of the other interviews. Kit enthusiastically embarked, in her adolescent way, on a litany of transgressions perpetrated by her grandmother: she was too possessive, too strict, not trusting, unappreciative, and didn't understand her, her music, her nose ring, or her need for leeway. And when she was done with this self-righteously indignant laundry list of wrongs, she then bowled me over with a sincere, if unexpected, declaration of love and appreciation for her grandmother. Once you scratched the brash surface and moved beyond her teenage swagger, she was clearly centered at the core by the knowledge that her grandmother was the one person that would always be there for her.

Like Kit, each grandchild had an agenda. They needed to get things off their chests, clear their individual air. They wanted to tell me about their struggles and grievances, and then once that was done, they moved on. It disturbed me at first, and then I realized that if you were to interview anyone about their childhood, they would do the same thing. They would tell you stories about the particularly hard row they had to hoe, the injustices they suffered, and the difficulties they had to overcome. Then they would wax poetic, about how good it was, how green, as no other, was their personal childhood valley. The adult children profiled here are no different. Here is what they want you to know about themselves, what they wish to tell other grandchildren in similar situations, and what it meant to them to be raised by grandparents.

PAUL

Traveling out to another far-flung valley, I pass lakes and hills with names like Mattawa and Monadnock, and swollen, rushing rivers with jagged, rocky beds that curl around hillside passes and race by cars like mine, wending cautiously down the narrow roads. In the summer, the rivers slow to an inviting gurgle; the killer rocks become stepping stones, skipping stones. But now, on the brink of spring, they are in a fury to get down the mountainous ridges—like reckless teenagers, impatient, thrilled with the wild ride, heedless of the end.

This area is a hunter's heaven, acres of dense forest and natural springs, unbroken miles of ancient deer paths and sheltered pools, scarred only by incipient duck blinds. It is beautiful. This is where tourists come in the fall to worship foliage, to buy corn, pumpkins, jars of put-up relish and homemade wild blueberry jam. They come to pick apples with the kids—Macoun, Baldwin, Rome Beauty, Winesap—jostling down mowed paths in hay wagons to bountiful, forgiving orchards. Some stay on for the peace, the pace, the endless, breathable space.

The Powickis have been here for generations, Paul Powicki nearly all his life. At thirty-six, Paul is a serene and steady young man of medium height and build, with dark, slightly receding hair, dark eyes, and skin the color of a late August tan. He is very soft spoken and deliberate in his speech, visibly measuring everything he says, and it is obvious he has given everything he says long, exhaustive thought.

Paul was adopted at six months of age by his maternal grandparents. I ask him if he knows the circumstances surrounding his adoption, and he replies, "I do *now*. It took a divorce, a lot of work, and dealing with who I consider to be my parents in trying to find out what was going on."

"My birth mom was going to school at Harvard, and she met my father who was a Chilean citizen. I was a result of that. She wanted to get married at the time, and he didn't. She was twenty-five. My grandmother, who has always been the dominant leader of the family, said, 'You are not going to give this baby up for adoption. We are going to raise him.' So what they did is they sent her to Ohio to get her out of the area, because they didn't want anybody to know about it. Because this is where all the Powickis and all the Guralniks were raised, and it was a big, big, big family secret.

"She went to live with a person I have always considered to be my brother and his wife. That's where I was born, and then about six or seven months after that, I was brought up to Brooksboro."

"So your birth mom had you for six months," I confirm.

"Yes."

"Was it difficult for her?" I ask, thinking it must have been absolutely wrenching to give up a baby after caring for him for six months.

"I've tried to talk to her about this. She just really does not want to deal with any of the issues around that. It was interesting, though. She was really kind of like a participant observer in my life for many, many years. I can remember being a very small boy and having her take me up to the pond behind the house. I can remember one time when she came home and we went for a walk up to the ledges, and she took a lot of pictures of me. I always looked at her as a sister. Everybody told me that."

"As you were growing up, did you sense that there was something else you weren't being told?" I ask, and he begins to unravel the threads of his childhood for me piece by piece.

"When I was nine years of age, I can remember getting off the bus. And there was a kid up the road, Billy, who I still know to this day, and he was teasing me, 'You're adopted, you're adopted!' And geez, I was really disturbed by this. I was like, 'What the hell's he talking about?' I didn't have any concept of that. After that, it felt that something was different. My mother and father always treated me as truly one of their own; there was never a question of that. But he started me wondering.

"It wasn't until I was twelve years of age, I was sitting down with my mom—my father was working the swing shift—and we were having pirogues; they are a Polish food. They're kind of like a ravioli, only big, and they're filled with cheese and potato and mushrooms, and you sauté them a little bit in butter. They're really nice. And I was sitting at the table. I was sitting in my father's chair, and she says, 'Your father and I wanted to tell you something. We've been thinking about this for a while, and we wanted to let you know you're adopted.' I was like, Oh? And it seemed like right after that she was asking me for the pepper to put on the pirogues—and that was it! I was just left with that. I was so shocked at the time. I . . . I could feel the coldness come over me. I was like, 'Oh my God, Billy was right after all these years.'"

"When they dropped that bomb on you, you didn't respond in any way?" I ask while Paul shakes his head sadly, no. "You probably had a million questions, but there was no way to ask?" Paul just continues to shake his head no.

"I thought it must be such a bad thing to be adopted. Because kids had been picking on me, like Billy. It wasn't a thing to be proud of in any sense. That's one of the things I learned from that situation. And you know, they kept it from me for so many years. I inferred it's not something to talk about, and I didn't talk about it, you know, to my friends or family members, for a long time.

"It's interesting that my parents were kind of on a little denial trip themselves. Because two years later, I was taken to a hospital in Boston to get some blood tests done. And when I asked, 'Why am I having these blood tests done?' my mother said, 'Well, you know your father has cancer, and we wanted to get you checked.' I knew it was odd, and I'm thinking, why am I really here? I was panicking!

"A couple of years after that, I discovered this letter. I can remember digging around my mother's drawers, and I found this letter that came from some attorney in Florida. And the letter said, 'This letter is in regards to the fourteen-year-old boy whose father is Miguel Cantera.' Miguel Cantera has a rare blood disorder, and he almost died on the operating table because he had an allergic reaction to an anesthetic. So that's why I was tested."

"So your birth father must have initiated the testing because he was concerned about you."

"Right."

"As time went on, I started to wonder, who is my mother? And where is she? And why is there this secrecy about it? I started to rebel. Through years of psychotherapy about it, I've learned that my rebellion was related to the confusion and the wondering. I can remember that one of the biggest ways I rebelled was to go into the service. All the other Powickis all went to college. When I told my mother, she cried, and my father gave me what's known as a Polish wave."

"What's a Polish wave?" I ask.

"A Polish wave is . . ." He laughingly demonstrates a dismissive gesture of the hand that suggests, 'Be gone with you then!'

After his tour in the service, he went on to college, got his master's degree, and now works as a rehabilitation counselor. He talks about some rocky years between the time he went into the service and the time he finally sought therapy—years of difficulty making commitments, engaging in acting-out behaviors, broken relationships, and an inability to trust.

"For me to sit here and do this today, I consider it a milestone. In the past it was like, 'Thou shalt *never* speak of this' was my view.

"When I started to go to school, it was like, 'This isn't an issue; it's not a problem for me.' A couple of times I asked my mother about my biological parents, and she'd say, 'Well, you know, we're really not sure.' And then came the Santa Claus story, I call it. My mother said, 'We went to the orphanage, and we saw this cute little monkey, and we knew you were the one for us.' And I was like, Geez, that's it?

"When I was about twenty-six, I asked again, and they gave me the same answer. And that was the story I was given consistently throughout my twenties."

"So when did you start your detective work?"

"My detective work started around the same time that my divorce happened. I was sitting across from a client one day. The person was really struggling, and I said to him, 'It seems like you've really got to be honest with yourself, honest with what you feel, and honest about what you want for yourself.' And when I went home, I realized, Wait a minute, what are you doing? How can I be prescribing this to a person, when I am not even doing it for myself?

"I called my brother, and I said, 'Tom, I've got some questions for you about my biological mother.' He said, 'I don't know anything; you've got to talk to Ma.' I said, 'I've talked to Ma; she gives me the same damn Santa Claus story.' He said, 'Well, Ma knows all the details. I was really young at the time. I really don't remember much.' I mean, there's a twenty-year difference between the two of us, so once again, I'm thinking he knows something; there's something else, and he just won't share it. I happened to stop by home, and my mother said, 'You've been doing a little detective work tonight, I hear. I hear you've been checking up on who your mother is. Your father and I had a talk, and we're going to talk to you about this tomorrow.' There was a part of me that was excited, and there was a part of me that was as scared as all hell.

"Of course my father didn't want anything to do with it. My mother was sitting on the couch and said, 'We've talked to your mother, and she said that it's okay if you know this information.' She was tearful as she was telling me this and just very upset. Finally she told me, 'Your sister Kay is your mother.'

"My response at that point was, 'Oh, thank God! Thank God I am a Powicki! Thank God she's alive! Thank God I know what my roots are!' Because, Deborah, that was the biggest thing, just that constant, constant wondering. It really felt like . . ." Paul gives a huge, heaving sigh. "Eighty pounds was lifted off my back at that point.

"I went home after that, and I was talking to my wife, and she said, 'Did you find out?' And I said, 'Yeah.' And she said, "I knew who it was.'

"She *knew*?" I ask, shocked.

"She knew. I really felt deceived. Here was a person that I had just married, and I really felt like she was in collusion with this whole cast of characters. I could feel, as time went on from that point, more and more that I just can't stay anymore." Paul soon left his wife, began therapy, and "started working on a lot of this stuff.

"I started picking up the self-help literature, books on psychology. I figured if I read enough, I could reduce the anxieties. That doesn't happen by just reading books. I think with a person getting into a therapeutic relationship, or having the family in a therapeutic relationship, and starting to see, 'Gee, this is really scary for me, this must be uncomfortable for *children*. This is hard for *me* to work on. I am unsure, and I'm struggling to recognize those feelings; imagine how hard it is for children.' And therapy is a real benefit not only for the child, but for the parent as well. In the process of therapy, I had my biological mom come to therapy, which was really difficult for her."

But all the years of burying the truth had taken their toll, and Paul's birth mother was unable to come to terms with the past. Paul asked his adoptive mother into therapy as well, but unfortunately she was uncomfortable with the whole idea of counseling and told him in no uncertain terms, "No, I don't want to do *that*!"

"I think the biggest thing that [therapy] did was allow me to get in touch with how I was feeling. Not just about being adopted, but about who I am, what I wanted." Because Paul had his master's in social work, he came into therapy with his own self-diagnosis. "Core identity issues, adjustment disorder with mixed emotional features . . . this is what's going on for me," Paul told his therapist. "But after a while, I put the diagnosis aside and started to work on things like, how am I feeling toward my biological mother, as well as my grandmother, as well as my grandfather, as well as my wife? I think therapy for me in the beginning was, 'Okay, let's see if we can ground you here,' because there was a part of me that just wanted to leave the area, there was a part of me that just wanted to sweep it back under the rug and not deal with it, and there was also another part of me that didn't want anything to do with my wife.

"As soon as I found out about my [birth] mom, I was on this other quest, [to find his birth father] with all the same feelings." When Paul tried to question his birth mother about his birth father, she was evasive. Fortunately for Paul, he worked part time at the police department. "There's a brotherhood and a sisterhood there." Paul tapped into information dug up through that valuable resource and subsequently found his birth father's address. He sent a card and a picture at Christmas of that year. "And the next thing I know, he called me at work. Since then we've developed a great relationship." Paul has siblings from his birth father's marriage, some of whom do not want to deal with having a half brother under these circumstances. With others, "We're still in the building stage.

"What's interesting is that not only do I have Polish in me, but there is also Chilean as well as Austrian," he says with wide-eyed wonder and pride.

"So you really have a rich heritage."

"Deborah, the moment I found out I was a Powicki, you can't imagine the amount of peace I felt in my life. In spite of the secrecy, there was a lot of consistency with the Powicki family. I deal with a lot of families today in my profession, and it's hurting to see the conditions that a lot of people are struggling with.

"I always knew the limits, and religion was a very big factor in our family. I have a hell of a work ethic, and that comes from Emily and Leo Powicki. My father is dead now, but I can remember many, many days that I'd be working with him, whether it was picking stones, driving the tractor, driving the truck, or making something in the shop. I was truly part of the family, and loved and shown right from wrong. I love my mother immensely, and she is still a big part of my life. Finding out the truth was almost healing in a way; it was so much easier to accept.

"It was the toughest year of my life, but at the same time, it's allowed me to become a much better husband [Paul has remarried], a much better friend. I'm much more open and honest with people. My Christianity has blossomed through this whole experience. I hate to use the term "born again," but I feel much more at peace. I am not in therapy now, but if I need to go back to therapy, I'm okay with that. So sitting here today, I feel extremely fortunate."

"Was there ever a rift within the family that occurred because of all that came out?"

"Not really. One of the offshoots of what happened is that we grew a lot closer. A lot of those resentments that I had on a deeper level seem to have abated because I was able to work through who my biological parents were and a lot of my relationship issues, and working out my feelings.

"If people learn one thing from this interview: *secrecy is destructive.* When kids start asking questions, tell them the truth. Don't bullshit around with this stuff. This is somebody's physiological and psychological makeup here we're dealing with. I can remember having my stomach in knots just wondering."

I ask Paul what he'd like to say to other grandchildren, and he whispers reverentially, almost like a prayer, "Be thankful. Be thankful for being kept where you are desired and loved."

LINDA

Linda was the last person I interviewed. She is a young woman who embodies everything grandparents hope for. She is successful, confident, gracious, and has come to appreciate the sacrifices her grandmother made. She remains solidly connected to her family. In some ways, however, she also reveals some aspects of what we grandparents hope against. Linda is a child divided. She remains in a struggle against the divisions of class, race, heritage, and loyalties. She combines the maturity to work through adolescent issues with her grandmother with a blind spot that pent-up anger has provided regarding the failings of her birth parents. She remains in denial over how deeply she has been wounded by her father's absence and focuses heavily, almost exclusively, on her birth mother's lack of racial sensitivity.

Linda is still unfolding; like the flowers closed down tight on the early spring afternoon I visited her, she is on the verge of blossoming. She needs to do the hard work of sorting through her complicated family structure and finding, identifying, examining, and putting to rest each of her feelings about her birth parents, one by one, before she can emerge unencumbered and bloom.

If Zeus walked among the mortals today, I am convinced he would be ensconced somewhere at Yale University; this place looks like it was built for the gods. Maybe he would borrow books from this library near where I'm sitting, a structure that looks like an ancient Roman cathedral. He would walk up to the megalithic, sinuous checkout desk, his mythic footfalls echoing through the cool, indifferent halls overlooked by soaring, stained-glass depictions of other more banal deities. He would stride along the bricked footpaths that lead past these majestic granite edifices. Zeus would feel at home among the domed, arched, turreted, spired castles that rise up in surreal side-by-side existence with students impossibly gliding by on rollerblades, toting lumpy backpacks, and wearing shredded jeans. He would look right here; the rest of us look wrong, like shabby, inconsequential, intruding ants.

I have time to ruminate on these things ad nauseam because I am sitting in front of the Sterling Memorial Library at Yale University thirty minutes early for my one o'clock meeting with Linda Swan, who is a student here.

It is the first perfect spring day of the year, the kind of day that makes you doubt winter. This spring has been slow in coming, laboring to break through mean drizzle and raw winds. Today the trees wave at the stringy clouds that drift by, and baby leaves shudder with delight at the fine blue sky and the fond, firm gaze of sunlight. However this interview turns out, I think, even if she doesn't show, I'm glad to be sitting here on this cool stone bench hugging my knees with the sun on my face.

I forgot to ask Linda what she looks like, so I play a private guessing game with every young black woman that passes, matching them up with the voice on the phone, the image I conjured. I check my watch, 12:55. I begin to think I am in the wrong place at the wrong time, so I abandon the only shady bench under lacy trees that border the walkway to the library steps to have a look around. I scan the sweeping grounds dotted with students stretched out in the grass, trying on the first real warmth of the season. I look all the way up and down first one walkway and then the other and slowly circle the sleek, black marble fountain—a refreshing antidote to the Greco-Roman glut. Then I see her. She is striding with long, confident legs toward the library steps, black leather backpack slung over a bared shoulder; a short, gauzy sundress the color of straw; and stacked espadrilles. She looks around a bit, never breaking stride, and enters the library with me trying to catch up on my shorter legs and comparatively Minnie Mouse-like steps. I rush to catch her—my last interview.

When we meet up, we move along to the dreary basement cafeteria to talk, the hidden underbelly of the ornate book temple above us. Linda is tall and slender, but strong looking and solid, as opposed to willowy or lanky. She has a perfectly oval face and large, shining eyes under well-defined, jet-black brows, sharp as arrows. Her hair is a close cap of small black swirls, and her skin is the color of warm.

She is very formal with me; her answers to my questions are short and to the point. Oh no, I think at first, this is like pulling teeth. I ladle out questions one after the other to sustain the flow. "And so . . . ," I keep saying, trying to draw her out. She is careful—friendly and pleasant, but guarded. I wonder what it is she holds so closely to herself. Her brown eyes, the same shade as mine, look ceiling-ward as she considers what she will say and how she will say it, exactly how much she will give me.

Linda has been with her grandmother since she was a baby. She tells me she sees both her birth parents regularly but says dryly, "They don't participate actively in my life as far as support, financial or emotional. My mom, she does try. However, considering the circumstances . . . um . . . that precipitated my being under my grandmother's guardianship, the need never arose for me to look to her for that support because I've never had it, so I never wanted it, and I don't care to have it now."

It takes my breath away, the force of her cool rationale. "So why don't we go back, if you want, and talk about what precipitated it," I suggest.

"Well, my mom is white. Italian American, third generation. My older brother was born out of wedlock, so at the time, that wasn't the best thing to happen. My father's family was much more receptive to my mother than my mother's family was to my father. So basically, she was disowned, had no money, nowhere to go, so she stayed with my grandmother. They got married later when I was born. She got really sick, ill. She was hospitalized for a couple of years, so my grandmother took us in. My father went into the Marines, and basically that was the end of their marriage."

She is rushing through this, not entirely comfortable, curt almost. I think she's wondering why the heck she ever agreed to do this interview. I ask her why her mother was hospitalized, and she replies coolly, "She had a breakdown."

"After she came back home, she didn't want to displace us again, so she just left us there." Her voice is smooth as cream, but there is a rough overlay that winks in and out of her speech, surfacing only now and then, scraping hard over a telling phrase; it bears down when she says, "left us there." I think she is totally unaware of this revealing lapse, and would be mighty displeased with herself if she knew.

"And she wasn't able really to take care of kids, never mind two black kids." There it is again, that harsh dip in tone, pursed lips, and downward turn at the corners of her mouth. "Her dad finally came around and took her back in. And he was a little bit more receptive to us as well. He was never like, *Grandpa*, but he let us come over weekends, and he cooked us dinner, and he was nice as he could be considering the circumstances. And that's it in a nutshell."

"When you say, 'He was nice as he could be considering the circumstances,' do you really think that's true?" I ask.

"I think that he had a lot of conflicting feelings. He was a very strong Catholic, so I think that his religious upbringing and convictions sort of conflicted with how he was treating his daughter's selection for a mate. Because whenever we went over there, he always got 'God' with us." She says this sarcastically, bitterly. "I think that he was trying to come around, but it was hard. All these racialized ideas had been inbred. I think he was definitely trying to come around because he loved his daughter, and if his daughter had black children, he had to love them as well, as much as he could." And there it is again, like sandpaper, or something deeper, like the serrated edge of a saw.

"Did you feel love from him?"

"Hmm . . . ," she muses, looking away from me, gazing off into the homely interior of the cafeteria, with its bald fluorescent lighting, scarred brown tables, and cold, spindle-legged chairs. She reminds me a lot of my eldest, with her intelligence and heads-up walk, her wide shoulders, and the curve of her slender arms, even the color and elegant consistency of her skin. My daughter tans easily and deeply, inheriting what I refer to as our "Italian skin"; I am half Italian, like Linda. My Italian heritage, though, has always brought me a wellspring of riches that I relish. I feel saddened that Linda feels only a negative connection there.

"Looking back now, I don't think so. Of course, he passed when I was thirteen. And when I came over, he was nice, he did all the superficial things, like he cooked us dinner and bought us

Christmas presents. So of course I thought, 'Wow, he really cares for us.' But looking back, he never went beyond that. But he never was an emotional man, he never went beyond that with my mom either."

"So until he passed away, do you think he was making an attempt to come to terms with his biases and make a peace with his daughter and his grandchildren?" I am pressing for an answer in the affirmative. It's something I need to hear.

"I think the only reason he was motivated to do that was out of love for his daughter. I think he was trying, but just basically to make things better for his daughter." The rough, sawing edge drags deeply over this, and she is just a little haughty. I think my daughter would behave the same way if she were the grandchild in these circumstances. She, too, would cover any sensitivities with a brave, brittle shell, daring anyone—with head held high and straight—to question her authority over the loose threads of her life.

"When you first went to live with your grandmother, did everyone think it was a temporary situation?"

"I don't think that was ever a concern, just because my grandmother's household has always been a very welcoming one. You know, relatives who come up from the South stay there, and when they get their finances going, they leave. It's sort of like, if you need a place, there's always a place there. It's just a very welcoming place. It's like family is family is family."

Linda was adopted at ten years of age. Before that, Linda believes it was an informal arrangement.

"I never missed having a nuclear family because I just never had one, so I never knew what it was like. A lot of people ask me, 'Are you bitter that things turned out the way it did?' and I'd say,

"No, I don't know any other way." And I'm just thankful that I did have someone there, so that never bothered me."

"Do you harbor any resentment for your birth mother?

"No."

"Or your birth father?"

"My birth father, yes. My mother I think I excuse just because of her mental incapacity. I understand she is just not able or equipped to raise a family. I have issues with her being white. My father on the other hand, he remarried, and he takes care of his other kids. And while I never really wanted any . . . um . . . ," she pauses, reaching for accuracy, precision, "emotional support from him, it's been a struggle going to school and being independent from my grandmother, whose only source of income is Social Security. I would have liked some help. But I understand that he's not rich. Actually he remarried and has seven other kids with his new wife. But never anything, never even like twenty bucks here and there, never! That bothers me." Interestingly, although she says this with righteous, static anger, that same low, dragging inflection that sometimes unintentionally surfaces is missing from her overtly angry remarks.

"It also bothers me that he never helped my grandmother out with little things. She was raising us by herself, and he could have helped with groceries—not even pay for them, just come by, pick us up, and take us to the store. Nothing. Nothing ever.

"I don't think he has any great disdain or dislike for us; I just don't think he knows how to be a father. I don't think he is any more of a father to the kids he's presently raising. I mean, he just doesn't know how to."

Author Jan Waldron's memoir, *Giving Away Simone*, depicts her experiences around giving her daughter up for adoption, their subsequent reunion, and the ongoing work of reconnecting. In the book, she works through many of the issues Linda has filtering through her own life. In a passage on absent birth fathers, she tells us, "Abandoning fathers, though personae non grata, are still woven seamlessly into our agenda of family liabilities. When men leave their families, they are called, frivolously, deadbeats. A missing father's breach is financial. His emotional and psychological debts are not even implied."[1] It appears that Linda glosses over the emotional cost of her father's absence. She dismisses, too quickly, the effect on her life of the miserly way in which he gave of himself.

"My mother made more of an effort to visit. Every weekend we would go out, and that was fine. We'd go to the movies or to her house for dinner. That was always nice, but it was more like a friend, because she was never there changing diapers or helping with homework. It was kind of cool, having a friend on the weekend. She knew that's how we viewed her, and there was nothing she could do about it."

"What did you call her?" I ask.

"Mummy," she says sweetly, just like a little girl.

"You say you have issues with her because she's white? Do you want to talk about that?"

"Sure. Initially I had a very warped view of my racial identity. I considered that because my mom was white and my dad was black, I enjoyed the best of both worlds. But society is not like that at all, and you really do have to choose. I grew up in a black neighborhood, I was treated as black, and I never really was accepted into the white world. There was just no way, no way. Just look at how my mother's family received us, my father. That was a big slap in the face."

I ask when she started to feel this way, and she answers, "I guess senior year in high school." Before that, "I was just very idealistic, and I just believed everyone could get along. I finally realized that was not the case.

"Even the little things that my mother says bother me." Linda is holding a pen, flopping it from side to side and tapping it on the table for emphasis. "I think that if a woman could marry a black man (tap) and have black children (tap)—and I know she would die for me right now, I know how much she loves me—and if *she* still harbored racist views, it's really hard for me to believe any white person can be sincere (tap).

"For instance, when I was applying to colleges, I said, "Yeah, Mummy, I'm applying to Yale and Princeton," and she's like, 'Well, are you sure? Maybe you shouldn't try, or aim as high.' All right . . . I let that alone. Then just recently I went to visit her with my niece. My niece is light skinned with long hair. I don't know if you're aware of this, but in the black community, they tend to give more privileges to black children that look white. Shauna's mom is very dark skinned with short, kinky hair, so she looks very black in a sense. So my mother was talking to her boyfriend, and she said, 'Shauna has a beautiful skin complexion, and she has really nice long hair even though her mother is *dark*.' And that really bothers me, but I never confront her with it, because I know she's not intellectually able to confront me with that. She has no awareness of that, and she's actually very bothered that I don't claim my Italian heritage, but I'm like, 'Mummy, it never claimed *me*.' But I never talk to her about racial issues because she's not really aware. I love her, but I just can't deal with her on a lot of different levels."

I offer my two cents worth in regard to her mother's discomfort about Linda's college choices. I tell her that it sounds to me like a typical scenario in which a mother fears her daughter may get hurt or disappointed. I've had similar concerns myself in the past. I ask her if her mother would acknowledge any bias, and she replies, "No! But I don't think that excuses it or makes it any less hurtful.

"I just became aware of it myself. I am sure there were numerous examples, but I was just too blind myself to see it. Lately I've kept my eyes open. But I tend not to talk to her about those things because I can't deal with it. She gets on my nerves. She thinks *I'm* crazy. She thinks I'm crazy." She laughs, but it is mirthless and dripping with irony.

"I think her racial views are very colored by her attraction to my father, because he was never much of a family man." She drags down heavily on these words too. "He was never much of a husband, or a father. So of course these ideas trickle down on how you treat other people of color (tap-tap). I think that has a lot to do with it."

I wonder how much of Linda's distress and focus on a perceived racial bias in her mother—though I wouldn't presume to doubt it—is really diverted anger over other less tangible issues. Jan Waldron has a lot to say about the mother-daughter rift in her book. There is one line that seems to me particularly fitting here: "All the language and behavior between my birth daughter and me is subject to a phantom translation, in our heads, by that awful spirit that presided over the day I walked away."[2] It would be understandable if Linda's buried abandonment issues influenced the way she reacts and interacts with her birth mother.

"Let's switch gears and talk about your grandmother. Tell me about her."

"She's a very industrious woman. She's very hardworking, and for her it's not really a choice; it's just how she grew up. Her dad was a sharecropper. Ever since she was young, she was out in the fields, and that work ethic has carried through. Even with all her kids, and however irresponsible they are with their parenting duties, she just takes it up. I don't know if I could be as strong. I don't know if I could do that, just seeing how much she struggled with raising me, my brother, my little cousin that she's raising now. I don't know if I could do it. I don't know if I'd want to do it.

"I understand that it's not the children's fault *at all*. It really disgusts me how parents do not take their job seriously, and I understand that there are a lot of circumstances that enter into the equation—financial, sometimes drug addiction, a lot of different factors. But people don't take child bearing, or child raising, seriously anymore.

"For me, family has become so important just because I see how hard she has worked to preserve her family, even though it's not a family in the traditional sense. For me, I very much want a husband. I want "two point five" kids; I want a house. Those are very important things for me, and I'm willing to work hard for that. She has inspired me. However, I don't think I could raise a family like she has. I would be drained; I'd just be *gone*. She's in her seventies now, and she's still raising kids!"

Most of her grandmother's children got "caught up" in drugs. Linda grew up in Dorchester but went to Tyndall, a private school in another part of Boston.

"I think that made all the difference. I really don't consider myself much different from the strain from which I emerged. I don't think I am much different from my family members who did get caught up. I think that my exposure to professional people, to achievement-oriented people, to the middle class, gave me the leverage I needed to work harder to get myself out of a bad situation.

"I know that I am in a very privileged position, basically going between both worlds. I do think both of them [mother and grandmother] do live vicariously through me. And that's hard, that's really hard. I feel added pressure; my degree is their degree. It bothers me when my grandmother boasts about me, because I feel like it creates a much deeper divide between me and my family. I know that, in a sense, I have strayed just because I am at Yale. But I don't want my little cousins and nieces and nephews to think that they can't achieve the same thing. By revering me, she's [unintentionally] putting them down."

I ask her how she wound up going to a private school.

"Actually, in fifth grade I had a pretty committed teacher who encouraged me to go to a private school. I didn't want to go. I wanted to be with my friends. But he encouraged me, and my grandmother encouraged me, so I went, and I hated it. But I wouldn't trade it for the world now."

"You mean you hated it initially, but then you . . . ," I begin.

"I always hated it. I went there seven years, and I appreciated it while I was hating it. It was a private, all girls' school. It was a big culture shock for me. For instance, I always thought I had it made, like I had everything in the world. I would go to school with these girls, and they'd be saying, 'I'm going skiing in Colorado this weekend,' or, 'My sister just got a new Volvo for her sixteenth birthday.' I remember I was talking about dialects, and my Latin teacher—there were two black girls in my class—my Latin teacher looked at both of us and said, 'Maybe Linda and Doreena can tell us a little bit about dialects.' That was hard because there was a race issue *and* there was a class issue. Even the black girls were very middle class. So it was hard to make friends. We lived in different places; our parents did different things. I had a totally different household than they did.

"It was strange because I thought that it was normal to have twelve people living in our house. And then when I went to visit them, it was mom and dad and brother. I was like, 'Where's every-body else? Don't you have uncles and cousins!' And they were like, 'Well, yeah but they don't live here.' It was that type of exposure that gave me the ability to see beyond my immediate surroundings, which a lot of my family members never had. I mean, a lot of them have just never been out of Boston, as simple as that is. So I think, had I not gone to private school, I would not have had the exposure I needed to prosper academically.

"A lot of the reason I'm here is basically because of her [her grandmother's] participation in my life. She worked up until I was in high school. Even when she wasn't working, she was so re-sourceful that we never struggled much. For instance, she always got us housing, and we were never hungry, and we never wanted much. For that, I am really thankful. For a long time I thought we were pretty rich, until I went to Tyndall. But I never wanted anything. She was there."

I ask her how she got through her teenage years being raised by a grandmother. "Actually, I was a pretty good kid, but of course I'm a little biased." She laughs warmly, happily for the first time, and I'm relieved to hear it. "I stuck to my studies without any pushing from her. I was very self-motivated. But there came a time when she didn't like my friends, and she told me I couldn't hang out with my friends. That was a big struggle; I was about fifteen. She didn't like my music."

Grandchildren—Having Their Say

"How about your clothes?"

"She never had a problem with it then. Now she does—my skirts are too short!" She laughs again. Now she loves all my friends. All my friends are either graduated, or working, or are presently in college. None of them have kids. We don't hang in the street, or go to seedy clubs; we're just college kids. I think she appreciates my choice of friendships."

"I am sure she loves to see that," I say. "It must be such a pleasure to see you going off with friends like that! Did you butt heads while you were growing up?"

"Yeah. Yeah, we did. It was difficult because we'd have so many people in the house, and I always resented it because you'd have to share your room; you don't have personal space to grow. I really believe you need physical space of your own. It's nice to feel like you're part of something larger, but if that's always being invaded, that's really hard. I was always a little bit resentful because of that, but then I understood what she was doing. Basically she had a bigger picture, and I was very self-focused and self-centered. That's what being a kid is about."

"What would you like to say to grandchildren being raised by grandparents?" I ask.

"It took me a long time to get to this point, but when I was an adolescent, I would always think in terms of my needs not being met, be it financial or emotional, what she could not do for me. Until recently, just a couple of years ago, I realized how hard it is for her. That was such a new thing for me, to think about her feelings, and I am still embarrassed about that. That was a big epiphany for me.

"Basically, she was done mothering, and she had to start from scratch. I was two days old; I'm twenty-one now, and she's still mothering me. Imagine how hard it was for her considering the big generation gap, considering how hurtful it probably is for her to know that the children she raised can't raise their own. Even though we never discussed it, I know it must really bother her. Whenever I am upset about something she's said or something she's done, I stop to think how strong she was to raise us, and then I'm not so indignant as I was initially. What I'm trying to say is, you need to make yourself more aware of why your grandparent is doing what they're doing. Because they care."

Linda interjects that one of the most important things that grandparents can accomplish is to make sure that birth parents are somehow involved in the children's lives. Even though she has had her share of difficulties with her birth parents, she is glad they are a part of her life. "Access to biological parents should always be there," she urges.

"As I've grown, I've been able to understand more why she has done what she's done, and it's only out of love and affection and wanting to preserve her family that she took me in. And if that's understood, you can get over the bumpy rides."

The need to claim a heritage, the need for a past and an identity, these are all critical and heartfelt themes demonstrated so poignantly by David, Kit, Paul, and Linda.

In all my years working with children and adults who have been part of the foster care system, I do not recall hearing anyone state, "Boy, growing up in foster care was great!" And while I have heard countless foster children share their appreciation for some of the quality, loving care they did receive while in foster care, they do, however, long for family bonds and lifelong connections. Like many other grandchildren, David, Kit, Paul, and

Linda were able, thanks to their grandparents, to maintain family connections and their roots.

The grandchildren who have spoken in these last pages have provided us with valuable insights, leaving images that will last long after we have put this book down. We have been given the opportunity to see with certainty that it is in the best interests of the child to receive their care and love from a supportive family member. The grandchildren themselves have made this powerful point loud and clear.

Will it always be an easy experience? No, but with openness, honesty, and mutual respect for the truth, the potholes and cracks in the road won't stop you from staying on course.

As Linda and I part, I feel at a loss. Standing at the foot of the library steps in the softened afternoon sunlight together, I want, suddenly, to ask her more questions, get to know her better. I embrace her before she leaves, patting her back like she was my own, and hesitate, asking her what she's going to do with the rest of the afternoon, with the summer, with her life. I hang on her words as if they contain some magic information for me, as if she might be a gypsy looking into a crystal ball telling my future, my grandchild's life swimming before her in the glass globe. "My degree is their degree," she told me earlier. Your degree is *my* degree, I think. Your success is *our* success; you represent the potential success of all our grandchildren, that it can be done. You are the reassurance that all will be well in the end. I want her to tell me something tangible and perfect as a jewel, something I can take with me like a talisman.

She is going to Princeton this summer, she says. She's interested in education reform, and they have programs there that will get her closer to her goal. I'm glad to hear it, and I'm happy for her, but that's not really what I want to hear.

I want to hear that it was wonderful to be raised by grandparents. That children's hearts can grow without scars, healed clean by the burning devotion of loving caregivers. That family connections have so grounded them that they never feel shaky in their shoes. That what they missed by not having birth parents to care for them was more than made up for by the stalwart affection of grandparents. That grandparents are really not second best, just a lateral alternate, like a quick two-step to the side, never breaking the rhythm or disturbing the healthy momentum of childhood. I need reassurance from Linda, from all the grandchildren I interviewed. That's really what I wanted all along.

In my head, I know better. There is no clear, happily-after-after path, only the road well traveled. I know that the work of raising emotionally secure children is so very difficult, and grandparents must use every tool available to accomplish their goal. I know that working to preserve our families is a way of life, not a part-time job, and that forgiveness is the best route to healing. In my head, I know that this work is never truly finished.

But in my heart, I wish to hold comforting assurances that all that we work for will have a satisfying payment, that there is nothing I can do that is more important than keeping my family together, and that I am blessed to have my family intact and moving forward toward the future. There is room in my heart for all these things.

Epilogue

As I crisscrossed New England conducting interviews, meeting families, getting to know grandparents, and talking with many others interested in the various issues involved when grandparents raise grandchildren, I very quickly realized that I could not be the objective journalist. This book became more than an exploration of an issue, more than a personally pertinent project; each step brought me closer to a kind of affirmation, and ultimately became an enlightening odyssey for me. In tapping into the stories and struggles, joys and heartaches of others, I was drawn into each family's story in a way that I had not intended; the thread of my experiences was woven tightly into the tapestry of theirs.

Walking with them as they relived their journeys, I reexperienced my own and was able to come home to a sense of peace and conviction that this was not merely an issue born out of individual failure, but one of triumph—of families who have faltered, rallied, and sustained.

When I began this book, my aim was to offer grandparents and grandchildren a look at what others have been through and survived. I hoped that through their examples, as well as the therapist's insights, grandparents would be better equipped to deal with challenges that might come their way and better navigate altered family dynamics. I knew it was important to raise awareness in others who may not realize the depth and complexity of this growing trend, and I tried to provide a commonsense outlook on the issues. In addition, I hoped to demonstrate that these are not strictly grandparent issues but *family* issues.

Finally, I wanted to dispel any complacent attitudes that may exist that would dismiss these problems as something on the periphery only, something that happens to "them" but not to "us." I believe the examples of the grandparents and adult children portrayed here will show that no one is immune to the destructive influence of drugs and alcohol, or the common vagaries of immaturity and irresponsibility, or even the ordinary twists and turns of everyday life.

Raising awareness is one of the most important missions of this book. Grandparents having to step in to raise their grandchildren is an enormous issue that permeates every segment of society, yet it is barely on anyone's radar screen. I hope this book will be instrumental in giving a boost to the efforts of those individuals involved in advocating for grandparents raising grandchildren, to those groups working toward rewriting social service policy, encouraging judicial reform, legislating regulations, and shaping society's attitudes toward child welfare and family preservation.

Systems in place that do not yet serve the specific needs of family helping family need to be rethought and reworked. Kinship Care and Kinship Adoption, as proposed by the Child Welfare League of America (CWLA), would leave room for birth parents in a legal reworking of custodial rights. In kinship caregiving arrangements, the grandparent or other kin could become the legal parent, while keeping intact the important connection of the birth parent and providing each with a legal designation for inclusion in the child's life. A spokesperson for the CWLA explained, "Many current policies, and even some proposed policies, fail to allow for what kinship care does best: support and affirm the extended family, without unnecessarily severing ties with the nuclear family."[1] The efforts of the CWLA represent a new, broader, more inclusive, and critically necessary way of thinking about family and family preservation.

The lifelong opus of family relationships is like an elaborate tango, sometimes close to the skin, warm and embracing, sometimes spinning apart in separate, self-absorbed revelries, sometimes flung together in hard, hurting passion. We move always in sync with, or in contrast to, the other participants in the intricate dance we call family. Out of step or in perfect time, what we do, what we are, is defined by not only the steps we take, but also by the steps taken by those closest to us. Whether they exist for us in body or spirit, whether they are tangible or bind us only as an unshakable psychic pull, they remain our partners in life, for life.

We are all inexorably wound together as individuals, as families, as communities, and as a society. We must take care to value, accommodate, and at times assist the variety and diversity, each unique facet, in the noble work—the blessed art—of family.

Notes

PREFACE

1. US Census Bureau News, Profile America, Facts for Features, CB12-FF.17, 31 July 2012.

2. The Stephen Lewis Foundation, Grandmothers Campaign, http://www.stephenlewisfoundation.org.

3. American Academy of Child and Adolescent Psychiatry, *Facts for Families, Grandparents Raising Grandchildren*, March 2011.

CHAPTER 4 HEALING THE WOUNDS

1. Child Help, National Child Abuse Statistics, 2012, http://www.childhelp-usa.com/pages/statistics.

2. *Child Abuse*, A study by League of Women Voters of Massachusetts, 1990.

CHAPTER 7 MOTHERS IN PRISON

1. Maya Angelou, *Wouldn't Take Nothing for My Journey Now* (New York: Random House, 1993). Reprinted by permission of Random House.

Notes

CHAPTER 8 GUARDIANSHIP— ADOPTION—LETTING GO

1. Child Welfare League of America, *A Blueprint for Fostering Infants, Children and Youths in the 1990s* (Washington, DC: Child Welfare League of America, 1995).

2. Hope Edelman, *Motherless Daughters: The Legacy of Loss* (New York: Addison-Wesley, 1994).

3. Joseph Califano Jr., "It's Drugs, Stupid," *New York Times Magazine*, 29 January 1995.

4. Edward M. Hallowell, MD, and John J. Ratey, MD, *Driven to Distraction* (New York: Pantheon, 1994).

CHAPTER 9 GRANDCHILDREN— HAVING THEIR SAY

1. Jan Waldron, *Giving Away Simone* (New York: Times Books, 1995).

2. Ibid.

EPILOGUE

1. *Brookdale Grandparent Caregiver Information Project Newsletter* (Berkeley, CA: University of California, October 1992).

Abbreviations

AARP	American Association of Retired Persons
ADD	attention deficit disorder
ADHD	attention deficit hyperactivity disorder
AFDC	Aid for Families with Dependent Children
Al-Anon	Support groups for family members of alcoholics
Alateen	Support groups for teenage family members of al-coholics
CHINS	Children in Need of Services
COA	Council on Aging
CPS	Child Protective Services
CWLA	Child Welfare League of America
DSS	Department of Social Services
DYS	Department of Youth Services
EOEA	Executive Office of Elder Affairs
FAS	fetal alcohol syndrome
GAL	guardian ad litem
GAP	Grandparents as Parents support group
GED	General Equivalency Degree
HHS	Health and Human Services

Abbreviations

OFC	Office for Children
PA	Parents Anonymous
PTSD	posttraumatic stress disorder
RAD	reactive attachment disorder
ROCC	Raising Our Children's Children support group
SAIN	Sexual Abuse Investigation Network
SSI	Supplemental Security Income
WIC	Women, Infants and Children nutrition program

Bibliography

PUBLICATIONS FOR ADULTS

Abrams, Justice Ruth I., and Chief Justice John M. Greaney. *Gender Bias Study of the Court System in Massachusetts*. Supreme Judicial Court, 1989.

Angelou, Maya. *I Know Why the Caged Bird Sings*. New York: Random House, 1970.

Angelou, Maya. *Wouldn't Take Nothing for My Journey Now*. New York: Random House, 1993.

Bolles, Richard. *What Color Is Your Parachute?* Berkeley, CA: Ten Speed Press, 1992.

Califano, Joseph, Jr. "It's Drugs, Stupid." *New York Times Magazine*, 29 January 1995, 40–41.

Chalfie, Deborah. *Going It Alone: A Closer Look at Grandparents Parenting Grandchildren*. Washington, DC: AARP Women's Initiative, 1994.

Child Welfare League of America. *A Blueprint for Fostering Infants, Children and Youths in the 1990s*. Washington, DC: Child Welfare League of America, 1995.

Creighton, Linda. "Silent Saviors." *U.S. News and World Report*, 16 December 1991, 80.

Bibliography

Donohue-King, Sheila, et al. *A Resource Guide for Massachusetts' Grand-parents Raising Their Grandchildren.* Boston: Massachusetts Executive Office of Elder Affairs, 1995.

Edelman, Hope. *Motherless Daughters.* New York: Addison-Wesley, 1994.

Hallowel, Edward M., MD, and John J. Ratey, MD. *Driven to Distraction.* New York: Pantheon, 1994.

Johnson, Ivory, et al. *Kinship Care: A Natural Bridge.* Washington, DC: Child Welfare League of America, 1994.

Melina, Lois Ruskai. *Making Sense of Adoption: A Parent's Guide.* New York: Harper and Row, 1989.

Minkler, Meredith, and Kathleen M. Roe. *Grandmothers as Caregivers: Raising Children of the Crack Cocaine Epidemic.* Newbury Park, CA: Sage, 1993.

Muse, Daphne. "Parenting from Prison." *Mothering,* September 1994, 99–105.

Sewel, Marilyn, ed. *Cries of the Spirit.* Boston: Beacon Press, 1991.

Tannen, Deborah, PhD. *You Just Don't Understand: Women and Men in Conversation.* New York: Random House, 1990.

Waldron, Jan L. *Giving Away Simone.* New York: Times Books, 1995.

Walker, Alice. *In Search of Our Mothers' Gardens: Womanist Prose.* New York: Harcourt Brace, 1984.

York, David, Phyllis York, and Ted Wachtel. *Toughlove.* New York: Bantam, 1990.

BOOKS FOR CHILDREN

Byrne, Gayle, and Mary Haverfield. *Sometimes It's Grandmas and Grandpas, Not Mommies and Daddies.* New York: Abbeville Kids.

Fraser, Debra. *On the Day You Were Born.* New York: Harcourt Brace Jovanovich, 1991.

Hoberman, Mary Ann, ed. *My Song Is Beautiful.* Boston: Little, Brown, 1992.

Bibliography

LaCure, Jeffrey R., PhD. *Adopted Like Me*. Franklin, MA: Adoption Advocate Publishing Company, 1992.

Pellegrini, Nina. *Families Are Different*. New York: Holiday House, 1991.

Warren-Lindsay, Jeanne. *Do I Have a Daddy?* Buena Park, CA: Morning Glory Press.

Warren-Lindsay, Jeanne. *School-Age Parents: Three Generation Living*. Buena Park, CA: Morning Glory Press.

Williams, Vera B. *More, More, More Said the Baby*. New York: New Greenwillow Books, 1990.

Resources

American Association for Marriage and Family Therapy (AAMFT)
112 Alfred Street
Alexandria, VA 22314
www.aamft.org

American Association of Retired Persons (AARP)
Grandfacts
601 E. Street, NW
Washington, DC 20049
www.aarp.org

American Bar Association Center for Children and the Law
1050 Connecticut Avenue, NW, Suite 400
Washington, DC, 20036
www.americanbar.org

Resources

Brookdale Foundation Group—Relatives as Parents Program (RAPP)
950 3rd Avenue, #1900
New York, NY 10022

Cambridge Documentary Films (CDF)
PO Box 390385
Cambridge, MA 02139
www.cambridgedocumentaryfilms.org

Defending Our Lives, produced by CDF and Peace at Home—an Academy Award–winning documentary film that portrays the severity of domestic violence.

CanGrands
Betty Cornelius, founder
R.R.1 McArthurs Mills, Ontario, CA K0L2M0
National kinship support for caregiver families across Canada.
www.cangrands.org.ca

Generations United
1331 H Street, NW, Suite 900
Washington, DC 20005
www.gu.org

Grandparents as Parents
Support group for grandparents raising grandchildren.
In US: www.grandparentsasparents.org
In UK: www.grandparentsasparents.org.uk

Resources

Grandparents as Parents Again
Grandparent support group in Australia.
www.grandparentsasparentsagain.org.au

National Kinship Alliance for Children
PO Box 1560
Troy, NY 12181
http://kinshipalliance.org

National Women's Law Center
11 Dupont Circle, NW, #800
Washington, DC 20036
www.nwlc.org